Second Language Learning
and Language Teaching

Second Language Learning and Language Teaching

Fourth Edition

Vivian Cook

HODDER
EDUCATION
AN HACHETTE UK COMPANY

First published in Great Britain in 2001 by Arnold.
This fourth edition published in 2008 by
Hodder Education, an Hachette UK Company,
338 Euston Road, London NW1 3BH.

www.hoddereducation.com

Hachette Livre UK's policy is to use papers that are natural, renewable and
recyclable products and made from wood grown in sustainable forests.
The logging and manufacturing processes are expected to conform to the
environmental regulations of the country of origin.

The advice and information in this book are believed to be true and accurate
at the date of going to press, but neither the authors nor the publisher can
accept any legal responsibility or liability for any errors or omissions.

British Library Cataloguing in Publication Data
A catalogue record for this book is available from the British Library

Library of Congress Cataloging-in-Publication Data
A catalog record for this book is available from the Library of Congress

ISBN: 978 0 340 95876 6

4 5 6 7 8 9 10

Cover © Marco Cristofori/zefa/Corbis

Typeset in 10/13 Stone Serif by Macmillan Publishing Solutions
(www.macmillansolutions.com)

Printed and bound in Great Britain by CPI Antony Rowe

What do you think about this book? Or any other
Hodder Education title? Please send your comments to
the feedback section on www.hoddereducation.com

Contents

Acknowledgements

The motto of this book, as before, comes from Otto Jespersen (1904): 'The really important thing is less the destruction of bad old methods than a positive indication of the new ways to be followed if we are to have thoroughly efficient teaching in modern languages.' The new edition has benefited from the feedback of students, colleagues and readers. Without the musical influence of EST, Polar Bear and Miles Davis, it would never have been finished.

Vivian Cook
January 2008

Note to teachers

This book provides an introduction to the application of second language acquisition (SLA) research to language teaching suitable for language teachers, student teachers and students on MA courses in applied linguistics, TESOL, methodology of modern language teaching, and so on. It presupposes no previous background and provides explanations and glossaries of important terms. Most sections of each chapter start with focusing questions and keywords and end with summaries of the area and of its application, as well as presenting discussion topics and further reading.

The scope of the book ranges from particular aspects of language and language teaching to broader contexts of second language acquisition and general ideas of language teaching. After the general background in Chapter 1, the next four chapters look at how people learn particular aspects of the second language: grammar in Chapter 2, vocabulary in Chapter 3, pronunciation in Chapter 4, and the writing system in Chapter 5. The next three chapters treat learners as individuals, dealing with learners' strategies in Chapter 6, listening and reading processes in Chapter 7, and individual differences in Chapter 8. Chapter 9 examines the characteristics of language teaching in classrooms. The remaining chapters adopt a wider perspective. Chapter 10 looks at the nature of the L2 user and the native speaker, Chapter 11 at goals of language teaching, and Chapter 12 at models of second language acquisition. The final Chapter 13 discusses different styles of language teaching and looks for their foundations in SLA research.

From my own teaching of this material I have found that the teaching sequence needs to vary to suit the interests and experience of the particular students on a course. For some it is better to start with the factual language materials in Chapters 2–5; those with more theoretical interests may start with the general models of second language acquisition in Chapter 12; students with less experience of teaching may need to start with sections of Chapter 13, which provide a quick background in teaching methods of the twentieth century; others may want to concentrate on the more controversial society-related issues of Chapters 10 and 11. Apart from the introductory Chapter 1, the chapters can stand alone and do not depend on previous chapters, though cross-references are made when necessary and a glossary of all key terms is given online.

The writing of the fourth edition has been guided largely by feedback from students, teachers and colleagues at Newcastle University. The broad framework and approach of the third edition have been maintained. An additional feature has been added, namely links to the website. For some time my website *SLA Topics* (http://homepage.ntlworld.com/vivian.c/SLA/index.htm) has offered a wide range of materials for SLA research. Recently, a portal has been created for users of this book which can be found at *www.hodderplus.com/linguistics*. This site contains support materials, notes, questionnaires, a glossary of keywords, samples of research techniques, further reading and lists of other related sites. The various questionnaires, summaries, data, and so on provided in the chapters are available online and can be downloaded and printed, usually as Microsoft® Word files. Links to a specific page on the website are indicated in the book by the mouse symbol. The links to other people's sites mentioned in the text are included on a single page of useful links on the website.

Background to second language acquisition research and language teaching

1

Language is at the centre of human life. We use it to express our love or our hatred, to achieve our goals and further our careers, to gain artistic satisfaction or simple pleasure, to pray or to blaspheme. Through language we plan our lives and remember our past; we exchange ideas and experiences; we form our social and individual identities. Language is the most unique thing about human beings. As Cicero said in 55 BC, 'The one thing in which we are especially superior to beasts is that we speak to each other.'

Some people are able to do some or all of this in more than one language. Knowing another language may mean: getting a job; a chance to get educated; the ability to take a fuller part in the life of one's own country or the opportunity to emigrate to another; an expansion of one's literary and cultural horizons; the expression of one's political opinions or religious beliefs; the chance to talk to people on a foreign holiday. A second language affects people's careers and possible futures, their lives and their very identities. In a world where probably more people speak two languages than one, the acquisition and use of second languages are vital to the everyday lives of millions; monolinguals are becoming almost an endangered species. Helping people acquire second languages more effectively is an important task for the twenty-first century.

1.1 The scope of this book

The main aim of this book is to communicate to those concerned with language teaching some of the ideas about how people acquire second languages that emerge from second language acquisition (SLA) research, and to make suggestions of how these might benefit language teaching. It is not a guide to SLA research methodology itself, or to the merits and failings of particular SLA research techniques, which are covered in other books, such as *Second Language Learning Theories* (Myles and Mitchell, 2004). Nor is it an overall guide to the methods and techniques of language teaching; only to those which are related to an SLA research perspective. It is intended for language teachers and trainee teachers. Most of the time it tries not to take sides in reporting the various issues; inevitably my own interest in the multi-competence approach is hard to conceal.

Much of the discussion concerns the L2 learning and teaching of English, mainly because this is the chief language that has been investigated in SLA research. English is used here, however, as a source of examples rather than forming the subject matter itself. The teaching and learning of other modern languages are discussed when appropriate. It should be remembered that the English language is often in a unique situation, being the only language that can be used almost anywhere on the globe between people who are non-native speakers. Most sections of each chapter start with focusing questions and a display of defining keywords, and end with discussion topics and further reading.

Contact with the language teaching classroom is maintained in this book chiefly through the discussion of published coursebooks and syllabuses, usually for teaching English. Even if good teachers use books only as a jumping-off point, they can provide a window into many classrooms. The books and syllabuses cited are taken from countries ranging from Germany to Japan to Cuba, though inevitably the bias is towards coursebooks published in England for reasons of accessibility. Since many modern language teaching coursebooks are depressingly similar in orientation, the examples of less familiar approaches have often been taken from older coursebooks.

This book talks about only a fraction of the SLA research on a given topic, often presenting only one or two of the possible approaches. It concentrates on those based on ideas about language, that is, applied linguistics, rather than those coming from psychology or education. Nevertheless it covers more areas of SLA research than most books that link SLA research to language teaching, for example, taking in pronunciation, vocabulary and writing, among other areas. It uses ideas from the wealth of research produced in the past twenty years or so, rather than just the most recent. Sometimes it has to go beyond the strict borders of SLA research itself to include topics such as the position of English in the world and the power of native speakers over their language.

The book is linked to an extensive website: *www.hoddereducation.com/viviancook*. This contains pages for this book, such as questionnaires, displays, language data, summaries, lists of links, and so on, as well as a great deal of other SLA information not specific to the book. The pages can be downloaded and printed. The main entry point is the index. The mouse symbol in the book indicates that there is a particular aspect available online; the more general pages are not signalled every time they might be useful.

1.2 Common assumptions of language teaching

Focusing question

- Answer the questionnaire in Box 1.1 to find out your assumptions about language teaching.

Keywords

first language: chronologically the first language that a child learns
second language: 'A language acquired by a person in addition to his mother tongue' (UNESCO)
native speaker: a person who still speaks the language they learnt in childhood, often seen as monolingual
Glosses on names of teaching methods are provided at the end of the chapter. Explanations of keywords throughout the book are available in the keyword glossary on the website.

Box 1.1 Assumptions of language teaching

Tick the extent to which you agree or disagree with these assumptions

	Strongly agree	Agree	Neither agree nor disagree	Disagree	Strongly Disagree
1 Students learn best through spoken, not written language.	❑	❑	❑	❑	❑
2 Teachers and students should use the second language rather than the first language in the classroom.	❑	❑	❑	❑	❑
3 Teachers should avoid explicit discussion of grammar.	❑	❑	❑	❑	❑
4 The aim of language teaching is to make students like native speakers.	❑	❑	❑	❑	❑

During the last quarter of the nineteenth century, a revolution took place that affected much of the language teaching used in the twentieth century. The revolt was primarily against the stultifying methods of grammatical explanation and translation of texts which were then popular. (In this chapter we will use 'method' in the traditional way to describe a particular way of teaching, with its own techniques and tasks; Chapter 13 replaces this with the word 'style'.) In its place, the pioneers of the new language teaching, such as Henry Sweet and Otto Jespersen, emphasized the spoken language and the naturalness of language learning, and insisted on the importance of using the second language in the classroom rather than the first (Howatt, 2004). These beliefs are largely still with us today, either explicitly instilled into teachers or just taken for granted. The questionnaire in Box 1.1 tests the extent to which the reader actually believes in four of these common assumptions.

If you agreed with most of the statements in Box 1.1, then you share the common assumptions of teachers over the past 120 years. Let us consider them in more detail.

Assumption 1: The basis for teaching is the spoken, not the written language

One of the keynotes of the nineteenth-century revolution in teaching was the emphasis on the spoken language, partly because many of its advocates were phoneticians. The English curriculum in Cuba, for example, insists on 'The principle of the primacy of spoken language' (Cuban Ministry of Education, 1999). The teaching methods within which speech was most dominant were the audio-lingual and audio-visual methods, which insisted on presenting spoken language from tape before the students encountered the written form. Later methods have continued to emphasize the spoken language. Communication in the communicative method is usually through speech rather than writing. The total physical response method uses spoken, not written, commands, and storytelling, not story reading. Even in the recent task-based learning approach, Ellis (2003: 6) points out: 'The literature on tasks, both research-based or pedagogic, assumes that tasks are directed at oral skills, particularly speaking.' The amount of teaching time that teachers pay to pronunciation far outweighs that given to spelling.

The importance of speech has been reinforced by many linguists who claim that speech is the primary form of language, and that writing depends on speech. Few teaching methods in the twentieth century saw speech and writing as being equally important. The problem with accepting this assumption, as we see in Chapter 5, is that written language has distinct characteristics of its own, which are not just pale reflections of the spoken language. To quote Michael Halliday (1985: 91), 'writing is not speech written down, nor is speech writing that is read aloud'. Vital as the spoken language may be, it should not divert attention from those aspects of writing that are crucial for students. Spelling mistakes, for instance, probably count more against an L2 user in everyday life than a foreign accent.

Assumption 2: Teachers and students should use the second language rather than the first language in the classroom

The emphasis on the second language in the classroom was also part of the revolt against the older methods by the late nineteenth-century methodologists, most famously through the direct method and the Berlitz method, with their rejection of translation as a teaching technique. In the 1990s the use of the first language in the classroom was still seen as undesirable, whether in England – 'The natural use of the target language for virtually all communication is a sure sign of a good modern language course' (DES, 1990: 58) – or in Japan – 'The majority of an English class will be conducted in English' (MEXT, 2003). This advice is echoed in almost every teaching manual: 'the need to have them practising English (rather than their own language) remains paramount' (Harmer, 1998: 129). One argument for avoiding the first language is that children learning their first language do not have a second language available, which is irrelevant in itself – infants do not play golf, but we teach it to adults. Another argument is that students should keep the two languages separate in their minds rather than linking them; this adopts a compartmentalized view of the languages in the same mind, which is not supported by SLA research, as we see everywhere in this book. Nevertheless, many English classes justifiably avoid the first language for practical reasons, whether because of the mixed languages of the students or because of the teacher's ignorance of the students' first language.

Assumption 3: Teachers should avoid explicit discussion of grammar

The ban on explicit teaching of grammar to students also formed part of the rejection of the old-style methods. Grammar could be practised through drills or incorporated within communicative exercises, but should not be explained to students. While grammatical rules could be demonstrated though substitution tables or situational cues, actual rules should not be mentioned. The old arguments against grammatical explanation were, on the one hand, the question of conscious understanding – knowing some aspect of language consciously is no guarantee that you can use it in speech – and, on the other, the time involved – speaking by consciously using all the grammatical rules means each sentence may take several minutes to produce, as those of us who learnt Latin by this method will bear witness. Chapter 2 describes how grammar has recently made something of a comeback.

Assumption 4: The aim of language teaching is to make students like native speakers

One of the assumptions that is most taken for granted is that the model for language teaching is the native speaker. Virtually all teachers, students and bilinguals have assumed that success is measured by how close a learner gets to a native speaker, in grammar, vocabulary and particularly pronunciation. David Stern (1983: 341) puts it clearly: 'The native speaker's "competence" or "proficiency" or "knowledge of the language" is a necessary point of reference for the second language proficiency concept used in language teaching.' Coursebooks are based on native language speakers; examinations compare students with the native speaker. Passing for a native is the ultimate test of success. Like all the best assumptions, people so take this for granted that they can be mortally offended if it is brought out into the open and they are asked, 'Why do you want to be a native speaker in any case?' No other possibility than the native speaker is entertained.

As we shall see, many of these background assumptions are questioned by SLA research and have sometimes led to undesirable consequences. Assumption 1, that students learn best through spoken language, leads to undervaluing the features specific to written language, as we see in Chapter 6. Assumption 2, that the L1 should be minimized in the classroom, goes against the integrity of the L2 user's mind, to be discussed later in this chapter and in Chapter 10. Assumption 3, on not teaching grammar, explicitly implies a particular model of grammar and learning, rather than the many alternatives shown in Chapter 2. The native speaker assumption 4 has come under increasing attack in recent years, as described in Chapter 10, on the grounds that a native speaker goal is not appropriate for all circumstances and is unattainable for the vast majority of students. Nevertheless, even if for the most part these assumptions are unstated, they continue to be part of the basis of language teaching, however the winds of fashion blow.

1.3 What *is* second language acquisition research?

Focusing questions

- Who do you know who is good at languages? Why do you think this is so?
- Do you think that everybody learns a second language in roughly the same way?

Keywords

Contrastive Analysis: this research method compared the descriptions of two languages in grammar or pronunciation to discover the differences between them; these were then seen as difficulties for the students that needed to be overcome

Error Analysis (EA): this method studied the language produced by L2 learners to establish its peculiarities, which it tried to explain in terms of the first language and other sources

As this book is based on SLA research, the obvious question is: what *is* SLA research? People have been interested in the acquisition of second languages since at least the ancient Greeks, but the discipline itself only came into being around 1970, gathering together language teachers, psychologists and linguists. Its roots were in the 1950s studies of Contrastive Analysis, which compared the first and second languages to predict students' difficulties, and in the 1960s Chomskyan models of first language acquisition, which saw children as creators of their own languages. Together these led to SLA research concentrating on the learner as the central element in the learning situation.

In the early days much attention focused on the language the learner produced. The technique of Error Analysis looked at the differences between the learner's speech and that of native speakers (Corder, 1981); it tried to establish what learner speech was actually like. The next wave of research tried to establish stages of development for the learner's language, say, the sequence for acquiring grammatical items like 'to', 'the' and '-ing', to be discussed in Chapter 2. Now people started to get interested in the qualities that learners brought to second language acquisition and the choices they made when learning and using the language. And they started to pay attention to the whole context in which the learner is placed, whether the temporary context of the conversation or the more permanent situation in their own society or the society whose language they are learning.

Nowadays SLA research is an extremely rich and diverse subject, drawing on aspects of linguistics, psychology, sociology and education. Hence it has many aspects and theories that are often incompatible. Most introductory books on second language acquisition will attest to the great interest that SLA researchers have in grammar. Yet many researchers are concerned exclusively with phonology or vocabulary, with their own specialist books and conferences. And still other groups are concerned with how Vygotsky's ideas link to modern language teaching, or how discourse and Conversation Analysis are relevant to second language acquisition. Much teaching-oriented SLA research now takes place at the interface between cognitive psychology and educational research, called 'usage-based learning' by Michael Tomasello (2003), leading to task-based learning. Though some SLA research is intended to be applied to teaching, most is either 'pure' study of second language acquisition for its own sake, or uses second language acquisition as a testing ground for linguistic theories.

The present book tries to be eclectic in presenting a variety of areas and approaches that seem relevant for language teaching rather than a single unified approach. Here are some 'facts' that SLA research has discovered; some of them will be explained and applied in later chapters; others are still a mystery:

- *English-speaking primary school children who are taught Italian for one hour a week learn to read better in English than other children.*
  Such a small exposure to a second language as one hour a week can have useful effects on other aspects of the child's mind and is potentially an important reason for teaching children another language. Language teaching affects more than the language in a person's mind.

- *People who speak a second language are more creative and flexible at problem solving than monolinguals (e.g. Einstein, Nabokov).*
  Research clearly shows L2 users have an advantage in several cognitive areas; they think differently and perceive the world differently. This benefit is discussed in Chapter 10.

- *Ten days after a road accident, a bilingual Moroccan could speak French but not Arabic; the next day Arabic but not French; the next day she went back to fluent French and poor Arabic; three months later she could speak both.*
  The relationship between the two languages in the brain is now starting to be understood by neurolinguists, yet the diversity of effects from brain injury is still largely inexplicable. The effects on language are different in almost every bilingual patient; some aphasics recover the first language they learnt, some the language they were using at the time of injury, some the language they use most, and so on.

- *Bengali-speaking children in Tower Hamlets in London go through stages in learning verb inflections; at 5 they know only '-ing' (walking); at 7 they also know /t/ 'walked', /d/ 'played' and 'ate' (irregular past tenses); at 9 they still lack 'hit' (zero past).*
  Learners all seem to go through similar stages of development of a second language, whether in grammar or pronunciation, as we see in other chapters. This has been confirmed in almost all studies looking at the sequence of acquisition. Yet, as in this case, we are still not always sure of the reason for the sequence.

- *The timing of the voicing of /t~d/ sounds in 'ten/den' is different in French people who speak English, and French people who do not.*
  The knowledge of the first language is affected in subtle ways by the second language that you know, so that there are many giveaways to the fact that you speak other languages, whether in grammar, pronunciation or vocabulary. L2 users no longer have the same knowledge of their first language as the monolingual native speaker.

- *L2 learners rapidly learn the appropriate pronunciations for their own gender, for instance, that men tend to pronounce the '-ing' ending of the English continuous form 'going' as '-in', but women tend to use '-ing'.*
  People quickly pick up elements that are important to their identity in the second language, say, men's versus women's speech – even if the teacher is probably

unaware of what is being conveyed. A second language is a complex new addition to one's roles in the world.

- *Remembering a fish tank they have been shown, Chinese people who also speak English will remember the fish more than the plants to a greater extent than Chinese monolinguals.*
  Different cultures think in different ways. Our cultural attitudes may be changed by the language we are acquiring; in this case, the Chinese attention to 'background' plants is altered by impact with the English attention to 'foreground' fish.

1.4 What a teacher can expect from SLA research

Focusing questions

- How do you think SLA research could help your teaching?
- Have you seen it applied to language teaching before?
- Who do you think should decide what happens in the classroom – the government, the head teacher, the teacher, the students, the parents, or someone else?

Let us take three examples of the contribution SLA research can make to language teaching: understanding the students' contribution to learning, understanding how teaching methods and techniques work, and understanding the overall goals of language teaching.

Understanding the students' contribution to learning

All successful teaching depends on learning; there is no point in providing entertaining, lively, well-constructed language lessons if students do not learn from them. The proof of the teaching is in the learning. One crucial factor in L2 learning is what the students bring with them into the classroom. With the exception of young bilingual children, L2 learners have fully formed personalities and minds when they start learning the second language, and these have profound effects on their ways of learning and on how successful they are. SLA research, for example, has established that the students' diverse motivations for learning the second language affect them powerfully, as we see in Chapter 8. Some students see learning the second language as extending the repertoire of what they can do; others see it as a threat.

The different ways in which students tackle learning also affect their success. What is happening in the class is not equally productive for all the students because their minds work in different ways. The differences between individuals do not disappear when they come through the classroom door. Students base what they do on their previous experience of learning and using language. They do not start from scratch without any background or predisposition to learn language in one way or another. Students also have much in common by virtue of possessing the same human minds. For instance, SLA research predicts that, however advanced they are, students will find that their memory works less well in the new language, whether they are trying to remember a phone number or the contents of an article. SLA research helps in understanding how apparently similar students react differently to the same teaching technique, while revealing the problems that all students share.

Understanding how teaching methods and techniques work

Teaching methods usually incorporate a view of L2 learning, whether implicitly or explicitly. Grammar-translation teaching, for example, emphasizes explanations of grammatical points because this fits in with its view that L2 learning is the acquisition of conscious knowledge. Communicative teaching methods require the students to talk to each other because they see L2 learning as growing out of the give-and-take of communication. For the most part, teaching methods have developed these ideas of learning independently from SLA research. They are not based, for example, on research into how learners use grammatical explanations or how they learn by talking to each other. More information about how learners actually learn helps the teacher to make any method more effective and can put the teacher's hunches on a firmer basis.

The reasons why a teaching technique works or does not work depend on many factors. A teacher who wants to use a particular technique will benefit by knowing what it implies in terms of language learning and language processing, the type of student for whom it is most appropriate, and the ways in which it fits into the classroom situation. Suppose the teacher wants to use a task in which the students spontaneously exchange information. This implies that students are learning by communicating, that they are prepared to speak out in the classroom and that the educational context allows for learning from fellow students rather than from the teacher alone. SLA research has something to say about all of these, as we shall see.

Understanding the goals of language teaching

The reasons why the second language is being taught depend on overall educational goals, which vary from one country to another and from one period to another. One avowed goal of language teaching is to help people to think better – brain training and logical thinking. Others are appreciation of serious literature; the student's increased self-awareness and maturity; the appreciation of other cultures and races; communication with people in other countries, and so on. Many of these have been explored in particular SLA research. For example, the goal of brain training is supported by evidence that people who know two languages think more flexibly than monolinguals (Landry, 1974). This information is vital when considering the viability and implementation of communicative goals for a particular group of students. SLA research can help define the goals of language teaching, assess how achievable they may be, and contribute to their achievement. These issues are debated in Chapter 11.

SLA research is a scientific discipline that tries to describe how people learn and use another language. It cannot decide issues that are outside its domain. While it may contribute to the understanding of teaching goals, it is itself neutral between them. It is not for the teacher, the methodologist or any other outsider to dictate whether a language should be taught for communication, for brain training, or whatever purpose, but for the society or the individual student to decide. One country specifies that group work must be used in the classroom because it encourages democracy. Another bans any reference to English-speaking culture in textbooks because English is for international communication, not for developing relationships with England or the USA. A third sees language teaching as a way of developing honesty and the values of good citizenship; a speaker at a TESOL conference in New York proclaimed that the purpose of TESOL was to create good American citizens (to the consternation of the British and Canadians present in the audience). SLA research as a discipline neither commends nor denies the value of these goals, since they depend on moral or political values rather than science. But it can offer advice on how these goals may best be achieved and what their costs may be, particularly in balancing the needs of society and of the individual.

Teachers need to see the classroom from many angles, not just from that of SLA research. The choice of what to do in a particular lesson depends on the teacher's assessment of the factors involved in teaching *those* students in *that* situation. SLA research reveals some of the strengths and weaknesses of a particular teaching method or technique and it provides information that can influence and guide teaching. It does not provide a magic solution to teaching problems in the form of a patented method with an attractive new brand name.

Insights from SLA research can help teachers, whatever their methodological slant. Partly this is at the general level of understanding; knowing what language learning consists of colours the teacher's awareness of everything that happens in the classroom and heightens the teacher's empathy with the student. Partly it is at the more specific level of the choice of teaching methods, the construction of teaching materials, or the design and execution of teaching techniques. The links between SLA research and language teaching made here are suggestions of what *can* be done rather than accounts of what *has* been done or orders about what *should* be done. Since SLA research is still in its early days, some of the ideas presented here are based on a solid agreed foundation; others are more controversial or speculative.

While this book has been written for language teachers, this is not the only way in which SLA research can influence language teaching. Other routes for the application of SLA research include:

1 Informing the students themselves about SLA research so they can use it in their learning. This has been tried in books such as *How to Study Foreign Languages* (Lewis, 1999) and *How to Be a More Successful Language Learner* (Rubin and Thompson, 1982).

2 Basing language examinations and tests on SLA research, a vast potential application but not one that has yet been tried on any scale, examination designers and testers usually following their own traditions.

3 Devising syllabuses and curricula using SLA research so that the content of teaching can fit the students better. We shall meet some attempts at this in various chapters here, but again, SLA research has not usually been the basis for syllabuses.

4 Writing course materials based on SLA research. Some coursebook writers do indeed try to use ideas from SLA research, as we shall see.

Often these indirect routes may have a greater influence on teaching than the teacher.

1.5 Some background ideas of SLA research

Focusing questions

- Do you feel you keep your two languages separate or do they merge at some point in your mind?
- Do you think students should aim to become as native-like as possible?

Keywords

multi-competence: the knowledge of more than one language in the same mind

the independent language assumption: the language of the L2 learner can be considered a language in its own right rather than a defective version of the target language (sometimes called 'interlanguage')

L2 user and L2 learner: an L2 user uses the second language for real-life purposes; an L2 learner is acquiring a second language rather than using it

second and foreign language: broadly speaking, a *second* language is for immediate use within the same country; a *foreign* language is for long-term future use in other countries

When SLA research became an independent discipline, it established certain principles that underlie much of the research to be discussed later. This section presents some of these core ideas.

SLA research is independent of language teaching

Earlier approaches to L2 learning often asked the question: which teaching methods give the best results? Is an oral method better than a translation method? Is a communicative method better than a situational one? Putting the question in this form accepts the status quo of what already happens in teaching rather than looking at underlying principles of learning: 'Is what happens in teaching right?' rather than 'What should happen in teaching?' A more logical sequence is to ask: how do people *learn* languages? Then teaching methods can be evaluated in the light of what has been discovered, and teaching can be based on adequate ideas of learning. The first step is to study learning itself; the second step is to see how teaching relates to learning, the sequence mostly followed in this book.

The teacher should be told from the start that there is no easy link between SLA research and language teaching methods, despite the claims made in some coursebooks or by some researchers. The language teaching approaches of the past 50 years, by and large, have originated from teaching methodologists, not from SLA research. The communicative approach, for example, was only remotely linked to the theories of language acquisition of the 1960s and 1970s; it came chiefly out of the insight that language teaching should be tailored to students' real-world communication needs. SLA research does not provide a magic solution that can be applied instantly to the contemporary classroom so much as a set of ideas that teachers can try out for themselves.

The new field did not blindly take over the concepts previously used for talking about L2 learning. Language teachers, for example, often contrast *second* language teaching (which teaches the language for immediate use within the same country, say, the teaching of French to immigrants in France) with *foreign* language teaching (which teaches the language for long-term future uses and may take place anywhere, but most often in countries where it is not an everyday medium, say, the teaching of French in England). While this distinction is often convenient, it cannot be taken for granted that learners in these two situations necessarily learn in two different ways without proper research evidence. Indeed, later we shall look at many other dimensions to the learning situation (see Chapter 10). (Also there seems to be some variation between British and American usage of 'foreign' and 'second'.)

The term *second language (L2) learning/acquisition* is used in this book to include all learning of languages other than the native language, in whatever situation or for whatever purpose: second simply means 'other than first'. This is the sense of *second language* defined by UNESCO: 'A language acquired by a person in addition to his mother tongue'. Nor does this book make a distinction between language 'acquisition' and language 'learning', as Stephen Krashen does (e.g. Krashen, 1981a).

A more idiosyncratic use here is the distinction between *L2 user* and *L2 learner*. An *L2 user* is anybody making an actual use of the second language for real-life purposes outside the classroom; an *L2 learner* is anybody acquiring a second language. In some cases a person is both user and learner – when an L2 learner of English in London steps out of the classroom, they immediately become an L2 user of English. The distinction is important for many countries where learners do not become users for many years, if ever. The prime motivation for the term *L2 user*, however, is the feeling that it is demeaning to call someone who has functioned in an L2 environment for years a learner rather than a user, as if their task were never finished. We would not dream of calling a 20-year-old adult native speaker an L1 learner, so we should not call a person who has been using a second language for 20 years an L2 learner!

The different spheres of SLA research and language teaching mean that the concepts of language they use are often different. The danger is when both fields use the same terms with different meanings. To SLA researchers, for instance, the term 'grammar' mostly means something in people's heads which they use for constructing sentences; to teachers it means a set of rules on paper which can be explained to students. The type of grammar used in SLA research has little to do with the tried and true collection of grammatical ideas for teaching that teachers have evolved, as will be illustrated in Chapter 2. It is perfectly possible, for example, for the same person to say 'I hate grammar' (as a way of teaching by explaining rules) and 'I think grammar is very important' (as the mental system that organizes language in the students' minds). It is dangerous to assume that words used by teachers every day, such as 'vocabulary', 'noun' or 'linguist', have the same meaning in the context of SLA research.

L2 learning is independent of L1 acquisition

Teaching methods have often been justified in terms of how children learn their first language, without investigating L2 learning directly. The audio-lingual method of teaching, for instance, was based primarily on particular views of how children learn their first language.

There is no intrinsic reason, however, why learning a second language should be the same as learning a first. Learning a first language is, in Halliday's memorable phrase, 'learning how to mean' (Halliday, 1975) – discovering that language is used for relating to other people and for communicating ideas. Language, according to Michael Tomasello (1999), requires the ability to recognize that other people have points of view. People learning a second language already know how to mean and know that other people have minds of their own. L2 learning is inevitably different in this respect from L1 learning. The similarities between learning the first and second languages have to be established rather than taken for granted. In some respects, the two forms of learning may well be rather similar, in others quite different – after all, the outcome is often very different. Evidence about how the child learns a first language has to be interpreted with caution in L2 learning and seldom in itself provides a basis for language teaching.

L2 learners, in fact, are different from children learning a first language since there is already one language present in their minds. There is no way that the L2 learner can become a monolingual native speaker *by definition*. However strong the similarities may be between L1 acquisition and L2 learning, the presence of the first language is the inescapable difference in L2 learning. So our beliefs about how children learn their first language cannot be transferred automatically to a second language; some may work, some may not. Most teaching methods have claimed in some sense to be based on the 'natural' way of acquiring language, usually meaning the way used by L1 children; however, they have very different views of what L1 children do, whether derived from the theories of language learning current when they originated or from general popular beliefs about L1 acquisition, say, 'Children are good at imitation, therefore L2 learners should have to imitate sentences.'

L2 learning is more than the transfer of the first language

One view of L2 learning sees its crucial element as the transfer of aspects of the first language to the second language. The first language helps learners when it has elements in common with the second language and hinders them when they differ. Spanish speakers may leave out the subject of the sentence when speaking English, saying 'Is raining' rather than 'It is raining', while French speakers do not. The explanation is that subjects may be omitted in Spanish, but they may not be left out in French. Nor is it usually difficult to decide from accent alone whether a foreigner speaking English comes from France, Brazil or Japan.

But the importance of such transfer has to be looked at with an open mind. Various aspects of L2 learning need to be investigated before it can be decided how and when the first language is involved in the learning of the second. Though transfer from the first language indeed turns out to be important, often in unexpected ways, its role needs to be established through properly balanced research rather than the first language taking the blame for everything that goes wrong in learning a second.

Learners have independent language systems of their own

Suppose a student learning English says, 'Me go no school'. Many teachers would see it as roughly the same as the native sentence, 'I am not going to school', even if they would not draw the student's attention to it overtly. In other words, this is what the student might say if he or she were a native speaker. So this student is 'really' trying to produce a present continuous tense 'am going', a first person sub-ject 'I', a negative 'not', and an adverbial 'to school', ending up with the native version 'I am not going to school'. But something has gone drastically wrong with the sentence. Perhaps the student has not yet encountered the appropriate forms in English or perhaps he or she is transferring constructions from the first lan-guage. The assumption is that the student's sentence should be compared to one produced by a native speaker. Sometimes this comparison is justified, as native-like speech is often a goal for the student.

This is what many students *want* to be, however, not what they *are* at the moment. It is judging the students by what they are *not* – native speakers. SLA research insists that learners have the right to be judged by the standards appropri-ate for them, not by those used for natives. 'Me go no school' is an example of learner language that shows what is going on in their minds. 'Me' shows that they do not distinguish 'I' and 'me', unlike native English; 'no' that negation consists for them of adding a negative word after the verb, unlike its usual position before the verb; 'go' that they have no grammatical endings such as '-ing', and so on. All these apparent 'mistakes' conform to regular rules in the students' own knowledge of English; they are only wrong when measured against native speech. Their sen-tences relate to their own temporary language systems at the moment when they produce the sentence, rather than to the native's version of English.

However peculiar and limited they may be, learners' sentences come from the learners' own language systems; their L2 speech shows rules and patterns of its own. At each stage learners have their own language systems. The nature of these learner systems may be very different from that of the target language. Even if they are idiosyncratic and constantly changing, they are nonetheless systematic. The starting point for SLA research is the learner's own language system. This can be called the 'independent language assumption': learners are not wilfully distorting the native system, but are inventing a system of their own. Finding out how stu-dents learn means starting from the curious rules and structures which they invent for themselves as they go along – their 'interlanguage', as Larry Selinker (1972) put it. This is shown in Figure 1.1.

Figure 1.1 The learner's independent language (interlanguage)

The interlanguage concept had a major impact on teaching techniques in the 1970s. Teaching methods that used drills and grammatical explanations had insisted on the seriousness of the students' mistakes. A mistake in an audio-lingual drill meant the student had not properly learnt the 'habit' of speaking; a mistake in a grammatical exercise meant the student had not understood the rule. The concept of the learner's own system liberated the classroom and in part paved the way for the communicative language teaching methods of the 1970s and 1980s, and the task-based learning of the 1990s. Learners' sentences reflect their temporary lan-guage systems rather than their imperfect grasp of the target language. If a student makes a 'mistake', it is not the fault of the teacher or the materials or even of the student, but an inevitable and natural part of the learning process. Teachers could now use teaching activities in which students talked to each other rather than to the teacher, because the students did not need the teacher's vigilant eye to spot what they were doing wrong. Their mistakes were minor irritants rather than major hazards. They could now work in pairs or groups, as the teacher did not have to supervise the students' speech continuously to pinpoint their mistakes.

In my own view, not yet shared by the SLA research field as a whole, the independent grammars assumption does not go far enough. On the one hand, we have the user's knowledge of their first language; on the other, their interlanguage in the second language. But these languages coexist in the same mind; one person knows both. Hence we need a name to refer to the overall knowledge that combines both the first language and the L2 interlanguage, namely *multi-competence* (Cook, 1992) – the knowledge of two languages in the same mind (shown in Figure 1.2). The lack of this concept has meant SLA research has still treated the two languages separately rather than as different facets of the same person, as we see from time to time in the rest of this book.

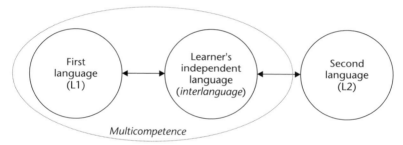

Figure 1.2 Multi-competence

Multi-competence

As this chapter has illustrated, one of the snags in discussing language teaching is the very word 'language', which has many meanings to many people. The opening sentence of this chapter said that 'language is at the centre of human life'; here 'language' is an abstract, uncountable noun used for a general property of human life ($Lang_1$), like vision, the meaning at stake in discussions of whether other species can use language. The next paragraph said, 'Some people are able to do all of this in more than one language'; here 'language' is a countable noun – there is more than one of it ($Lang_2$); this meaning covers the English language, the French language, and so on; that is to say, an abstraction describing one particular group of people, often a nation, rather than another. Later in this chapter we said that 'knowing some aspect of language consciously is no guarantee that you can use it in speech'; here 'language' has shifted meaning to the psychological knowledge in an individual human mind, what Chomsky (1965) meant by 'linguistic competence' ($Lang_5$). Then we talked about 'the language the learner produced', where 'language' now means the actual sentences that someone has said or written ($Lang_3$). Later still we commented that 'language is used for relating to other people'; 'language' also means something that is used for social reasons as part of society ($Lang_4$).

It is always important, therefore, when discussing language teaching and language acquisition, to remember which meaning of language we have in mind (Cook, 2007) – and there are doubtless many more meanings one could find. Sometimes misunderstandings occur simply because people are using different meanings of 'language' without realizing it. For example, an individual native speaker may know the English language in the psychological sense, but probably knows only a fraction of the words in any dictionary of the English language; students often feel frustrated because they measure their knowledge of a language against the grammar book and the dictionary (Lang$_2$) rather than against what an individual speaker knows (Lang$_5$).

Box 1.2 Meanings of 'language' (Cook, 2007)

- Lang$_1$: a representation system known by human beings – 'human language'
- Lang$_2$: an abstract entity – 'the English language'
- Lang$_3$: a set of sentences – everything that has been or could be said – 'the language of the Bible'
- Lang$_4$: the possession of a community – 'the language of French people'
- Lang$_5$: the knowledge in the mind of an individual – 'I have learnt French as a foreign language for eight years'

Discussion topics

1 What do you think is going on in the student's head when they are doing, say, a fill-in exercise? Have you ever checked to see if this is really the case?

2 In what ways are coursebooks a good source of information about what is going on in a classroom, and in what ways are they not?

3 Do your students share the language teaching goals you are practising or do you have to persuade them that these are right? Do you have a right to impose the goals you choose on them?

4 Why do you believe in the teaching method you use? What evidence do you have for its success?

5 Are there more similarities or dissimilarities between L1 acquisition and L2 learning?

6 What should an L2 speaker aim at if not the model of the native speaker?

7 What factors in a teaching technique do *you* think are most important?

8 What is wrong with the following sentences from students' essays? If you were their teacher, how would you correct them?

   a Anyone doesn't need any deposit in my country to rent an apartment. (Korean student)

   b I play squash so so and I wish in Sunday's morning arrange matches with a girl who plays like me. (Italian)

   c Everytimes I concentrate to speak out, don't know why always had Chinese in my mind. (Chinese)

d Raelly I am so happy. I wold like to give you my best congratulate. and I wold like too to till you my real apologise, becuse my mother is very sik. (Arabic)

e I please you very much you allow me to stay with you this Christmas. (Spanish)

Further reading

Good technical introductions to L2 learning and bilingualism can be found in Myles and Mitchell, *Second Language Learning Theories* (2004) and VanPatten and Williams (2006) *Theories in Second Language Acquisition*; a brief overview can be found in 'Linguistics and second language acquisition: one person with two languages' (Cook, 2000) in *The Blackwell Handbook of Linguistics*. Useful books with similar purposes but covering slightly different approaches to second language acquisition are: Lightbown and Spada (2006) *How Languages are Learned* and Cohen (1990) *Language Learning*. Some useful resources to follow up SLA and teaching on the web are the *Second Language Acquisition Bibliography* (SLABIB) at http://homepage.ntlworld.com/vivian.c/Vivian%20Cook.htm; the *European Second Language Association* (EUROSLA) at http://eurosla.org; and Dave's ESL Café at www.eslcafe.com Those interested in the nineteenth-century revolution in language teaching should go to Howatt (2004) *A History of English Language Teaching*. More information is available on the website for this book, *www.hoddereducation. com/viviancook*. The issue of the meanings of 'language' is treated at greater length in Cook (2007).

Glosses on language teaching methods

audio-lingual method: this combined a learning theory based on ideas of habit formation and practice with a view of language as patterns and structures; it chiefly made students repeat sentences recorded on tape and practise structures in repetitive drills; originating in the USA in the 1940s, its peak of popularity was probably the 1960s, though it was not much used in British-influenced EFL (**Note**: it is not usually abbreviated to ALM since these initials belong to a particular trademarked method)

audio-visual method: this used visual images to show the meaning of spoken dialogues and believed in treating language as a whole rather than divided up into different aspects; teaching relied on filmstrips and taped dialogues for repetition; it emerged chiefly in France in the 1960s and 1970s

communicative teaching: this based language teaching on the functions that the second language had for the student and on the meanings they wanted to express, leading to teaching exercises that made the students communicate with each other in various ways; from the mid-1970s onwards this became the most influential way of teaching around the globe, not just for English

direct method: essentially any method that relies on the second language throughout

grammar-translation method: the traditional academic style of teaching which placed heavy emphasis on grammar explanation and translation as a teaching technique

task-based learning: this approach sees learning as arising from particular tasks the students do in the classroom and has been seen increasingly as a logical development from communicative language teaching

The details of many of these are discussed further in Chapter 13.

Learning and teaching different types of grammar

2

A language has patterns and regularities which are used to convey meaning, some of which make up its grammar. One important aspect of grammar in most languages is the order of words: any speaker of English knows that 'Mr Bean loves Teddy' does not have the same meaning as 'Teddy loves Mr Bean'. Another aspect of grammar consists of changes in the forms of words, more important in some languages than others: 'This bush flowered in May' means something different from 'These bushes flower in May' because of the differences between 'This/these', 'bush/bushes' and 'flowered/flower'. The glossary on page 44 defines some grammatical terms.

Many linguists consider grammar to be the central part of the language in the Lang₅ sense of the knowledge in an individual mind, around which other parts such as pronunciation and vocabulary revolve. However important the other components of language may be in themselves, they are connected to each other through grammar. Chomsky calls it the 'computational system' that relates sound and meaning, trivial in itself but impossible to manage without.

Originally the word 'glamour' came from the same root as 'grammar'; the person who knew grammar was glamorous and could cast mysterious spells. In the fifteenth-century ballad 'King Estmere', it is said of two brothers, 'And aye their swordes soe sore can byte, Through help of gramarye.' Grammar is indeed one of the mysteries of human life.

Grammar is the most unique aspect of language. It has features that do not occur in other mental processes and that are not apparently found in animal languages. According to linguists (though psychologists often disagree), grammar is learnt in different ways from anything else that people learn.

In some ways, as grammar is highly systematic, its effects are usually fairly obvious and frequent in people's speech or writing – one reason why so much SLA research has concentrated on grammar. This chapter first looks at different types of grammar and then selects some areas of grammatical research into L2 learning to represent the main approaches.

2.1 What *is* grammar?

Focusing questions

- What *is* grammar?
- How do you think it is learnt?
- How would you teach it?

Keywords

prescriptive grammar: grammar that 'prescribes' what people should or should not say

traditional grammar: 'school' grammar concerned with labelling sentences with parts of speech, and so on

structural grammar: grammar concerned with how words go into phrases, and phrases into sentences

grammatical (linguistic) competence: the knowledge of language stored in a person's mind

---

Glosses on some grammatical terminology are given at the end of the chapter and appear on the website.

To explain what the term 'grammar' means in the context of L2 learning, it is easiest to start by eliminating what it does *not* mean.

Prescriptive grammar

One familiar type of grammar is the rules found in schoolbooks, for example, the warnings against final prepositions in sentences, 'This can't be put up with', or the diatribes in letters to the newspaper about split infinitives, 'To boldly go where no one has gone before'. This is called *prescriptive grammar* because it prescribes what people ought to do. Modern grammarians have mostly avoided prescriptive grammar because they see their job as describing what the rules of language *are*, just as the physicist says what the laws of physics are. The grammarian has no more right to decree how people *should* speak than the physicist has to decree how electrons should move; their task is to describe what happens. Language is bound up with human lives in so many ways that it is easy to find reasons why some grammatical forms are 'better' than others, but these are based on criteria other than the grammar itself, mostly to do with social status; for example, that you should not say 'ain't'. The grammarian's duty is to decide what people actually say; after this has been carried out, others may decide that it would be better to change what people say. Hence all the other types of grammar discussed below are 'descriptive' in that they claim to describe the grammar that real people know and use, even if sometimes this claim is given no more than lip service.

Prescriptive grammar is all but irrelevant to the language teaching classroom. Since the 1960s people have believed that you should teach the language as it *is*, not as it *ought to be*. Students should learn to speak real language that people use, not an artificial form that nobody uses – we all use split infinitives from time to time when the circumstances make it necessary, and it is often awkward to avoid them. Mostly, however, these prescriptive dos and don'ts about 'between you and me' or 'it is I' are not important enough or frequent enough to spend much time thinking about their implications for language teaching. If L2 learners need to pander to these shibboleths, a teacher can quickly provide a list of the handful of forms that pedants object to.

One area where prescriptive grammar still thrives is spelling and punctuation, where everyone believes there is a single 'correct' spelling for every word: spell <receive> as <recieve> or <news> as <new's> at your peril. Another is word processing; the program I use for writing this warns me against using final prepositions and passives, common as they are in everyday English. A third is journal editors, who have often been nasty about my sentences without verbs – to me a normal variation in prose found on many pages of any novel.

Traditional grammar

A second popular meaning of 'grammar' concerns the parts of speech: the 'fact' that 'a noun is a word that is the name of a person, place, thing, or idea' is absorbed by every school pupil in England. This definition comes straight from *Tapestry Writing 1* (Pike-Baky, 2000), a course published in the year 2000, but which differs little from William Cobbett's definition in 1819: 'Nouns are the names of persons and things'.

Analysing sentences in this approach means labelling the parts with their names and giving rules that explain in words how they may be combined. This is often called *traditional grammar*. In essence it goes back to the grammars of Latin, receiving its English form in the grammars of the eighteenth century, many of which in fact set out to be prescriptive. Grammarians today do not reject this type of grammar outright so much as feel that it is unscientific. After reading the definition of a noun, we still do not know what it is, in the way that we know what a chemical element is: is 'fire' a noun? 'opening'? 'she'? The answer is that we do not know without seeing the word in a sentence, but the context is not mentioned in the definition. While the parts of speech are indeed relevant to grammar, there are many other powerful grammatical concepts that are equally important.

 A useful modern source is the *NASA Manual* in the list of links on the website, which provides sensible advice in largely traditional terms, such as: 'The subject and verb should be the most important elements of a sentence. Too many modifiers, particularly between the subject and verb, can over-power these elements.'

Some language teaching uses a type of grammar resembling a sophisticated form of traditional grammar. Grammar books for language teaching often present grammar through a series of visual displays and examples. A case in point is the stalwart *Basic Grammar in Use* (Murphy, 2002, 2nd edn). A typical unit is headed 'flower/flowers' (singular and plural). It has a display of singular and plural forms ('a flower > some flowers'), lists of idiosyncratic spellings of plurals ('babies, shelves'), words that are unexpectedly plural ('scissors'), and plurals not in '-s' ('mice'). It explains: 'The plural of a noun is usually '-s'.' In other words, it assumes that students know what the term 'plural' means, presumably because it will translate into all languages. But Japanese does not have plural forms for nouns; Japanese students have said to me that they only acquired the concept of singular and plural through learning English. Languages like Tongan, or indeed Old English, have *three* forms: singular, plural and dual ('two people'). The crucial question, for linguists at any rate, is how the subject of the sentence agrees with the verb in terms of singular or plural, which is not mentioned in Murphy's text, although two out of the four exercises that follow depend on it.

Even main coursebooks often rely on the students knowing the terms of traditional grammar. In the very first lesson of an EFL course for beginners called *Changes* (Richards, 1998: 16), the grammar summary uses the technical terms in English 'subject pronouns', 'possessive adjective', 'contraction' and 'statement'. Goodness knows how the students are supposed to have learnt these technical terms in another language; modern language teachers in UK schools lament that pupils are no longer equipped with this framework of traditional grammatical terminology. Nor would switching to the students' first language necessarily be much help: in countries like Japan grammar does not come out of the Latin-based European traditional grammar, and it uses quite different terms and concepts.

Structural grammar

Language teaching has also made use of *structural grammar* based on the concept of phrase structure, which shows how some words go together in the sentence and some do not. In a sentence such as 'The man fed the dog', the word 'the' seems somehow to go with 'man', but 'fed' does not seem to go with 'the'. Suppose we group the words that seem to go together: 'the' clearly goes with 'man', so we can recognize a structure '(the man)'; 'the' goes with 'dog' to get another '(the dog)'. Then these structures can be combined with the remaining words: 'fed' belongs with '(the dog)' to get a new structure '(fed the dog)', not with 'the man' in 'the man fed'. Now the two structures '(the man)' and '(fed the dog)' go together to assemble the whole sentence. This phrase structure is usually presented in tree diagrams that show how words build up into phrases and phrases build up into sentences (see Figure 2.1).

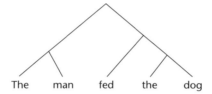

The   man   fed   the   dog

Figure 2.1 An example of a phrase structure tree

Structural grammar thus describes how the elements of the sentence fit together in an overall structure built up from smaller and smaller structures.

Teachers have been using structural grammar directly in substitution tables since at least the 1920s. A typical example can be seen in the Bulgarian coursebook *English for the Fifth Class* (Despotova *et al.*, 1988) (see Figure 2.2).

They	can draw a	black	dog
I		white	car
You		red	rose

Figure 2.2 A typical substitution table

Students form sentences by choosing a word from each column: 'I. . . can draw a. . . black. . . rose'. They are substituting different words within a constant grammatical structure. Substitution tables are still common in present-day coursebooks and grammar books, though more today as graphic displays of grammar, as Chapter 13 illustrates.

Such exercises have long been a staple of language teaching in one guise or another. Structure drills and pattern practice draw on similar ideas of structure, as in the following exercise from my own *Realistic English* (Abbs *et al.*, 1968):

You can go and see him.
Well, if I go. . .
He can come and ask you.
Well, if he comes. . .
They can write and tell her.
Well, if they write. . .

The students replace the verb each time within the structure 'Well, if *pronoun verb*', dinning in the present tense for possible conditions. Chapter 13 provides further discussion of such drills.

Grammar as knowledge in the mind

SLA research relies mainly on another meaning of 'grammar' – the knowledge of language that the speaker possesses in the mind, known as *linguistic* or *grammatical competence*, originally taken from Chomsky's work of the 1960s. A more recent definition is as follows:

> By 'grammatical competence' I mean the cognitive state that encompasses all those aspects of form and meaning and their relation, including underlying structures that enter into that relation, which are properly assigned to the specific subsystem of the human mind that relates representations of form and meaning. (Chomsky, 1980: 59)

All speakers know the grammar of their language in this Lang₅ sense of 'language' as a mental state without having to study it. A speaker of English knows that 'Is John is the man who French?' is wrong, without looking it up in any book – indeed few grammar books would be much help. A native speaker knows the system of the language. He or she may not be able to verbalize this knowledge clearly; it is 'implicit' knowledge below the level of consciousness.

Nevertheless, no one could produce a single sentence of English without having English grammar present in their minds. A woman who spontaneously says 'The man fed the dog' shows that she knows the word order typical of English in which the subject 'The man' comes before the verb 'fed'. She knows the ways of making irregular past tenses in English – 'fed' rather than the regular '-ed' ('feeded'); she knows that 'dog' needs an article 'the' or 'a'; and she knows that 'the' is used to talk about a dog that the listener already knows about. This is very different from being able to talk about the sentence she has produced, only possible for people who have been taught explicit 'grammar'.

A parallel can be found in a teaching exercise that baffles students – devising instructions for everyday actions. Try asking the students, 'Tell me how to put my coat on.' Everyone knows how to put a coat on in one sense, but is unable to describe their actions. There is one type of knowledge in our mind which we can talk about consciously, another which is far from conscious. We can all put on our coats or produce an English sentence; few of us can describe *how* we do it. This view of grammar as knowledge treats it as something stored unconsciously in the mind – the native speaker's competence. The rationale for the paraphernalia of grammatical analysis such as sentence trees, structures and rules is ultimately that they describe the competence in our minds.

As well as grammatical competence, native speakers also possess knowledge of how language is used. This is often called *communicative competence* by those who see the public functions of language as crucial (Hymes, 1972), rather than the ways we use language inside our minds. Sheer knowledge of language has little point if speakers cannot use it appropriately for all the activities in which they want to take part – complaining, arguing, persuading, declaring war, writing love letters, buying season tickets, and so on. Many linguists see language as having private functions as well as public – language for dreaming or planning a day out. Hence the more general term *pragmatic competence* reflects all the possible uses of language rather than restricting them to communication (Chomsky, 1986): praying, mental arithmetic, keeping a diary, making a shopping list, and many others. In other words, while no one denies that there is far more to language than grammar, many linguists see it as the invisible central spine that holds everything else together.

Box 2.1 shows the typical grammatical elements in beginners' English coursebooks. This gives some idea of the types of structure that are taught to beginners in most classrooms around the world. The grammar is the typical medley of traditional and structural items. A clear presentation of this can be found in Harmer (1998). Many of these items are the basis for language teaching and for SLA research.

Box 2.1 Grammar for beginners

Here are the elements of English grammar common to lessons 1–5 of three modern beginners' books for adults, with examples:

1 present of to be: It's in Japan. I'm Mark. He's Jack Kennedy's nephew.
2 articles a/an: I'm a student. She is an old woman. It's an exciting place.
3 subject pronouns: She's Italian. I've got two brothers and a sister. Do you have black or white coffee?
4 in/from with places: You ask a woman in the street the time. I'm from India. She lives in London.
5 noun plurals: boys / parents / sandwiches.

2.2 Structure words, morphemes and sequences of acquisition

Focusing questions

- What do you understand by a structure (function) word?
- What do you think are the main characteristics of beginners' sentences in English or another modern language?

Keywords

content words such as 'table' or 'truth' have meanings that can be found in dictionaries and consist of nouns, verbs, adjectives and (possibly) prepositions

structure (function) words such as articles 'the' and 'a' exist to form part of phrases and structures and so have meanings that are difficult to capture in the dictionary

morpheme: the smallest unit of grammar, consisting either of a word ('toast') or part of a word ("'s" in 'John's')

morphology and syntax: morphology is the branch of linguistics that deals with the structure of morphemes; syntax is the branch that deals with the structure of phrases above the level of the word

grammatical morphemes are morphemes such as '-ing' and 'the' that play a greater part in structure than content words such as 'horse' (lexical morphemes)

order of difficulty: the scale of difficulty for particular aspects of grammar for L2 learners

sequence of acquisition: the order in which L2 learners acquire the grammar, pronunciation, and so on of the language

Box 2.2 Types of grammar

Grammar can be:

1 a way of telling people what they ought to say, rather than reporting what they do say (prescriptive grammar);
2 a system for describing sentence structure used in English schools for centuries, based on grammars of classical languages such as Latin (traditional grammar);
3 a system for describing sentences based on the idea of smaller structures built up into larger structures (structural grammar);
4 the knowledge of the structural regularities of language in the minds of speakers (linguistic/grammatical competence);
5 EFL grammar combining elements of (2) and (3).

An important distinction for language teaching has been that between 'content' words and 'structure' words, also known as 'function' words. Here is a quotation from a Theodore Sturgeon story that combines made-up content words with real structure words:

So on Lirht, while the decisions on the fate of the miserable Hvov were being formulated, gwik still fardled, funted and fupped.

The same sentence with made-up structure words might have read:

> So kel Mars, dom trelk decisions kel trelk fate mert trelk miserable slaves hiv polst formulated, deer still grazed, jumped kosp survived.

Only the first version is comprehensible in some form, even if we have no idea how you fardle and funt.

Content words have meanings that can be looked up in a dictionary and they are numbered in many thousands. 'Beer' or 'palimpsest' are content words referring to definable things. A new content word can be invented easily; advertisers try to do it all the time – 'Contains the magic new ingredient kryptonite'.

Structure words, on the other hand, are limited in number, consisting of words like 'the', 'to' and 'yet'. A computer program for teaching English needs about 220 structure words; the ten most common words in the British National Corpus 100 million sample are all structure words, as we see in Chapter 3. Structure words are described in grammar books rather than dictionaries. The meaning of 'the' or 'of' depends on the grammatical rules of the language, not on dictionary definitions. It is virtually impossible to invent a new structure word because it would mean changing the grammatical rules of the language, which are fairly rigid, rather than adding an item to the stock of words of the language, which can easily take a few more. Science fiction novelists, for example, have a good time inventing new words for aliens, ranging from 'Alaree' to 'Vatch'; new nouns for new scientific ideas, ranging from 'noocyte' (artificially created intelligent cells) to 'iahklu' (the Aldebaranian ability to influence the world through dreams). Where Lewis Carroll once coined nouns like 'chortle', William Gibson now contributes 'cyberpunk' to the language. But no writer dares invent new structure words. The only exception perhaps is Marge Piercy's non-sexist pronoun 'per' for 'he/she' in the novel *Woman on the Edge of Time*, first coined by the psychologist Donald McKay.

Table 2.1 shows the main differences between content and structure words. As can be seen, the distinction is quite powerful, affecting everything from the spelling to speech production. Nevertheless, this simplistic division needs to be made far more complicated to catch the complexities of a language like English, as we shall see.

As well as words, most linguists' grammars use a unit called the morpheme, defined as the smallest element that has meaning. Some words consist of a single morpheme – 'to', 'book', 'like' or 'black'. Some words can have morphemes added to show their grammatical role in the sentence, say 'books' (book+s) or 'blacker' (black+er). Other words can be split into several morphemes: 'mini-supermarket' might be 'mini-super-market'; 'hamburger' is seen as 'ham-burger' rather than 'Hamburg-er'. When the phrase structure of a sentence is shown in tree diagrams, the whole sentence is at the top and the morphemes are at the bottom: the morpheme is the last possible grammatical fragment at the bottom of the tree. The structure and behaviour of morphemes are dealt with in the area of grammar called morphology.

In some SLA research, grammatical inflections like '-ing' are grouped together with structure words like 'to' as 'grammatical morphemes'. In the 1970s Heidi Dulay and Marina Burt (1973) decided to see how these grammatical morphemes were learnt by L2 learners. They made Spanish-speaking children learning English describe pictures and checked how often they supplied eight grammatical morphemes in the appropriate places in the sentence. Suppose that at a low level, L2

Content words	Structure words
are in the dictionary: 'book'	are in the grammar: 'the'
exist in large numbers, 615,000 in the *Oxford English Dictionary*	are limited in number, say, 220 in English
vary in frequency: 'book' versus 'honved'	are high frequency: 'to', 'the', 'I'
are used more in written language	are used more in spoken language
are more likely to be preceded by a pause in speech	are less likely to be preceded by a pause in speech
consist of nouns 'glass'; verbs 'move'; adjectives 'glossy', etc.	consist of prepositions 'to'; articles 'a'; pronouns 'he', etc.
are always pronounced and spelt the same: 'look' /lʊk/	vary in pronunciation for emphasis, etc.: 'have' /hæv, hǝv, ǝv, v/
have a fixed stress or stresses: 'pilot'	are stressed for emphasis, etc.: 'the' /ði: ~ ðǝ/
have more than two letters: 'eye', 'Ann'	can consist of one or two letters: 'I', 'an'
are pronounced with an initial voiceless 'th': 'theory' /θ/	are pronounced with an initial voiced 'th': 'there' /ð/
can always be invented: 'cyberpunk'	can seldom be invented

Table 2.1 Content words and structure words

learners say sentences with two content words, like 'Girl go'. How do they expand this rudimentary sentence into its full form?

1 *Plural '-s'*. The easiest morpheme for them was the plural '-s', getting 'Girls go'.
2 *Progressive '-ing'*. Next easiest was the word ending '-ing' in present continuous forms like 'going', 'Girls going'.
3 *Copula forms of 'be'*. Next came the use of 'be' as a copula, that is, as a main verb in the sentence ('John is happy') rather than as an auxiliary used with another verb ('John is going'). Changing the sentence slightly gets 'Girls *are* here'.
4 *Auxiliary form of 'be'*. After this came the auxiliary forms of 'be' with '-ing', yielding 'Girls *are* going'.
5 *Definite and indefinite articles 'the' and 'a'*. Next in difficulty came the definite and indefinite articles 'the' and 'a', enabling the learners to produce '*The* girls go' or '*A* girl go'.
6 *Irregular past tense*. Next were the irregular English past tenses such as 'came' and 'went', that is, those verbs that do *not* have an '-ed' ending pronounced in the usual three ways /d/, /t/ or /ɪd/, 'played', 'learnt' and 'waited', as in 'The girls *went*'.
7 *Third person '-s'*. Next came the third person '-s' used with verbs, as in 'The girl go*es*'.

8 *Possessive "s'*. Most difficult of the eight endings was the "s' ending used with nouns to show possession, as in 'The girl*'s* book'.

The sequence from 1 to 8 mirrors the order of difficulty for the L2 learners Dulay and Burt studied. They had least difficulty with plural '-s' and most difficulty with possessive "s'. The interesting discovery was the similarities between the L2 learners. It was not just Spanish-speaking children who have a sequence of difficulty for the eight grammatical morphemes. Similar orders have been found for Japanese children and for Korean adults (Makino, 1980; Lee, 1981), though not for one Japanese child (Hakuta, 1974). The first language does not seem to make a crucial difference: all L2 learners have much the same order. This was quite surprising in that people had thought that the main problem in acquiring grammar was transfer from the first language; now it turned out that learners had the same types of mistake whatever the first language they spoke. The other surprise was that it did not seem to matter if the learners were children or adults; adults have roughly the same order as children (Krashen *et al.*, 1976). It does not even make much difference whether or not they are attending a language class (Larsen-Freeman, 1976). There is a strong similarity between all L2 learners of English, whatever the explanation may be. This research with grammatical morphemes was the first to demonstrate the common factors of L2 learners so clearly.

While grammatical morphemes petered out as a topic of research in the 1990s, it was the precursor of much research to do with the acquisition of grammatical inflections such as past tense '-ed' which is still common today. Yet there are still things to learn from this area. Muhammad Hannan (2004), for instance, used it to find a sequence of acquisition for Bengali-speaking children in East London, as mentioned in Chapter 1. At the age of 5, they knew only '-ing', as in 'looking'; by 6 they had added past tense /t/ 'looked'; by 7 irregular past tenses such as 'went', and regular /d/ 'played'; by 8 past participles '-en' 'been'; by 9 the only persistent problem was with 'zero' past 'hit'. Clearly these children made a consistent progression for grammatical morphemes over time.

This type of research brought important confirmation of the idea of the learner's independent language, interlanguage. Learners from many backgrounds seemed to be creating the same kind of grammar for English out of what they heard, and were passing through more or less the same stages of acquisition. They were reacting in the same way to the shared experience of learning English. While the first language made some difference, its influence was dwarfed by what the learners had in common. Indeed, at one point Dulay and Burt (1973) dramatically claimed that only 3 per cent of learners' errors could be attributed to interference from the first language. While later research has seldom found such a low incidence, nevertheless it became clear that much of the learning of a second language was common to all L2 learners rather than being simply transfer from their first language.

One of the best demonstrations of the independence of interlanguage came from a research programme that investigated the acquisition of five second languages by adult migrant workers in Europe, known as the ESF (European Science Foundation) project. Researchers found a basic grammar that all L2 learners shared, which had three simple rules; a sentence may consist of:

- a noun phrase followed by a verb, optionally followed by another noun phrase 'girl take bread';

- a noun phrase followed by a copula and another noun phrase or an adjective 'it's bread';
- a verb followed by a noun phrase 'pinching its'.

Box 2.3 Early acquisition of grammar

- Content and structure words differ in many ways, including the ways they are used in sentences and how they are pronounced.
- Grammatical morphemes (structure words and grammatical inflections) are learnt in a particular sequence in L2 acquisition.
- L2 learners acquire the same basic grammar regardless of the first and second languages involved.

L2 learners not only have an interlanguage grammar, they have the *same* interlanguage grammar, regardless of the language they are learning. In other words, all that teachers can actually expect from learners after a year or so is a sparse grammar having these three rules; whatever the teacher may try to do, this may be what the learners achieve.

2.3 The processability model

Focusing questions

- Do you find problems in following certain structures in your L2, or indeed your L1?
- Why do you think you find some structures more difficult to follow than others?

Keywords

movement: a way of describing some sentences as being based on moving various elements about

processability: sequences of acquisition may reflect the ease with which certain structures can be processed by the mind

sequence of development: the inevitable progression of learners through definite stages of acquisition

the teachability hypothesis: 'an L2 structure can be learnt from instruction only if the learner's interlanguage is close to the point when this structure is acquired in the natural setting' (Pienemann, 1984: 201)

The problem with research into sequences of acquisition was that it tended to say *what* the learners did rather than *why* they did it. During the 1980s an attempt was made to create a broader-based sequence of development, first called the *multidimensional model*, later the *processability model*, which believed that the explanation

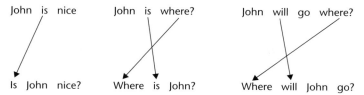

Figure 2.3 Examples of movement in syntax

for sequences must lie in the expanding capacity of the learner's mind to handle the grammar of L2 sentences. The core idea was that some sentences are formed by moving elements from one position to another. English questions, for example, move the auxiliary or the question word to the beginning of the sentence, a familiar idea to language teachers. So 'John is nice' becomes 'Is John nice?' by moving 'is' to the beginning; 'John is where?' becomes 'Where is John?' by moving 'where' and 'is'; and 'John will go where?' becomes 'Where will John go?' by moving both 'where' and 'will' in front of 'John'.

The multidimensional model sees movement as the key element in understanding the learning sequence. The learner starts with sentences without movement and learns how to move the various parts of the sentence around to get the final form. The learner ascends the structural tree from bottom to top, first learning to deal with words, next with phrases, then with simple sentences, and finally with subordinate clauses in complex sentences.

Stage 1

To start with, the learners can produce only one word at a time, say, 'ticket' or 'beer', or formulas such as 'What's the time?' At this stage the learners know content words but have no idea of grammatical structure; the words come out in a stream without being put in phrases and without grammatical morphemes, as if the learners had a dictionary in their mind but no grammar.

Stage 2

Next learners acquire the typical word order of the language. In both English and German this is the subject verb object (SVO) order – 'John likes beer', 'Hans liebt Bier'. This is the only word order that the learners know; they do not have any alternative word orders based on movement such as questions. So they put negatives in the front of the sentence as in 'No me live here' and make questions with rising intonation such as 'You like me?', both of which maintain the basic word order of English without needing movement.

In the next stages the learners discover how to move elements about, in particular to the beginnings and ends of the sentence.

Stage 3

Now the learners start to move elements to the beginning of the sentence. So they put adverbials at the beginning – 'On Tuesday I went to London'; they use wh-words at the beginning with no inversion – 'Who lives in Camden?'; and they move auxiliaries to get yes/no questions – 'Will you be there?' Typical sentences at this stage are 'Yesterday I sick' and 'Beer I like', in both of which the initial element has been moved from later in the sentence.

Stage 4

At the next stage, learners discover how the preposition can be separated from its phrase in English – 'the patient he looked after' rather than 'the patient after which he looked' – a phenomenon technically known as preposition-stranding, which is the antithesis of the prescriptive grammar rule. They also start to use the '-ing' ending – 'I'm reading a good book'.

Stage 5

Next come question-word questions such as 'Where is he going to be?'; the third person grammatical morpheme '-s', 'He likes'; and the dative with 'to', 'He gave his name to the receptionist'. At this stage the learners are starting to work *within* the structure of the sentence, not just using the beginning or the end as locations to move elements to. Another new feature is the third person '-s' ending of verbs, 'He smokes'.

Stage 6

The final stage is acquiring the order of subordinate clauses. In English this sometimes differs from the order in the main clause. The question order is 'Will he go?' but the reported question is 'Jane asked if he *would go*', not 'Jane asked if *would he go*', to the despair of generations of EFL students. At this stage the learner is sorting out the more untypical orders in subordinate clauses after the ordinary main clause order has been learnt. In addition, this stage includes structures such as 'He gave me the book', where the indirect object precedes the direct object, as opposed to 'He gave the book to me' with the reverse order.

The multidimensional model stresses that L2 learners have a series of interim grammars of English – interlanguages. Their first grammar is just words; the second uses words in an SVO order; the third uses word order with some elements moved to the beginning or end, and so on. As with grammatical morphemes, this sequence seems inexorable: all learners go through these overall stages in the same order. The recent development of the multidimensional model has been called the *processability model* because it explains these sequences in terms of the grammatical processes involved in the production of a sentence, which are roughly as follows:

1 The learner gets access to individual content words 'see. car.'
2 The learner gets access to grammatical structure words 'see. the car.' (called the 'category procedure').
3 The learner assembles these into phrases 'he see. the car.' (the 'phrasal procedure').
4 The learner puts the phrases together within the sentence 'he will see the car' (the 'S-procedure').
5 The learner can work with both main clauses and subordinate clauses: 'If he looks out of the window, he will see the car' (the 'subordinate clause procedure').

In a sense, the teacher is helpless to do much about sequences like the grammatical morphemes order. If all students have to acquire language in more or less the same sequence, the teacher can only fit in with it. This processability model leads to the *teachability hypothesis*: 'an L2 structure can be learnt from instruction only if the learner's interlanguage is close to the point when this structure is acquired in the natural setting' (Pienemann, 1984: 201). So teachers should teach according to the stage that their students are at. To take some examples from the above sequence:

- Do not teach the third person '-s' ending of present tense verbs in 'He likes' at early stages as it inevitably comes late.
- In the early stages concentrate on the main word order of subject verb object (SVO), 'Cats like milk', and do not expect learners to learn the word order of questions, 'What do cats like?', and so on, until much later.
- Introduce sentence-initial adverbials, 'In summer I play tennis', as a way into the movement involved in questions, 'Do you like Brahms?'

These are three possible suggestions out of the many that arise from the research. They conflict with the sequence in which the grammatical points are usually introduced in textbooks; '-s' endings and questions often come in opening lessons; initial adverbial phrases are unlikely to be taught before questions. It may be that there are good teaching reasons why these suggestions should not be taken on board. For instance, when people tried postponing using questions for the first year of teaching to avoid movement, this created enormous practical problems in the classroom, where questions are the lifeblood. But these ideas are nevertheless worth considering in the sequencing of materials, whatever other factors may overrule them.

Let us compare the sequence of elements in a typical EFL course with that in the processability model. A typical modern course is *Flying Colours* (Garton-Sprenger and Greenall, 1990), intended for adult beginners. Unit 1 of *Flying Colours* starts with the student looking for 'international words' such as 'bar' and 'jeans', and repeating short formulas such as 'What's your name?' and 'I don't understand'. Thus it starts with words rather than structures, as does the processability model. Unit 2, however, plunges into questions: 'What is your phone number?', 'Would you like some French onion soup?', 'What does Kenneth Hill do?' In terms of the processability model these come in stages 3 and 5 and should not be attempted until the students have the main subject verb object structure of English fixed in their minds. Certainly this early introduction of questions is a major difference from the processability model. Unit 3 introduces the present continuous tense – 'She's wearing a jacket and jeans'. While this is already late compared to courses that introduce the present continuous in lesson 1, it is far in advance of its position in the processability model sequence at stage 4. Subordinate clauses are not mentioned in *Flying Colours*, apart from comparative clauses in Unit 6. Looking through the text, however, one finds in Unit 1 that the students have to understand sentences such as 'When he goes to a foreign country, he learns. . .' ('when' clause), 'Listen and say who is speaking' (reported speech clause), 'Boris Becker wins after a hurricane stops the match' ('after' clause), 'The only other things I buy are a map and some postcards' (relative clause). Clearly subordinate clauses are not seen as particularly difficult; the processability model, however, insists that they are mastered last of all.

Some other differences between the L2 stages and the sequences in EFL coursebooks are:

- The textbook collapses two L2 stages into one. *Atlas 1* (Nunan, 1995), for example, teaches auxiliary questions 'Can you come to my birthday party tomorrow?', copula questions 'Are you Michael Shaw?', wh-questions 'Where are you from?' and reported questions 'Talk about where you are from' all in Unit 1 of a 'beginning' course, despite the fact that in the processability model these would be scattered across stages 3 to 6.

- The textbook goes against some aspects of the order. For example, *Tapestry 1 Writing* (Pike-Baky, 2000) for 'high beginning' students uses subordinate clauses from the outset, despite their apparent lateness in acquisition. Chapter 2 has instructions 'Think about where you go every day', text sentences 'So he designed an environment where people "can take their minds off" their problems', and completion sentences 'I believe that Feng Shui. . .', all of which would be impossible for students below the most advanced stage of the processability model.

- The coursebook omits some stages, for instance, not teaching initial adverbs and preposition-stranding, unmentioned in the grammatical syllabuses for, say, *New Cutting Edge* (Cunningham *et al.*, 2005), *New Headway* (Soars and Soars, 2002) or *Just Right* (Harmer, 2004), even if they doubtless creep in somewhere.

- When coursebooks make use of grammatical sequences at all, they tend to rely on a skeleton of tenses and verb forms, by no means central to the processability model or indeed to any of the approaches found in SLA research. For instance *International Express* (Taylor, 1996) for pre-intermediates follows the sequence present simple (Unit 1), present continuous (2), past simple (3), present perfect (6), future 'will' (9), passives (12) – a typical EFL teaching sequence for most of the twentieth century but virtually unconnected to any of the L2 learning sequences.

One problem is very hard for language teaching to resolve. Learners' interlanguages contain rules that are different from the native speaker's competence. The student may temporarily produce sentences that deviate from native correctness, say, stage 2 'No me live here'. Many teaching techniques, however, assume that the point of an exercise is to get the student to produce sentences from the very first lesson that are completely correct in terms of the target language, even if they are severely restricted in terms of grammar and vocabulary. The students are *not* supposed to be producing sentences like 'No me live here' in the classroom. Teaching materials similarly only present sentences that are possible in terms of the target language, never letting learners hear sentences such as 'No me live here'. Hence the classroom and the textbook can never fully reflect the stages that interlanguages go through, which may well be quite ungrammatical in terms of the target language for a long time – just as children only get round to fully grammatical sentences in their first language after many years. There is an implicit tension between the pressure on students to produce well-formed sentences and the natural stages that students go through. Should learners be allowed to produce these 'mistakes' in the classroom, since they are inevitable? Or should the teacher try to prevent them? The answers to these questions also affect when and how the teacher will correct the student's 'mistakes'.

Box 2.4 Processability

- Learners acquire a second language in a sequence of six grammatical stages.
- These stages relate to the learners' growing ability to process language in their minds.
- Sequences of teaching currently do not fit these six stages and may place undue demands on learners.

2.4 Principles and parameters grammar

Focusing questions

- Do you think that you learnt your first language entirely from your parents or do you think some of it was already present in your mind?
- If you came from Mars, what would you say all human languages had in common?

Keywords

Universal Grammar: the language faculty built into the human mind consisting of principles and parameters

principles of language: aspects of human language present in all human minds, for example, the locality principle – why you cannot say 'Is John is the man who happy?'

parameters: aspects that vary from one language to another within tightly set limits, whether or not subjects are required in the sentence – the pro-drop parameter

So far, this chapter has discussed grammar in terms of morphemes, content and structure words, and movement. All these capture some aspect of L2 learning and contribute to our knowledge of the whole. A radically different way of looking at grammar that has become popular in recent years, however, tries to see what human languages have in common. This is the Universal Grammar theory associated with Noam Chomsky. Universal Grammar (UG) sees the knowledge of grammar in the mind as made up of two components: 'principles' that all languages have in common and 'parameters' on which they vary. All human minds are believed to honour the common principles that are forced on them by the nature of the human mind that all their speakers share. They differ over the settings for the parameters for particular languages. The overall implications of the UG model are given in Chapter 12.

Principles of language

One principle that has been proposed is called locality. How do you explain to a student how to make English questions such as 'Is Sam the cat that is black?' One possible instruction is to describe the movement involved: 'Start from the sentence: "Sam is the cat that is black" and move the *second* word "is" to the beginning.'

This works satisfactorily for this one example. But if the students used this rule, they would go completely wrong with sentences such as 'The old man is the one who's late', producing 'Old the man is the one who's late?' Something obvious must be missing from the explanation.

To patch it up, you might suggest: 'Move the copula "is" to the beginning of the sentence.' So the student can now produce 'Is the old man the one who's late?' But suppose the student wanted to make a question out of 'Sam is the cat that is black'? As well as producing the sentence 'Is Sam the cat that is black?' the rule also allows 'Is Sam is the cat that black?' It is obvious to us all that no one would ever dream of producing this question; but *why* not? It is just as possible logically to move one 'is' as the other.

The explanation again needs modifying to say: 'Move the copula "is" *in the main clause* to the beginning of the sentence.' This instruction depends on the listeners knowing enough of the structure of the sentence to be able to distinguish the main clause from the relative clause. In other words, it presupposes that they know the structure of the sentence; anybody producing a question in English takes the structure of the sentence into account. Inversion questions in English, and indeed in all other languages, involve a knowledge of structure, not just of the order of the words. But they also involve the locality principle which says that such movement has to be 'local', that is, within the same area of structure rather than across areas of structure that span the whole sentence. There is no particular reason why this should be so; computer languages, for instance, do not behave like this, nor do mathematical equations. It is just an odd feature of human languages that they depend on structure. In short, the locality principle is built into the human mind. The reason why we find it so 'obvious' that 'Is Sam is the cat that black?' is ungrammatical is because our minds work in a particular way; we literally cannot conceive a sentence that works differently.

This approach to grammar affects the nature of interlanguage – the knowledge of the second language in the learner's mind. From what we have seen so far, there might seem to be few limits on how the learners' interlanguage grammars develop. Their source might be partly the learners' first languages, partly their learning strategies, partly other sources. However, if the human mind always uses its built-in language principles, interlanguages too must conform to them. It would be impossible for the L2 learner, say, to produce questions that did not depend on structure. And indeed no one has yet found sentences said by L2 learners that break the known language principles. I tested 140 university-level students of English with six different first languages on a range of structures including locality; 132 of them knew that sentences such as 'Is Sam is the cat that black?' were wrong, while only 76 students knew that 'Sam is the cat that is black.' and 'Is Sam the cat that is black?' were right. Second language learners clearly have few problems with this deviant structure compared to other structures. Interlanguages do not vary without limit, but conform to the overall mould of human language, since they are stored in the same human minds. Like any scientific theory, this may be proved wrong. Tomorrow someone may find a learner who has no idea that questions depend on structure. But so far no one has found clear-cut examples of learners breaking these universal principles.

Parameters of variation

How do parameters capture the many grammatical differences between languages? One variation is whether the grammatical subject of a declarative sentence has to be actually present in the sentence. In German it is possible to say 'Er spricht' (he speaks), but impossible to say 'Spricht' (speaks); declarative sentences must have subjects. The same is true for French, for English and for a great many languages. But in Italian, while it is possible to say 'Il parla' (he talks), it is far more usual to say 'Parla' (talks) without an expressed subject; declarative sentences are not required to have subjects. The same is true in Arabic and Chinese and many other languages. This variation is captured by the *pro-drop parameter* – so-called for technical reasons we will not go into here. In 'pro-drop' languages such as Italian, Chinese or Arabic, the subject does not need to be actually present; in 'non-pro-drop' languages such as English or German, it must always be present in declarative sentences. The pro-drop parameter variation has effects on the grammars of all languages; each of them is either pro-drop or non-pro-drop.

Children learning their first language at first start with sentences without subjects (Hyams, 1986). Then those who are learning a non-pro-drop language such as English go on to learn that subjects are compulsory. The obvious question for L2 learning is whether it makes a difference if the first language does not have subjects and the second language does, and vice versa. Lydia White (1986) compared how English was learnt by speakers of French (a non-pro-drop language with compulsory subjects) and by speakers of Spanish (a pro-drop language with optional subjects). If the L1 setting for the pro-drop parameter has an effect, the Spanish-speaking learners should make different mistakes from the French-speaking learners. Spanish-speaking learners were much more tolerant of sentences like 'In winter snows a lot in Canada' than were the French speakers. Oddly enough, this effect does not necessarily go in the reverse direction: English learners of Spanish do not have as much difficulty with leaving the subject out as Spanish learners of English have with putting it in.

One attraction of this form of grammar is its close link to language acquisition, as we see in Chapter 12. The parts of language that have to be learnt are the settings for the parameters on which languages vary. The parts which do not have to be learnt are the principles that all languages have in common. Learning the grammar of a second language is not so much learning completely new structures, rules, and so on, as discovering how to set the parameters for the new language – for example, whether you have to use a subject, what the word order is within the phrase – and acquiring new vocabulary.

Another attraction is that it provides a framework within which all languages can be compared. It used to be difficult to compare grammars of different languages, say, English and Japanese, because they were regarded as totally different. Now the grammars of all languages are seen as variations within a single overall scheme. Japanese can be compared to English in its use of locality (unnecessary in Japanese questions because Japanese does not form questions by moving elements of the sentence around); in terms of the pro-drop parameter (English sentences must have subjects, Japanese do not have to); and in terms of word order parameters (Japanese has the order phrase + head of phrase, for example, noun phrase followed by postposition 'Nihon ni' (Japan in), English phrases have the order head + noun phrase, for example, preposition followed by noun phrase 'in London'). This helps with the description of learners' speech, which fits within the same framework regardless of their first language and reveals things they have in common. Chinese, Arabic or Spanish students all have problems with the subject in English because of their different setting for the pro-drop parameter.

The implications of this overall model for language learning and language teaching are described in greater detail in Chapter 11. For the moment we need to point out that the study of grammar and of acquisition by linguists and SLA researchers in recent years has been much more concerned with the development of abstract ways of looking at phenomena like pro-drop than with the conventional grammar of earlier sections. Language teaching will eventually miss out if it does not keep up with such new ideas of grammar (Cook, 1989).

Box 2.5 L2 learning of principles and parameters grammar

- L2 learners do not need to learn principles of Universal Grammar as they will use them automatically.
- L2 learners need to acquire new parameter settings for parameters such as pro-drop, often starting from their first language.
- All L2 learners can be looked at within the same overall framework of grammar as it applies to all languages.

2.5 L2 learning of grammar and L2 teaching

Focusing questions

- What do you think is easy grammar for a beginner?
- What do you think is the best order for teaching grammar?

Teachers are often surprised by what 'grammar' means in SLA research and how much importance is given to it. While the grammar used here has some resemblance to the traditional and structural grammars with which teachers are familiar – 'structures', 'rules', and so on – the perspective has changed. The SLA research category of grammatical morphemes, for instance, cuts across the teaching categories of prepositions, articles and forms of 'be'. Principles and parameters theory puts grammar on a different plane from anything in language teaching. Hence teachers will not find any quick help with carrying out conventional grammar teaching in such forms of grammar. But they will nevertheless understand better what the students are learning and the processes they are going through. For example, sentences without subjects are not only common in students' work, but can also be explained simply by the pro-drop parameter. It is an insightful way of looking at language which teachers have not hitherto been conscious of.

Let us gather together some of the threads about grammar and teaching introduced so far in this chapter. If the syllabus that the student is learning includes grammar in some shape or form, this should be not just a matter of structures and rules but a range of highly complex phenomena, a handful of which have been discussed in this chapter. The L2 learning of grammar has turned out to be wider and deeper than anyone supposed. It ranges from morphemes such as 'the', to processes of sentence production, to parameters about the presence of subjects. Above all, grammar is knowledge in the mind, not rules in a book – Lang$_5$ in the sense of language given in Chapter 1; the crucial end-product of much teaching is that students should 'know' language in an unconscious sense so that they can put it to good use. Teaching has to pay attention to the internal processes and knowledge the students are subconsciously building up in their minds.

Grammar is also relevant to the sequence in which elements of language are taught. Of necessity, language teaching has to present the various aspects of language in order, rather than introducing them all simultaneously. The conventional solution used to be to sequence the grammar in terms of increasing complexity, say, teaching the present simple first 'He cooks', and the past perfect continuous passive last 'It has been being cooked', because the former is much 'simpler' than the latter. Box 2.6 gives the teaching sequence for grammatical items in *Move* (Bowler and Parminter, 2007), a recent beginners' course. This is typical of the sequences that have been developed for EFL teaching over the past hundred years, based chiefly on the tense system. While it has been tested in practice, it has no particular justification from SLA research.

Box 2.6 The grammatical sequence in *Move* (Bowler and Parminter, 2007)

1 articles and determiners
2 present simple
3 present continuous
4 countable and uncountable nouns
5 simple past
6 present perfect
7 comparative and superlative

As Robert DeKeyser (2005) points out, it is almost impossible for researchers to agree on which forms are more complex, which comparatively simple. When language use and classroom tasks became more important to teaching, the choice of a teaching sequence was no longer straightforward, since some way of sequencing these non-grammatical items needed to be found. SLA research has often claimed that there are definite orders for learning language, particularly for grammar, as we have seen. What should teachers do about this? Four extreme points of view can be found:

1 *Ignore the parts of grammar that have a particular L2 learning sequence*, as the learner will follow these automatically in any case. Nothing teachers can do will help or hinder the student who is progressing through the grammatical morpheme order from plural '-s' to irregular past tense to possessive ''s'. Teachers should therefore get on with teaching the thousand and one *other* things that the student needs, and should let nature follow its course.

2 *Follow the L2 learning order as closely as possible* in the teaching. There is no point in teaching 'not' with 'any' to beginners 'I haven't got any money', because the students are not ready for it. So the order of teaching should follow the order found in L2 learning as much as possible. Language used in the class might then be geared to the learners' stage, not of course by matching it exactly

since this would freeze the learner at that moment in time, but by being slightly ahead of the learner all the time, called by Krashen (1985) 'i+1' (one step on from the learner's current language).

3 *Teach the last things in an L2 learning sequence first.* The students can best be helped by being given the extreme point of the sequence and by filling in the intermediary positions for themselves. It has been claimed, for example, that teaching the most difficult types of relative clauses is more effective than teaching the easy forms, because the students fill in the gaps for themselves spontaneously rather than needing them filled by teaching.

4 *Ignore grammar altogether.* Some might argue that, if the students' goals are to communicate in a second language, grammar is an optional extra. Obviously this depends on the definition of grammar: in the Lang$_5$ sense that any speaker of a language knows the grammatical system of the language, then grammar is not dispensable in this way, but plays a part in every sentence anybody produces or comprehends for whatever communicative reason.

As with pronunciation, an additional problem is which grammar to use. Typically the description seems to be slanted towards the grammar of written language with its complete 'textual' sentences, rather than spoken language with its elliptical 'lexical' sentences (Cook, 2003). For example, English teachers have spent considerable energy on teaching students to distinguish singular 'there is' from plural 'there are', yet the distinction barely exists in spoken language, which uses /ðəz/ for both. The publisher of my first EFL coursebook objected to the sentence 'Good book that' occurring in a dialogue, an unremarkable spoken form; of course, the publisher won.

Traditionally for English the model has been taken to be that of a literate educated native speaker from an English-speaking country. This, however, ignores the differences between varieties of English spoken in different countries. An Irishman means something quite different from an Englishman by 'she's after doing it', and an Indian by 'I am thinking it'; North Americans have past tenses like 'dove' and past participles like 'gotten' that no longer exist in British speech. Nor does it encompass variation between people in one country, for example, the people of Norwich, who do not use the singular 's' on verbs 'he ride', or the Geordie who distinguishes singular 'you' from plural 'yous'. And it treats English as having a singular genre; you must always have a subject in the sentence, even if it is perfectly normal to leave it out in diaries and emails, 'Went out' or 'Like it'. And similar issues arise in choosing a grammatical model for most languages that are used across a variety of countries: should French be based on Parisians and ignore the rest of France, along with the Frenches spoken in Switzerland, Quebec and Central Africa?

No one would probably hold completely to these simplified views. The fuller implications of the L2 order of learning or difficulty depend on the rest of teaching. Teaching must balance grammar against language functions, vocabulary, classroom interaction, and much else that goes on in the classroom to find the appropriate teaching for *those* students in *that* situation. Teachers do not necessarily have to choose between these alternatives once and for all. A different decision may have to be made for each area of grammar or language and each stage of acquisition. But SLA research is starting to provide information about sequences based on the processes going on in the learners' minds, which will eventually prove a gold mine for teaching.

> ## Box 2.7 Alternative ways of using L2 sequences in language teaching
>
> - Ignore the parts of grammar that have a particular L2 learning sequence, as the learner will follow these automatically anyway.
> - Follow the L2 learning order as closely as possible in the teaching.
> - Teach the last things in an L2 learning sequence first.
> - Ignore grammar altogether.

2.6 The role of explicit grammar in language teaching

Focusing questions

- Did hearing about grammar from your teacher help you learn a second language? In what way?
- How aware are you of grammar when you are speaking (a) your first language (b) your second language?

Keywords

consciousness-raising: helping the learners by drawing attention to features of the second language

language awareness: helping the learners by raising awareness of language itself

sensitization: helping the learners by alerting them to features of the first language

focus on FormS: deliberate discussion of grammar without reference to meaning

focus on form (FonF): discussion of grammar and vocabulary arising from meaningful language in the classroom

It is one thing to make teachers aware of grammar and to base coursebooks, syllabuses and teaching exercises on grammar. It is something else to say that the students themselves should be aware of grammar. Indeed, Chapter 1 showed that the nineteenth- and twentieth-century teaching tradition has avoided explicit grammar in the classroom. This section looks at some of the ideas that have been raised about using grammatical terms and descriptions with the student. Though the discussion happens to concentrate on grammar, the same issues arise about the use of phonetic symbols in pronunciation teaching, the class discussion of meanings of words, or the explanations of language functions, all of which depend on the students consciously understanding the rules and features of language.

One issue is the extent to which grammatical form and meaning should be separated. Mike Long (1991) makes a distinction between *focus on FormS*, which is deliberate discussion of grammatical forms such as ''s' or the past tense, and *focus on form (FonF)*, which relates the form to the meaning arising from language in the classroom. A linguist might object that grammar is a system for encoding and decoding particular meanings; any teaching of grammar that does not involve meaning is not teaching grammar at all. However, the distinction between FormS and FonF does focus attention away from grammar explanation for its sake, towards thinking how grammar may contribute within the whole context of language teaching methodology, as described in Chapter 13.

Explicit grammar teaching

This revives the classical debate in language teaching about whether grammar should be explained to the students, as mentioned in Chapter 1. Usually the kind of grammar involved is the traditional or structural grammar described earlier, exemplified in books such as *Basic Grammar in Use* (Murphy, 2002); seldom does it mean grammar in the sense of knowledge of principles and parameters such as locality and pro-drop. Hence it has often been argued that the problem with teaching grammar overtly is not the method itself but the type of grammar that has been used. Most linguists would regard these grammars as the equivalent to using alchemy as the basis for teaching chemistry.

Other types of grammar are hardly ever used. The pro-drop parameter, for example, is a simple idea to explain and might well be a useful rule for students of English from Japan or Greece, or indeed for learners of the vast majority of the world's languages; yet it is never mentioned in materials that teach grammar. If the grammar content were better, perhaps explicit grammar teaching would be more effective.

The use of explicit explanation implies that L2 learning is different from L1 learning, where it never occurs. The belief that L2 learning can potentially make use of explanation underlies distinctions such as those made by Harold Palmer (1926) between 'spontaneous capacities' for acquiring speech and 'the studial capacity' through which people study language, and by Krashen (1981a) between 'acquisition' and 'learning' (the latter being conscious and available only to older learners), as well as by many others.

The main issue is the connection between conscious understanding of a rule and the ability to use it. Any linguist can tell you facts about languages such as Japanese or Gboudi that their native speakers could not describe. This does not mean the linguists can say a single word, let alone a sentence, of Japanese or Gboudi in a comprehensible way. They have acquired a pure 'academic' knowledge of the languages. In their case this satisfies their needs. Grammatical explanation is a way of teaching facts about the language – that is to say, a form of linguistics. If the aim of teaching is academic knowledge of language, conscious understanding is acceptable as a form of L2 learning. But students who want to use the language need to transform this academic knowledge into the ability to use it, going beyond the Lang$_5$ mental sense to the Lang$_4$ social sense of 'language'.

Grammatical explanation in the classroom has relied on the assumption that rules which are learnt consciously can be converted into unconscious processes of comprehension and production. Some people have questioned whether academic knowledge ever converts into the ability to use the language in this way. The French subjunctive was explained to me at school, not just to give me academic knowledge of the facts of French, but to help me to write French. After a period of absorption, this conscious rule was supposed to become part of my unconscious ability to use the language – unfortunately not so much enabling me to use it easily as making me freeze whenever I anticipated a subjunctive coming over the horizon.

Stephen Krashen (1985), however, has persistently denied that consciously learnt rules change into normal speech processes in the same way as grammar that is acquired unconsciously, sometimes called the non-interface position, that is, that learnt grammar does not convert into the acquired grammar that speech depends on. If Krashen's view is accepted, people who are taught by grammatical explanation can only produce language by laboriously checking each sentence against their conscious repertoire of rules, as many had to do with Latin at school – a process that Krashen calls 'monitoring'. Or they can use it for certain 'tips' or rules of thumb, such as 'i before e except after c or before g'. Conscious knowledge of language rules in this view is no more than an optional extra. This mirrors the traditional teaching assumption, summed up in the audio-lingual slogan 'teach the language not about the language', more elegantly phrased by Wilma Rivers (1964) as 'analogy provides a better foundation for foreign language learning than analysis', as discussed in Chapter 13.

Convincing as these claims may be, one should remember that many graduates of European universities who learnt English by studying traditional grammars turned into fluent and spontaneous speakers of English. I asked university-level students of English which explicit grammar rules they had found useful; almost all said that they still sometimes visualized verb paradigms for English to check what they were writing. This at least suggests that the conversion of conscious rules to non-conscious processes does take place for some academic students; every teaching method works for someone somewhere.

Language awareness

An alternative possibility is that raising awareness of language in general helps second language learning. Eric Hawkins (1984) suggested that the learners' general awareness of language should be raised before they start learning the L2, partly through grammar. If the students know the kind of thing to expect in the new language, they are more receptive to it. Hawkins advocates 'an exploratory approach' in which the pupils investigate grammar, for example, by deciding where to insert 'see-through' in the sentence 'She put on her cosy, old, blue, nylon, blouse'. They invent their own labels for grammar, rather than being taught a pre-established system. As Hawkins puts it, 'grammar approached as a voyage of discovery into the patterns of the language rather than the learning of prescriptive rules, is no longer a bogey word'. It is not the teaching of particular points of grammar that matters, but the overall increase in the pupil's language sensitivity. The textbook *Learning to Learn English* (Ellis and Sinclair, 1989) provides some exercises to make EFL learners more aware of their own predilections, for instance, suggesting ways for the students to discover grammatical rules themselves. Philip Riley (1985) suggested *sensitization* of the students by using features of the first language to help them understand the second, say, by discussing puns to help them see how speech is split up into words. Increasing awareness of language may have many educational advantages and indeed help L2 learning in a broad sense. Raised awareness of language is in itself a goal of some language teaching. It has no particular seal of approval from the types of grammar considered in this chapter, however.

Focus on form (FonF)

An issue in recent research is how focus on form contributes to the student's learning. As Mike Long (1991: 45–6) puts it, 'focus on form . . . overtly draws students' attention to linguistic elements as they arise incidentally in lessons whose overriding focus is on meaning or communication'. Several ways exist of drawing the students' attention to grammar without actually explaining grammar explicitly. Grammatical items or structures may be brought to the students' attention by some graphic or auditory device, provided it does not distort the patterns of the language – stressing all the grammatical morphemes in speech to draw attention to them, for example, would be a travesty – 'IN THE town WHERE I WAS born lived A man WHO sailed TO sea'. In L1 research James Morgan (1986) showed that adults used pauses and intonation to provide children with clues to the structure of the sentence so that they could tell which noun was the subject of the sentence, that is, indicating that the sentence 'The cat bit the dog' has the structure seen in (The cat) (bit the dog) not (The cat bit) (the dog).

SLA research by Joanna White (1998) drew the students' attention to grammatical forms such as pronouns by printing them in italic or bold face, for instance, '*She* was happy when *she* saw her ball'. However, she found variation between individuals rather than a consistent pattern. The minor problem is that italic and bold letter-forms are used for emphasis in English and, however much the students' pronouns might improve, it could have bad effects on their knowledge of the English writing system. Jessica Williams and Jacqueline Evans (1998) contrasted two structures, participial adjectives such as the familiar confusion between 'He is interesting/interested' and passives such as 'The lake was frozen'. One group heard language with many examples of these structures; another group was given explicit explanation of their 'form, meaning, and use'; a third had no special teaching. The group who were given explanations did indeed do better than the other groups for the adjectives, but there were only slight effects for passives. Hence there seems to be a difference in the extent to which grammatical forms lend themselves to focus on form: participial adjectives do, passives do not. Of course, not too much should be made of the specific grammatical points used here; some accounts of English, after all, put participle adjectives like 'interested' and passives such as 'frozen' on a continuum rather than seeing them as entirely different. Nevertheless, the point is that all the parts of grammar cannot be treated in the same way. Because we can help students by clearing up their confusions over past tense endings, we cannot necessarily do the same with relative clauses.

The teaching applications of FonF are discussed at greater length in Chapter 13 as part of task-based teaching. The overall feeling is that judicious use of focus on form within other activities may be useful, rather than full-scale grammar explanation. Having once seen a teacher explain in English the differences between 'must' and 'have to' to a class of Japanese children for 45 minutes, I can only agree that explicit grammar instruction is hugely ineffective; even as a native speaker, I cannot remember the differences she explained. The focus on form (FonF) argument combines several different threads, all of which are fruitful for teachers to think about: how they can highlight features of the input, subtly direct attention to grammatical errors through recasting, and slip grammatical discussion in as support for other activities, all of which are sound classroom practice. None of them, however, is novel for practising teachers who have probably always from time to time stressed words to draw the students' attention, paraphrased the students' mistakes, or given a quick grammatical explanation during the course of a communicative exercise. The overall question is whether these activities have anything to do with 'form'; calling them 'focus on meaning' would be as suitable, given that grammatical form is there to serve meaning. Nor does it answer the question of which type of grammar is appropriate for language teaching. Much teaching simply uses structural or traditional grammar without realizing that there are alternative approaches, or indeed that such approaches are not taken seriously as grammar today.

Box 2.8 Grammar and language teaching

- Teachers have to be aware of the many ways in which grammar comes into language learning and use, and the many types of grammar that exist in choosing which grammar to teach and how to teach it.
- L2 learners go through distinct stages of acquisition, for reasons still only partially understood. Teaching can utilize the known facts about these stages in several ways.
- Many aspects of grammar do not need to be taught as they are already present in the learner's mind and need instead to be activated.
- Conscious explanation of the L2 grammar is seen as beneficial in some circumstances, as is raising of language awareness.

Discussion topics

1 Here are seven techniques for teaching grammar. Decide in the light of the various approaches in this chapter what the chief advantage or disadvantage may be for each.

Grammar teaching technique	Advantage	Disadvantage
explanation	......	......
use of context/situation	......	......
fill-in-the-blank exercises	......	......
drilling	......	......
substitution tables	......	......
'games'	......	......
consciousness-raising, etc.	......	......

2 Take any current coursebook you have to hand, and look at one or two grammar-based exercises. What type of grammar does it employ? How successfully?

3 What aspects of grammar do you feel strongly about? For example, what things do you feel people should *not* say? For example, 'between you and I'? Why?

4 How important are grammatical morphemes to the student? How much attention do they receive in teaching? How much *should* they receive?

5 Do the learners you know conform to the stages of the processability model?

6 If you should only teach what a student is ready to receive, how do you establish what the student is actually ready for?

7 SLA research thinks that the order of acquisition is a very important aspect of learning. How important do you think that order of presentation is to language teaching?

8 Are there occasions when it would be right to start by teaching the students the most difficult or most complex aspect of grammar rather than the easiest or simplest?

9 What aspects of grammar that you have acquired consciously do you think are useful?

10 What ways of making other aspects of language conscious are there, for example, pronunciation, intonation or speech functions? Would this be a good idea?

Further reading

A good overview of grammatical morphemes research is in Goldschneider and DeKeyser (2001). An introduction to principles and parameters grammar can be found in Cook and Newson (2007) *Chomsky's Universal Grammar: An Introduction*. Various viewpoints on grammar and language teaching are summarized in Odlin (1994) *Pedagogical Grammar*. Otherwise the reader is referred to the books and articles cited in the text. The processability model is in Pienemann (1998) *Language Processing and Second-language Development: Processability Theory*. A good collection on focus on form is Doughty and Williams (eds) (1998) *Focus on Form in Classroom Second Language Acquisition*. The most accessible of Chomsky's own recent writings on Universal Grammar is probably Chomsky (2000) *The Architecture of Language*.

Some grammatical terms

(See also the glossary on the website.)

articles: specifiers of nouns divided in English into definite articles '*the* man in the photo', indefinite articles '*a* man came in', and zero article (i.e. none) 'Man is mortal'

grammar: the system of relationships between elements of the sentence that links the 'sounds' to the 'meanings', using word order, word forms, and so on

number: this is a way of signalling how many entities are involved, for example, through the forms of nouns, pronouns and verbs. English has two numbers: singular (*he*) and plural (*they*); other languages do not have grammatical number (Japanese), have three numbers (Old English), and so on

passive and active: passive sentences express similar meanings to active sentences by shifting focus from the agent doing the object to the object enduring the action 'I broke the mirror'/ 'The mirror was broken'

phrase structure: one way of linking all the parts of a sentence together in a structure like that of a family tree, by splitting the sentence into smaller and smaller bits

preposition: prepositions are words like *to*, *by* and *with* which come before nouns to make preposition phrases; when they come after a noun, as in Japanese, they are called 'postpositions' 'Nippon ni' (Japan in)

subject pronouns: some languages show the role of nouns in the sentences with different case forms; in English this only applies to the pronouns – 'she' is the subject form, 'her' is the object form, and so on

tense: the relationship between the sentence and time is indicated by tense, English having present and past tenses but no future; in English the two tenses are shown by inflections '-s' and '-ed', with several regular and irregular forms

wh-questions: many languages make a difference between questions that demand a yes or no answer 'Can you drive a lorry?' and questions that are open-ended 'What can you drive?'; the latter are called question word questions, or wh-questions, in English because question-words mostly happen to start with 'wh', such as 'when' and 'who'

word order: for many languages the order of the main elements in the sentence is crucial, whether subject (S) verb (V) object (O), as in English, SOV in Japanese, VSO in Arabic, or whatever; other word order variations are whether the language has prepositions 'in New Orleans' or postpositions 'Nippon ni' (Japan in) and whether questions or subordinate clauses have distinctive word orders.

Learning and teaching vocabulary

3

The acquisition of vocabulary at first sight seems straightforward; we all know you need a large number of words to speak a language. Just how many is anybody's guess: one estimate claims 20,000 word 'families', that is, counting related words as one word – 'teacher' / 'teaches' / 'teaching'/ 'taught', and so on.

But there is far more to acquiring vocabulary than the acquisition of words. Since the late 1980s there has been a massive explosion in research into the acquisition of vocabulary, seen in books such as Nation (2001). However, much of it is concerned with the acquisition of isolated words in laboratory experiments and is tested by whether people remember them, not whether they can use them. While such research gives some hints, much of it has little to say about how we can teach people to use a second language vocabulary.

3.1 Word frequency

Focusing questions

- What do you think are the ten most frequent words in English? Would you teach them all to beginners?
- Why do you think frequency is important?

Keywords

word frequency: simply measured by counting how often a word or word form occurs in a large sample of spoken or written language, such as the British National Corpus (BNC) (www.natcorp.ox.ac.uk)

Much teaching has been based on the idea that the most frequently used words in the target language should be taught first. Almost all beginners' books restrict the vocabulary they introduce in the first year to about a thousand of the most frequent items. My beginners' coursebook *People and Places* (Cook, 1980), for instance, had about 950 separate words; the American course *I Love English* (Capelle *et al.*, 1985) lists about 750 words. Traditional syllabuses for language teaching usually include lists of the most frequent words.

The French course *Voix et Images de France* (CREDIF, 1961) was perhaps the first to choose its vocabulary by actually counting how often words were used by native speakers. The *COBUILD English Course* (Willis and Willis, 1988; COBUILD stands for 'Collins and Birmingham University International Data Base') similarly bases itself on a corpus of speech. Its first lesson teaches 91 words including 'person' and 'secretary', unlikely to be in the opening lessons of most coursebooks. Now that vast collections of language are easily accessible on the computer, counting the frequencies of words is fairly simple. The list below cites the 50 most frequent words in the British National Corpus (BNC) sample of 100 million words. The most frequent word 'the' occurs no less than 6,187,267 times and the 50th word 'her' 218,258 times. The top 100 words account for 45 per cent of all the words in the BNC; in other words, knowing 100 words would allow you at least to recognize nearly half of the words you meet in English.

1 the	11 I	21 are	31 which	41 their
2 of	12 for	22 not	32 or	42 has
3 and	13 you	23 this	33 we	43 would
4 a	14 he	24 but	34 an	44 what
5 in	15 be	25 's (poss)	35 n't	45 will
6 to	16 with	26 they	36 's (verb)	46 there
7 it	17 on	27 his	37 were	47 if
8 is	18 that (conj)	28 from	38 that (det)	48 can
9 was	19 by	29 had	39 been	49 all
10 to (prep)	20 at	30 she	40 have	50 her

The first surprise on looking at this list is that most of the words feature in the discussion of grammar in Chapter 2 since they are structure words, such as articles 'the', pronouns 'it', auxiliaries 'would' and forms of the verb 'be'. Usually the teaching of structure words is seen as part of grammar, not vocabulary. Frequency is taken to apply more to content words. Nevertheless we should not forget that the most frequent words in the language are mostly structure words: the top 100 words only include three nouns.

The 20 most frequent words in the BNC for three types of content word are given in Table 3.1 overleaf.

This list also has some surprises for teachers. The nouns 'government' and 'system', the verbs 'become' and 'seem', and the adjectives 'social' and 'public' are seldom taught in beginners' courses, despite their high frequency. Many of the nouns have vague, general meanings, like 'people' and 'thing'; many words are abstract, like 'seem' or 'available', or involve subjective evaluation, 'think' and 'good'. The first lesson of the elementary course *Move* (Bowler and Parminter, 2007) concentrates on specific concrete nouns like 'cinema' and 'shops', and verbs for actions such as 'study' or 'visit'.

While word frequency has some relevance to teaching, other factors are also important, such as the ease with which the meaning of an item can be demonstrated ('blue' is easier to explain than 'local') and its appropriateness for what the students want to say ('plane' is more useful than 'system' if you want to travel). Indeed the frequency-based French course *Voix et Images* needed to amplify the list of frequent words with those that were 'available' to the speaker, which may not necessarily be very common. The word 'surname' found in lesson 1 of *Changes*

Position	Nouns	Verbs	Adjectives
1	time	say	new
2	people	know	good
3	way	get	old
4	year	go	different
5	government	see	local
6	day	make	small
7	man	think	great
8	world	take	social
9	work	come	important
10	life	use	national
11	part	give	British
12	number	want	possible
13	children	find	large
14	system	mean	young
15	case	look	able
16	thing	begin	political
17	end	help	public
18	group	become	high
19	woman	tell	available
20	party	seem	full

Table 3.1 The 20 most frequent nouns, verbs and adjectives in English

Box 3.1 Test how many words you know

Complete these definitions, then look at the answers at the end of the chapter on page 65.

  1 a round object often used as a toy is a b_____
  2 something you carry and put things in is a b_____
  3 a pipe or channel through which things flow is a c_____
  4 to give way to someone is to y_____
  5 a person who works without being paid is a v_____
  6 a preparation for preventing infectious disease is a v_____
  7 a heavy glass with a handle is known as a t_____
  8 a type of brain chemical is s_____
  9 a sailor's word for a clumsy fellow is a l_____
  10 the effects of wind, rain, and so on, on objects is w_____
  11 a heavy wheel used to store power is a f_____
  12 something engraved on stone is l_____

and module 1 of *New Cutting Edge* is far from frequent, in fact number 19,467 on the BNC list, but it is certainly available to speakers and, quite rightly, needs to be taught in the very early stages, particularly when the naming systems differ between languages and it is unclear which of a person's names might count as their surname in English; the use of 'last name' in Unit 1 of *Touchstone* (McCarthy, 2005) seems particularly dubious given that family names come first in Chinese. Carter (1988) has proposed that a language has a 'core' vocabulary found in all its uses, plus 'subject' cores specific to specialist subject matters, and a non-core vocabulary.

Influential as frequency has been in teaching, it has not played a major role in SLA research. It belongs more to the descriptive Lang$_3$ sense of 'language' as a collection of sentences. It is true that you are more likely to remember a word you meet every day than one you only meet once. But there are many other factors that make students learn words. A swear word '****' said accidentally when the teacher drops the tape recorder is likely to be remembered by the students for ever, even if it is never repeated. Common words like 'because' and 'necessary' are still spelt wrongly after students have been meeting them for many years.

Frequency of vocabulary has been applied in teaching mainly to the choice of words to be taught. In a sense, the most useful words for the student are obviously going to be those that are common. But it is unnecessary to worry about frequency too much. If the students are getting reasonably natural English from their coursebooks and their teachers, the common words will be supplied automatically. The most frequent words do not differ greatly from one type of English to another; the commonest five words in Jane Austen's novels are 'the', 'to', 'and', 'of', 'a'; in 7-year-old native children's writing 'and', 'the', 'a', 'I', 'to'; in the BNC 'the', 'of', 'and', 'a', 'in'; and in Japanese students of English 'I', 'to', 'the', 'you', 'and'. Any natural English the students hear will have the proper frequencies of words; it is only the edited texts and conversations of the classroom that do not have these properties, for better or worse.

Box 3.2 Frequency of words

- Frequency is usually established nowadays from a large corpus of a language, such as the BNC for English.
- Words vary extremely in how often they are used.
- Frequency is only one factor in the choice of words to teach.

3.2 Knowledge of words

Focusing questions

- What do you know about a word like 'man' if you speak English?
- When you teach students the meaning of a word, what do you mean by 'meaning' and how do you teach it?

> ### Keyword
>
> **argument structure**: the aspect of a word that dictates the structures in which it may be used, for example, the verb 'give' requires an animate subject, a direct object and an indirect object: 'Peter gave a stone to the wolf'

Most people assume that knowing a word is a matter of knowing that 'plane' in English means ✈ or that the English word 'plane' means the same as 'l'aereo' in Italian. Learning vocabulary means acquiring long lists of words with their meanings, whether through some direct link or via translation into the first language. Coursebooks often have vocabulary lists that organize the words in the course alphabetically, sometimes with brief translations. The Italian coursebook *Ci Siamo* (Guarnuccio and Guarnuccio, 1997) indeed lists **'l'aereo** plane'.

However, a word in the Lang$_5$ sense of language as knowledge in the mind is more than its meaning. Let us illustrate some aspects of vocabulary by using the word 'man'. What does any person who knows English know about 'man'?

Forms of the word

- *Pronunciation.* We know how to pronounce 'man' as /mæn/. Each word is associated in our memory with a specific pronunciation and is tied in to the pronunciation rules of the language; for instance, 'man' is pronounced /mən/ in compounds such as 'chairman'.

- *Spelling.* If we can read, we know that the word is spelled as <man>. Words have specific spellings and are linked to the spelling rules of the language. The letter <n> in <man>, for example, needs to be doubled when followed by <-ing>: 'Overmanning is a real problem in the car industry'.

Grammatical properties

- *Grammatical category.* We know that the word 'man' is either a noun ('a man') or a verb ('to man'), that is to say, we know the grammatical category or categories that each word belongs to. This dictates how it behaves in the structure of the sentence; as a noun 'man' can be part of a noun phrase acting as the subject or object of the sentence 'The man left', 'They shot the man'; if it is a verb, it can be part of the verb phrase 'They manned the barricades'. Like most nouns, it will have a possessive form 'man's' and a plural 'men'. While 'man' as a noun occurs 58,769 times in the BNC, as a verb it only occurs 12 times.

- *Possible and impossible structures.* We know the types of structure that 'man' can be used in. When 'man' is a verb, the sentence must have a subject that is animate '*She* manned the barricades', not '*It* manned the barricades'; and it must have an object 'They manned *the barricades*', not 'They manned'. This is called the 'argument structure' of the verb – which arguments (subject, object, etc.) may or may not go with it in the structure of the sentence. The Universal Grammar model of language acquisition, described in Chapter 12, claims that the argument structure of words is pivotal in language acquisition. Maurice Gross (1991) found 12,000 'simple' verbs in French of which no two could be used in exactly the same way in sentences.

- *Idiosyncratic grammatical information.* The plural spoken form of 'man' is /men/; the written form is <men>, that is, we know that it is an exception to the usual rules for forming noun plurals in English. In addition, the noun 'man' can be either countable 'A man's a man for a' that' or uncountable 'The proper study of Mankind is Man', depending on the sense with which it is used.

- *Word building.* There is a whole family of related words to 'man', such as 'mannish', 'manlike', 'unmanly'. These are made by adding various prefixes such as 'un-' and suffixes such as '-ish' to the stem 'man'.

Lexical properties

- *Collocations.* We know many more or less set expressions in which the word 'man' conventionally goes with other words, such as 'my good man', 'man in the street', 'man to man', 'Man of God', 'to separate the men from the boys', 'my man Jeeves', and many others.

- *Appropriateness.* 'my man' may be used as a form of address 'Hi my man'. The prime minister might be surprised at being greeted with 'Hi my man', a pop star might not. We have to know when and to whom it is appropriate to use a word.

Meaning

- *General meanings.* We know general properties about the meaning of 'man', such as 'male', 'adult', 'human being', 'concrete', 'animate'. These aspects of meaning, called 'semantic features' or 'components of meaning', are shared with many other words in the language.

- *Specific meanings.* We know a range of specific senses for 'man'. The OED has 17 main entries for 'man' as a noun, ranging from 'A human being (irrespective of sex or age)' to 'One of the pieces used in chess'.

Acquiring a word is not just linking a form with a translated meaning '**man** l'uomo, il signore', as in the *Ci Siamo* wordlist. It is acquiring a complex range of information about its spoken and written form, the ways it is used in grammatical structures and word combinations, and diverse aspects of meaning. Knowing that 'man' equals 'l'uomo' is only one small part of the total knowledge necessary for using it. Of course, nobody completely knows every aspect of a word. I may know how to read something but not how to say it; for years I assumed 'dugout' was pronounced /dʌguːt/ rather than /dʌgaʊt/ by analogy with 'mahout'. Nor does any individual speaker possess all the dictionary meanings for a word. The OED meaning for 'man' of 'a cairn or pile of stones marking a summit or prominent point of a mountain' would not be known by many people outside Cumbria.

Hence the message for language teaching is that vocabulary is everywhere. It connects to the systems of phonology and orthography through the actual forms of the words, to the systems of morphology and grammar through the ways that the word enters into grammatical structures and through grammatical changes to the word's form, and to the systems of meaning through its range of general and specific meanings and uses. To quote Noam Chomsky (1995: 131), 'language acquisition is in essence a matter of determining lexical idiosyncrasies'. Effective acquisition of vocabulary can never be just the learning of individual words and their meanings in isolation. The pre-intermediate course *International Express*

(Taylor, 1996) admirably has a section in the very first unit entitled 'Learning vocabulary', which encourages students to organize words in topics, word groups and word maps, and gets them to keep a vocabulary notebook for recording meaning and pronunciation. Later units have sections on 'word-power', mostly treating vocabulary in topic groups such as 'food', or word families such as 'business headlines'. As in most coursebooks, the main emphasis here is on learning vocabulary as meaning, organized in a systematic, logical fashion, rather than on the other aspects mentioned above, which are usually dealt with incidentally in the texts and dialogues rather than in specific vocabulary work.

Box 3.3 Knowing a word

- Knowing a word means its spoken and written forms, its grammatical and lexical properties and its meaning.
- Vocabulary impinges on all areas of language acquisition and is not just learning sets of words and meanings.

3.3 One word-store or two in the L2 user's mind?

Focusing questions

- When you learn a new word in a second language, do you try to keep it separate from your first language words?
- When you teach a new word do you try to link it to words in the first language, say, by translation, or do you keep it separate?

The fundamental question in SLA vocabulary research is how the words of the two languages are stored in the mind. The various alternatives are set out below.

1 *Separate stores*. The vocabulary of the second language is kept entirely separate from that of the first: an English person who learns the word 'libre' in French keeps it separate from the English word 'free'.

2 *L2 store dependent on L1 store*. The two word-stores are tightly linked so that L2 words are always related to L1 words; to think of the French word 'libre' means thinking first of the English word 'free'.

3 *Overlapping stores*. There is an overlapping system so that some words are shared, some not; 'libre' in French might be associated with English 'free', 'liberty' or 'liberal'.

4 *Single store*. There is a single overall word-store for both languages; French 'libre' and English 'free' are stored together.

At the moment it is far from certain which of these possibilities is correct. People with two languages are still aware of the words of one language when the other is not being used. Using a word like 'coin' with a different meaning in English (money) and French (corner), bilinguals were shown to have access to both meanings rather

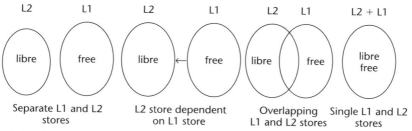

Figure 3.1 Different ways of storing the vocabulary of two languages in the mind

than just to the one specific to the language being used; one language is not totally deactivated when you are speaking the other (Beauvillain and Grainger, 1987). So it seems unlikely that there are entirely separate stores. People take about the same time to say whether a 'table' is 'furniture' in their first language as in their second language (Caramazza and Brones, 1980). On the other hand, speed of mental access to a word is helped by hearing another word in the same language rather than a word in the speaker's other language (Kirsner *et al.*, 1980), suggesting the two stores are separate in the mind. So the question of one dictionary or two is unanswerable at the moment. What seems clear is that the extreme models ('separate' versus 'single store') are unlikely to be true; and that there is overlap at many points.

Box 3.4 Words in the L2 user's mind

- The L1 and the L2 sets of vocabulary in the L2 user's mind may be related in various ways, ranging from completely separate to completely integrated.
- Research suggests that in many cases the two vocabulary stores are closely linked.

3.4 Types of meaning

Focusing questions

- What do you mean by meaning?
- What nouns can you remember learning first in your first language? In your second?

Keywords

components of meaning: general aspects of meaning which are shared by many words; 'boy' has the components 'male', 'human', 'young', and so on
prototype theory: words have whole meanings divided into basic level ('car'), subordinate level ('Ford') and superordinate level ('vehicle')

It seems easy enough to say what a word means. To an English speaker 'plane' means ✈, 'dog' means 🐕; indeed many SLA researchers are content to explore how this type of meaning is acquired in a second language, that is, how 'avion' comes to mean ✈ and 'chien' 🐕 for the English person who knows French. Linguists have spent at least a century exploring the different types of meaning that words can have. Here we look at three types that have been linked to L2 acquisition.

Components of meaning

Often the meaning of a word can be broken up into smaller components. Thus the meaning of 'girl' is made up of 'female', 'human' and 'non-adult'. The meaning of 'apple' is made up of 'fruit', 'edible', 'round', and so on. The components view of meaning was used to study the development of words such as 'before' and 'big' in English children. At one stage they know one component of the meaning but not the other. They know 'big' and 'small' share a meaning component to do with size, but think they both mean 'big'; or they know that 'before' and 'after' are to do with 'time' but do not know which one means 'prior' (Clark, 1971). Indeed, L2 beginners in English found it much easier to understand 'Mary talks before Susan shouts' than 'Caroline sings after Sally dances' (Cook, 1977); they had not acquired the component 'prior'. Paul Nation (1990) describes learners of Samoan who confuse 'umi' (long) with 'puupuu' (short) because they have acquired the component 'length' for both but have not sorted out which is which.

Students are learning components of meaning for a word, not necessarily all of the word's meaning at once. An informal version of this components approach can be found in coursebooks such as *The Words You Need* (Rudzka *et al.*, 1981). Students look at a series of 'Word study' displays showing the different meaning components of words. For example, a chart gives words that share the meaning 'look at/over' such as 'check', 'examine', 'inspect', 'scan' and 'scrutinise'. It shows which have the component of meaning 'detect errors', which 'determine that rules are observed', and so on. Students are encouraged to use the meaning components to build up their vocabulary while reading texts.

Lexical relations

Words do not exist by themselves, however, but are always in relationship to other words. The meaning of 'hot' relates to 'cold'; the meaning of 'run' to 'walk', of 'high' to 'low', of 'pain' to 'pleasure', and so on. When we speak, we choose one word out of all those we have available, rejecting all the words we could have said: 'I love you' potentially contrasts with 'I hate you'. Words function within systems of meaning.

A metaphor for meaning that is often used is traffic lights. When a traffic light has two colours, red and green, red means 'stop', contrasting with green 'go'. Hence 'red' does not just mean 'stop', it also means 'not green', that is, 'don't go', a system with two options. Add another colour, called 'amber' in England, and the whole system changes, with amber acting as a warning that something is going to change, having two possibilities: amber alone, officially 'stop' (unofficially, 'prepare to stop'), and amber and red together, officially 'stop' (unofficially 'prepare to go'). If a simple three-colour system can lead to such complexity of meanings (and indeed traffic accidents), think what happens with the thousands of words in any human language.

In his book *Lexical Semantics* Cruse (1986) brought out many relationships between words. Words can be *synonyms* if they have the same meaning – 'truthful' and 'honest'; *hyponyms* if they belong to the same group with a single superordinate name – 'dogs', 'cats' and 'horses' are kinds of animals. Each category may have many variations. For example, *antonyms* are pairs with the opposite meaning – 'good' versus 'bad'. But there are several ways in which words can be opposites: 'top' and 'bottom' form a scale with extremes (called antipodals); 'concave' and 'convex' have reverse directions (counterparts); 'rise' and 'fall' are movements in opposite directions (reversives); 'above' and 'below' are the relationship of one direction to another (converses). And doubtless many more.

Prototypes

Some aspects of meaning cannot be split up into components but are taken in as wholes. According to Eleanor Rosch's *prototype* theory (Rosch, 1977), an English person who is asked to give an example of a typical bird is more likely to say 'sparrow' than 'penguin' or 'ostrich'; sparrows are closer to the prototype for 'birds' in the mind than penguins and ostriches. Rosch's theory suggests that there is an ideal of meaning in our minds – 'birdiness' in this case – from which other things depart. Speakers have a central form of a concept and the things they see and talk about correspond better or worse with this prototype.

Prototype theory claims that children first learn words that are 'basic' because they reflect aspects of the world that stand out automatically from the rest of what they see – prototypes. 'Sparrow' is a 'basic-level' term compared to a 'superordinate-level' term like 'bird', or a 'subordinate-level' term like 'house sparrow'. The basic level of vocabulary is easier to use and to learn. On this foundation, children build higher and lower levels of vocabulary. Some examples of the three levels of vocabulary are seen in Table 3.2.

Superordinate terms	furniture	bird	fruit
Basic-level terms	table, chair	sparrow, robin	apple, strawberry
Subordinate terms	coffee table, armchair	field sparrow	Golden Delicious, wild strawberry

Table 3.2 Three levels of vocabulary

L1 children learn basic-level terms like 'apple' before they learn the superordinate term 'fruit' or the subordinate term 'Golden Delicious'. They start with the most basic level as it is easiest for the mind to perceive. Only after this has been learnt do they go on to words that are more general or more specific. Some of my own research (Cook, 1982) showed that L2 learners first of all acquire basic terms such as 'table', second, more general terms like 'furniture', and finally, more specific terms like 'coffee table'. Rosch's levels are therefore important to L2 learning as well as to first language acquisition.

This sequence of levels, however, is different from the usual order of presentation in language teaching in which the teacher introduces a whole group of words simultaneously. For example, in Unit 4 of *New English File* (Oxenden *et al.*, 2004: 48), the heading 'clothes' is followed by the instructions 'Match the words and pictures', with drawings of a jacket, jeans, and so on. According to prototype theory, this is misguided; the superordinate term 'clothes' should come *after* the students have the basic-level terms such as 'jacket' and 'jeans', not before.

The most important early words are basic-level terms. The human mind automatically starts from this concrete level rather than from a more abstract level or a more specific one. Starting with vocabulary items that can be shown easily in pictures fits in with the Rosch theory; grouping them prematurely into superordinate categories does not. A drawing can be readily recognized as a chair but is less easy to see as an armchair or as furniture. Hence prototype theory ties in with the audio-visual method of language teaching that introduces new vocabulary with a picture of what it represents, in an appropriate cultural setting. This theory has particular implications for teaching of vocabulary at the beginning stages.

Are meanings universal?

So far as meaning is concerned, the interesting question that has been raised over the years is whether speakers of all languages possess the same concepts, despite variation in the words used to express them, or whether meanings vary from one language to another as well as the words that convey them. The well-known example is how people see colours. Languages have rather different colour vocabularies; Greek, Italian and many other languages have two 'blue' colours where English people see only light blue and dark blue; Japanese has names for colours that to an English eye are either in between two colours or are different shades of the same colour. Originally research showed that languages could be arranged on a single scale, as seen in Figure 3.2 (a colour version can be found on the website).

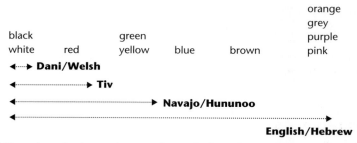

Figure 3.2 The universal colour scale, according to Berlin and Kay (1969)

This means that the two languages Dani and Welsh only have two basic colour words, for black and white; Tiv has three, black white and red; Navajo and Hununoo have five, adding green and yellow; English and Hebrew have eleven. All the languages of the world fit into this scale somewhere. Learning another language may mean dropping some colour distinctions, say, 'red' if you are learning Welsh, adding some colour distinction, say, 'blue' if you are a Navajo learning English. Again, it is not just the words that you are learning in another language but their meaning relationships; 'black' in Welsh means 'not white', in English, additionally, 'not red/blue/. . .': the borders may be different. For example, to an English eye the green in a Japanese traffic light looks blue; an Englishman who had never driven in Japan stopped at a traffic light and his wife said, 'Don't forget to go when the green light comes on'; he sat without moving off for some time till she said, 'Why don't you go?' and he replied, 'There's a blue light but it hasn't turned green yet.'

So do people who speak Japanese see the world differently from those who speak English? Or do they see it in the same way but speak differently? This question is called linguistic relativity; is the world seen differently from different points of view? Since the late 1990s a fair amount of research has shown that differences in thinking go with differences in language. Most human languages talk about a speaker's location in terms of 'front/back' and 'left/right'; the whiteboard is behind me, the students are in front of me, the door is on my left, the window is on my right. Speakers of Australian Aboriginal languages talk about location as 'north/south' and 'east/west'. Now the whiteboard is in the east, the students in the west, the door on the north, the window on the south. Does this make a difference to people's thinking? Try blindfolding two speakers of Aboriginal and English and abandoning them in the middle of a forest; who would you think finds their way out first?

If you know two languages, what happens to your thinking? Will you always think like speakers of the L1 or will you shift to thinking like speakers of the L2, or will you think like neither of them? SLA research has been investigating this issue in controlled experiments in recent years. Greeks who know English separate the two blues differently from Greeks who do not know English (Athanasopoulos, 2001). Japanese who know English tend to categorise things more as 'shapes' in an English way than as 'substances' in a Japanese way (Cook *et al.*, 2006). Hence learning another language can have more far-reaching effects on the learner than anybody imagined; you may think in a slightly different way if you know another language.

Box 3.5 Ways of meaning

- Words have many different kinds of meaning, whether sharing general components, linked in lexical relations or related to prototypes and levels.
- While some aspects of meaning are universal, there are differences between languages in how they express concepts of colour, and so on, which may affect the thinking of L2 users.

3.5 Strategies for understanding and learning vocabulary

Focusing questions

- If you meet a new word, how do you go about finding out its meaning and remembering it?
- How do you use a dictionary in your second language? In your first?

Keywords

false friends: words that are more or less the same in two languages but have different meanings

mnemnotechnics: ways of remembering new information by deliberately organizing it and linking it to existing information in the mind

---

Box 3.6 Vocabulary learning task

Here are some German words for you to learn. Spend three minutes on this and then do the test at the end of the chapter on page 66.

1	2	3	4	5
die Schere	das Telefon	die Hand	das Flugzeug	der Mann

6	7	8	9	10
das Fahrrad	das Fernsehapparat	der Schüssel	der Bleistift	das Segelboot

---

Students are often acutely aware of their ignorance of vocabulary in a way they are unaware of their ignorance of grammar and phonology. When you want to say something in a second language, it is the words that you feel you struggle for rather than the grammar or pronunciation. Hence L2 users have devised strategies to compensate for words they do not know, discussed in Chapter 6. Here we shall look at some of the vocabulary strategies students use, with or without their teacher's approval. First test yourself on the task in Box 3.6.

Strategies for understanding the meaning of words

One main issue is learning the meaning of new words. Most recent teaching methods, such as task-based learning or communicative language teaching, have relied either on the context to make sense of the word or on traditional techniques such as pictures, explanation or translation into the students' L1. Conveying the meaning of new words is crucial to language teaching; for example, it is the vital stage in Krashen's natural approach, Dodson's bilingual method and the audio-visual method.

Suppose that someone says to you in a restaurant in Italy, 'Scusi, è occupato questo posto?' You think you can work out everything in the sentence apart from the word 'posto' (Excuse me, is this **** occupied?). What do you do?

Guess from the situation or context

The situation is sitting at a restaurant table; the person is a stranger – what could the sentence be? 'Are you waiting for somebody?' 'Can I borrow the mustard?' 'Could I borrow this chair?' 'Can I sit down here?' Looking at the probabilities you decide that the word 'posto' must mean 'seat' in English. This is the natural process of getting meaning for unknown words that we use all the time in our first language: if we encounter a new word in our reading, how often do we bother to check precisely what it means in a dictionary? Checking back on a novel I have just started, I discover that pages 1 and 2 had 'baulks of sheer-sided soil', 'a severe weather advisory' and 'a layer of regolith'; none of the three nouns, 'baulk', 'advisory' and 'regolith', are part of my vocabulary and yet I had not noticed this while reading. I had presumably deduced enough from the context not to interfere with reading: 'baulk' must be a pile of some kind, 'advisory' must be an advice-notice (according to the OED this is North American usage) and 'regolith' must be some geological term for a layer of stone.

Guessing is a much-used strategy in a second language. But of course it can go wrong. On the one hand, we may come to quite the wrong conclusion: one of my postgraduate students gave a seminar talk in which she distinguished 'schema' theory from 'schemata' theory, having deduced these were different words rather than the singular and plural of the same word. On the other hand, much language is unpredictable from the situation; in a German supermarket the only remark that was addressed to me was, 'Könnten Sie bitte das Preisschildchen für mich lesen da ich meine Brille zu Hause gelassen habe?' (Could you read this label to me as I have left my glasses at home?)

Use a dictionary

The most popular way of getting the meaning of a new word like 'posto' is to look it up in a dictionary, according to Norbert Schmitt's survey of students (Schmitt, 1997). The use of dictionaries in language teaching has always been controversial to some extent. There is inevitably a question of choosing which type of dictionary to use:

- **monolingual** dictionaries versus **translation** dictionaries. If you believe that the word-stores of the two languages must be kept distinct in the mind, you will go for monolingual L2 dictionaries. If you believe that the words for the two languages are effectively kept in one joint store, you will prefer translation dictionaries.

- **reception** dictionaries versus **production** dictionaries such as the *Language Activator* (1993). Production dictionaries permit one to hunt for the precise word to express something one wants to say. If you decide to talk about your problems, you look up the concept 'problem' and see which of the 12 related ideas (e.g. 'ways of saying that a person causes problems') best expresses what you want to say; a version of this is found in the thesaurus that forms part of word-processing programs – mine tells me that other ways of saying 'dictionary' are 'lexicon', 'word list' and 'glossary', though unlike a production dictionary it does not tell me the differences in meaning between them.

- **corpus-based** dictionaries such as COBUILD versus **example-based** dictionaries such as the OED. Traditional dictionaries such as the OED depended on collecting a large sample of words from many sources, including other dictionaries. Recent dictionaries have been based on large-scale collections of real spoken and written language processed by computer. The OED may give the precise technical meaning of a word, COBUILD its everyday use. For example, according to the OED 'bronchitis' is 'Inflammation of the bronchial mucous membrane', according to COBUILD 'An illness like a very bad cough, in which your bronchial tubes become sore and infected'. One definition gives an accurate medical definition; the other suits a layperson's understanding.

Dictionary use can only be minimal during speech, however important it may be during reading and writing. At best students can use it as a prop for the occasional word, say, in a lecture, as many of my overseas students seem to do with their pocket electronic dictionaries.

Make deductions from the word form

Another way of discovering the meaning of a word is to try to deduce it from its actual form; 69 per cent of students in Schmitt's survey found this a useful strategy. The Italian word 'posto' may not be very helpful in this respect, as it provides few clues to its structure. The English example 'regolith' is more useful. I have encountered other words with the morpheme 'lith' before, such as 'megalith', which I understand to be a big stone, and 'Neolithic', which I understand to mean 'stone age'; hence I guess that 'lith' is something to do with stone. 'rego' provides no help – in fact if I had simply related it to the English word 'rug' I wouldn't have been far out according to the OED, which claims it was indeed a mistaken interpretation of the Greek for 'blanket'. Again, it is easy to go wrong in making these deductions; my interpretation of 'regolith' as 'layer of stone' gave me sufficient understanding to read a novel but would hardly impress a geologist. *International Express* (Taylor, 1996) practises word forms by getting the students to do the reverse operation of adding prefixes such as 'un-' or 'in-' to words such as 'efficient' and 'sociable'.

Link to cognates

One more way is to resort to a language that one already knows, popular with 40 per cent of Schmitt's students. Many languages have words that are similar in form, particularly if the languages are closely related, English 'chair' versus French 'chaise' or English 'day' versus German 'Tag'. Students often seem to avoid such cognates (Lightbown and Libben, 1984), perhaps to keep the two languages separate in their minds. Hakan Ringbom (1982) found that Finnish learners of English in fact preferred words from Swedish rather than from Finnish: 'I can play pingis' for 'table tennis' or 'This is a very beautiful stad' for 'town'. Given the relationships between many European languages and the amount of word-borrowing that affects modern languages everywhere, there may well be some links between the L2 word and something in the second language. With 'posto' there may be few clues; there are some meanings of 'post' such as 'leave your post' which suggest a fixed location such as a seat, but most of the meanings are more to do with the mail or with fence-posts. With other words a reasonable guessing strategy may nevertheless be to try to relate them to the L1, provided of course there is a relationship between the two languages – it does not work for English speakers trying to read street signs in Hungary. In the past, language teachers have often put students on their guard against 'false friends' – to the neglect of 'true friends' whose resemblance is not accidental, which are utilized in methods such as the new concurrent approach described in Chapter 13.

Strategies for acquiring words

It is one thing to be able to work out the meaning of a word on one occasion; it is another to remember the word so that it can be used on future occasions. Some of the strategies that learners use are set out below.

Repetition and rote learning

The commonest approach is perhaps sheer practice: repeat the word again and again until you know it by heart. Typically this is done by memorizing lists of words or by testing yourself repeatedly on piles of flashcards, eliminating the ones you know until none are left. However, much of this work may be in vain. Harry

Bahrick (1984) has shown that the most important thing in learning a word is the first encounter; he found effects of this eight years later. Practice may not be able to make up for a disastrous first encounter.

Organizing words in the mind

Much teaching of vocabulary implies that the effective way of learning vocabulary is to organize the words into groups in our mind. Hence we saw coursebooks using vocabulary sets even when Rosch's work suggests this is not the normal way of learning. *Touchstone* (McCarthy *et al.*, 2005) tells the students in Lesson 2, 'Here are some things students take to class', and then lists 'umbrella', 'pencil', and so on – that is, reversing Rosch's sequence by starting with a superordinate category.

Organizing may consist of putting related words in a 'word map'. *International Express* (Taylor, 1996) gets students to fill in empty bubbles in a diagram that links 'Air travel' to 'Luggage', 'Documents', and so on. Or it may mean thinking about aspects of the word form, say word endings such as '-er' or prefixes such as 'con-'. Organizing words in groups by common morphology linked to meaning may be a useful way of remembering them. *Tapestry 1 Listening and Speaking* (Benz and Dworak, 2000), for instance, asks students to characterize nouns for professions both as '-or' (actor), '-ist' (typist), or '-ian' (musician) and then as different types of career (medical careers, entertainers, public service, and so on). The book does not, however, point out that 'driver' has now made the transition from human being to machine that many '-er' words take, such as 'computer', 'typewriter' and 'reader'.

Linking to existing knowledge

The commonest way of remembering new vocabulary is to exploit the different memory systems in our minds for linking new information to old. Learning an entirely new item may be very hard; it will be a single isolated piece of knowledge that will rapidly fade. The information that 'posto' = 'seat' soon disappears if is not linked to our experience in one way or another. The ancient Greeks first devised memory systems to help with delivering speeches. One invention was 'loci': store information you want to remember in a carefully visualized location. You imagine a palace with many rooms; you enter the palace and turn to the left into the west wing; you go up the stairs, find a corridor and go into the third room on the left; you put your piece of information on the second bookcase on the left, second shelf up, on the left. To retrieve the information you mentally retrace your footsteps to the same point. Adaptations of the loci theory are still in use today by people who entertain with feats of memory; it is also supposed to be useful for card players.

Other ways of remembering information link what you are learning to something you already know through mental imagery. In *Tapestry 1 Listening and Speaking* (Benz and Dworak, 2000), students are told, 'To remember new vocabulary words, think about a picture that reminds you of the word.' One system is to link the new vocabulary to a pre-set scheme. First you need to memorize a simple scheme for storing information; then you need to link the new information to the scheme you already know. New information is hooked in to old. The version I have used involves students memorizing a short poem for the numbers from one to ten: 'One's a bun; two's a shoe; three's a tree; four's a door; five's a hive; six's sticks; seven's heaven; eight's a gate; nine's a line; ten's a hen.' Then they remember ten items by making an incongruous mental image connecting each item with a number on the list; if no. 1 is an elephant, then they have to invent an image of an elephant eating a bun or an elephant inside the bun. And so on for nine other items. Things remembered in this way can be quickly recovered from memory, even out of sequence. Elaborate schemes exist for handling more items at a time.

There are still other ways of making the links, such as the psychology-inspired 'mnemotechnics' techniques. In one, students acquire L2 words by associating them with incongruous images or sounds in the L1. The French 'hérisson' (hedgehog) is remembered through an image of the English sound-alike 'hairy son' (Gruneberg, 1987). The original keyword approach described by Atkinson (1975) suggests that, to learn the Spanish word 'pato' (duck), you might invent the image of a duck wearing a pot on its head. When you think of the English word 'duck', this brings to mind the pot-wearing duck, which in turn causes the Spanish word 'pato' to be produced. One consequence is the fantasy word-store created in the L2 user's mind, inhabited by hairy sons and eccentric ducks, quite unlike the word-store of a monolingual native speaker. This complicated chain of associations may prove difficult to use in actual speech. Indeed, these strategies treat a word as being paired with a single meaning and thus ignore not only all the depth of meaning of the word but also all the other aspects outlined earlier. They amount to a sophisticated form of list learning. It may also depend on the target language having a reasonable phonological similarity to the first language, as Ernesto Macaro (2006) points out: the Polish word 'szalenstwo' (madness) may have little recognizable for an English speaker to cling on to.

Box 3.7 Vocabulary strategies

- To understand an unfamiliar L2 word, people make use of a variety of strategies, such as guessing, using dictionaries, deducing meaning from the word's form and relating it to cognates.
- To acquire new L2 words, people use strategies such as repetition, organizing them in the mind, and linking them to existing knowledge.

3.6 Vocabulary and teaching

Focusing questions

- How would you teach a new word such as 'trombone' to a student?
- Do you use any 'local' words in your first language or in your second that people from other areas do not understand?

What we have been saying impinges on teaching in at least four main ways.

Demonstrating meaning

One of the central issues of language teaching is how to get the meaning of a new word across to the student. This depends on what we believe meaning to be and on the nature of the particular word. Audio-visual teaching thought that you conveyed new meaning by providing students with a picture: 'der Mann' = ⬆.

Traditional language teaching thought you provided it by means of a translation: 'der Mann' = 'the man'. Communicative language teaching and task-based learning provide no techniques for demonstrating meaning at all; the meaning of 'der Mann' is built up out of hearing it in different interactional contexts over time.

All these techniques assume that getting meaning is simply associating a word with a unique meaning. But a single 'word' may have many meanings; we have to pair 'man' with 'human being', with 'a piece in chess' and with the other 15 meanings found in the OED; the number of pairs between words and meanings in a language vastly exceeds the number of actual words.

Moreover, if you treat words as discrete coins in this manner, you overlook the many aspects of meaning they share, such as 'animate'; and the many relationships they have with other words such as 'woman' and 'boy'; and the other aspects of meaning discussed above such as collocations like 'a man-to-man talk'. The links between 'der Mann' and ♀ or 'man' are only the first stage in getting the word. My *People and Places* (Cook, 1980) tried to teach meaning by getting the students to use the word actively almost immediately; just after hearing 'beautiful' for the first time, the students had to decide whether Paul Newman, Barbra Streisand and Stan Laurel are beautiful.

Teaching the complexity of words

L2 learning of vocabulary is not just learning a word once and for all, but learning the range of information that goes with it. It is unlikely that everything about a word is learnt simultaneously; we might not know its spelling; we might be missing some of the components of its meaning; we certainly will not know all the word combinations in which it can occur. The problems associated with going from the first language to the second are not just the transfer of the actual words, but also the relationships and overtones they carry in the L1. As an English speaker, I cannot conceive how 'postpone' and 'reject' could be the same word in another language, as they are in Hebrew 'lidchot' (Levenston, 1979). Most uses of vocabulary in textbooks imply that words have single meanings: books that have vocabulary lists usually give single-word translations. The German course *English for You* (Graf, 1983), for instance, lists one translation for 'bar' (Bar) and one for 'write' (schreiben), where many might be necessary.

An aspect of vocabulary that has become important in recent years is how the word fits in to the structure of the sentence. Partly this is the argument structure of the verb described earlier, which for example, forces the verb 'faint' to have a grammatical subject 'Martin fainted', but never an object 'Martin fainted John', and requires the verb 'meet' to have an object 'He met John', not 'He met'. In addition, some verbs are followed by subordinate clauses, 'I hoped Mary would go' rather than grammatical objects 'I hoped Mary'. A speaker of English knows not only what a word means and how it is pronounced, but also how it fits into sentences.

Teaching cannot ignore that the student has to learn not just the meaning and pronunciation of each word, but how to use it. One simple way of doing this is the traditional task of getting the students to make up sentences using particular words. For example, in *Just Right* (Harmer, 2004), students have to say which words in a word list, 'absolutely . . . pirate . . . water tank', they already know and then to 'Write some sentences using them'.

Words are multifaceted; we do not know a word properly until we have learnt its forms, its different types of meaning and the ways in which it is used in sentences. Vocabulary teaching has been diminished by being considered the provision of a list of separate items, each with a specific meaning. Instead it is building up the richness of vocabulary in the students' minds.

Box 3.8 Vocabulary and teaching

- Teach the complexity of words.
- Fit in with the students' strategies.
- Teach basic-level words first.
- Teach lexical relationships.
- Think about the *first* presentation of the word.
- Teach some words through components of meaning.
- Remember that it is how the word is practised, not how often, that is important.
- Remember that students transfer L1 meanings as well as the words themselves.
- Put words in their structural context.

Fitting in with students' strategies

The third major implication is how teaching can fit in with the students' ways of learning vocabulary. For example, teachers implicitly draw on many of the strategies we have just outlined when they introduce new vocabulary. Showing a picture of a train may allow the students to guess what 'train' means from the context. Miming the action of flying may demonstrate the meaning of 'fly'. The teacher's attempts to explain a word through examples or definitions are similar to providing a human dictionary. Getting the students to sort vocabulary into sets relies on the strategy for organizing things in their minds.

Whose vocabulary is the learner acquiring?

Finally, as usual there is the issue not of what vocabulary the learner should be acquiring, but whose vocabulary? If students want to be like native speakers, we have to define *which* native speakers. Vocabulary differs from one country to another; what North Americans call an 'elevator' is a 'lift' to the rest of the world; Indian speakers use 'peon' to mean an office clerk, where English people mean a kind of peasant, and 'flower bed' where others would say 'marriage bed'. Vocabulary varies from region to region within a country; an alleyway is a 'chare' in Newcastle, a 'folly' in Colchester, and a 'lane' in the Isle of Wight; 'gravy' seems to be made with milk in Texas and with meat juice in the rest of the USA. Even if the variation in vocabulary is not extensive, language teaching still has to consider which native speaker is most appropriate.

But what if the student's aim is not to be a native speaker, but an efficient user of English as a second language – an L2 user? The words they need may be those that are understood by fellow L2 users, not by native speakers. Much of the Far East seems to use 'cider' for any fizzy drink rather than one made of apple; perhaps it is more useful for the student to acquire the general term rather than the specifically native usage. Some things we have hitherto considered mistakes may in fact be useful – if other L2 users all make the same 'mistake'. For example, I have spent a lifetime querying students who claim, 'I was very interesting in the class', by pointing out that this actually means something different from 'I was very interested in the class'. Perhaps I have been wasting my time: if all the L2 users know perfectly well what they mean by 'interesting', what I understand by it is beside the point, unless they want to communicate with me and my fellow natives rather than with each other.

Discussion topics

1   Take a lesson or a page from the textbook you are most familiar with: what new words are taught, and how?

2   What strategies would you now encourage in your students for learning vocabulary?

3   To what extent can we learn the words of another language without learning a new way of thinking to go with them?

4   How useful are dictionaries for students?

5   Decide how you would teach a beginners' class these high-frequency words:
  • *Nouns*: time, people, way, year, government, day, man, world, work, life.

  • *Verbs*: say, know, get, go, see, make, think, take, come, use.

  • *Adjectives*: new, good, old, different, local, small, great, social, important, national.

Further reading

An interesting book with many exercises for vocabulary teaching is Lewis (1993) *The Lexical Approach*. Useful books on vocabulary are: Nation (2001) *Learning Vocabulary in Another Language*, Cohen (1990) *Language Learning*, and Singleton (1999) *Exploring the Second Language Mental Lexicon*.

Answers to Box 3.1

1 a round object often used as a toy is a *ball*	☐	0–2,000 level
2 something you carry and put things in is a *bag*	☐	
3 a pipe or channel through which things flow is a *conduit*	☐	up to 10,000
4 to give way to someone is to *yield*	☐	
5 a person who works without being paid is a *volunteer*	☐	up to 20,000
6 a preparation for preventing infectious disease is a *vaccine*	☐	
7 a heavy glass with a handle is known as a *tankard*	☐	up to 50,000
8 a type of brain chemical is *serotonin*	☐	

9 a sailor's word for a clumsy fellow ☐ ⎫
   is a *lubber*

10 the effects of wind, rain, and so on, ☐ ⎬ up to 100,000
   on objects is *weathering* ⎭

11 a heavy wheel used to store power ☐ ⎫
   is a *flywheel*

12 something engraved on stone is ☐ ⎬ up to 150,000
   lapidary ⎭

You can now see roughly how many words you know by taking the last level at which you score both right. A full version of this test is on the website.

Box 3.9 German word test

In German what is the word for?:

1 🚲   2 ✋   3 ✏️

4 👤   5 ✈️   6 scissors

7 telephone   8 key   9 television

10 yacht

How did you try to learn these words? Tick the strategies you used:

1 Linking L2 sounds to sounds of the L1 word.
2 Looking at the meaning of part of the word.
3 Noting the structure of part of the word.
4 Putting the word in a topic group.
5 Visualizing the word in isolation.
6 Linking the word to a situation.
7 Creating a mental image of the word.
8 Associating a physical sensation with the word.
9 Associating the word with a keyword.

Check your answers against page 58.

Acquiring and teaching pronunciation

4

Focusing questions

Think of a speech sound in your first language:

- How do you think you make it?
- How do you think an L2 student learns it?
- How would you teach it to an L2 student?

Keywords

phonetic alphabet: a way of transcribing the sounds of speech through a carefully designed set of symbols, as in the IPA (International Phonetics Alphabet)

phonology and phonetics: phonology is the branch of linguistics that deals with the sound systems of language, including phonemes and intonation; phonetics is the branch that deals with the sheer sounds themselves

Language conveys meanings from one person to another through spoken sounds, written letters or gestures. Speakers know how to pronounce the words, sentences and utterances of their native language. At one level they can tell the difference in pronunciation between 'drain' and 'train', the sound patterns of the language; at another they know the difference between 'Fine', 'Fine?' and 'Fine!', the intonation patterns in which the voice rises and falls. The phonologies of languages differ in terms of which sounds they use, in the ways they structure sounds into syllables, and in how they use intonation, hard as this may be for many students to appreciate, and difficult as it may be for teachers to teach. It is impossible to imagine a non-disabled speaker of a language who could not pronounce sentences in it.

Talking about the sounds of language necessitates some way of writing down the sounds without reference to ordinary written language. For over a century the solution for researchers and teachers in much of the world has been the International Phonetic Alphabet (IPA), which supplies symbols for all the sounds that could occur in human languages. The full version is given in many books and the latest official revision can be downloaded from the International Phonetic Association; there is also an online version at the University of California, Los Angeles, that gives demonstrations of how the sounds are pronounced. This then gives a way of showing the sheer sounds of language, known as phonetics.

Any language, however, only makes use of a small selection of these sounds for its sound system, its phonology. So the version of IPA that is normally encountered in teaching is that used for transcribing a particular language, for instance the sounds of English, included somewhere in most coursebooks. A transcript that records sheer phonetic sounds is independent of language and so uses the full IPA chart; usually this is put in square brackets, for example [tin]. A transcript of the significant sounds in the phonological systems of a particular language is usually given in slant brackets, say, English /tɪn/.

Box 4.1 instant accent test for English consonants

Carry out the following test. (**Note**: it only covers the consonants of English as the vowels would be more complicated to test and have far more variations from one native speaker to another.) A version of this test that can be printed out is available on the website.

Find a non-native speaker of English and get them to read the following words aloud rapidly. Point to words at random rather than in sequence. Score each selected consonant as; (1) native-like accent; (2) comprehensible but not fully native; (3) non-native pronunciation. Note any peculiarities on the right. Do *not* pay attention to vowels.

phoneme	allophones					misc
	initial		medial		final	cluster (CC) etc.
1. /p/	pin ❐		supper ❐		map ❐	spit ❐
2. /b/	bin ❐		suburb ❐		rub ❐	bleed ❐
3. /t/	tip ❐		bitter ❐		pet ❐	sting ❐
4. /d/	doll ❐		rudder ❐		fed ❐	drain ❐
5. /k/	cash ❐		tucker ❐		luck ❐	create ❐
6. /g/	goat ❐		rugger ❐		mug ❐	glade ❐
7. /tʃ/	chew ❐		Richard ❐		rich ❐	
8. /dʒ/	joke ❐		lodger ❐		fudge ❐	
9. /f/	fast ❐		differ ❐		off ❐	flame ❐
10. /v/	view ❐		river ❐		of ❐	
11. /θ/	thigh ❐		rethink ❐		bath ❐	three ❐
12. /ð/	then ❐		rather ❐		bathe ❐	
13. /s/	soon ❐		lesson ❐		mess ❐	strain ❐
14. /z/	zoom ❐		razor ❐		was ❐	sizzle ❐
15. /ʃ/	show ❐		usher ❐		fish ❐	shrine ❐
16. /ʒ/	genre ❐		measure ❐		rouge ❐	
17. /h/	who ❐					
18. /l/	lip ❐		pillar ❐		hill ❐	plain ❐
19. /r/	read ❐		direct ❐		far (0) ❐	there is ❐
20. /m/	mix ❐		summer ❐		aim ❐	dims ❐
21. /n/	nod ❐		dinner ❐		sin ❐	likes ❐
22. /ŋ/			banger ❐		sang ❐	finger ❐
23. /j/	yes ❐		reunite ❐			student ❐
24. /w/	wet ❐		dissuade ❐			saw it ❐

What does this test tell you about (a) the person's first language (b) the person's first writing system?

4.1 Phonemes and second language acquisition

Focusing questions

- What do you think are the crucial sounds in your first language?
- How do you think you learnt them?

Keywords

phonemes: the sounds of a language that are systematically distinguished from each other, for example, /s/ from /t/ in 'same' and 'tame'
allophones: different forms of the phoneme in particular contexts, for example, the aspirate /p/ (with a puff of air) in 'pill' versus the unaspirated /p/ (without a puff of air) in 'lip'
distinctive feature: the minimal difference that may distinguish phonemes, such as voice and aspiration in 'din' and 'tin'
voice onset time (VOT): the moment when voicing starts during the production of a consonant

Each language uses a certain number of sounds called phonemes that distinguish words and morphemes from one other. The spoken word 'sin' is different from the word 'tin' because one has the phoneme /s/, the other the phoneme /t/; 'sin' differs from 'son' in that one has the phoneme /ɪ/, the other the phoneme /ʌ/. And so on for all the words of the language – 'bin', 'kin', 'din', 'gin', 'soon', 'sawn', 'seen', ... Phonemes signal the difference between words and meanings: the spoken distance between 'I adore you' and 'I abhor you' is a single phoneme, /d/ versus /b/.

A phoneme is a sound which is conventionally used to distinguish meanings in a particular language. Any language only uses a small proportion of all the sounds available as phonemes; English does not have the /x/ phoneme heard in German words like 'Buch', or the click sounds used in South African languages; Japanese does not have two phonemes for the /l/ in 'lip' and the /r/ in 'rip'; nor does French recognize a distinction between short /ɪ/ in 'bin' and long /iː/ in 'been'. Human languages have between 11 and 141 phonemes, English being about average with 44 or so (depending on accent).

As well as phonemes, there are allophones – variant pronunciations for a phoneme in different situations. For instance, in English the phoneme /l/ has three main allophones. At the beginning of a word such as 'leaf', it is a so-called 'clear' [l], sounding more like a front high vowel. At the end of a word such as 'feel', it can be pronounced as a 'dark' [l], sounding lower and more like a back low vowel. For many British speakers it is nowadays pronounced as /w/, that is, 'tell' is pronounced /tew/. It is not going to affect the meaning if you pronounce 'leaf' with the wrong dark /l/ but it will certainly convey a particular foreign accent.

The problem for second language acquisition is that each language has its own set of phonemes and allophones. Two phonemes in one language may correspond to two allophones of the same phoneme in another language, or may not exist at all: the two Polish phonemes that distinguish 'prosie' (pig) from 'prosze' (please) sound like allophones of /ʃ/ (ship) to an English ear, while the two English phonemes /θ/ 'thigh' and /ð/ 'thy' seem to be allophones of one phoneme to a Spanish speaker.

When the phonemes of spoken language connect one-to-one to the letters of alphabetic written language, the writing system is called transparent, as in Finnish or Italian. The English writing system is far from transparent because there are many more sounds than letters to go round: 44 phonemes will not go into 26 letters. So pairs of written letters go with single sounds, like 'th' for /θ/ in 'three' or 'ea' for /iː/ in 'bean'; or single letters go with two sounds, like 'x' for /ks/ 'six'; or letters have multiple pronunciations, like the <a> in 'pat' /æ/, 'atomic' /ə/, 'ska' /aː/ and 'swan' /ɒ/. And of course letters are used very differently in the spelling of, say, English, Polish and Arabic.

In the early days of the direct method, such phonetic scripts were often used directly for language teaching, and they are still common at advanced levels where people are often taught 'ear-training' by transcribing spoken language. Most EFL coursebooks use a phonetic script as a resource to be consulted from time to time rather than as the main vehicle for teaching; charts of the phonetic alphabet for English can be seen pinned up in many classrooms. The elementary coursebook *New Headway Beginners* (Soars and Soars, 2002) has a chart of the symbols for English at the end of the book and uses them in the vocabulary lists, but only a handful of exercises in the book actually use them. Joanne Kenworthy's *The Pronunciation of English: A Workbook* (2000), intended more for teachers than students, uses phonetic symbols to train the listener to locate and discuss phonemes in authentic English speech.

Over the years the concept of the phoneme has proved useful in organizing materials for teaching pronunciation, even when it has been largely superseded in much phonological research. Pronunciation textbooks like *Ship or Sheep?* (Baker, 1981) present the student with pairs of words: 'car' /kaː/ versus 'cow' /kaʊ/ or 'bra' /braː/ versus 'brow' /braʊ/. This technique originated from the 'minimal pairs' technique used by linguists to establish the phonemes of a language from scratch; you present the native speaker with a series of likely or unlikely pairs of words and ask them whether they are different. This allows you, in principle, to build up the whole phoneme inventory – in practice, it is very hard to do, as I discovered when I naively tried to demonstrate it in a lecture with a native speaker of a language I did not know (Russian).

In typical pronunciation materials the student learns how to distinguish one phoneme from another by hearing and repeating sentences with a high concentration of particular phonemes, such as 'I've found a mouse in the house' or 'This is the cleanest house in town', or traditional tongue-twisters such as 'He ran from the Indies to the Andes in his undies'. Like the teaching of structural grammar, this activity emphasizes practice rather than communication and sees pronunciation as a set of habits for producing sounds. The habit of producing the sound /n/ is believed to be acquired by repeating it over and over again and by being corrected when it is said wrongly. Learning to pronounce a second language means building up new pronunciation habits and overcoming the bias of the first language. Only by saying 'car' /kaː/ and 'cow' /kaʊ/ many times is the contrast between /aː/ and /aʊ/ acquired. In other areas of language teaching, such as grammar, people would scorn making students simply repeat sentences. Nevertheless it remains a popular technique for pronunciation teaching.

> **Box 4.2 Characteristics of speakers of different L1s using English**
>
> **German**: devoicing of final voiced plosives: /bɪk/ for /bɪg/ (big)
> **Japanese**: use of /l/ for /r/: /led/ ~ /red/ (red)
> **Arabic**: devoicing final voiced consonants: /spuːns/ for /spuːnz/
> **Chinese** (Mandarin): use of /v/ for /w/: /vɪð/ for /wɪð/ (with)
> **Spanish**: adding vowels: /esneik/ for /sneik/ (snake)
> **Italian**: vowel shortening: /plɪz/ for /pliːz/ (please)
> **Hindi**: use of /b/ for /w/: /biː/ for /wiː/ (we)
> **Hungarian**: devoicing final consonants: /faif/ for /faiv/ (five)
> **Fante**: velar fricative /h/: /xə/ for /hə/ (her)
> **Finnish**: vowel raising: /æsk/ for /aːsk/ (ask)
>
> *Examples derived from the Speech Accent Archive.*

Phoneme learning

Traditionally, much research into the L2 acquisition of phonology has focused on the phoneme. One classic example is the work of Wilfried Wieden and William Nemser (1991), who looked at phonemes and features in the acquisition of English by Austrian schoolchildren. They found that some phonemes improved gradually over time while others showed no improvement. Beginners, for example, perceived the diphthong /əʊ/ in 'boat' only 55 per cent correctly, but managed 100 per cent after eight years; the sound /ə/ at the end of 'finger', however, gave students as much trouble after eight years as it did at the start. The learners went through three stages:

1 *Presystemic.* At this stage learners learn the sounds in individual words but without any overall pattern, that is, they may learn the /əʊ/ in 'no' but not the /əʊ/ in 'coat'.

2 *Transfer.* Now the learners start to treat the second language sounds systematically as equivalent to the sounds of their first language, that is, they see the second language sounds through the lens of the first.

3 *Approximative.* Finally the learners realize their native sounds are not good enough and attempt to restructure the L2 sounds in a new system; they realize that the sounds are not just variants of their native sounds.

This example shows the important role of transfer from one language to another in acquiring pronunciation. It is not, however, a simple matter of transferring a single phoneme from the first language to the second, but of carrying over general properties of the first language. The phonemes of the language do not exist as individual items but are part of a whole system of contrasts. Practising a single phoneme or pair of phonemes may not tackle the underlying issue. Though some of the learners' pronunciation rules are related to their first language, they nevertheless still make up a unique temporary system – an interlanguage.

Learning below the phoneme level

For many purposes the phoneme cannot give the whole picture of pronunciation. As well as the allophone, mentioned above, the elements which make up a phoneme also need to be taken into account. Seemingly different phonemes share common features which will present a learning problem that stretches across several phonemes.

Let us take the example of voice onset time (VOT), which has been extensively researched in SLA research. One of the differences between pairs of plosive consonants such as /p~b/ and /k~g/ is the VOT – the interval of time between the consonant and the following vowel. The voicing of the vowel can start more or less at the same moment as the release of the obstruction by the tongue or the lips; this will then sound like a voiced /b/ 'boss' or /g/ 'go'. Or voicing can start a few milliseconds *after* the release of the plosive, yielding voiceless /p/ 'pod', /k/ 'cod'. The difference between voiced and voiceless plosives is not a matter of *whether* voicing occurs but *when* it occurs, that is, of timing relative to the moment of release. The distinction between voiced and voiceless plosives is a matter of convention rather than absolute. Hence it varies from one language to another: the Spanish /k~g/ contrast is not exactly the same as the English /k~g/ because English /k/ has VOT that starts +80 milliseconds, but Spanish /k/ has VOT of only +29 milliseconds, almost overlapping with the English /g/.

An interesting question is whether there are two separate systems to handle the two languages or one system that covers both. French learners of English, for example, pronounce the /t/ sound in French with a longer VOT than monolinguals (Flege, 1987). Spanish/English bilinguals use more or less the same VOT in both English and Spanish (Williams, 1977). It makes no difference to their perception of stops which language is used. As Watson (1991: 44) sums up: 'In both production and perception, therefore, studies of older children (and adults) suggest that bilinguals behave in ways that are at once distinct from monolinguals and very similar to them.' L2 users are not imitation native speakers but something unique – people who simultaneously possess two languages. We should not expect them to be like natives, but like people who can use another language efficiently in their own right – L2 users with multi-competence, not imitation native speakers with monolingual competence.

Many theories of phonology see the phoneme as built up of a number of distinctive features. The English /p~b/ contrast is made up of features such as:

- *fortis/lenis*: /p/ is a fortis consonant, said with extra energy, like /k~t/, while /b/ is a lenis consonant, said with less energy, like /g~d/.
- *voice*: /p/ is a voiceless consonant in which the vocal cords do not vibrate, like /t~k/, while /b/ is a voiced consonant during which the vocal cords vibrate, like /g~d/.
- *aspiration*: /p/ is aspirated (i.e. has a long VOT), like /t/, while /b/ is unaspirated, like /d/.

And other features as well.

These distinctive features do not belong just to these six phonemes, but potentially to all phonemes; other voiced consonants, for instance, include /l/ 'let' and /m/ 'mouth'; other fortis consonants include /k/ and /f/. All the differences between phonemes can be reduced to about 19 of these distinctive features, though no two lists seem to agree – aspiration is not usually on the list. Getting the distinctive features right or wrong can then affect not just one phoneme but many; producing the right voicing contrast affects /ʃ/ 'shirt', /dʒ/ 'job' and /p/ 'pie' and many others. The danger, again, is that in some languages a distinctive feature may be crucial to a phonemic difference, while in others it may contribute to an allophone; the difference between English aspirated /p/ 'pot' and unaspirated /p/ 'stop' is allophonic and depends on position in the word. In Hindi, however, aspiration is phonemic and /pʰəl/ (fruit) and /pəl/ (moment) are different words, one with, one without aspiration.

The characteristics of a foreign accent often reside in these distinctive features. In German, for example, tenseness is important for consonant pairs like /t~d/, not voice; hardly surprisingly, German speakers have problems with all the voiced and voiceless consonants in English, /t~d/, /ð~θ/, /s~z/, and so on, not just with individual phonemes or pairs of phonemes. It is often the feature that gives trouble, not the individual phoneme. The Speech Accent Archive at George Mason University details the typical pronunciations of many accents of English, both native and non-native.

However useful phonemes may be for organizing teaching, they do not in themselves have much to do with learning pronunciation. The phoneme is not an entity in itself but an abstract way of bundling together several aspects of pronunciation. The phonemes of a language are made up of distinctive features. Learning another language means acquiring not just each phoneme as a whole, but the crucial features. Minimal pairs like 'din/tin' are deceptive in that there are often several differences between the two members of the pair, each of which may pose a separate learning problem for the student.

Box 4.3 Phonemes and distinctive features

- Much learning of pronunciation depends on aspects other than the phoneme, for example, distinctive features.
- L2 learners gradually acquire the L2 way of voicing stop consonants.
- Their first language is affected by their knowledge of the second language, as well as their second being affected by their first.

4.2 Learning syllable structure

Focusing questions

- How many syllables are there in 'constitution'? in 'fire'? in 'autosegmentalism'?
- How do you think syllables work in your own speech?

Keywords

syllable: a unit of phonology consisting of a structure of phonemes, stresses, and so on

syllable structure: how consonants (C) and vowels (V) may be combined into syllables in a particular language; for example, English has CVC syllables while Japanese has CV

epenthesis: padding out the syllable by adding extra vowels or consonants; for example, 'Espain' for 'Spain'

In Chapter 2 we saw how elements of language such as morphemes build up into sentences through phrases and structures. The same is true of phonology: phonemes are part of the phonological structure of the sentence, not just items strung together like beads on a necklace. In particular they form part of the structure of syllables.

One way of analysing syllables is in terms of consonants (C) such as /t/, /s/, /p/, and so on, and vowels (V) such as /ɪ/ or /ai/. The simplest syllable consists of a vowel V /ai/ 'eye'; this structure is found in all languages. In English, all syllables must have a vowel, with the occasional exception of syllabic /n/ in /bʌtn̩/ ('button') and /l/ in /bɒtl̩/ ('bottle').

Another type of syllable combines a single consonant with a vowel, CV as in /tai/ 'tie'. In languages such as Japanese all syllables have this CV structure with few exceptions, hence the familiar-looking pattern of Japanese words such as 'Miyazaki', 'Toyota' or 'Yokahama'.

A third syllable structure allows combinations of CVC as in /tait/ 'tight'. CVC languages vary in how many consonants can come at the beginning or end of the syllable. Chinese allows only one of each, again resulting in familiar-looking names like 'Chan' and 'Wong'.

One difficulty for the L2 learner comes from how the consonants combine with each other to make CC – the permissible consonant clusters. English combines /p/ with /l/ in 'plan' and with /r/ in 'pray' /prei/, but does not combine /p/ with /f/ or /z/; there are no English words like 'pfan' or 'pzan'. In German, however, /pn/ and /ps/ are possible combinations, as in 'Psychologie' (psychology) and 'Pneu' (tyre). Aliens in Larry Niven science fiction stories can be identified because their names have non-English clusters – 'tnuctipun' /tn/ and 'ptavvs' /pt/. English does not allow 'tn' at the beginning of a word and doubles /v/ in the spelling of a handful of words, such as 'skivvy'.

The compulsory vowel in the English syllable can be preceded or followed by one or more consonants. So 'lie' /lai/, which has a consonant/vowel (CV) structure, and 'sly' /slai/, which starts with a two-consonant cluster /sl/ (CC), are both possible, as are 'eel' /iːl/ with VC and 'eels' /iːlz/ with VCC. Longer clusters of three or four consonants can also occur, for example, at the end of 'lengths' /leŋkθs/ or the beginning of 'splinter' /splintə/. The ultimate seems to be the five final consonants in the /mpfst/ of 'Thou triumphst!' The syllable structure of some languages allows only a single consonant before or after the vowel. Japanese, for instance, has no consonant clusters and most syllables end in a vowel, that is, it has a bare CV syllable structure; the English word 'strike' starting with CCC becomes 'sutoraki' in Japanese, in conformity with the syllable structure of the language.

L2 learners often try by one means or another to make English clusters fit their first languages. Examples are Koreans saying /kəlaːs/ for 'class', and Arabs saying /bəlæstik/ for 'plastic'. They are inserting extra vowels to make English conform to Korean or Arabic, a process known as epenthesis. So British Indian children in Yorkshire pronounce 'blue' as /bəluː/ not /bluː/, 'friend' as /fərend/ not /frend/, and 'sphere' as /səfiə/ not /sfiə/, all with epenthetic vowels (Verma *et al.*, 1992).

An alternative strategy is to leave consonants out of words if they are not allowed in the LI – the process of 'simplification'. Cantonese speakers, whose L1 syllables have no final consonants, turn English 'girl' /gəːl/ into 'gir' /gəː/ and 'Joan' /dʒəʊn/ into 'Joa' /dʒəʊ/. Arabic syllables too can be CV but not CCV, that is, there are no two-consonant clusters. 'Straw' /strɔː/ is an impossible syllable in

Arabic because it starts with a three-consonant cluster /str/ CCC. Indian children in Yorkshire simplify the /nd/ of 'thousand' and the /dz/ of 'Leeds' to /d/ (Verma *et al.*, 1992).

Egyptian-Arabic learners of English often add an epenthetic vowel /ə/ to avoid two or three-consonant clusters. 'Children' /tʃɪldrən/ becomes 'childiren' /tʃɪldɪrən/ in their speech because the CC combination /dr/ is not allowed. 'Translate' /trænzleɪt/ comes out as 'tiransilate' /tɪrænzɪleɪt/ to avoid the two consonant CC sequences /tr/ and /sl/. Part of their first language system is being transferred into English.

So the clash between the syllable structures of the first and second languages is resolved by the expedient of adding vowels or leaving out consonants, a true interlanguage solution. It is not just the phonemes in the sentence that matter, but the abstract syllable structure that governs their combination. Indeed, some phonologists regard the syllable as the main unit in speaking or listening, rather than the phoneme, one reason being that the sheer number of phonemes per second is too many for the brain to process and so some other unit must be involved.

Box 4.4 Syllables

- A crucial aspect of language acquisition is the mastery of syllable structure.
- Learners often try to make their second language syllable structure fit the structure of their first language, by adding or omitting vowels and consonants.

4.3 General ideas about phonology learning

Focusing questions

- Do you think your own accent gives away where you come from in your L1? In your L2?
- How important do you think the first language is in learning L2 pronunciation?

Keywords

transfer: carrying over elements of one language one knows to another, whether L1 to L2 or L2 to L1 (reverse transfer)

accent versus **dialect**: an accent is a way of pronouncing a language that is typical of a particular group, whether regional or social; a dialect is the whole system characteristic of a particular group, including grammar and vocabulary, and so on, as well as pronunciation

---

Let us now look at some general issues about the learning of L2 pronunciation.

L1 and transfer

Usually it is very easy to spot the first language of a non-native speaker from their accent; German speakers of English tend to say 'zing' when they mean 'thing', Japanese 'pray' when they mean 'play'. Chapter 10 asks whether this matters: after all, we can tell instantly whether a native speaker of English comes from Texas, Glasgow or Sydney, but this does not mean we see their accent as wrong. In the second language very few people manage to acquire an accent that can pass for native; at best, L2 users have boasted to me of being mistaken for a native speaker of some variety other than that of the person they are talking to; for example, a Swedish speaker of English might be taken to be an American in England. Foreign accent is all but ineradicable – but then so are many local accents of English.

The components of foreign accent may be at different levels of phonology. The most salient may be the apparent use of the wrong phoneme. I ordered 'bière' (beer) in France and was surprised when the waiter brought me 'Byrhh' (a reinforced wine). This carries perhaps the greatest toll for the L2 user as it involves potential misunderstandings. Next comes the level of allophones; saying the wrong allophone will not interfere with the actual meaning of the word, but may increase the overall difficulty of comprehension if the listener always has to struggle to work out what phoneme is intended. And it certainly gives rise to characteristic accents. Consonant clusters may be a difficulty for some speakers; Spanish does not have an initial /st/ cluster, so Spanish speakers tend to say 'estation' for 'station'. And we have seen that syllables and clusters pose problems for many.

The reason for these pronunciation problems has been called cross-linguistic transfer: a person who knows two languages transfers some aspect from one language to another; in other words, this is language in a $Lang_5$ sense of linguistic competence. What can be transferred depends, among other things, on the relationship between the two languages. Fred Eckmann *et al.* (2003) have drawn up three possibilities:

1 *The first language has neither of the contrasting L2 sounds.* Korean, for example, does not have any phonemes corresponding to English /f~v/ as in 'fail/veil'. A Korean learning English has to learn two new phonemes from scratch.

2 *The second language has one of the L2 sounds.* Japanese, for instance, has a /p/ sound corresponding to English /p/ in 'paid', but no /f/ phoneme corresponding to that in 'fade'. Japanese learners of English have to learn an extra phoneme.

3 *The second language has both sounds as allophones of the same phoneme.* In Spanish, plosive /d/ and fricative /ð/ are both allophones of the phoneme /d/. Spanish learners of English have to learn that what they take for granted as alternative forms of the same phoneme are in fact different phonemes in English. Similarly, /l/ and /r/ are allophones of one phoneme in Japanese.

Which of these creates the most problems for learners? Logically it would seem that missing sounds would create problems: German has two fricatives /ç/ in 'Tuch' (towel) and /x/ 'Mach' (make), almost totally absent from English, apart from the isolated 'foreign' words 'loch' and 'Bach' for some people. So English people should have a problem acquiring these German phonemes; but this is not the case. By and large, totally new sounds do not create particular problems. One exception might be click phonemes in some African languages, which speakers of non-click languages find it hard to master, though young babies are very good at it.

The combination that appears the trickiest to deal with is in fact when two allophones of one L1 phoneme appear as two phonemes in the second language, as we saw with Japanese problems with /l~r/. Once you have classed a particular sound as the same as that in your first language, that is, Japanese /l/ goes with English /l/, you find it difficult to split its allophones into two phonemes. The more similar the two phonemes may be in the L1 and the L2, the more deceptive it may be.

The first language phonology affects the acquisition of the second through transfer because the learner projects qualities of the first language onto the second. The same happens in reverse in that people who speak a second language have a slightly different accent in their first language from monolinguals. The VOT research has shown subtle influences on L1 timing from the L2; for example, French people who know English tend to have slightly longer VOTs for /t/ in French, their first language, compared to monolinguals.

L2 and universal processes of acquisition

As well as transfer, L2 learners make use of universal processes common to all learners. Some problems are shared by L2 learners because of the similar processes of language processing and acquisition engraved on their minds.

For example, the simplification of consonant clusters happens almost regardless of L1. The earlier example of Germans having trouble with English voicing may be due not to transfer from German, but to a universal preference for 'devoicing' of final consonants. Similarly, the use of CV syllables by many L2 learners could reflect a universal tendency rather than transfer from specific first languages. While epenthesis often depends on the structure of the first language, it nevertheless appears to be available to all L2 learners.

A number of models have been put forward to explain L2 phonological acquisition in a second language. The ontogeny phylogeny model of language acquisition put forward by Roy Major (2002) claims that the early stages of L2 learning are characterized by interference from the second language. Then the learner starts to rely on universal processes common to all learners. The L2 elements themselves increase over time until finally the learner possesses the L2 forms. This is shown in the stages captured in Figure 4.1.

Figure 4.1 The ontogeny phylogeny model (OPM) (Major, 2002)

Major (2002) takes the example of English speakers learning the Spanish trilled [r]. They start with the English sound, written phonetically as [ɹ] (stage 1). In the next stages, though the Spanish [r] starts to appear, they also use an uvular trilled [ʀ] based on their universal processes. Spanish [r] continues to increase until it reaches 100 per cent, while [ɹ] and [ʀ] decrease until they reach zero in stage 5. Learning pronunciation then depends on three different components – L1 transfer, universal processes and L2. The relationship between these varies according to the learner's stage.

Box 4.5 Processes in acquiring L2 phonology

- A crucial element in L2 phonology acquisition is transfer from the L1, which depends partly on the nature of the two phonological systems.
- Nevertheless, phonological acquisition also depends on universal processes of language acquisition available to the human mind.

4.4 Choosing a model for teaching pronunciation

Focusing questions

- What do you think is a status accent for your L1? Do you speak it?

Keywords

RP (received pronunciation): the usual accent of British English given in books about English, spoken by a small minority in England

English as lingua franca (ELF): English used as a means of communication among people with different first languages rather than between natives

The underlying issue with pronunciation is who the students want to sound like – which model should they strive to emulate, in the Lang$_3$ sense of 'language' as an abstract entity? Usually this is taken to be some type of native speaker, an assumption questioned in Chapter 10. The issue of the target affects pronunciation more than grammar, spelling or vocabulary, as accent shows far more variation between native varieties of languages; written language may hardly ever give away the writer's dialect.

The usual model for teaching is a status form of the language within a country: you are supposed to speak French like the inhabitants of Paris, not of Marseilles or Brittany. Regional accents are not taught, nor are class dialects other than that of the educated middle class. For English the status accents are non-regional: in the USA Standard American English (SAE), in the UK received pronunciation (RP), both of them spread across regions, even if SAE is mostly in the north-east USA, RP mostly in southern England. Hence L2 students are rarely supposed to sound like Texans from Dallas, Glaswegians from Glasgow or Scouses from Liverpool. These status accents are spoken by a small minority of speakers, even if many others shift their original accents towards them to get on, say, in politics or broadcasting.

The goal for teaching British English has long been RP, which is spoken by a small minority even in England; my students in Newcastle grumble that they never hear it outside the classroom. The claimed advantages of RP were that, despite its small number of speakers located in only one country, it was comprehensible everywhere and had neutral connotations in terms of class and region. True as this may be, it does sound like a last-ditch defence of the powerful status form against the rest. A more realistic British standard nowadays might be Estuary English, popular among TV presenters and pop stars; the chief characteristics are the glottal stop [ʔ] for /t/, inserted /r/ in words like 'sawing', and the vowel-like /w/ for /l/ as in /bjuːʔɪfuw/ 'beautiful'. So the phonemes and intonation of a particular language that are taught to students should vary according to the choice of regional or status form. Most native speaker teachers have some problems in consistently using the appropriate model; I had to modify my pronunciation of 'often' as /ɔːftən/ by getting rid of the /t/ and changing the vowel to /ɒ/ to get the RP version /ɒfən/ because my students protested.

An additional problem in choosing a model comes when a language is spoken in many countries, each of which has its own status form, say, French used officially in 28 countries, Arabic in 18 or English in 43. Should the target for French be a francophone African one, a Canadian one or a French one? The English-speaking countries, from Australia to Canada, Scotland to South Africa, each have their own variety, with its own internal range; outside these countries there are well-established varieties of English spoken in countries such as Singapore and India, now mostly recognized as forms of English in their own right, like Singlish and Hinglish. A global language such as English faces the problem not just of which local variety *within* a country to teach, but of which country to take as a model – if any. The choice of which national model to use can seldom be made without taking into account the political nature of language, particularly in ex-colonial countries, a topic developed in Chapter 10.

Overall the student's target needs to be matched with the roles they will assume when using the second language. If they want to be baristas in coffee bars, teach them an appropriate accent (in England Italian might be an advantage); if they are training to be doctors in London, teach them how London doctors and patients speak. One problem is native speaker expectation: natives often expect non-natives to have an approximation to a status accent. Many students in England have complained to me that they did not want to acquire an RP accent because of its snobbish middle-class associations. It is up to the teacher to decide whether the students' wishes to sound like Michael Caine or Elton John, for example, are in their best interests.

As we see throughout this book, recently people have been challenging the centrality of the native speaker as a model. In terms of pronunciation, apart from those living in English-speaking countries, what is the point of making learners of English understand and use a native standard accent like RP when virtually everybody they will meet is a fellow non-native speaker? The goal should be an accent that is maximally comprehensible by non-native speakers, leaving the native speaker out of the equation except for those who have to deal with them.

Jenny Jenkins (2000, 2002) has been proposing a syllabus for English pronunciation based on what non-native speakers of English as a lingua franca (ELF) need. In terms of consonants, for example, there is no point belabouring the difference between /ð/ 'this' and /θ/ 'thistle' as it rarely causes any misunderstanding (and affects only a small group of function words in any case). It would also be helpful if students were taught the 'rhotic' /r/ used in SAE (or regional English dialects) in front of consonants /bɜrd/ and preceding silence /sentər/ rather than the non-rhotic RP, which has no /r/ in these positions /bɜd/ and /sentə/. It is also interesting to note what she does *not* think is important, such as the difference between clear and dark allophones of /l/ in 'lip' and 'pill', and the intonation patterns, both of which teachers have laboured over for generations.

Some of her other points are shown in Box 4.6. It should be noted, however, that these are primarily derived from the analysis of learner English, that is to say the language of students, rather than from the language of successful L2 users. If you take the ELF idea seriously, you need to teach what is important for international uses of English, not for talking with native speakers, as we see in Chapter 10, nor just for talking to fellow students in a classroom. For amusement only, look at my web page *Speech Reform*, which satirizes spelling reform by suggesting we could get by in English speech with 11 consonants /p t k s ʃ ð ʃ m n r w/ and three vowels /i e a/.

Box 4.6 The lingua franca pronunciation core

Elements of English pronunciation that need to be right to avoid problems between students with different L1s (Jenkins, 2000: 159):

1 all consonants except for /ð~θ/ which can be dispensed with.
2 aspiration after voiceless plosives /p~t~k/ needs to be maintained in 'spy', 'sting', 'scorn', etc.
3 simplification of initial clusters should be avoided e.g. 'product' as /pɒdʌk/.
4 pure vowels should be longer before voiced consonants than before voiceless consonants in, say, 'bad/bat', 'league/leak', 'bard/bart'.
5 the placement of the nuclear tone in the tone-groups is vital; 'John is *here*'/ 'John *is* here'/ '*John* is here', but not choice of tone.

Box 4.7 Models of pronunciation

• In teaching a native speaker variety, the choice has to be made between national varieties and between different local and class accents.
• In teaching an international language like English (ELF), the choice is which forms work best among non-native speakers from different countries.

4.5 Learning and teaching pronunciation

What does this mean for teaching? Most language teachers use 'integrated pronunciation teaching', as Joanne Kenworthy (1987) calls it, in which pronunciation is taught as an incidental to other aspects of language, similar to the focus on form described in Chapter 2. *The Pronunciation Book* (Bowen and Marks, 1992), for example, describes including pronunciation work within activities primarily devoted to other ends, such as texts and dialogues. Some teachers correct wrong pronunciations when they arise on an ad hoc basis. Such incidental correction probably does not do much good directly if it concentrates on a single phoneme rather than on the role of the phoneme in the whole system; it may only improve the students' pronunciation of a single word said in isolation. It also relies on direct correction being a good way of teaching, something which has been out of fashion in other areas of language teaching for generations. Correction may indirectly serve to raise the students' awareness of pronunciation, but may also succeed in embarrassing all but the most thick-skinned of students.

One clear implication from SLA research is that the learning of sounds is not just a matter of mastering the L2 phonemes and their predictable variants. At one level, it means learning the rules of pronunciation for the language, such as those for forming syllables; at another level, it is learning precise control over VOT. While phonemes are indeed important, pronunciation difficulties often have to do with general effects; in the case of English we have come across a problem with voicing for German students, syllable structure for Arabic students, VOT for Spanish students, and so on. Language teaching should pay more attention to such general features of pronunciation rather than the phoneme.

Learners have their own interlanguage phonologies – temporary rules of their own. The sounds of the language are not just separate items on a list to be learnt one at a time, but are related in a complex system. An English /p/ is different from a /b/ because it is voiced and fortis, different from a /t/ because it involves the lips, different from a /v/ because it is a stop consonant rather than a fricative, and so on. Teaching or correcting a single phoneme may not have much effect on the students' pronunciation, or may even have the wrong effect. It is like taking a brick out of a wall and replacing it with another. Unless the replacement fits exactly, all the other bricks will move to accommodate it or, at worst, the wall will fall down. Understanding how to help students' pronunciation means relating the faults first to their current interlanguage and only secondly to the target. The differences between their speech and that of native speakers should not be corrected without taking into account both the interlanguage and the target system. The Austrian research suggests that teachers should be aware which sounds are going to improve gradually and which are never going to improve, so that these can be treated differently. It also suggests that pronunciation teaching should relate to the particular stage the learner is at, emphasizing individual words at the beginning, relating pronunciation to the first language for intermediates, and treating the sound system of the new language in its own right for advanced students.

Let us go through some standard techniques for teaching pronunciation in the light of what we have been saying.

Use of phonetic script

At advanced levels, students are sometimes helped by looking at phonetic transcripts of spoken language using IPA or by making transcripts of speech themselves. As we see throughout this book, it is disputable whether such conscious awareness of pronunciation ever converts into the unconscious ability to speak, useful as it may be as an academic activity for future teachers. At the more practical level, a familiarity with phonetic script enables students to look up the pronunciation of individual words, say, London place names such as 'Leicester Square' /lestə/ or 'Holborn' /həʊbən/ (even if a booking clerk once said to me distinctly /həʊlbɜrn/ with an /l/ and an /r/).

Imitation

Repetition of words or phrases has been the mainstay of pronunciation teaching: it is not only Henry Higgins who says 'Repeat after me, "The rain in Spain stays mainly on the plain"'; the elementary coursebook *New English File* (Oxenden *et al.*, 2004), for example, asks students to 'Listen and repeat the words and sounds' and 'Copy the rhythm' – whatever that means. At one level, this is impromptu repetition at the teacher's command; at another, repetition of dialogues in the language laboratory sentence by sentence. Of course, repetition may not be helpful without feedback: you may not know you are getting it wrong unless someone tells you so. Sheer imitation is not thought to be a productive method of language learning, as we see throughout this book. It also ignores the fact that phonemes are part of a system of contrasts in the students' minds, not discrete items.

Discrimination of sounds

Audio-lingual teaching believed that, if you cannot hear a distinction, you cannot make it. This led to minimal pair exercises in which the students have to indicate whether they hear 'lice', 'rice' or 'nice' in the sentence 'That's …'. The dangers include the unreality of such pairs as 'sink/think' taken out of any context, the rarity of some of the words used (I once taught the difference between 'soul' and 'thole'), and the overdependence on the phoneme rather than the distinctive feature and the syllable, for example. Again, useful if it is treated as building up the overall pronunciation system in the students' minds, not as learning the difference between two phonemes, such as /ɪ/ and /iː/.

Consciousness raising

Given the rise of such approaches as FonF discussed in Chapter 2, we can use exercises to make students more aware of pronunciation in general, say, listening to tapes to discover aspects such as the speaker's sex, age, education, region, or the formality of the situation. In other words, rather than concentrating on specific aspects of speech, the students' ears are trained to hear things better. For example, Eric Hawkins (1984) used to get students to listen to noises he made by hitting objects; they had to invent a transcription system so that they could 'play back' the noises he had made. Certainly an awareness of the range of phonological systems may help the student – the importance of the syllable may be news to them.

Communication

In principle, pronunciation materials could use the actual problems of communication as a basis for teaching. For instance, both natives and non-natives confuse 'fifty' /fɪftɪ/ and 'fifteen' /fɪftiːn/ in real-world situations of shops, and so on, presumably because the final /n/ sounds like a nasalized vowel rather than a consonant.

4.6 Learning and teaching intonation

Focusing questions

- What do you convey to someone else when you say 'John' with your voice rising rather than falling?
- Do you notice when you make a mistake in intonation in the second language?

Keywords

intonation: the systematic rise and fall in the pitch of the voice during speech
nuclear tone: significant changes in pitch on one or more syllables
tone language: a language in which words are separated by intonation, for instance, Chinese

Intonation is the way that the pitch of the voice goes up and down during speech. Many ways of describing it have been tried. The analysis in Box 4.8 shows a 'British' style analysis based on nuclear tones – significant changes in pitch on one or more syllables, here reduced to seven tones.

Box 4.8 English intonation

High Fall	$^{y}e_{s}$	`yes	High Rise	$y^{e^{s}}$	´yes?
Low Fall	$^{y}e_{s}$	ˏyes	Low Rise	$y^{e\ s}$	ˏyes
Fall Rise	$y_{e}{}^{s}$	˅yes.	Rise Fall	$y^{e}s$	^yes
Level	*c o o e e*	‾cooee			

The problem is that, while people agree that intonation is important, they disagree on its function. Some say that it is used for making grammatical distinctions: 'He's `going' with falling intonation is a statement; 'He's ´going?' with rising intonation is a question. Indeed, rising intonation is perhaps the most frequent way of making questions in French. But this explanation is only partially successful as some questions tend not to have rises – wh-questions such as 'What's the `time?' usually have falls. Others think that intonation is used to convey emotion and attitude: 'He`llo' with a high fall sounds welcoming, with a low fall 'Heˏllo' cold, with a fall-rise 'He˅llo' doubtful, and so on.

Intonation also varies between speakers. There is an overall difference between British and American patterns: apparently British men sound effeminate to American ears because of our use of a higher pitch range. Younger people around the world use rising intonation for statements, 'I like ˏbeer' where older people use a fall 'I like `beer'. Even within the UK there are differences (Grabe and Post, 2002). People living in Cambridge use 90 per cent falls for declaratives, those in Belfast 80 per cent rises. People in western areas such as Liverpool cut off the end of falling tones in short vowels. People in eastern areas such as Newcastle compress them, that is, make the fall more rapid.

The languages of the world fall into two groups: intonation languages and tone languages. Chinese is a 'tone' language that separates different words purely by intonation: '´li zi' (rising tone) means 'pear'; '˅li zi' (fall rise) means 'plum', and '`li zi' (falling) means 'chestnut'. In tone languages a tone functions like a phoneme in that it distinguishes words with different meanings. Indeed, this means that Chinese tones are stored in the left side of the brain along with the vocabulary, while English intonation is stored in the right side along with other emotional aspects of thinking. In intonation languages the intonation pattern has a number of functions; it may distinguish grammatical constructions, as in question '´Beer?' versus statement '`Beer'; it may show discourse connections, for example, a new topic starting high and finishing low; it may hint at the speakers' attitudes, say, polite 'Good`bye' versus rude 'Good`bye!'

Adult L2 learners of Chinese have no problem in distinguishing Chinese tones, though with less confidence than native speakers of Chinese (Leather, 1987). Adults learning Thai, another tone language, were worse at learning tones than children (Ioup and Tansomboon, 1987).

L2 learners may have major problems when going from an intonation language such as English to a tone language such as Chinese, and vice versa. Hence people have found Chinese speaking English to be comparatively unemotional, simply because the speakers are unused to conveying emotion though intonation patterns, while in reverse, English learners of Chinese make lexical mistakes because they are not used to using intonation to distinguish lexical meanings.

With languages of the same type, say, English speakers learning Spanish, another intonation language, there are few problems with intonation patterns that are similar in the first and second languages. The problems come when the characteristics of the first language are transferred to the second. My hunch is that our interpretation of intonation patterns by L2 users is responsible for some national stereotypes – Italians sound excitable and Germans serious to an English ear, because of the meaning of their first language patterns when transferred to English.

It is also a problem when a pattern has a different meaning in the second language. A student once said to me at the end of a class, 'Good`bye!'; I assumed she was mortally offended. However, when she said it at the end of every class, I realized that it was an inappropriate intonation pattern transferred from her first language – which reveals the great danger of intonation mistakes: the listener does not realize you have made a straightforward language mistake like choosing a wrong word, but ascribes to you the attitude you have accidentally conveyed. Intonation mistakes are often not retrievable, simply because no one realizes that a mistake has been made.

As with VOT, there may be a reverse transfer of intonation back on to the learner's first language. Dutch people who speak Greek have slightly different question intonation from monolinguals (Mennen, 2004), and the German of German children who speak Turkish is different from those who do not (Queen, 2001). Once again, the first language is affected by the second.

Teaching intonation

Specialized intonation coursebooks, like my own *Active Intonation* (Cook, 1968), often present the learner with a graded set of intonation patterns for understanding and for repetition, starting, say, with the difference between rising '´Well?' and falling '`Well', and building up to more complex patterns through comprehension activities and imitation exercises. But the teaching techniques mostly stress practice and repetition; students learn one bit at a time, rather than having systems of their own; they repeat, they imitate, they practise, all in a very controlled way.

Some teaching techniques for intonation aim to make the student aware of the nature of intonation rather than to improve specific aspects. Several examples can be found in *Teaching English Pronunciation* (Kenworthy, 1987). For instance, Kenworthy suggests getting two students to talk about holiday photographs without using any words other than 'mmm', 'ah' or 'oh'. This makes them aware of the crucial role of intonation without necessarily teaching them any specific English intonation patterns – the objective underlying the communicative inton-ation exercises in my own textbook *Using Intonation* (Cook, 1979). Dickerson (1987) made detailed studies of the usefulness of giving pronunciation rules to L2 learners, concluding that they are indeed helpful.

Other teaching exercises can link specific features of intonation to communica-tion. For example, the exercise 'Deaf Mr Jones' in *Using Intonation* (Cook, 1979) provides students with a map of Islington and asks them to play two characters: Mr Jones, who is deaf, and a stranger. Mr Jones decides which station he is at on the map and asks the stranger the way. Hence Mr Jones will constantly be produc-ing intonation patterns that check what the stranger says within a reasonably nat-ural conversation.

Box 4.9 Learning intonation

- A major L2 learning problem is moving between the two major ways of using intonation in the world's languages: tone languages where intonation shows difference in lexical meaning, and intonation languages where into-nation shows grammar, attitude, and so on.
- Intonation mistakes can be dangerous because it is not obvious to the par-ticipants that a mistake has been made.

Box 4.10 Pronunciation and teaching

- Pronunciation teaching should recognize the diversity of levels of pronunci-ation in a language, including phonemes, allophones, syllables, intonation, and so on.
- The learning of pronunciation involves aspects of the learner's first language, universal learning processes and aspects of the second language.
- Teaching has mostly made use of conventional techniques of phonetic scripts, imitation, sound discrimination and communication.
- Students can also be made more aware of sound features of language.

Discussion topics

1   How important is a native-like accent to using a second language? Which native accent?

2   How could teachers best exploit the kinds of stages that students go through in the acquisition of pronunciation?

3   How much of the difficulty of acquiring L2 phonology is due to the learner's first language?

4   Do you accept that English is now different from other languages because it functions like a lingua franca?

5   What uses can you find in coursebooks for phonetic script? What other uses can you think of?

Further reading

There are few readily accessible treatments of the areas covered in this chapter. Kenworthy (1987) *Teaching English Pronunciation* provides a readable and trustworthy account of pronunciation for teachers. Further discussion of phonology can be found in Cook (1997) *Inside Language*. Web links include a clickable IPA chart(http://hctv.humnet.ucla.edu/departments/linguistics/VowelsandConsonants/course/chapter1/chapter1.html) and an IPA chart for English (www.teachingenglish.org.uk/download/pron.shtml), as well as the amazing *Speech Accent Archive* (http://accent.gmu.edu).

Acquiring and teaching a new writing system 5

Chapter 1 points out how both SLA research and language teaching have assumed that writing depends on speech rather than being another mode of language. This has led to the unique skills of written language being undervalued and to a lack of attention to the demands that writing places on the student in a second language. A spelling mistake is as important as a pronunciation mistake; indeed it is more so, in that bad spelling carries overtones of illiteracy and stupidity which bad pronunciation does not.

Just as pronunciation involves both lower-level skills and higher-order structures, so writing goes from physical skills involving forming letters, to higher-level skills such as spelling, to the highest level of discourse skills involved in writing essays, and so on. The present chapter provides more background information than the other chapters because of the lack of information about writing systems in most teachers' backgrounds. More information on the English writing system can be found in Cook (2004), and on writing systems in general in Cook and Bassetti (2005).

5.1 Writing systems

Focusing questions

- Which words do you have trouble spelling? Why? What do you do to improve your spelling?
- What spelling mistakes do your students make? Why? What do you do to improve your students' spelling?

Keywords

meaning-based writing system: a form of writing in which the written sign (character) connects directly to the meaning, as in Chinese characters

sound-based writing system: a form of writing in which the written sign connects to the spoken form, whether through syllables (Japanese, Korean) or consonant phonemes alone (Arabic, Hebrew), or both vowels and consonants (alphabetic languages like Greek, Urdu or English)

correspondence rules: the rules in sound-based writing systems for connecting sounds to letters, that is, the English phoneme /ei/ to the letter <a> and vice versa <a> to /ei/, /æ/, and so on

The big division in the writing systems of the world is between those based on meaning and those based on sounds, as seen in Figure 5.1. The Chinese character-based system of writing links a written sign to a meaning; the character 人 means a person, the sign 象 an elephant; it is not necessary to know how 人 is pronounced or even to know what the Chinese spoken word actually is in order to read it. A Chinese-English dictionary does not tell you the spoken form: 口 is simply given as 'mouth'. Hence speakers of different dialects of Chinese can communicate in writing even when they cannot understand each other's speech.

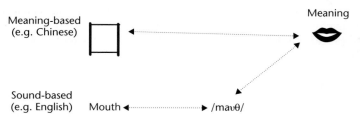

Figure 5.1 Meaning-based and sound-based writing

The other main type of writing system in the world links the written sign to its spoken form rather than its meaning. The English word <table> corresponds to the spoken form /teibl/; the meaning is reached via the spoken form. Knowing the written form of the word tells you how it is pronounced, but knowing that 'table' is pronounced /teibl/ gives you no idea what it means. (**Note**: when words or letters are cited purely for their orthographic form they are enclosed in angle brackets <table>, parallel to slant brackets for phonological form /teibl/.)

Though these routes between writing and meaning are distinct in principle, in practice they are often mixed. Numbers function like a meaning-based system regardless of the language involved: '1, 2, 3…' have the same meaning in most languages, so that you do not have to know Greek to know what '1' means on an airport departure board in Greece. Some keyboard signs familiar from computers behave in similar ways: they either have spoken forms that virtually nobody uses in English such as <&> (ampersand) or <~> (tilde), or their spoken forms vary from place to place or person to person without changing their meaning; <#> is called 'flat' by some people, 'the pound sign' in the USA, 'hash' in England and, supposedly, 'octothorpe' in Canada, after a Mr Thorpe who invented it and the prefix 'octo' after its eight points. It is the meaning of these signs that counts, not how they are pronounced. Even a sound-based writing system like English is full of written symbols that can only be read aloud if you know the words they correspond to – <£, @, $, % … >. An interesting example is arithmetic, where everyone knows what <=> means in '2 + 2 = 4', but some people say '2 and 2 make 4', some '2 plus 2 is/are 4', some '2 and 2 equals 4'.

Indeed, both the meaning-based and sound-based writing routes are used by everybody to some extent, whichever their language. Try the e-deletion test in Box 5.1 to test this. Frequent English words such as 'the' and 'are' take the meaning-based route as wholes, rather than being converted to sounds letter by letter; other words go through the sound-based route. Usually, with tests like this, most native speakers fail to delete all 50 <e>s, mostly because they do not 'see' the <e> in 'the' (13 examples), only the whole word <the>. In fact, non-natives are

Box 5.1 Exercise: spot the 'e's

Here is the opening of Charles Dickens' *The Pickwick Papers* (1837). Read through it quickly and cross out all the letter <e>s.

The first ray of light which illumines the gloom, and converts into a dazzling brilliancy that obscurity in which the earlier history of the public career of the immortal Pickwick would appear to be involved, is derived from the perusal of the following entry in the Transactions of the Pickwick Club, which the editor of these papers feels the highest pleasure in laying before his readers, as a proof of the careful attention, indefatigable assiduity, and nice discrimination, with which his search among the multifarious documents confided to him has been conducted.

Now check your copy against page 103 at the end of the chapter.

better at crossing out this <e> than natives – one of the few cases where non-native speakers beat natives because they have had less practice.

The sound-based route is nevertheless always available: given new words like 'Hushidh', 'Zdorab' or 'Umene' (characters in a science fiction novel), we can always have a stab at reading them aloud, despite never having seen them before, using the sound-based route. Nevertheless, very common words such as 'the' or 'of', or idiosyncratic words like 'yacht' /yɒt/ or 'colonel' /kənl/ or 'lieutenant' /leftenənt/ (in British English) have to be remembered as individual word shapes. English writing is not just sound-based but uses the meaning-based route as well.

Sound-based writing systems have many variations. Some use written signs for whole syllables; for example, the Japanese hiragana system uses た to correspond to the whole syllable 'ta', な to 'na', and so on (rather like text messages in English 'Gr8 2 c u'). Other systems use written signs only for spoken consonants, so that Hebrew ד ר gives the consonants 'd' and 'r' (in a right-to-left direction), and the reader has to work out whether this corresponds to the word pronounced /diʁ/ (stable) or to /daʁ/ (mother-of-pearl).

Many languages use the alphabetic system in which a written sign stands for a phoneme in principle, even if there are different alphabets in Urdu, Russian and Spanish. Languages vary, however, in how straightforwardly they apply the alphabetic system. If a language has one-to-one links between letters and sounds, it is called 'transparent', popularly 'phonetic'. Italian or Finnish, for example, have highly transparent writing systems. But even in Italian <c> corresponds to two different sounds depending on which vowel comes next, /k/ in 'caffè' or /tʃ/ in 'cento'. English is much less transparent and has complicated rules for connecting letters and sounds. The diphthong /ei/ can be spelt in at least twelve ways: 'lake', 'aid', 'foyer', 'gauge', 'stay', 'café', 'steak', 'weigh', 'ballet', 'matinée', 'sundae' and 'they'. In reverse, the letter <a> can be pronounced in at least eleven ways: 'age' /eidʒ/, 'arm' /aːm/, 'about' /əbaʊt/, 'beat' /biːt/, 'many' /menɪ/, 'aisle' /ail/, 'coat' /kəʊt/, 'ball' /bɔːl/, 'canal' /kənæl/, 'beauty' /bjuːtɪ/, 'cauliflower' /kɒlɪflaʊə/. The rules for connecting letters to sounds and vice versa are known as correspondence rules. In a sense, Chinese and Japanese characters are least transparent of all as they have little connection to their pronunciation, particularly in Japanese.

Even the ways in which people make the marks on the page vary from language to language. In some countries children are told to form letters by making horizontal strokes first and vertical strokes second; in others the reverse. The consequences can be seen in English 'to', written by a Japanese $\mathcal{T}_{\mathcal{O}}$, and capital <E>, written by a Chinese $\mathcal{E}$, in both of which the horizontal strokes have clearly been made before the vertical. The actual way of holding the writing instrument may be different too. According to Rosemary Sassoon (1995), a typical brush-hold for Chinese may damage the writer's wrist if used as a pen-hold for writing English. Language teachers should be on the alert for such problems when they are teaching students who have very different scripts in their first language.

The direction that writing takes on the page is also important. Some writing systems use columns, for instance, traditional Chinese and Japanese writing; others use lines, say French, Cherokee and Persian. Within those writing systems that use lines, there is a choice between the right-to-left direction found in Arabic and Urdu, and the left-to-right direction found in Roman and Devanagari scripts. While this does not seem to create major problems for L2 learners, students have told me about Arabic/English bilingual children who try to write Arabic from left-to-right. Rosemary Sassoon (1995) found a Japanese child who wrote English on alternate lines from right-to-left and from left-to-right, a system called boustrophedon, now known only from ancient scripts.

Box 5.2 L1 and L2 writing systems

Students may have problems transferring various aspects of their L1 writing system to another language, such as:

- whether it is a sound-based or meaning-based writing system;
- the direction in which writing goes on the page;
- the ways of making letters.

5.2 Spelling

Focusing questions

- Do you think English spelling is a 'near optimal system', as Noam Chomsky calls it?
- Can you remember any spelling rules for English?

Keywords

orthographic regularities: rules that govern how letters behave in English, such as <ck> corresponding to /k/ occurring at the ends of syllables 'back', <c> at the beginning 'cab'

silent letter: a letter that does not correspond directly to a speech sound but often has indirect effects, for example, silent <e> 'fat' versus 'fate', and silent <u> 'guess' versus 'gesture'

The major problem with English for many students, however, is the correspondence rules that govern how letters are arranged in words, in other words, spelling. English is far from having a straightforward, transparent system in which one letter stands for one sound. The letter <h>, for example, plays an important role in consonant pairs such as <th, sh, gh, ph, ch, wh>, without being pronounced as /h/ in any of them. The sound /tʃ/ is usually spelled <ch> with two letters at the beginning of words as in 'chap', but <tch> with three letters at the end as in 'patch'; indeed the extra letter gives people the impression that there are more sounds in 'patch' than in 'chap'.

The popular belief is that English spelling is chaotic and unsystematic – 'the evil of our irregular orthography' according to Noah Webster, the dictionary maker – usually based on the ideal, fully transparent alphabetic system. English is far from transparent: it additionally involves not only a system of linking whole items to meanings, as in 'of' and 'yacht', but also a system of orthographic regularities, such as <wh> only occurring initially, as in 'white' and 'when'. Hence it should not be forgotten that native speakers of English also have problems with spelling, some the same as L2 users, some different. On my website the spelling test called 'The most difficult words' has been taken by over 100,000 people, yet at the time of writing only 14 have emailed me to say that they scored 100 per cent (and those mostly worked for publishers).

The charge of being unsystematic ignores the many rules of English spelling, only some of which we are aware of. The one spelling rule that any native speaker claims to know is 'i before e except after c', which explains the spelling of 'receive'. There are exceptions to this rule, such as plurals 'currencies' and when <c> corresponds to /ʃ/, as in 'sufficient'. The rule applies at best to ten base forms in the hundred million running words of the British National Corpus, along with their

---

Box 5.3 Structure word spelling rules

1 The three-letter rule

Structure words have fewer than three letters; content words can be any length, from three letters upwards (but must *not* have fewer than three letters):

so:sew/sow	to:two/too	we:wee	oh:owe	by:bye/buy	no:know
an:Ann	I:eye/aye	in:inn	be:bee	or:ore/oar/awe	

2 The 'th' rule

In structure words, the initial <th> spelling corresponds to /ð/, 'this' and 'they'; in content words, initial <th> corresponds to /θ/, as in 'thesis' and 'Thelma'.

the:therapy	than:thank	thou:thousand	this:thistle	thy:thigh
though:thought	that:thatch	those:thong	them:thematic	

3 The titles rule

In titles of books, films, and so on, content words usually start with capital letters, structure words with lower case.

The Case of the Stuttering
  Bishop
Strangers on a Train
I Wish I could Shimmy like my Sister Kate

Handbook of Bilingualism
The Tragedy of King
  Richard the Second

derived forms: 'receive', 'ceiling', 'receipt', 'perceive', 'conceive', 'deceive', 'conceit', 'transceiver', 'fluorescein' and 'ceilidh'.

Nevertheless, there are rules that do work better for English. One set is the structure word rules, given in Box 5.3. Teachers are usually aware how structure words such as 'of' and 'the' behave in English sentences compared to content words such as 'oven' and 'drive'; how they are pronounced in specific ways, such as the voiced /ð/ 'these' compared to the unvoiced /θ/ in 'think' and 'thesis'; and how they have stressed versus weak forms, /ði:/ versus /ðə/, as mentioned in Chapters 2 and 3, but they are unaware that they are also spelt in particular ways.

The **three-letter rule** describes how only structure words can consist of a single letter – 'I' and 'a' – or two letters – 'an' and 'no'; content words have three letters or more. If a content word could be spelt with one or two letters, extra letters have to be added to make it up to three or more – 'eye', 'Ann', 'know'. While this three-letter rule seems perfectly obvious once it has been explained, most people have no idea it exists. There are exceptions, of course: 'go' and 'ox' have two letters but are content words (even if 'go' can act like an auxiliary 'I am going to see him'); American 'ax' is an exception, British 'axe' is not. Nevertheless, the rule is a small generalization about English spelling that works nearly all the time.

The **'th' rule** for structure words similarly reflects the fact that the only spoken English words that start with /ð/ are structure words like 'these' and 'them'; hence the spelling rule that in structure words alone initial <th> corresponds to /ð/, all the rest have /θ/. Again, this fact about the spelling of structure words seems obvious once it is understood. The exceptions are, on the one hand, a small group of words in which initial <th> corresponds to /t/ such as 'Thai' and 'Thames', on the other, the unique structure word 'through' in which <th> corresponds to /θ/.

The third rule of spelling that affects structure words is the **titles rule**. This affects the use of capital letters in titles of books, songs, and so on, where content words are given initial capitals but structure words are not, as in *<Context and Culture in Language Learning>*, *<Focus on Form in Classroom Second Language Acquisition>* and *<Sociocultural Theory and the Genesis of Second Language Development>*, to take three books that happen to be lying on my desk. This convention is not always adhered to and some book lists avoid all capitals in book titles. But if you cannot identify structure words you will not be able to apply it at all.

Perhaps the most complex set of spelling rules in English are the **vowel correspondence rules**, from which Box 5.4 gives a small selection. As RP English has 5 vowel letters and about 20 vowel phonemes, considerable ingenuity has been devoted over the centuries to telling the reader how vowel letters are said. The **silent 'e' rule** gives the sound correspondence of the preceding vowel. If there is a silent <e> following a single consonant, the preceding vowel is 'long': the letter <a> will correspond to /ei/ 'Dane', <e> to /i:/ 'Pete', <i> to /ai/ 'fine', <o> to /əʊ/ 'tote', <u> to /ju:/ 'dune'. If there is no <e>, the vowel is 'short': <a> corresponds to /æ/ 'Dan', <e> to /e/ 'pet', <i> to /ɪ/ 'fin', <o> to /ɒ/ 'tot', <u> to /ʌ/ 'dun'.

The terms 'short' and 'long' vowels do not have the same meaning here as in phonetics, since three of the so-called 'long' vowels are in fact diphthongs. For this reason, some people prefer to call the five short vowels 'checked', the five long vowels 'free'. This rule has become known as the **Fairy E rule**, after the way that it is explained to children: 'Fairy E waves its wand and makes the preceding vowel say its name'; the long vowel sounds here happen to be the same as the names for the five vowel letters. People who attack silent <e>, like the <e> in 'fate' /feɪt/, as being useless are missing the point: the silent <e> letter acts as a

---

Box 5.4 Vowel correspondence rules

1 Silent 'e' rule

A silent <e> following a single consonant shows that the preceding vowel letter corresponds to a long vowel; lack of an <e> shows a short vowel.

	long free vowels	**short checked vowels**
'a'	/eɪ/ Dane	/æ/ Dan
'e'	/iː/ Pete	/e/ pet
'i'	/aɪ/ fine	/ɪ/ fin
'o'	/əʊ/ tote	/ɒ/ tot
'u'	/(j)uː/ dune	/ʌ/ dun

2 Consonant doubling rule

A double consonant shows that the preceding vowel corresponds to a short vowel rather than a long one.

	Single consonant	**Double consonant**
'a'	/eɪ/ planing	/æ/ planning
'e'	/iː/ beta	/e/ better
'i'	/aɪ/ biter	/ɪ/ bitter
'o'	/əʊ/ hoping	/ɒ/ hopping
'u'	/(j)uː/ super	/ʌ/ supper

---

marker showing that the preceding <a> is said /eɪ/ not /æ/, that is, it is different from the <a> in 'fat'.

The same relationship between long and short vowels underlies the **consonant doubling rule** in Box 5.4. A doubled consonant in writing, say <tt> in 'bitter' or <nn> in 'running', has nothing to do with saying the consonant twice, but shows that the correspondence of the preceding vowel is short: the <pp> in 'supper' shows that the preceding <u> corresponds to /ɪʌ/, the <p> in 'super' that <u> is the long /uː/. This version of the doubling rule is highly simplified and ignores the fact that some consonants never double, <h, j>, or rarely double, <v> and <k> ('revving' and 'trekker'), and that British and North American spelling styles are slightly different, as we see below. As always, there are exceptions, such as doubled consonants after long vowels, as in 'small' and 'furry'. What the rules we have discussed show, however, is that there *is* a system to English spelling. It may be complicated, but it is probably simpler than the system for speaking English.

SLA research has mostly tackled the problems which arise in acquiring a second language that has a different overall writing system from one's first language, whether going from a meaning-based route to a sound-based one, as in Chinese students of English, or from a sound-based route using only consonant letters to one using both vowels and consonants, as in Hebrew students of English, or from one type of alphabetic script to another, say, Greek to English or English to German. Chikamatsu (1996) found that English people tended to transfer their L1 sound-based strategies to Japanese as an L2, Chinese people their L2 meaning-based strategies. In the reverse direction, the Chinese meaning-based system handicaps reading in English; upper high school students in Taiwan read at a speed of 88 words per minute, compared to 254 for native speakers (Haynes and Carr, 1990). Students' difficulties with reading may have more to do with the basic characteristics of their L1 writing system than with grammar or vocabulary. Indeed the characteristics of the writing system you learn first may affect you in other ways; Chinese people, for example, are more visually dominated than English people, probably due in part to their character-based writing system.

Box 5.5 gives examples of the spelling mistakes made by L2 users of English. Many of them are similar to those made by native speakers. This tends to show that the English spelling system itself is to blame rather than the difficulties of writing in a second language. 'accommodate' is often spelt wrong because people are unsure of the consonant doubling rules and gamble that consonants would not be doubled twice in the same word – similarly for 'address'. The vowel correspondence rules cause problems for native speakers as well as non-native users of English; what does the final spoken /ə/ in 'grammar' correspond to in writing? <ar>, <a>, <ah> and <er> would all be equally plausible if sound correspondences were all that mattered. Research of my own showed that adult L2 user university students made about as many spelling errors as 15-year-old English native children. In one sense this is disappointing in that they are not writing like native adults. In another way it is encouraging; the students would probably be very pleased to be told that they spoke English as well as 15-year-old native children.

Box 5.5 Mistakes with English spelling

The words most commonly misspelled by L2 users of English

accommodating, because, beginning, business, career, choice, definite, describe, develop, different, government, integrate, interest(ing), kindergarten, knowledge, life, necessary, particular, professional, professor, really, study/student, their/ there, which, would

Some typical L2 mistakes

address: adres, adress, adresse
because: beause, beaucause, becase, becaus, becouse, becuase, beacause, begause, becuse, becuas
business: busines, bussines, buisness, bussiness
grammar (etc.): gramma, grammatikal, grammartical, grammer
professional: profesional, professinal, proffessional, proffesional
sincerely: sinarely, sincerelly, sincerley, sincersly
student (etc.): studet, stuienet, studing, studyed, stuent

Just as an L2 user's accent can betray their first language, so their spelling can indicate not only the kind of L1 writing system they were taught first, but also the phonology of their first language. An Arabic student may well leave out vowels from their spellings, say 'coubrd' (cupboard) or 'recive' (receive), showing that this is a feature of the consonantal Arabic writing systems: they may also add vowels 'punishment' showing that <shm> is not a possible consonant sequence in Arabic. Box 5.6 gives some examples of typical spelling mistakes from different L2 learners. These do indeed reveal something about the learners' L1 and L1 writing systems. The French obviously double consonants differently, the Greek clearly have different letters, the Dutch have double <k>.

Box 5.6 Problems for users of specific L1 writing systems

Arabic: substituted vowels 'obundant'; additional 'epenthetic' vowels 'punishe-ment'; phonological mistakes 'manshed' (mentioned). Unique: <c> for <q> 'cuickly'.

Chinese: omission of consonants 'subjet'; addition of <e> 'boyes'.

Dutch: double <kk> 'wekk'.

French: wrong double consonants 'comming '; vowel substitution 'definetely'.

German: omission of <a> 'h'ppened'; substitution of <i> for <e> 'injoid'. Unique: 'telephon'.

Greek: consonant substitution, <d>/<t> 'Grade Britain'; double unnecessarily 'sattisfaction'; transposition 'sceince'. Unique <c> for <g> 'Creek' (Greek).

Italian: consonant omission 'wether' (whether); failure to double 'biger'.

Japanese: consonant substitution 'gramatikal'; epenthetic vowels 'difficulty'; CV transposition 'prospretiy'. Unique <l> and <r> 'grobal'.

Korean: consonant omission 'fators'; lack of doubling 'poluted'; omitted vowels 'therefor'.

Spanish: consonant omission 'wich'; lack of doubling 'til'; unnecessary doubling 'exclussive'.

Urdu: vowel omission 'somtimes' and final <d> and <t> 'woul', 'lef'.

Thanks to Cambridge English, I collected 18,000 spelling mistakes made with verbs from First Certificate of English (FCE) examination scripts from many languages. The most common type of mistake was letter doubling (both consonant and vowel) with 35 per cent 'speciallize', followed by letter omission with 19 per cent 'exlaimed', using the wrong letter with 18 per cent 'enjoiing', and adding an extra letter with 10 per cent 'boreing'. Clearly, teaching could take these overall patterns of spelling mistakes into account. Something more is needed than correction of individual mistakes as and when they occur.

Box 5.7 Spelling and L2 learning

- The English spelling system has a number of specific rules such as structure word rules.
- L2 learners of English make spelling mistakes based in part on their L1 writing system, in part on lack of knowledge of the English spelling rules.

5.3 Punctuation

Focusing questions

- Are you confident about your punctuation?
- What do you think punctuation is for?

While some teachers are aware of spelling and do try to correct individual errors, the area of punctuation has been virtually ignored. Punctuation consists of the use of additional marks as well as the letters of the alphabet, such as commas <,> or full stops <.>, known in American style as periods. Many writing systems have similar punctuation marks, with slight variations in their form. Quotation marks, for instance, vary between English <" ">, Italian goosefeet <« »> and Swiss goosefeet <» «>. Spanish uses inverted question marks < ¿ > and exclamation marks < ¡ > at the beginning of phrases. Chinese has a hollow full stop < ∘ >, Catalan a raised one < · >.

The most important English punctuation mark is literally invisible. Compare:

WillyoustillneedmewillyoustillfeedmewhenImsixtyfour?

with:

Will you still need me, will you still feed me, when I'm sixty-four?

Apart from punctuation, the difference is word spaces: modern English writing separates words with a space, recognized as a character in computer jargon – look at the word count results provided in Microsoft® Word to see this. Spaces are not intrinsic to alphabetic writing. In Europe the use of spaces between words only became widespread in the eighth century AD. Sound-based writing systems do not necessarily have word spaces, such as Vietnamese, or may use word spaces for different purposes, such as Thai. Character-based writing systems like Chinese and Japanese do not have word spaces but put spaces between characters, which may or may not correspond to words. Some have seen the invention of the word as crucial to the ability to read.

Another little considered aspect of punctuation is the actual forms of letters. Starting a sentence with a capital letter is one familiar use. In English, capitals are used for proper names, <Bill> rather than <bill>, and for certain groups of words like months <January>, and for content words in the titles rule seen in Box 5.3 on page 91. In German, capital letters are used for all nouns, a practice occasionally found in seventeenth-century English. Underlining and italics are used for questions of emphasis and for book titles in academic references. Underlining is disliked by typographers and rarely found in books because it destroys the descender of the letter below the line in letters like <p, g, y> and so makes it less legible: <I'm trying to pay the mortgage> versus <I'm trying to pay the mortgage>.

The perpetual debate about punctuation is what it is for. Punctuation is used in both the sound-based and the meaning-based routes. On the one hand, punctuation has sometimes been seen as a guide to reading aloud. The eighteenth-century rule for English was that a full stop <.> meant a full pause, a colon <:> was half that, a semicolon <;> half that, and a comma <,> half that, rather like the relationship between musical notes. While the colon and semicolon may now be rare, people reading aloud may still use pauses of different lengths for the full stop and the comma. The sentence final punctuation marks <.?!> correspond roughly to intonation patterns in reading aloud – <?> to rising intonation, <.> to falling, <!> to extra movement or rise-fall intonation. Within the sentence, commas in lists may show rising intonation: 'I bought some apples, some pears, and some bananas'.

On the other hand, punctuation has also been seen as a guide to grammatical structure. At one level, it separates different constructions, whether sentences with full stops, or phrases with commas. But it also provides a structure for complex written prose where large sentences can be constructed out of smaller sentences by using colons and semicolons, to yield sentences such as those seen in Box 5.8, or indeed the Dickens' sentence in Box 5.1 on page 89. This is a unique feature of written language, vaguely related, perhaps, to discourse intonation in speech. Without the ability to put together such higher-level sentences, a writer will come across as lightweight and over-simple.

Box 5.8 Sample punctuation sentence

Add the appropriate punctuation marks and capital letters to this sentence. (Answer at the end of the chapter on page 103.)

now of old the name of that forest was greenwood the great and its wide halls and aisles were the haunt of many beasts and of birds of bright song and there was the realm of king thranduil under the oak and the beech but after many years when well nigh a third of that age of the world had passed a darkness crept slowly through the wood from the southward and fear walked there in shadowy glades fell beasts came hunting and cruel and evil creatures laid there their snares

J.R.R. Tolkien (1977) The Silmarillion

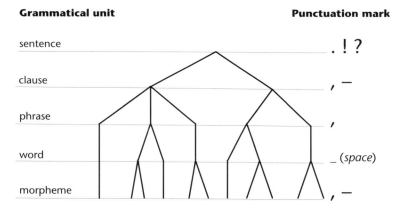

Though Peter's sight improved, the eye-doctor operated.

Figure 5.2 Punctuation and phrase structure in English

Box 5.9 Punctuation

- Punctuation is used both as a guide for reading the sentence aloud and as a way of showing sentence structure.
- Punctuation includes punctuation marks, use of capitals, word spaces and other features, all of which can vary between writing systems.

What do students need to learn about second writing systems?

We can summarize what L2 students need to learn, assuming that they are already literate in one writing system, that is, that it is not the L2 teacher's job to cope with basic literacy problems, which would be a different issue.

The appropriate direction of reading and writing

Arabic students learning English need to acquire the left-to-right direction; English students learning Arabic that it goes from right to left. If the second language uses a different direction, this may be quite a burden on the student.

Making and recognizing the actual letter or character shapes

English people learning Russian need to learn the Cyrillic script; Japanese people learning German the Roman alphabet. Again, it may be difficult to go from Chinese characters to the Roman alphabet, from a German script to Arabic letters. In principle, the number of letters or signs needed will depend on the writing system involved, whether the scores needed for alphabetic systems or the tens of thousands needed for character-based systems.

Using the phonological processing route

Learning a sound-based L2 writing system means primarily learning that <t> corresponds with /t/, and so on. Depending on the writing system, this will be a matter of syllables, all the phonemes or the consonants alone. Moving from an L1 writing system that prioritizes the meaning route to an L2 writing system that emphasizes the sound-based route may be a considerable step, as is moving in the opposite direction.

Using the lexical, morpheme-based processing route

Learning a meaning-based writing system means mostly learning that 人 means 'person', and so on. Switching one's preferred route between L1 writing system and L2 writing system can be a difficult feat.

Orthographic regularities in less transparent writing systems

Less transparent sound-based writing systems like English are not just straightforward correspondences between letters and sounds, but make use of complex spelling rules, which have to be learnt.

Using punctuation marks and other typographic features

Differences in punctuation and typography of the L2 from the L1, whether of form such as quotation marks or of use such as capitals, have to be learnt.

5.4 The writing system and language teaching

Focusing questions

- How important do you think issues of the writing system are for the teacher?
- Do you think students of English should be taught British or American styles of spelling?

So what should the language teacher do about teaching the writing system? This vital and complex area has been virtually ignored by teachers and coursebook writers.

One possibility in English is to exploit the two routes: the lexical route and the phonological route. Most high-frequency words in English are stored as wholes and not treated by the correspondence rules. So the best course of action may be to check whether the students know how to spell the most frequent words and the most often misspelt words by getting them to memorize and practise the words they do not know as one-off items – 'there/their', and so on. Eliminating mistakes with a few hundred words would wipe out most of the glaring mistakes in students' work. For instance, the verbs that FCE students made most mistakes with were forms of 'choose', 'study', 'travel', 'develop', 'begin' and 'plan'. This could simply be dealt with on a one-off basis, or it could be related to the rules for consonant doubling, *not* changing <y> to <i>, and so on. Certainly students have to learn many idiosyncratic words as wholes, whether high-frequency words such as 'of' /ɒv/ and 'there' /ðɛə/, or lower-frequency oddities such as 'sandwich' /sæmwɪdʒ/ or place names 'Edinburgh' /edɪmbrə/. Again, there is little that students can do other than memorize these words individually; there is no point in trying to relate them to spelling rules.

Many student mistakes relate to their L1 writing system. Arabic speakers reveal the syllable structure of Arabic, not just in their pronunciation, but also in their use of written vowels as in 'punishement'. The Greek tendency to substitute one consonant for another, as in <d> for <t> in 'Grade Britain', is due to the phonology of Greek. Japanese difficulties with spoken /l/ and /r/ extend to spelling, as in 'grobal' (global) and 'brack' (black). Inevitably, teachers need to pay attention to L1-specific spelling problems, caused by the phonological system and the spelling of the students' first languages, directly, by explaining to students the link between spelling and their L1 phonology and writing system; and indirectly, by practising their typical errors.

Other mistakes reflect the complexity of the rules of English spelling for natives and non-natives alike. Indeed, one piece of research found that English children learning German made fewer spelling mistakes in German than in English (Downing, 1973). Both natives and L2 learners have particular problems with consonant doubling. <l> is wrongly doubled by both groups, as in 'controll', 'allready', 'carefull' and 'propell', the first two being from L2 learners, the second two from natives; <l> is also left out of doubled <l> as in 'filed' for 'filled' (L2 user) and 'modeled' (native speaker). Vowels are substituted for other vowels, for example, in word endings with '-an' or '-en' such as 'frequantly', 'relevent', 'appearence' and 'important', with '-el' or '-al' as in 'hostal' and 'leval', and with '-ate' or '-ite' as in 'definately' and 'definetely'. Again, in general, the choice amounts to explaining rules directly – safe if the teacher has a grasp of the descriptive rules of spelling beyond the school tradition – or to carrying out specific practice with spelling rules.

The discussion of pronunciation in Chapter 4 raises the issue of which accent to use as a model. For English, the choice in spelling comes down to British style or North American style. Box 5.10 tests which style people use; a fuller version is online (http://homepage.ntlworld.com/vivian.c/TestsFrame.htm). Mostly the differences of American English style from British style come down to Noah Webster's decision to emphasize USA identity when he chose spellings for the first edition of his dictionary in 1828. The main differences are:

- <-er> **versus** <-re>: American 'center', 'theater', 'fiber' versus British 'centre', 'theatre', 'fibre'

- <-or> versus <-our>: American 'labor', 'color', 'neighbor' versus British 'labour', 'colour', 'neighbour'
- <-ize> versus <-ise>: American 'realize', 'recognize', 'organize' versus British 'realise', 'recognise', 'organise'

Box 5.10 American or British style of spelling?

		American	British
1	color	❐	❐
2	theatre	❐	❐
3	catalyze	❐	❐
4	labor	❐	❐
5	travelling	❐	❐
6	moustache	❐	❐
7	dialogue	❐	❐
8	molt	❐	❐
9	sulphur	❐	❐
10	vigour	❐	❐
11	skeptic	❐	❐
12	catalog	❐	

American: 1, 3, 4, 8, 11, 12
British: 2, 5, 6, 7, 9, 10

In many cases, British style has two spellings for a word, often with different meanings – 'meter/metre', 'kerb/curb' – where American style has one. There is also variation between the conventions adopted by particular publishers, say over <-ise>~<-ize> in words such as 'socialise'.

The American/British divide in spelling affects most countries in the world that use English. For example, Australia uses both British 'labour' and American 'labor' in different contexts; Canada laid down the spelling 'colour' by Order-in-Council in 1890. Yet the number of words that differ between the two styles is a handful compared to the totality of the language. The choice of which style to teach usually comes down to overall attitudes towards British and American culture within a particular educational setting. And any computer spell-checker will soon alert you if you are not conforming to a particular spelling style.

Spelling is hardly ever covered systematically in language teaching, vital as it may be to the students' needs. The extent of the help in the beginners' book *Changes* (Richards, 1998) is practising names for letters, and occasional advice such as 'Listen and practice. Notice the spelling'. Little specific teaching of the writing system appears in main coursebooks. *New English File* (Oxenden *et al.*, 2004), however, does have a useful chart of correspondences between 'Sounds and spelling'. A supplementary book for an EFL context, called *Making Sense of Spelling and Pronunciation* (Digby and Myers, 1993), is concerned with the links between sounds and letters to the exclusion of other aspects of spelling. A typical section first explains 'th' ('At the beginning of a word **th** is usually pronounced /θ/ (e.g. thing …) …', then practises it through labelling and distinguishing /ð/ and /θ/ in pictures ('thumb', 'tooth', etc.), and matching words with definitions ('thorough', 'athletics', etc.). In terms of the

---

Box 5.11 Spell it Right/Write/Rite/Wright

Word Test 1

1 He is a very   (a) careful driver.
                (b) carefull

2 She   (a) payed the bill.
                (b) paid

. . .

Remember the right spelling

1 careful
[one <l> in words that end in <ful>, two <l>s in the word 'full' itself.]
One careful man is worth two full of care.
2 paid
[a small group of irregular verbs in <ay> have <aid> in the past tense]
He paid the fine out of his pay.

…

Which past tense in each pair is spelt right?

paid	❐	payed	❐
staid	❐	stayed	❐
prayed	❐	praid	❐
layed	❐	laid	❐

Reason: a small group of verbs have irregular past forms with <aid> in written English; 'paid', 'said', 'laid'. Be careful about these verbs; English people often make mistakes with 'paid'.

Answers: paid, stayed, prayed, laid

---

distinctions made in Chapter 2, this is *FormS*, that is to say, deliberate teaching of spelling forms, rather than *FonF* (focus on form), where such discussion arises out of other activities. Some books for native speakers, such as *Test Your Spelling* (Parker, 1994) and *Handling Spelling* (Davis, 1985), go slightly beyond this and liven up what can be a boring topic with cartoons and quizzes. But none incorporate the basic insights about the sound and visual routes in spelling, about mistakes specific to particular first languages and about the actual rules of spelling. None, for example, mentions the most obvious rule of English, the three-letter rule.

A few years ago I attempted some teaching materials called *Spell It Right (Write/Rite/Wright)*, which tried to provide a systematic approach to spelling but only reached a pilot stage. A sample is shown in Box 5.11 and can be found on the website. Exercises consisted of word tests to see what mistakes the students made. Each wrong answer led them to a set of advice about how to avoid this mistake, and to sets of exercises that practised the particular point.

The official syllabuses for teaching language nowadays do tend to make some gesture towards teaching the writing system. The Malaysian Year 1 syllabus (Pusat Perkembangan Kurikulum, 2003), for instance, specifies mastering 'the mechanics

---

Box 5.12 Adult ESOL Core Curriculum: Spelling (extract)

An adult will be expected to:

ENTRY LEVEL 1	ENTRY LEVEL 2	ENTRY LEVEL 3
spell correctly some personal key words and familiar words	spell correctly the majority of personal details and familiar common words	spell correctly common words and relevant key words for work and special interest
write the letters of the alphabet, using upper case	produce legible text for grammar and spelling	proofread and correct writing
produce legible text and lower case		

Box 5.13 Writing systems and teaching

Teachers need to teach:

- the type of writing system, direction, letter formation, and so on, to students whose first writing system is different;
- the rules and orthographic regularities of spelling;
- the punctuation and capitalization rules;
- individual spellings of frequent words and of frequently misspelt words.

---

of writing so that they form their letters well', and learning 'individual **letter sounds** of the alphabet'. However, useful as the names of the letters are for all sorts of language tasks, they are highly misleading as a guide to their correspondences in speech, as the vowel correspondence rules on page 92 show. Indeed, some of the letter names vary from place to place. <z> is /ziː/ in American, but not Canadian, style and /zed/ in British style. The name for the letter <h> is becoming /heitʃ/ rather than /eitʃ/; children on a television game called *Hard Spell* were penalized for spelling words wrong but allowed to get away with saying /heitʃ/, previously considered an uneducated variant. Sticking to letters, the Common European Framework (2008) goes so far as to mention the need to recognize the difference between 'printed and cursive forms in both upper and lower case', that is, <a>, <ɑ>, <A> and <*A*>.

While in general these syllabuses make a start, they reflect common sense more than ideas about how people use and acquire writing systems. Box 5.12 gives the parts that concern spelling that I could find in *The Adult ESOL Core Curriculum* (DfES, 1999). The word 'correctly' appears in each level, the students being expected to go from correct spelling of 'personal key words' at level 1, to 'familiar common words' at level 2, to 'relevant key words' at level 3; that is, the curriculum is dominated by the meaning-based one-word-at-a-time route, with no use of spelling rules. The other strand is an emphasis on legibility and proofreading. But that is all that is said about a major component of English – not a curriculum that pays any attention to the massive work done on the English writing system in the past few years.

Discussion topics

1 How much attention should writing system topics receive in language teaching?

2 To what extent are people's problems with English spelling because of English or because of their first language?

3 Are spelling problems in English worse or better than those in another language you know?

4 How much do you care about proper spelling rather than proper pronunciation?

5 How should examinations and tests accommodate mistakes with the writing system?

6 Do you prefer a British or American style of spelling? Why?

Further reading

The background on writing systems can be found in books like Coulmas (1996) *The Blackwell Encyclopaedia of Writing Systems*; an overview of English is in Cook (2004) *The English Writing System*, on which the current chapter draws, particularly for punctuation. There is a separate set of pages on the writing system on my website (http://homepage.ntlworld.com/vivian.c/index.htm). The details of English spelling can be found in Carney (1994) *A Survey of English Spelling*, and Venezky (1999) *The American Way of Spelling*. L2 writing systems are described in Cook and Bassetti (2005) *Second Language Writing Systems*.

Answer to Box 5.1

The Pickwick Papers, *extract without the 'e's (see page 89)*

> ThX first ray of light which illuminXs thX gloom, and convXrts into a dazzling brilliancy that obscurity in which thX XarliXr history of thX public carXXr of thX immortal Pickwick would appXar to bX involvXd, is dXrivXd from thX pXrusal of thX following Xntry in thX Transactions of thX Pickwick Club, which thX Xditor of thXsX papXrs fXXls thX highXst plXasurX in laying bXforX his rXadXrs, as a proof of thX carXful attXntion, indXfatigablX assiduity, and nicX discrimination, with which his sXarch among thX multifarious documXnts confidXd to him has bXXn conductXd.

Total: 50 <e>s, 13 <the>s

Answer to Box 5.8

Sample punctuation sentence (see page 97)

> Now of old the name of that forest was Greenwood the Great, and its wide halls and aisles were the haunt of many beasts and of birds of bright song;

and there was the realm of King Thranduil under the oak and the beech. But, after many years, when well nigh a third of that age of the world had passed, a darkness crept slowly through the wood from the southward, and fear walked there in shadowy glades; fell beasts came hunting, and cruel and evil creatures laid there their snares.

J.R.R. Tolkien (1977) The Silmarillion

Strategies for communicating and learning

Most of the time teachers think they know best: they make the students carry out various activities; they select the language they are going to hear or read; they prescribe the language they should produce, all hopefully in their best interests. But as human beings students have minds of their own; ultimately they decide how they are going to tackle the tasks of the classroom and the aims of their learning. Sometimes their choices are visible to us – they put electronic dictionaries on their desks – sometimes they are invisible decisions in their privacy of their own heads – they work out translations in their minds. This independence of the learner from the teacher has been recognized by the tradition of strategies research, which tries to discover the choices that students are making and to recognize them in language teaching.

Of course, there are extreme methodological problems with this, as Ernesto Macaro (2006) has shown. Measuring the invisible contents of the mind has always been difficult. One way is to ask people what they think they are doing – 'how do you try to remember new vocabulary?' The answer, however, may not accurately reflect what you actually do, since so much of our language behaviour is subconscious and not available to our conscious minds. Imagine asking a 5-year-old, for example, 'How do you learn new words?' The answer would be meaningless and bear no connection to how the child is really learning vocabulary. Yet the child probably has a bigger vocabulary than most L2 students. Introspection is a potentially suspect source of evidence.

Another way of investigating strategies is to look for outward signs of behaviour: does a student sit at the back of the class or are they always the first to ask a question? The problem with this observational evidence is interpretation; we have to connect what the student appears to be doing with some process in their minds – an extremely difficult feat scientifically: is a silent student someone who is bored, deep in concentration or naturally shy? And we have to observe their behaviour in a consistent way so that someone else would make the same deduction from it. Of course, we could ask students what is going through their minds, but then we are back to introspection.

A third way is to get the students to carry out a specific task and to see what language they produce: 'Describe this picture to someone over the phone.' While this should yield clear linguistic evidence, the technique is limited to strategies visible from language production; many powerful strategies may have no obvious linguistic consequences. Furthermore, it is open to the objection that it is essentially the technique of the psychological laboratory; do the results tell us anything about the real learning or use situations that the students encounter?

These doubts should be borne in mind when looking at strategies research and may well be insoluble: exploring the private world of people's minds is a problem for any research. Nevertheless, potentially, strategies research leads to interesting results for language teaching, as we shall see. This chapter looks at strategies for communication and for learning; vocabulary and listening strategies are dealt with in the relevant chapters.

6.1 Communication strategies

Focusing question

- How would you explain to someone the type of nut you need to repair your car? Would your strategy be different in your first or second language?
- Should students have to talk about things for which they do not know the words or should they always have the vocabulary available to them?

Keywords

communication strategies can be:

- mutual attempts to solve L2 communication problems by participants (Tarone, 1980)
- individual solutions to psychological problems of L2 processing (Faerch and Kasper, 1984)
- ways of filling vocabulary gaps in the first or second language (Poulisse, 1990)

L2 learners are attempting to communicate through a language that is not their own. L2 learning differs from L1 learning because mental and social development go hand in hand with language development in the L1 child's life. Hence, unlike L1 children, L2 learners are always wanting to express things for which they do not have the means in the second language; they know there are things they cannot say, while L1 children do not. First we look at three different approaches to communication strategies. The detailed lists of strategies used by these approaches are summarized in Box 6.3 on page 112, which can be referred to during this section.

Communication strategies as social interaction

Elaine Tarone (1980) emphasizes social aspects of communication. Both participants in a conversation are trying to overcome their lack of shared meaning. She sees three overall types of strategy: communication, production and learning, the first of which we will consider here. When things go wrong, both participants try to devise a communication strategy to get out of the difficulty.

One type of strategy is to **paraphrase** what you want to say. Typical strategies are:

- *Approximation.* Someone who is groping for a word falls back on a strategy of using a word that means approximately the same, say 'animal' for 'horse', because the listener will be able to deduce what is intended from the context.
- *Word coinage.* Another form of paraphrase is to make up a word to substitute for the unknown word – 'airball' for 'balloon'.
- *Circumlocution.* L2 learners talk their way round the word – 'when you make a container' for 'pottery'.

All these strategies rely on the speaker trying to solve the difficulty through the second language.

A second overall type of communication strategy is to fall back on the first language, known as **transfer**. Examples are:

- *Translation from the L1.* A German-speaking student says 'Make the door shut' rather than 'Shut the door'.
- *Language switch.* 'That's a nice tirtil' (caterpillar). This is distinct from codeswitching because the listener does not know the L1.
- *Appeal for assistance.* 'What is this?'
- *Mime what you need.* My daughter succeeded in getting some candles in a shop in France by singing 'Happy Birthday' in English and miming blowing out candles.

A third overall type of strategy is **avoidance**: do not talk about things you know are difficult to express in the second language, whether whole topics or individual words.

Ellen Bialystok (1990) compared the effectiveness of some of these strategies and found that listeners understand word coinage more than approximation, circumlocution or language switch, though in terms of sheer frequency word coinage was very rare, the commonest strategy being circumlocution.

These types of strategy are particularly important to the teacher who is aiming to teach some form of social interaction to the students. If they are to succeed in conversing with other people through the second language, they need to practise the skill of conducting conversations in which they are not capable of saying everything they want to. This contrasts with some older language teaching techniques which tried to ensure that the students never found themselves doing what they had not been taught. The ability to repair the conversation when things go wrong is vital to using the second language. Maximally the suggestion would be that the teacher specifically teaches the strategies rather than letting them emerge out of the students' own attempts. In this case there would be specific exercises on approximation or word coinage, say, before the students had to put them together in a real conversation.

Communication strategies as psychological problem solving

The approach of Faerch and Kasper (1984) concentrates on the psychological dimension of what is going on in the L2 speaker's mind. L2 learners want to express something through the second language; they make a plan for how to do it, but they encounter a hitch. To get round this psychological difficulty, they resort to communication strategies. Faerch and Kasper divide these into two main groups: achievement (trying to solve the problem) and avoidance (trying to avoid it).

Achievement strategies

These subdivide into *cooperative* strategies, such as appealing to the other person for help, which are mostly similar to Tarone's list, and *non-cooperative* strategies, where the learner tries to solve the problems without recourse to others. One form of non-cooperation is to fall back on the first language when in trouble by:

- *Codeswitching*. The speaker skips language – 'Do you want to have some ah Zinsen?' (the German word for 'interest').
- *Foreignerization*. A Dane literally translating the Danish word for vegetables into English as 'green things'.

These strategies seem likely to occur when the listener knows both languages, as in many situations where codeswitching takes place.

Another overall grouping is interlanguage strategies, based on the learner's evolving L2 system rather than on the L1. Among these, Faerch and Kasper include:

- *Substitution*. Speakers substitute one word for another, say 'if' for 'whether' if they cannot remember whether 'whether' has an 'h'.
- *Generalization*. L2 speakers use a more general word rather than a more particular one, such as 'animal' for 'rabbit', that is, shifting up from the basic level of vocabulary described in Chapter 3 to the superordinate.
- *Description*. Speakers cannot remember the word for 'kettle' and so describe it as 'the thing to cook water in'.
- *Exemplification*. Speakers give an example rather than the general term, such as 'cars' for 'transport', that is, shift down a level.
- *Word coining*. That is, making up a word when a speaker does not know it, such as inventing an imaginary French word 'heurot' for 'watch'.
- *Restructuring*. The speaker has another attempt at the same sentence, as in a learner struggling to find the rare English word 'sibling': 'I have two – er – one sister and one brother'.

Avoidance strategies

These Faerch and Kasper divide into:

- *Formal avoidance*. The speaker avoids a particular linguistic form, whether in pronunciation, in morphemes or in syntax.
- *Functional avoidance*. The speaker avoids different types of function.

Again, this approach, in general, reminds the teacher of the processes going on in the students' minds when they are trying to speak in a new language. Practice with communication techniques, such as information gap games, forces the students to use these types of communication strategy, whether they want to or not, provided that they have to say things that are just beyond their current level of functioning in the second language.

Box 6.1 Test of communication strategies

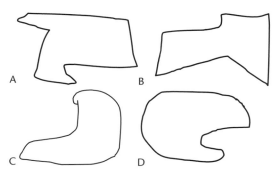

Figure 6.1 Describe either (i) A or B or (ii) C or D in writing, so that other people could distinguish it from the other member of the pair (without, of course, being told 'left' or 'right'). Then check against the types of strategies on page 112. Some examples of students' responses are given at the end of the chapter on page 120.

Compensatory strategies

To some extent, Tarone's social communicative strategies and Faerch and Kasper's psychological strategies are complementary ways of coping with the problems of communicating in a second language. But as we have seen, they end up as rather long and confusing lists. Eric Kellerman and his colleagues (1987) feel that these approaches can be considerably simplified. The common factor to all communication strategies is that the L2 learner has to deal with not knowing a word in a second language; it is lack of vocabulary that is crucial. The strategies exist to plug gaps in the learners' vocabulary by allowing them to refer to things for which they do not know the L2 words; a better name, then, is **compensatory strategies** – L2 learners are always having to compensate for the limited vocabulary at their disposal.

Nanda Poulisse (1990) set up an experiment in which Dutch learners of English had to carry out tasks such as retelling stories and describing geometrical shapes. She ended up with a new division of strategies into two main types, called archistrategies, each with two subdivisions, according to the way that they coped with words they did not know.

Conceptual archistrategy

This involved solving the problem by thinking of the meaning of the word and attempting to convey it in another way:

- *Analytic strategy*. Here the learner tries to break up the meaning of the word into parts, and then to convey the parts separately: so a student searching for the word 'parrot' says 'talk uh bird', taking the two parts 'bird that talks'.

- *Holistic strategy.* Here the learner thinks of the meaning of the word as a whole and tries to use a word that is the closest approximation; for example, seeking for the word 'desk', a student produces 'table', which captures all the salient features of 'desk' apart from the fact that it is specifically for writing at.

Linguistic archistrategy

Here the students fall back on the language resources inside their head, such as:

- *Morphological creativity.* One possibility is to make up a word using proper endings and hope that it works; for instance, trying to describe the act of 'ironing', the student came up with the word 'ironise'.
- *L1 transfer.* The students also have a first language on tap. It is possible for them to transfer a word from the first to the second language, hoping that it is going to exist in the new language. Thus a Dutch student trying to say 'waist' says 'middle' – the Dutch word is in fact 'middel'.

This approach led to an interesting conclusion. The linguistic transfer strategy requires knowledge of another language and hence is unique to L2 learning. However, the conceptual strategies are the same as those used in native speech when speakers cannot remember the word they want to use. Describing to a mechanic which parts of my car needed repairing, I said, 'There's oil dripping from that sort of junction in the pipe behind the engine' – an analytic strategy. This not only allowed me to communicate without knowing the correct words; it also means I never need to learn them – I still do not know what this part of the car is called and never will. Such strategies occur more frequently in the speech of L2 learners only because they know fewer words than native speakers. The strategies are used by native speakers in the same way as L2 learners when they too do not know the words, as any conversation overheard in a shop selling do-it-yourself tools will confirm. Kellerman and his colleagues believe that these compensatory strategies are a part of the speaker's communicative competence that can be used in either language when needed, rather than something peculiar to L2 learning (Kellerman *et al.*, 1990). Poulisse indeed showed that people had preferences for the same type of strategy when they were faced with finding a word they did not know in both the first and the second language; the only difference is that this situation arises far more frequently in a second language!

So it is not clear that compensatory strategies need to be taught. L2 learners resort to these strategies in the situation outside the classroom when they do not know words. This does not mean that it may not be beneficial for students to have their attention drawn to them so that they are reminded that these strategies can indeed be used in a second language; Zoltan Dornyei (1995), however, has demonstrated that Hungarian students who were taught communication strategies improved in their ability to define words, compared to control groups. In a sense, such strategies form part of the normal repertoire of the students' communicative competence. In any teaching activity that encourages the learners to speak outside their normal vocabulary range, they are bound to occur. An exercise in *Keep Talking* (Klippel, 1984) suggests that the students describe their everyday problems, such as losing their keys and not being able to remember names, and other students suggest ways of solving them. If the students do not know the word for 'key', for example, they might ask the teacher (a cooperative strategy) or look it up in a dictionary (a non-cooperative strategy), or they might attempt an analytical archistrategy: 'the thing you open doors with'.

To give some idea of what students actually do, look at the transcript of a conversation in Box 6.2. Are the strategies we have described actually being used, and how important are they to the students' interaction?

Box 6.2 Transcript of students doing an information gap exercise

M is a stranger asking the way round Oxford; W is the local providing help from a map.

1 W: I want to go er I am en smallest street called Merton Street and I want to visit the Rege Readerculf er ca Camera.
2 M: You are in?
3 W: Yes please.
4 M: Merton College, you said?
5 W: Yeah called Merton Street.
6 M: Merton Street.
7 W: Yes please.
8 M: And you are going to?
9 W: To visit the Redcliff Camera.
10 M: The?
11 W: Camera yeah.
12 M: Can you spell it?
13 W: R A D C L I Double F E Camera.
14 M: Radcliffe yes, Radcliffe camera, it's number 4. And you are?
15 W: In um a small street called Merton Street.
16 M: Called Merton.
17 W: Yeah Merton Street.
18 M: You are here. Merton Street.
19 W: Yes.
20 M: Yes. And er Radcliffe camera is I can't say (Long pause). Sorry. You must to ask another people.
21 W: It doesn't matter.
22 M: 'Cos I don't know.

With the exception of dictionary use, most of the communication strategies that have been listed can be safely ignored by the teacher. They are there if the students need them, but they need not form the teaching point of an exercise. One danger with teaching activities that make the students communicate spontaneously is that sheer lack of vocabulary forces the students back onto these strategies, as we see in the transcript in Box 6.2. Hence the teacher should keep the likely vocabulary load of non-teacher-controlled activities within certain limits, ensuring that students already know enough of the vocabulary not to be forced back onto compensatory strategies for too much of the time. Alternatively, the teachers can treat them as ways of discovering and teaching the vocabulary the students lack. There is further discussion of the teaching of strategies in general in the next section.

Box 6.3 Different approaches to L2 communication strategies

Socially motivated strategies for solving mutual lack of understanding (Tarone, 1980):

- paraphrase (approximation, word coinage, circumlocution)
- falling back on L1 translation, language switch, appeal for assistance, mime
- avoidance

Psychologically motivated strategies for solving the individual's L2 problems of expression (Faerch and Kasper, 1984):

1 Achievement strategies:
- cooperative strategies (similar to list above)
- non-cooperative strategies
- codeswitching
- foreignerization
- interlanguage strategies (substitution, generalization, description, exemplification, word coining, restructuring)
2 Avoidance strategies:
- formal (phonological, morphological, grammatical)
- functional (actional, propositional, modal)

Compensatory strategies to make up for a lack of vocabulary (Poulisse, 1990).

Archistrategies:

- conceptual analytic (breaks down the meaning of the word)
- conceptual holistic (tries for a word that is closest overall in meaning)
- linguistic morphological creativity (makes up a new word by adding an appropriate ending)
- linguistic transfer (uses a word from the first language instead)

Box 6.4 Communication strategies and language teaching

- Communication strategies are a natural part of conversational interaction that people fall back on when they have difficulty in getting things across.
- Students mostly fall back on the first language strategies, so teaching can heighten students' awareness of which of their natural strategies are useful in a second language.

6.2 Learning strategies: how do learners vary in their approaches to L2 learning?

Focusing question

When you are learning another language, what special means do you use for:

- pronunciation?
- getting meanings from contexts?
- making oral presentations?
- using the language socially outside the classroom?

Keywords

learning strategy: a choice that the learner makes while learning or using the second language that affects learning: 'steps taken by the learner to make language learning more successful, self-directed and enjoyable' (Oxford, 1990)
good language learner strategies: the strategies employed by people known to be good at L2 learning
metacognitive strategies: involve planning and directing learning at a general level
cognitive strategies: involve specific conscious ways of tackling learning
social strategies: involve interacting with other people

The choices made by the student for using the language (communication strategies) can logically be separated from the choices that the student makes about learning the language (learning strategies). This section looks at the learning strategies used by L2 learners. As with communication strategies, there is considerable difficulty in investigating these invisible strategies: on the one hand, introspectively, for the same reasons that the students may not be consciously aware of them or able to verbalize them adequately; on the other hand, objectively, as it is unclear what the visible effects on their behaviour might be. This means there is little consensus among researchers about the definition of learning strategies; a useful version is 'steps taken by the learner to make language learning more successful, self-directed and enjoyable' (Oxford, 1990). A list of learning strategies is given on page 115.

Good language learner strategies

People who are good at languages might tackle L2 learning in different ways from those who are less good, or they might behave in the same way but more efficiently. One interesting theme is the good language learner (GLL) strategies. Naiman *et al.* (1978/1995) tried to see what people who were known to be good at learning languages had in common. They found six broad strategies shared by GLLs.

GLL strategy 1: find a learning style that suits you

Good language learners become aware of the type of L2 learning that suits them best. Though they conform to the teaching situation to start with, they soon find ways of adapting or modifying it to suit themselves. Thus some GLLs supplement audio-lingual or communicative language teaching by reading grammar books at home, if that is their preference. Others seek out communicative encounters to help them compensate for a classroom with an academic emphasis.

GLL strategy 2: involve yourself in the language learning process

GLLs do not passively accept what is presented to them, but go out to meet it. They participate more in the classroom, whether visibly or not. They take the initiative and devise situations and language learning techniques for themselves. Some listen to the news in the second language on the radio; others go to see L2 films.

GLL strategy 3: develop an awareness of language both as system and as communication

GLLs are conscious not only that language is a complex system of rules, but also that it is used for a purpose; they combine grammatical and pragmatic competence. In other words, GLLs do not treat language solely as communication or as academic knowledge, but as *both*. While many learn lists of vocabulary consciously, many also seek out opportunities to take part in conversations in the second language – one Canadian even driving a lorry for the L2 opportunities it yielded.

GLL strategy 4: pay constant attention to expanding your language knowledge

GLLs are not content with their knowledge of a second language, but are always trying to improve it. They make guesses about things they do not know; they check whether they are right or wrong by comparing their speech with the new language they hear; and they ask native speakers to correct them. Some are continually on the lookout for clues to the second language.

GLL strategy 5: develop the second language as a separate system

GLLs try to develop their knowledge of the second language in its own right, and eventually to think in it. They do not relate everything to their first language, but make the second language a separate system. One common strategy is to engage in silent monologues to practise the second language. I have sometimes told students to give running commentaries in the second language to themselves about the passing scene, for example, as they travel on a bus.

GLL strategy 6: take into account the demands that L2 learning imposes

GLLs realize that L2 learning can be very demanding. It seems as if you are taking on a new personality in the second language, and one which you do not particularly care for. It is painful to expose yourself in the L2 classroom by making foolish mistakes. The GLL perseveres in spite of these emotional handicaps. 'You've got to be able to laugh at your mistakes,' said one.

Osamu Takeuchi (2003) took a different approach to finding out the strategies of good learners by analysing books in which 160 Japanese speakers described how they had successfully learnt another language. To Japanese it is particularly important to immerse themselves in the new language, 'pushing' themselves into the new language as often and as hard as possible.

Some qualifications need to be made to this line of research. First of all, it only describes what GLLs are aware of; this is what they *say* they do, rather than what they actually do – introspective evidence. The magic ingredient in their L2 learning may be something they are unaware of, and hence cannot emerge from interviews or autobiographies. Second, the strategies are similar to what teachers already supposed to be the case, that is, it states the obvious. This is partly a limitation of the original research. Most of the GLLs studied were highly educated people themselves working in education, probably rather similar to the readers of this book. The strategies are familiar because we are looking at ourselves in a mirror. As with aptitude, there may be an alternative set of strategies employed in natural settings by people who are non-academic GLLs. Third, as Steve McDonough (1995) points out, the GLL strategies are not so much strategies in the sense of a deliberate approach to solve problems, as 'wholesome attitudes' that good learners have towards language learning. Macaro (2006) reinforces this by pointing out that it is still unresolved whether GLLs have better strategies than weaker students or are better at using the same strategies.

Types of learning strategies

Extensive research that goes deeper into learning strategies has been carried out by O'Malley and Chamot (1990) within an overall model of L2 learning based on cognitive psychology. They have defined three main types of strategy used by L2 students:

1 *Metacognitive strategies* involve planning and thinking about learning, such as planning one's learning, monitoring one's own speech or writing, and evaluating how well one has done.

2 *Cognitive strategies* involve conscious ways of tackling learning, such as note-taking, resourcing (using dictionaries and other resources) and elaboration (relating new information to old).

3 *Social strategies* mean learning by interacting with others, such as working with fellow students or asking the teacher's help.

They found that cognitive strategies accounted for the majority of those reported by ESL students, namely 53 per cent, the most important being *repetition* (14.8 per cent), *note-taking* (14.1 per cent) and *questions for clarification* (12.8 per cent) (O'Malley *et al.*, 1985). Metacognitive strategies accounted for 30 per cent, the most important being *self-management* – as one student put it, 'I sit in the front of the class so I can see the teacher's face clearly' – and *advance preparation* – 'You review before you go into class'. Social strategies made up the remaining 17 per cent, consisting about equally of cooperative efforts to work with other students and of questions to check understanding. The type of strategy varies according to the task the students are engaged in (O'Malley and Chamot, 1990). A vocabulary task calls forth the metacognitive strategies of self-monitoring and self-evaluation, and the cognitive strategies of resourcing and elaboration. A listening task leads to the metacognitive strategies of selective attention and problem identification, as well as self-monitoring, and to the cognitive strategies of note-taking, inferencing and summarizing, as well as elaboration. The use of strategies also varied according to level: intermediate students used slightly fewer strategies in total, but proportionately more metacognitive strategies.

The most influential research on learning strategies is that carried out by Rebecca Oxford. In 1990, she published a method for finding out the strategies used by learners called the *Strategy Inventory for Language Learning* (SILL). SILL turned into a benchmark for strategies research for many years, was used in many circumstances around the world, and still forms the basis for many an MA thesis. SILL asks the student to rate 50 statements such as: 'I think of relationships between what I already know and new things I learn in English' on a scale going from (1) 'Never true of me', to (5) 'Always true of me'. It includes between 6 and 18 items for six broad classes of strategies, divided into 'Direct' and 'Indirect'.

Direct

1 *Memory strategies*, that is, remembering more effectively, say by visualizing the spelling of a new word in your mind.

2 *Cognitive strategies*, that is, using all your mental processes, for instance by looking for patterns in the new language.

3 *Compensation strategies*, that is, compensating for missing knowledge, for example by trying to anticipate what the other person is going to say next.

Indirect

1 *Metacognitive strategies*, that is, organizing and evaluating your knowledge, for example, by preparing in advance what is going to come up in the next class.

2 *Affective strategies*, that is, managing your emotions, say, by trying to relax when speaking.

3 *Social strategies*, that is, learning with others, for instance, by asking the other person to slow down.

Oxford originally used SILL mostly as an aid to teachers in evaluating what their students were actually doing, and in developing teaching methods. Since then, SILL has been used to study students in a variety of situations in different parts of the world. The research has been assessed by Ernesto Macaro (2006); his summary is displayed in Box 6.5. This makes it apparent that we have to exercise caution in applying strategies research: it can show some benefits, but there is great variation between learners in the strategies they use and in the extent to which teaching them is of benefit.

Box 6.5 Claims from learning strategy research (Macaro, 2006)

1 Strategy use appears to correlate with various aspects of language learning success.
2 There are group differences and individual differences in learner strategy use.
3 The methodology for eliciting learner strategy use, although imperfect, is at an acceptable level of validity and reliability.
4 Despite some setbacks … and some reservations … learner strategy instruction (or 'training') appears to be successful if it is carried out over lengthy periods of time and if it includes a focus on metacognition.

Box 6.6 Language learning strategies

The good language learner (GLL) strategies (Naiman *et al.*, 1978/1995):

1 Find a learning style that suits you.
2 Involve yourself in the language learning process.
3 Develop an awareness of language both as system and as communication.
4 Pay constant attention to expanding your language.
5 Develop the second language as a separate system.
6 Take into account the demands that L2 learning imposes.

Learning strategies (O'Malley and Chamot, 1990):

1 Metacognitive strategies: planning learning, monitoring your own speech, self-evaluation, etc.
2 Cognitive strategies: note-taking, resourcing, elaboration, etc.
3 Social strategies: working with fellow students or asking the teacher's help.

Strategy Inventory for Language Learning (SILL) (Oxford, 1990):

1 Remembering more effectively.
2 Using all your mental processes.
3 Compensating for missing knowledge.
4 Organizing and evaluating your knowledge.
5 Managing your emotions.
6 Learning with others.

Learning strategies and language teaching

How can teachers make use of learning strategies? The chief moral is that the students often know best. It is the learners' involvement, the learners' strategies and the learners' ability to go their own ways that count, regardless of what the teacher is trying to do. Poor students are those who depend most on the teacher and are least able to fend for themselves. The students must be encouraged to develop independence inside and outside the classroom. Partly this can be achieved through 'learner training': equipping the students with the means to guide themselves by explaining strategies to them. The idea of learner training leads on to autonomous, self-directed learning, in which the students take on responsibility for their own learning. They choose their goals; they control the teaching methods and materials; they assess how well they are doing themselves. This is dealt with further in Chapter 13.

It may simply not have occurred to students that they have a choice of strategies for conducting their learning. Teaching can open up their options. My intermediate course *Meeting People* (Cook, 1982) asked students to discuss four GLL strategies. The intention was to make them aware of different possibilities, rather than specifically to train them in any strategy. A more thorough approach is seen in *Learning to Learn English* (Ellis and Sinclair, 1989), which aims 'to enable learners of English to discover the learning strategies that suit them best'. One set of activities practises metacognitive strategies. The opening questionnaire, for instance, asks the students: 'Do you hate making mistakes?' 'Do you like to learn new grammar rules, words, etc. by heart?' and so on. The results divide the students into 'analytic', 'relaxed' and 'a mixture'. A second set of activities practises cognitive as well as metacognitive strategies. Teaching speaking, for instance, starts with reflection ('How do you feel about speaking English?'), knowledge about language ('What do you know about speaking English?'), and self-evaluation ('How well are you doing?'). As a guide for teachers, *Language Learning Strategies* (Oxford, 1990) provides a wealth of activities to heighten the learners' awareness of strategies and their ability to use them; for example: 'The old lady ahead of you in the bus is chastising a young man in your new language; listen to their conversation to find out exactly what she's saying to him.'

Strategy training assumes that conscious attention to learning strategies is beneficial and that the strategies are teachable. While the idea that GLLs need to 'think' in the second language may strike the students as a revelation, this does not mean they can put it into practice. Indeed, they may find it impossible or disturbing to try to think in the second language, and so feel guilty that they are not living up to the image of the GLL. For example, the GLLs studied in Canadian academia clearly had above-average intelligence; less intelligent learners may not be able to use the same GLL strategies. Many strategies cannot be changed by the teacher or the learner, however good their intentions. Bialystok (1990) argues in favour of training that helps the students to be aware of strategies in general, rather than teaching specific strategies.

O'Malley and Chamot (1990) provide some encouragement for strategy training. They taught EFL students to listen to lectures using their three types of strategy. One group was trained in cognitive strategies such as note-taking, and social strategies such as giving practice reports to fellow students. A second group was trained, in addition, in metacognitive strategies, for example, paying conscious attention to discourse markers such as 'first', 'second', and so on. A third group was not taught any strategies. The metacognitive group improved most for speaking, and did better on some, but not all, listening tasks. The cognitive group was better than the control group. Given that this experiment only lasted for eight 50-minute lessons spread over eight days, this seems as dramatic an improvement as could reasonably be expected. Training students to use particular learning strategies indeed improves their language performance. But as O'Malley and Chamot (1990) found, teachers may need to be convinced that strategy training is important, and may themselves need to be trained in how to teach strategies. However, to dampen excessive enthusiasm, it should be pointed out that there is still some doubt about how useful strategies really are: Oxford *et al.* (1990) found that Asian students of English used fewer 'good' strategies than Hispanics, but improved their English more!

Most of the learning strategies mentioned suit any academic subject. It is indeed a good idea to prepare yourself for the class, to sit near the teacher and to take notes, whether you are studying physics, cookery or French. Those who believe in the uniqueness of language, however, feel language learning is handled by the mind in ways that are different from other areas. Some consciously accessible learning strategies that treat language as a thing of its own may be highly useful for L2 learning, say, the social strategies. But metacognitive or cognitive strategies treat language like any other part of the human mind. Hence they may benefit students with academic leanings who want to treat language as a subject, but may not help those who want to use it for its normal functions in society, that is unless, of course, such knowledge translates into the practical ability to use the language – one of the controversies discussed in Chapter 12.

A coursebook that relies on the SILL approach is *Tapestry 1 Listening and Speaking* (Benz and Dworak, 2000). Some are language learning strategies – 'Practice speaking English with classmates as often as possible'. Some are called 'Academic power strategies' – 'Learn how to address your teachers'. As the level of the course is claimed to be 'high beginning', there is a discrepancy between the level of the language the students are supposed to be learning, namely greetings and polite forms of address, and the level of language they are using for discussing it. This is a problem with any teaching that involves explicit discussion of strategies, unless it can take place in the students' first language. The other problem is the extent to which the presentation of strategies in a class situation puts students in the position of practising strategies that are inappropriate for their particular learning style and which they would never choose voluntarily. Chapter 4 of *Tapestry*, for example, emphasizes 'graphic organisers', that is to say associations of ideas in doodled networks, popular in the UK through the work of Tony Buzan books such as *Use Your Head* (1995). Useful as these may be for some students, those who do not think graphically and do not consciously store information through such mental networks are going to waste their time. Group teaching of strategies is inevitably in conflict with the individual's right to choose the best strategies for them.

Box 6.7 Learning strategies and language teaching

- Exploit the GLL strategies that are useful to the students.
- Develop the students' independence from the teacher with learner training or directed learning.
- Make students aware of the range of strategies they can adopt.
- Provide specific training in particular strategies.
- Remember the similarities and differences between learning a second language and learning other school subjects.

Discussion topics

1   Choose a type of learning strategy and decide how you would teach it.

2   How important is the idea of strategies to language teaching?

3 How do you think it is possible to test whether students have learnt effective communication and learning strategies?

4 What differences are there between strategies used by beginners and advanced learners?

5 How might strategies teaching best be incorporated into textbooks?

6 Are compensatory strategies the same or different from learning strategies?

7 How can we combine the students' right to choose strategies with the teacher's duty to direct their learning?

Further reading

One perspective on communication strategies can be found in Bialystok (1990) *Communication Strategies*. The Nijmegen communication strategies are best described in Poulisse (1990) *The Use of Compensatory Strategies by Dutch Learners of English*. A useful collection is Kasper and Kellerman (1997) *Communication Strategies: Psycholinguistic and Sociolinguistic Perspectives*. The starting point for learning strategies is Oxford (1990) *Language Learning Strategies: What Every Teacher Should Know*. The leading current work is reflected in Macaro (2003) *Teaching and Learning a Second Language: A Guide to Recent Research*.

Answers to Box 6.1

Student responses to the shapes in the test of communication strategies in Box 6.1 (see page 109).

- Looks like arrow
- Left-hand to show letter c
- 7 angles, rectangular top left and bottom right some parts eliminated; looks like an ox
- Kidney shape
- Looks like a seal without eyes
- 7 lines
- Nine angles; bottom looks like a foot.

Listening and reading processes

7

7.1 Meaning and reading

Focusing question

- What do you think are the typical elements involved in going to a restaurant?
- What do you think are the main aims of an academic essay?

Keywords

schema (pl. *schemas* or *schemata*): the background knowledge on which the interpretation of a text depends

script: 'a predetermined stereotyped sequence of actions that defines a well-known situation' (Schank and Abelson, 1977)

Reading, like speaking, occurs in a context rather than in isolation. The meaning of a text is not found just in the sentences themselves, but is derived from the previous knowledge stored in the reader's mind and the processes through which the reader tackles it. 'We do not find meaning lying in things nor do we put it into things, but between us and things it can happen' (Buber, 1947).

I look out of my window and see an empty road, as anybody else would do sitting in the same position. However, to me the emptiness means my wife has gone out, since the family car is not there; to my son it means the bus for school has not yet arrived; to my daughter it means the postman is late. The same scene is interpreted in different ways according to our background information and predilections.

Schema theory

A famous experiment by Bransford and Johnson (1982) asked people to read texts such as the following:

The procedure is actually quite simple. First you arrange things into different groups depending on their makeup. Of course, one pile may be sufficient depending on how much there is to do. If you have to go somewhere else due to lack of facilities that is the next step, otherwise you are pretty well set. It is important not to overdo any particular endeavour. That is, it is better to do too few things at once than too many.

To make sense of this text, a particular piece of information is required: the passage is about washing clothes. A person who does not have this information does not get much out of the text. Once the topic is known, the passage is straightforward and the comprehension level is much higher. The sentences themselves do not change when we know the topic, but the interpretation they have in our minds does. The background knowledge into which a text fits, sometimes called the schema, plays a large role in how it is read.

L2 readers also need to know what the passage is about. Adams (1983) gave American students of French the same texts as Bransford and Johnson, and tested whether they were better or worse at learning new vocabulary when they were told what the passage was about. Her results showed first that they were better at learning vocabulary in the first language, and second that knowing what the passage was about helped them equally in both languages. Hence this kind of background knowledge is relevant to both L1 and L2 processing. Patricia Carrell (1984) tested L2 learners of English with the same texts to see not only whether the presence or absence of context made a difference to how much they could understand, but also the importance of whether the text had precise words like 'clothes' and 'washing machine', or vague words like 'things' and 'facilities'. Both advanced learners and natives once again found lack of context affected their comprehension. However, intermediate L2 learners also found the use of vague words was a hindrance, even if, as we saw in the last chapter, such words are often of high frequency. The provision of context varied in importance according to the stage of L2 learning. At the early stages of L2 learning, linguistic aspects of the words are as important to understanding as context. One interesting side effect of Carrell's research was that, while native speakers had a fair idea of how difficult the passages were for them to understand, non-natives did not! However, later research by Roller and Matombo (1992) did not get the same results: speakers of Shona actually remembered more of the Bransford and Johnson texts in English than in their first language.

'Scripts' and discourse

A crucial element in the understanding of discourse was given the name of 'script' by Roger Schank in the 1970s (Schank and Abelson, 1977). The concept of the script came out of attempts to build computer programs that would understand human languages. The problem was that the computer did not know obvious things that human beings take for granted. Suppose a text reads, 'Bill had some hamburgers in a restaurant.' Straightforward as this sentence seems, our understanding of it relies on several unconscious assumptions about restaurants. What did Bill do with the hamburgers? He ate them, because that is what you go to restaurants for. Did he cook the hamburgers? Of course he did not. Did he fetch them himself? Probably not. Did Bill pay for them? Of course he did. In our minds there is a script for restaurants that specifies that they are places where they provide you with food that you pay for. None of this information needs to be given in the text as our minds supply it automatically. Only if the actual event does not conform with our background knowledge for restaurants will it be mentioned – if it is self-service, if they have run out of food, or if Bill sneaks out without paying his bill. The mind supplies such information automatically from the background script in its memory. A script, then, according to Schank and Abelson (1977), is 'a predetermined, stereotyped sequence of actions that defines a well-known situation'. While in recent years Schank has developed his ideas beyond this, the script has remained an influential view of how memory is organized.

Some scripts are virtually the same for speakers of different languages; others differ from one country to another. The script for eating out may require all restaurants to have waitress service, or to be takeaway, or to have cash desks by the exit, or other variations. I remember once arguing that US hotels are not proper hotels because they have large entrance lobbies rather than cosy lounge areas; my British script for hotels implies lounges. Wherever there are such differences between two scripts, the L2 learners will be at a loss. In an American novel, the hero visits London and asks his friend at a pub 'Have you settled up at the bar?' – an unthinkable concept in virtually all English pubs since each round is paid for at the time. L2 learners unwittingly have different expectations and they have an unpleasant shock when something turns out differently. A self-service restaurant that calls for payment in advance by naming the dishes you want can be a trial for visitors to Italy. Or indeed the script may be totally absent; I have no script for a Finnish sauna. Many of the stereotyped problems of foreign travel that people recount show conflicts between scripts – eating snakes, loos for mixed sexes, tipping taxi drivers, asking if food tastes good, are all absent from the scripts in particular cultures. An example can be found in the script for doctor/patient interaction (Ranney, 1993): English-speaking patients expect to ask questions of the doctor, Hmong patients do not; English speakers prefer to talk to the doctor informally, Hmong speakers prefer to show respect. Similarly, Australian doctors are reported to be unsympathetic towards ethnic minority women who scream in childbirth, having different cultural scripts about the expression of pain.

An important aspect of discourse is how the background information contributed by the script relates to the purposes of conversation. Say someone is attempting to book a plane ticket in a travel agent's. The participants have their own ideas of what they expect to get out of the conversation; the travel agent needs to know what information he needs to find out and how to ask the customer to supply it. There is an expected framework of information necessary for the task of booking a ticket to be accomplished. The customer has to supply bits of information to fit this framework. Both participants are combining background knowledge of what goes on in a travel agent's with the specific goal of booking a ticket – almost a definition of task-based teaching!

Scripts and schema theory in teaching

Patricia Carrell (1983) produced a set of recommendations for language teachers, based on her own research and that of others. She points to the importance of vocabulary, revealed in her experiments with tests outlined earlier. The L2 learner needs to be supplied with the vocabulary that the native takes for granted. Carrell also sees teaching as building up the learner's background knowledge. Thus she stresses pre-reading activities that build up background knowledge, partly through providing learners with appropriate vocabulary through activities such as word association practice. The techniques she suggests develop processing strategies for the text, such as flow-charting or diagramming activities. Materials should not only be interesting, but also conceptually complete; a longer passage or an in-depth set of passages on a single topic is better than short unconnected passages.

Perhaps none of these ideas will be completely new to the practising teacher. Reading materials have after all been stressing content and background for some time. Pre-reading exercises are now standard. Com-municatively oriented reading tasks meet many of her requirements. In the textbook *True to Life* (Collie and Slater, 1995), for example, pairs of students prepare for a reading passage on reflexology by looking at diagrams of feet and by formulating questions about its history and practice; they read the text and check whether they were asking the right questions; they discuss their views about it and then report them to the group. All the desirable ingredients seem to be there, even if the balance and overall sequence are slightly different.

The benefit for the teacher is an increased awareness of the difficulties that L2 learners face with texts. These are not just a product of the processing of the text itself, but of the background information that natives automatically read into it. L2 learners have 'cognitive deficits' with reading that are not caused so much by lack of language ability as by difficulties with processing information in a second language. At advanced levels, L2 learners still cannot get as much out of a text as in their first language, even if on paper they know all the grammar and vocabulary. Cambridge University students tested by John Long and Edith Harding-Esch (1977), for example, not only remembered less information from political speeches in French than in English, but also added more false information. Furthermore, advanced L2 learners still read their second language much more slowly than they read their first (Favreau and Segalowitz, 1982), particularly when they are changing from one overall writing system to another, as we saw in Chapter 5 (Haynes and Carr, 1990). The problem with reading is not just the language, but the whole process of getting meaning from texts.

The importance of background information through scripts and similar mental structures is much wider than the area of reading. The processing of written texts is distinctive in that the reader has to depend only on his or her own script. In speaking, someone else is usually there to help or hinder by interacting with the speaker in one way or another. As with pronunciation, reading involves important low-level processes as well as high-level comprehension. The discussion here has not been about the teaching of reading itself, that is, literacy, but about teaching L2 students to read in a new language, which is a rather different issue. The literacy skills themselves become important either when the L2 learners cannot read in their own language or when the writing system of their first language is very different, as discussed in Chapter 5.

A particular problem for L2 students occurs in the use of academic language. Never mind the language problems, think of the schemas. Ruqaiya Hasan (1996) pointed out that the crucial problem for the non-native student studying in an English setting is what counts as knowledge: one culture may prize the views of well-known authorities; another the views of the individual student. So the schema for an essay may be a collection of quotations strung together in a fairly arbitrary order; or it may be a personal argument built up from existing sources. The main problem for the non-native speaker of English studying in England who has previously studied in other academic systems is the nature of the essay, not the grammatical structures, vocabulary, and so on. In my own experience this is true of students coming from Greece, Iran and Hong Kong, to take a random sample.

An interesting approach to teaching schemas comes from the field of cross-cultural psychology, which has developed a technique called cross-cultural training (Cushner and Brislin, 1996). This presents the students with a key intercultural problem, for which they are given alternative solutions; they decide which of them is most likely and check this against interpretations supplied by native speakers. For example, one case study features an American student in Germany who is worried by her apparent rejection by German students; the most likely reason is her lack of interest in politics. Another example is a foreign student in the USA who cannot get women to go out with him; the correct explanation is that he should ask them out via their women friends rather than directly, a surprising custom to a non-American. This approach is a variety of focus on form in which the students' attention is directed to the specific cultural nature of the situation rather than its grammar or functions.

Box 7.1 Reading and memory processes

- Knowledge of conventional situations (scripts) is important to L2 use.
- Background knowledge (schemata) is important to L2 learners.
- Use of 'vague words' hinders lower-level learners.

7.2 Listening processes

Focusing questions

- When you listen to something in a second language, do you try to work out the meaning of every word or are you content with the gist?
- Do you believe listening comes before or after speaking in the sequence of teaching the language skills?

Keywords

parsing: the process through which the mind works out the grammatical structure and meaning of the sentence

top-down versus **bottom-up**: starting from the sentence as a whole and working down to its smallest parts, versus starting from the smallest parts and working up

decoding versus **codebreaking**: processing language to get the 'message', versus processing language to get the 'rules'

Guides to the teaching of listening appear almost every year; some textbooks are aimed specifically at listening, others include listening components. Yet listening does not even figure as a topic in most introductions to SLA research. This section looks first at the process of listening itself and then develops the use of listening as a vehicle for learning – the most discussed aspect in recent years.

Elements of listening

Most introductions to the comprehension of speech stress three elements: access to vocabulary, parsing and memory processes.

Access to words

At one level, in order to comprehend a sentence you have to work out what the words mean. The mind has to relate the words that are heard to the information that is stored about them in the mind, as described in Chapter 3. For example, a native speaker can answer the question, 'Is the word "blint" English?' almost instantaneously, somehow working through many thousands of words in a few moments. Such feats show the human mind is extraordinarily efficient at organizing the storage of words and their interconnections. The context automatically makes particular meanings of words available to us. To a person reading a research article, the word 'table' means a layout of figures. To someone reading about antiques, it means a piece of furniture. To someone reading a surveyor's report, it means the depth at which water appears in the ground, and so on. Somehow the context limits the amount of mental space that has to be searched to get the right meaning.

Take the sentence, 'The dog was hit by a bus.' As people listen to it, they are retrieving information about the words. They know that 'the' is an article used with certain meanings, here probably indicating the dog is already relevant to the conversation or known to the listener. Next, 'dog' summons up the meanings of 'dog' important to this context, its relationships to other words such as 'bark', and the probable other words that contrast with it or come in the same context, such as 'cat'. The word 'hit' connects in our mental word-store with the verb 'hit', with its range of meanings and its irregular past form, and to expectations that it is going to be followed by a noun phrase object, here made more complicated by being in the passive voice. In addition there are links between the L1 vocabulary and the L2 vocabulary, as seen in Chapter 3.

Parsing

Parsing refers to how the mind works out the grammatical structure and meaning of the sentences it hears, that is to say, the term is only loosely connected to its meaning in traditional grammar. Take a sentence such as 'The man ate breakfast.' To understand the sentence fully means being able to tell who is carrying out the action and what is affected by the action, and to realize that 'ate breakfast' goes together as a phrase, while 'man ate' does not. Even if our minds are not consciously aware of the grammatical technicalities, they are automatically working out the structure of the sentence. Grammar is not just in the back of our minds, but is active all the time we are listening.

Ideas of parsing in psychology and computational models rely on the phrase structure idea described in Chapter 2, but tackle it in two opposite directions, either bottom-up or top-down. Let us start with the sentence, 'The man ate breakfast.'

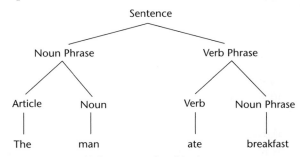

Figure 7.1 Phrase structure tree of 'The man ate breakfast'

Bottom-up parsing involves building up the sentence in our minds bit by bit, putting the sounds into words, the words into phrases, the phrases into a whole sentence, that is to say, working from the bottom to the top of the tree. So 'the' is put with 'man' to get a noun phrase 'the man'; 'ate' goes with 'breakfast' to get a verb phrase 'ate breakfast'; and the noun phrase 'the man' and the verb phrase 'ate breakfast' go together to yield the structure of the whole sentence.

Box 7.2 Bottom-up parsing

Step 1: the + man → (the man)	*article + noun = noun phrase*
Step 2: ate + breakfast → (ate breakfast)	*verb + noun = verb phrase*
Step 3: (the man) + (ate breakfast) → (the man ate breakfast)	*noun phrase + verb phrase = sentence*

'Top-down' parsing, on the other hand, means breaking down the whole sentence into smaller and smaller bits, that is, going from the top of the tree to the bottom, as represented in Box 7.3. Given 'The man ate breakfast', the top-down process tries to find the whole structure of an SVO sentence. It first tries to find a noun phrase, which in turn means trying to find, first, an article 'the', and then a noun, 'man'. If it succeeds, the next step is to find a verb phrase, which means trying to find a verb 'ate' and a noun phrase 'breakfast'. If the quest to find a noun phrase and a verb phrase succeeds, it has parsed the whole sentence, complete with its structure. The list in the figure is in fact a mirror of a computer program to parse sentences in a computer language like Prolog. The schema theories mentioned earlier are top-down in that they see how the sentence fits in with whole patterns in the mind.

Box 7.3 Top-down parsing

→**?** sentence *The man ate breakfast*
[means: is there a noun phrase plus a verb phrase?]

→**?** a noun phrase →**?** an article *the* ✓
→**?** a noun *man* ✓

→✓a noun phrase (the man)
[means: yes, there is a noun phrase consisting of article+ noun (the man)]
→**?** a verb phrase →**?** a verb *ate* ✓
→**?** a noun phrase →**?** an article ✗
→**?** a noun *breakfast* ✓
→✓ a noun phrase (breakfast)
→ ✓ a verb phrase (ate breakfast)
[means: yes, there is a verb phrase verb + noun phrase (ate breakfast)]

→✓ a sentence

[means: yes, there is a sentence because there is a noun phrase plus a verb phrase (the man)(ate breakfast)]

In principle, the mind could parse the sentence in either direction, bottom-up or top-down. In practice, listeners use both types of process. Features such as the intonation pattern allow them to fit words and phrases within an overall structure, a top-down process. Particular words such as articles indicate the start of a phrase and allow them to build it up word by word, a bottom-up process. The top-down/bottom-up dichotomy, then, is only true in ideal terms. Some parsing experts talk in terms of left-corner parsing, that is to say, starting with the lowest word in the left corner of the tree, then going *up* to the first branching node and *down* to the next word, up the next node, then down again, rather like a yoyo. J. Michael O'Malley and his colleagues (1985) found that effective L2 learners used both top-down strategies listening for intonation or phrases and bottom-up strategies listening for words, while ineffective listeners concentrated on the bottom-up process. When parsing failed, they fell back on a range of other strategies, the least effective being translation.

Memory processes and cognition

Listening relies on much the same memory processes discussed in Section 7.1. All comprehension depends on the storing and processing of information by the mind. Call (1985), for instance, found that sheer memory for digits was less important to comprehension than memory for sentences. The extent of the memory restriction in a second language depends on how close the task is to language. Hence getting the students to perform tasks that are not concerned with language may have less influence on their learning than language-related tasks. For example, comprehension activities using maps and diagrams may improve the learners' problem-solving abilities with maps and diagrams, but may be less successful at improving those aspects of the learners' mental processes that depend on language.

A further point that applies to listening as much as to reading is that vital aspects of the process are contributed by the listener. At the lowest level, the actual 'p' sounds of speech have to be worked out by the mind. While the sounds in 'pit', 'spit' and 'top' differ in terms of VOT, as seen in Chapter 4, the English person nevertheless hears a /p/ in each of them, that is, recognizes a phoneme; the listener's ear somehow imposes the idea of a /p/ on the sound waves it hears. The meaning of words such as 'bus' and 'breakfast' is not present in the sentence itself, but is retrieved from the listener's mental dictionary to match the sequence of sounds that is heard. The sentence also has to be actively parsed by the listener to discover the phrases and constructions involved. As with reading, the listener's knowledge of the context of situation and background knowledge of the culture and society are crucial to listening comprehension. I once asked British students to fill in a chart showing what listening they were doing at different times of day; I was surprised when the 9.30 a.m. slot was left blank by most of them, the explanation they gave me being that none of them was actually awake at that hour except when they had a lecture.

The scripts and schemas discussed in relation to reading are equally involved in listening. Our mental pictures of restaurants and stations come into play as soon as the appropriate situation is invoked. Any sentence listeners hear is matched against their mental scripts and schemas. If the models of speaker and listener differ too much, they have problems in comprehending each other. O'Malley *et al.* (1989) found that effective listeners helped themselves by drawing on their knowledge of the world, or on their personal experiences, or by asking questions of themselves.

The teaching of listening

How does this view of listening compare with that in teaching guides such as Mary Underwood's *Teaching Listening* (1989)? She recognizes three stages of teaching:

- *pre-listening*, where the students activate their vocabulary and their background knowledge;
- *while-listening*, where 'they develop the skill of eliciting messages';
- *post-listening*, which consists of extensions and developments of the listening task.

Some of the elements are similar. It is rightly considered important to get the students' background scripts working and the appropriate vocabulary active in their minds. What seems overlooked is parsing. Listeners do need to know the structure of the sentence in some way. Teaching has mostly ignored the process of syntactic parsing, perhaps because of its unwelcome overtones of grammar. But, as with reading, some attempt could be made to train both top-down and bottom-up parsing skills.

One development has been task-based teaching of listening. The students carry out a task in which they have to listen for information in a short piece of discourse and then have to fill in a diagram, check a route on a map or correct mistakes in a text. The *COBUILD English Course 1* (Willis and Willis, 1988), for example, asks the students to listen to tapes of people speaking spontaneously and to work out information from them. Lesson 9 has a recording of Chris telling Philip how to get to his house in Birmingham. The students listen for factual information, such as which buses could be taken; they make a rough map of the route, and they check its accuracy against an A–Z map of Birmingham.

One teaching motivation is the practical necessity of checking that comprehension is taking place. Unfortunately, in normal language use, there is rarely any visible feedback when someone has comprehended something. A visible sign of comprehension is useful to the teacher to see if the student has understood. This check can range from a straightforward question to an action based on what has happened. If you shout 'Fire' and nobody moves, you assume they have not understood. Much teaching of listening comprehension has made the student show some sign of having comprehended, whether through answering questions, carrying out tasks, or in some other way.

In task-based listening activities, information is being transferred for a communicative purpose. Task-based listening stresses the transfer of information rather than the social side of language teaching. In the *COBUILD* example, the student is practising something that resembles real-world communication. The information that is being transferred in such activities, however, is usually about trivial topics or is irrelevant to the students' lives. The factual information the students learn in the *COBUILD* exercise is how to get around in Birmingham, somewhere only a few of them are ever likely to go. Often such exercises deal with imaginary towns, or even treasure islands. Task-based exercises often neglect the educational value of the content that can be used in language teaching, as discussed in Chapter 13, although much psychological research shows that, the more important the information is to the listener, the more likely it is to be retained. Box 7.4 gives an example of a teaching exercise that solves this problem by choosing a topic of 'manufacturing systems' appropriate to ESP students, and making the students employ an integrated range of skills and strategies to achieve the point of the task.

> **Box 7.4 A strategy and task-based exercise for ESP (Flowerdew and Miller, 2005)**
>
> 1 Teacher introduces topic of 'manufacturing systems' and gets students to discuss it.
> 2 Teacher plays video; students listen for general ideas.
> 3 Teacher plays video again; students listen for specific stages in the system.
> 4 Students work in small groups to establish particular points.
> 5 Students fill in a skeleton handout.
> 6 Students practise giving oral summaries of the video in pairs.

Many listening techniques do not so much teach listening as decorate the listening process with a few frills. They suggest that conscious attention to information will improve all the other aspects of listening – hardly justified by the research described here. If word access, parsing and memory processes are improved by these activities, this is an accidental by-product. Perhaps listening cannot be trained directly and the best the teacher can do is devise amusing activities during which the natural listening processes can be automatically activated.

Another approach to listening, pioneered by Mary Underwood in the 1970s, relies on authentic tapes of people talking. After some introductory focusing activities, students were played the tape and then did follow-on comprehension activities. For instance, in *The Listening File* (Harmer and Ellsworth, 1989), a unit on 'The Historic MP, Diane Abbott' first makes the students think about the House of Commons and the problems that an MP might face. Then they listen to the tape and check whether their initial guesses were right; they listen again and answer a series of detailed factual questions; they go on to follow-up activities in discussion and writing – literally a textbook example of Mary Underwood's three phases.

In my own *English Topics* (1975), I used recordings of English people carrying out the same tasks or having the same kinds of conversation as the students. For example, a unit on 'Buying a House' had an authentic recording of someone describing how complicated they had found the whole process. Students listened to it as often as they liked and then their comprehension was checked by asking them to agree or disagree with statements such as 'He paid for the house immediately'. This led to discussion points and a transcript of the speech that the students could look at. The checking element was then kept as minimal as possible so that it did not add difficulties to the actual comprehension. Students were using top-down listening as the starting point for their own discussion and opinions. The transcript was available not only for the students' benefit, but also for the teacher's.

Clearly, authentic speech tries to encourage top-down listening by getting the students to visualize an overall context for the speech before they hear it; nevertheless, they are also doing some bottom-up processing on their second listening in that they have to deal with specific pieces of information. One snag is that such teaching edges towards testing memory rather than listening itself; if the students have to remember the content for any period longer than a handful of seconds, they are being tested on what they can remember, not on what they actually understood. While this may be a very valuable skill, it is not characteristic of ordinary listening. I once tried out the teaching materials I was using for the

Cambridge First Certificate with native speakers and found that they did less well than my students. The explanation was that I had trained the students in the specific task of storing information from the text; the natives were untrained.

A further incidental problem comes back to the power struggle in conversational discourse. An interview is a very specific type of speech; the interviewer is allowed to play the leader and to ask all the questions, but must remain neutral; the interviewee has to respond to whatever happens. I remember once seeing the film star Danny Kaye being interviewed on television after he had arrived at a London airport; he asked the interviewer why she had come to the airport and about her life and opinions. The effect was hilarious because it broke the usual conventions of the interview. While all of us are passively familiar with interviews from the media, we are seldom called on to take part in them ourselves. Listening materials should not stress interviews too much as they are a rather untypical and unequal encounter, as described in Chapter 9. It would be better to use examples of genuine monologues, whether lectures or stand-up comedians, or real-life two-person encounters in more everyday settings – the supermarket, the library, and so on. And it is vital to give the students situations involving successful L2 users, so that they can see models to aim at that are not just monolingual native speakers.

Listening-based methods of teaching

So far listening has been taken as a process of decoding speech – working out the 'message' from the sentence you hear, just as a spy decodes a secret message by using a code he or she already knows. However, recent discussions of teaching methodology have focused on listening as a way of learning rather than as a way of processing language. Logically, L2 learners cannot learn a language if they never hear it; the sounds, the words, the structures, have to come from somewhere. This process can be called codebreaking – listening means working out the language code from the 'message', just as a cryptographer works out an unknown code from an intercepted message. Decoding speech has the aim of discovering the message using processes that are already known. Codebreaking speech has the aim of discovering the processes themselves from a message.

One of the first to interpret listening as codebreaking was James Asher's total physical response method (TPR) (Asher, 1986), which claimed that listening to commands and carrying them out was an effective way of learning a second language. A specimen TPR exercise consists of the teacher getting the students to respond to the following (Seely and Romijn, 1995):

1 You get a present from a friend.
2 Look it over.
3 Feel it.
4 Shake it and listen to it ...

... and so on. The students follow the directions given by the teacher. This can now be done through an interactive CD-ROM called *Live Action English* (Romijn and Seely, 2000).

TPR came out of psychological theories of language learning and was based on extensive research. Its unique twist on listening is the emphasis on learning through physical actions. As Asher puts it, 'In a sense, language is orchestrated to a choreography of the human body.' TPR gradually leads in to student production of language. According to Seely and Romijn (1995), TPR relies on four main exercises:

1 *single unrelated commands* such as 'Grapple with your opponent';
2 *action series* like the one above;
3 *natural action dialogues* based on a short script;
4 *action role-playing* without a script, that is, a freer version of (3).

These lead in to a technique called TPR storytelling, in which students retell familiar stories through the second language. TPR is discussed further in Chapter 13.

During the 1980s there was much talk of listening-based methods, summed up under the slogan of 'Listening First' (Cook, 1986). Postovsky (1974) had described how students who were taught Russian by methods that emphasize listening were better than students taught in a conventional way. According to Gary and Gary (1981a; 1981b), the benefits of concentrating on listening are that students do not feel so embarrassed if they do not have to speak; the memory load is less if they listen without speaking; and classroom equipment such as tape recorders can be used more effectively for listening than for speaking. Classroom research has confirmed that there are distinct advantages to listening-based methods, as shown in the collection by Winitz (1981). A major schism in communicative teaching is between those who require students to practise communication by both listening and speaking, and those who prefer students to listen for information without speaking.

Krashen brought several disparate listening-based methods together through the notion of 'comprehensible input'. He claims that 'acquisition can take place only when people understand messages in the target language' (Krashen and Terrell, 1983). Listening is motivated by the need to get messages out of what is heard. L2 learners acquire a new language by hearing it in contexts where the meaning is made plain to them. Ideally, the speech they hear has enough 'old' language that the student already knows and makes enough sense in the context for the 'new' language to be understood and absorbed. How the teacher gets the message across is not particularly important. Pointing to one's nose and saying 'This is my nose', working out 'nose' from the context in 'There's a spot on your nose', looking at a photo of a face and labelling it with 'nose', 'eyes', and so on, are all satisfactory provided that the student discovers the message in the sentence. Steve McDonough (1995) neatly summarizes the process as 'the accretion of knowledge from instances of incomprehension embedded in the comprehensible'.

Stephen Krashen claims that all teaching methods that work utilize the same 'fundamental pedagogical principle' of providing comprehensible input: 'if x is shown to be "good" for acquiring a second language, x helps to provide CI [comprehensible input], either directly or indirectly' (Krashen, 1981b).

Krashen's codebreaking approach to listening became a strong influence on language teachers. It is saying, essentially, that L2 acquisition depends on listening: decoding *is* codebreaking. It did not, however, oddly enough, lead to a generation of published listening-based main coursebooks in the teaching of English, though some examples exist for teaching other languages in the *Two Worlds* series by

Tracey Terrell and others (Terrell *et al.*, 1993), and in 'More English Now!', an appendix to the Gary and Gary (1981b) materials discussed in Chapter 13.

But Krashen's theory does not say what the processes of decoding are and how they relate to codebreaking. The statement that teaching should be meaningful does not in itself get us very far. Most teachers have always tried to make their lessons convey messages, whatever method they may be using, even the conversational interaction drills mentioned in Chapter 2. Comprehensible input is too simplistic and too all-embracing a notion to produce anything but general guidelines on what a teacher should do. It pays little heed to the actual processes of listening or learning, but promises that everything will be all right if the teacher maximizes comprehensible input. As advice, this is too vague; the teacher can do anything, provided the students have to make sense of the language that is addressed to them – at least anything but make the students produce language, thus eliminating most of the 'British' communicative methods.

Box 7.5 L2 learning and listening processes

- L2 listening is an active process involving background schemas, and so on.
- Both top-down and bottom-up parsing are involved.
- Ineffective L2 students rely too much on bottom-up parsing.

Box 7.6 Listening, reading and teaching

- Build up students' background knowledge.
- Vocabulary should be emphasized in the teaching of texts.
- Allow for students' inherent loss of efficiency in processing the L2.
- Help students to appreciate different cultural schemas.

Teaching involves getting students both to decode messages and to codebreak the language system from what is heard.

Discussion topics

1   How important do you now feel memory is for the student?

2   Do conventional teaching techniques strain students' memory? If so, what can we do about it?

3   What mental scripts pose a particular problem for L2 learners? Are these covered satisfactorily in the classroom?

4   How can one go about supplying the background information students would need for a particular text?

5   Do you agree from your own experience that codebreaking and decoding are separate processes, or do you feel, like Krashen, that they are essentially the same process?

6   Do you approve or disapprove of students codeswitching between their first and their second language in the classroom?

Further reading

For the areas of short-term memory processes, reading and listening, readers can go to the original sources referred to in the chapter, as no book-length SLA research treatments exist that cover the areas adequately. Intercultural training is provided in Cushner and Brislin (1996) *Intercultural Interactions: A Practical Guide.*

Individual differences in L2 users and L2 learners

Mostly this book concentrates on the factors that L2 learners have in common. Teachers usually have to deal with students in groups rather than as individuals; it is what all the class do that is important. However, at the end of the lesson, the group turns into 25 individuals who go off to use the second language for their own needs and in their own ways. Particular features of the learner's personality or mind encourage or inhibit L2 learning. The concern of the present chapter is with how L2 learners vary as individuals, mostly dealing with language in a Lang₅ sense of knowledge in the mind.

This is clearly one difference between first and second language learning. Apart from a handful of children with specific language impairment (SLI), everybody manages to learn to speak their first language, more or less by definition – human language is whatever human beings learn to speak. However, we are all aware of vast differences in how well people can speak a second language. On the one hand you have the Czech-born financier Robert Maxwell, who was able to pass for English, on the other you have Henry Kissinger, forever sounding German. Every teacher knows that some students will learn a second language effortlessly, others will struggle for ever. Some of the explanation for this undoubtedly lies in the different situations; children learn their L1 naturally in the intimate situations of their family; school learners learn an L2 formally in the public situation of the classroom.

However, there still seems to be an element that can only be attributed to the individual; some people can, others cannot. Whatever the teaching method used, some students will prosper, some will not, often despite their best intentions. This chapter will look at some of the ways in which individuals differ that have been linked to how well they learn a second language in the classroom. Some have already been seen in Chapter 6: individuals choose for themselves how to process or learn language. It should be noted that much of this research is applied psychology rather than applied linguistics, making use of concepts and measures from psychology rather than from disciplines to do with language. This sometimes means it treats language teaching as if it were the teaching of any other subject on the curriculum, rather than concentrating on its unique nature.

8.1 Motivation for L2 learning

One reason for some L2 learners doing better than others is undoubtedly because they are better motivated. The child learning a first language does not have good or bad motivation in any meaningful sense. Language is one means through which all children fulfil their everyday needs, however diverse these may be. One might as well ask what the motivation is for walking or for being a human being. In these terms, the second language is superfluous for many classroom learners, who can already communicate with people and use language for thinking. Their mental and social life has been formed through their first language.

The usual meaning of motivation for the teacher is probably the interest that something generates in the students. A particular exercise, a particular topic, a particular song, may interest the students in the class, to the teacher's delight. Obvious enjoyment by the students is not necessarily a sign that learning is taking place – people probably enjoy eating ice cream more than carrots, but which has the better long-term effects? 'What interests the students is not necessarily in the students' interests' (Peters, 1973). Motivation in this sense is a short-term affair, from moment to moment in the class. Vital as it is to the classroom, SLA research has as yet paid little attention to it, as Crookes and Schmidt (1991) point out.

So why do people learn languages? A survey of schools in six countries of the European Union (Bonnet, 2002) found that 94 per cent of children thought that learning English was an advantage for 'communication abroad', 86 per cent for 'facilitation of computer work' and 'comprehension of music texts', down to 64 per cent 'sounds better in English', and 51 per cent 'no expression in national language'. The inclusion of musical lyrics is interesting, showing the continuing influence of pop music sung in English.

Another survey shows the nine most popular reasons across the EU for learning a new language (EuroBarometer, 2006), shown in Figure 8.1; a UK report came up with 700 reasons for studying modern languages (Gallagher-Brett, n.d.). Clearly the reasons why people learn new languages are far wider than for their personal careers.

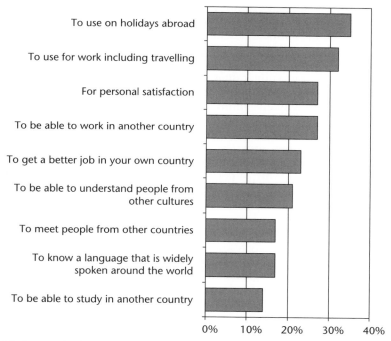

Figure 8.1 Reasons for learning a new language held by Europeans 2005 (Eurobarometer 243)

Motivation in L2 learning, however, has mostly been used to refer to long-term stable attitudes in the students' minds, in particular integrative and instrumental motivation, introduced by Robert Gardner and Wallace Lambert in a series of books and papers (Gardner and Lambert, 1972; Gardner, 1985, 2007). A discussion of the socio-educational model within which these two factors are crucial is provided in Chapter 12. The integrative motivation reflects whether the student identifies with the target culture and people in some sense, or rejects them. The statement in the Focusing questions at the beginning of this section, 'Studying a foreign language is important to my students because they will be able to participate more freely in the activities of other cultural groups', was taken from one used by Gardner for testing integrativeness in the AMTB (Attitudes and Motivation Test Battery), which can be found in full online; a short version is also on the website. The more that a student admires the target culture – reads its literature, visits it on holiday, looks for opportunities to practise the language, and so on – the more successful they will be in the L2 classroom.

Instrumental motivation means learning the language for an ulterior motive unrelated to its use by native speakers – to pass an examination, to get a certain kind of job, and so on; the statement in the Focusing questions, 'Studying a foreign language can be important for my students because it will some day be useful in getting a good job' also comes from Gardner's test battery. I learnt Latin at school because a classical language was at the time an entry requirement for university, and for no other reason.

Some people want to learn a second language with an integrative motivation such as 'I would like to live in the country where it is spoken', or with an instrumental one such as 'For my future career', or indeed with both, or with other motivations entirely. The relative importance of these varies from one part of the world to another. In Montreal, learners of French tend to be integratively motivated, in the Philippines learners of English tend to be instrumentally motivated (Gardner, 1985).

I have been using the Gardner questionnaire with L2 learners in different countries, as seen on the website. English schoolchildren learning French, for example, score 77 per cent for integrative motivation and 70 per cent for instrumental; adult English students score 87 per cent for integrative motivation and 66 per cent for instrumental. Whether the country is Belgium, Poland, Singapore or Taiwan, the integrative motive comes out as more important than the instrumental. Surprisingly, the highest scores for integrative motivation are Taiwan with 88 per cent; the lowest Belgium with 74 per cent. In other words, people want to learn a language for getting on with people more than they do for job opportunities. Coleman (1996) too found that students did better with integrative motivation than with instrumental.

The distinction between integrative and instrumental motivation has been used as a point of reference by many researchers. Zoltan Dornyei (1990) argues that it is biased towards the Canadian situation where there is a particular balance between the two official languages, English and French. He therefore tested the motivation of learners of English in the European situation of Hungary. He found that an instrumental motivation concerned with future careers was indeed very powerful. Though an integrative motivation was also relevant, it was not, as in Canada, related to actual contact with native groups, but to general attitudes and stereotypes; it became more important as the learners advanced in the language, as was the case in England. In addition, he identified two factors relating to classroom learning. One was the need for achievement – trying to improve yourself in general, more specifically to pass an examination; the other, attributions about past failures – whatever else the learners blame their failures on.

Motivation and teaching

Students will find it difficult to learn a second language in the classroom if they have neither instrumental nor integrative motivation, as is probably often the case in school language teaching, or if they feel negatively about bilingualism or are too attached to monolingualism. Schoolchildren have no particular contact with the foreign culture and no particular interest in it, nor do their job prospects depend on it; their attitudes to L2 users may depend more on the stereotypes from their cultural situations than on any real contact. Only 36 per cent of pupils in England thought learning French would be useful to them, according to the Assessment of Performance Unit (1986). Teachers of French in England try to compensate for this lack by stressing the career benefits that knowledge of a second language may bring, or by building up interest in the foreign culture through exchanges with French schools or bringing croissants to class, that is, by cultivating both types of motivation in their students.

Otherwise teachers may have to go along with the students' motivation, or at least be sufficiently aware of the students' motivation so that any problems can be smoothed over. Coursebooks reflect the writer's assessment of the students' motivation. The coursebook *Touchstone* (McCarthy *et al.*, 2005) reflects a world of young people, some overseas students, meeting in the park or living with their parents, babysitting for their friends, interested in TV and films, celebrities and the Internet. This will be valuable to students interested in this lifestyle and an alienating experience for those who prefer something else. *The Beginner's Choice* (Mohamed and Acklam, 1992) features the lives of multi-ethnic students in England with cosmopolitan interests and worldwide contacts for house exchanges and holidays. While this may be motivating for multilingual adult classes in the UK, it is less relevant for single language groups of children in other countries.

In my own coursebook series *English for Life*, the location of the first book *People and Places* (Cook, 1980), is a non-specific fictional English-speaking town called Banford, with a range of old-age pensioners, children, teachers and businessmen. The second book, *Meeting People* (1982), used English in specific locations in different parts of the world, such as Hong Kong, London and New York. The third book, *Living with People* (1983), took the specific location of Oxford in England and used the actual supermarkets, hospitals, radio stations, and so on, as background, including interviews with people who worked in them. The aim was that students at the beginners' level would be motivated by a non-specific English for use anywhere; at the next stage they wanted to use English anywhere in the world; at the advanced stage they might envisage living in an English-speaking country. Coursebooks differ according to whether they prefer integrative or instrumental motivation from the outset, reflecting educational priorities in particular countries, as seen in Chapter 7. An integrative motivation for English may not be admissible in Israel or mainland China, for example.

In a teacher's ideal world, students would enter the classrooms admiring the target culture and language, wanting to get something out of the L2 learning for themselves, eager to experience the benefits of bilingualism and thirsting for knowledge. In practice, teachers have to be aware of the reservations and preconceptions of their students. What they think of the teacher, the course and L2 users in general heavily affects their success. These are the factors that teachers can influence, rather than the learners' more deep-seated motivations.

Motivation also goes in both directions. High motivation is one factor that causes successful learning; in reverse, successful learning causes high motivation. The process of creating successful learning which can spur high motivation may be under the teacher's control, if not the original motivation. The choice of teaching materials and the information content of the lesson, for example, should correspond to the motivations of the students. As Lambert (1990) puts it while talking about minority group children, 'The best way I can see to release the potential [of bilingualism] is to transform their subtractive experiences with bilingualism and biculturalism into additive ones.'

Box 8.1 Motivation and L2 learning

- Both integrative and instrumental motivations may lead to success, but lack of either causes problems.
- Motivation in this sense has great inertia.
- Short-term motivation towards the day-to-day activities in the classroom and general motivations for classroom learning are also important.

8.2 Attitudes

Focusing questions

- What do you think are people's typical reactions to foreigners? To bilinguals? To monolinguals?
- Mark how much you agree with these statements:

It is important to be able to speak two languages.

strongly agree	slightly agree	neither agree nor disagree	slightly disagree	strongly disagree
❑	❑	❑	❑	❑

I will always feel more myself in my first language than in my second.

strongly agree	slightly agree	neither agree nor disagree	slightly disagree	strongly disagree
❑	❑	❑	❑	❑

Keywords

additive bilingualism: L2 learning that adds to the learner's capabilities in some way

subtractive bilingualism: L2 learning that takes away from the learner's capabilities

acculturation: the ways in which L2 users adapt to life with two languages

---

The roots of the motivations discussed in the last section are deep within the students' minds and their cultural backgrounds. One issue is how the student's own cultural background relates to the background projected by the L2 culture. Lambert (1981, 1990) makes an important distinction between 'additive' and 'subtractive' bilingualism. In additive bilingualism, the learners feel they are adding something new to their skills and experience by learning a new language, without taking anything away from what they already know. In subtractive bilingualism, on the other hand, they feel that the learning of a new language threatens what they have already gained for themselves. Successful L2 learning takes place in additive situations; learners who see the second language as diminishing themselves will not succeed. This relates directly to many immigrant or multi-ethnic situations; a group that feels in danger of losing its identity by learning a second language does not learn the second language well. Chilean refugees I taught in the 1970s often lamented their lack of progress in English. However much they consciously wanted to learn English, I felt that they saw it subconsciously as committing themselves to permanent exile and thus to subtracting from their identity as Chileans. It is not motivation for learning as such which is important to teaching, but motivation for learning a particular second language. Monolingual UK children in a survey conducted by the Linguistic Minorities Project (1983) showed a preference in order of popularity for learning German, Italian, Spanish and French. Young people in the European Community as a whole, however, had the order of preference English, Spanish, German, French and Italian (Commission of the European Communities, 1987).

A useful model of attitudes that has been developed over many years is acculturation theory (Berry, 1998). This sees the overall attitudes towards a second culture as coming from the interaction between two distinct questions:

1 Is it considered to be of value to maintain cultural identity and characteristics?

In my experience as a teacher in London, Hungarian students of English tended to merge with the rest of the population; they did not maintain their separate cultural identities. Polish students, on the other hand, stayed within their local community, which had Polish newspapers, theatres, churches and a Saturday school; they were clearly maintaining their cultural differences. What the Poles valued, the Hungarians did not.

2 Is it considered to be of value to maintain relationships with other groups?

Again from my own experience, some students keep to themselves, others mix freely. Greek students in England, for example, usually seem to mix with other Greeks; one of the Essex university bars is informally known as the Greek bar. Japanese students, on the other hand, seem to mix much more with other people, and I am often surprised that two Japanese students in the same university class do not know each other.

According to the acculturation model, both questions could be answered 'yes' or 'no', though of course these would be questions of degree rather than absolute differences. The different combinations of 'yes' and 'no' yield four main patterns of acculturation, as shown in Figure 8.2: integration (Q1 'yes', Q2 'no'), assimilation (Q1 'no', Q2 'yes'), separation (Q1 'yes', Q2 'yes') and marginalization (Q1 'no', Q2 'no').

There are then four possible patterns of acculturation. Marginalization is the least rewarding version, corresponding loosely to Lambert's subtractive bilingualism. Assimilation results in the eventual dying out of the first language – the so-called melting-pot model once used in the USA. Separation results in friction-prone situations like Canada or Belgium, where the languages are spoken in physically separate regions. Integration is a multilingual state where the languages exist alongside each other in harmony.

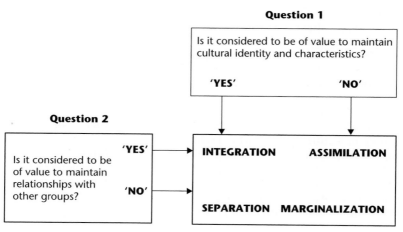

Figure 8.2 The acculturation model

This model is mainly used for groups that have active contact within the same country. My examples come from the use of English in England, not of English in Japan. When there are no actual contacts between the two groups, the model is less relevant, particularly for classroom learners who have no contact with the L2 culture except through their teacher, and whose experience of the L2 culture is through the media or through the stereotypes in their own culture.

A crucial aspect of attitudes is what the students think about people who are L2 users or monolinguals. I asked adults and children in different countries to rate how much they agreed with statements such as 'It is important to be able to speak two languages'. As we see in Figure 8.3, most groups have fairly positive attitudes towards speaking two languages, but the British adults, who were university students, are clearly more positive.

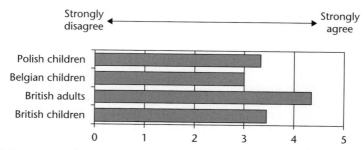

Figure 8.3 Responses to 'It is important to be able to speak two languages'

The same groups were asked about monolingualism. Their answers to the question 'I will always feel more myself in my first language than in my second' are shown in Figure 8.4.

The British children feel less comfortable in the second language than the others; they feel more threatened by the new language.

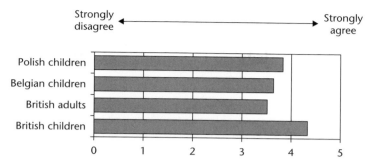

Figure 8.4 Responses to 'I will always feel more myself in my first language than in another language'

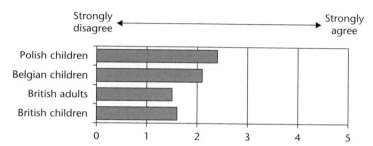

Figure 8.5 Responses to 'People who go to live in a new country should give up their own language'

In this case, rather few of the people feel that learning a second language means forfeiting the first language, a topic developed in the context of language teaching goals in Chapter 11.

Attitudes and language teaching

One crucial point coming out of this is how teaching reinforces unfavourable images of L2 users. Virtually all the L2 users represented in coursebooks, for example, are either students who are in the process of learning the second language or ignorant foreigners using tourist services. Students never see successful L2 users in action and so have no role model to emulate other than the native speaker, which they will very rarely match. The famous people whose photos proliferate in coursebooks tend to be people who are not known as anything other than monolinguals, such as George Clooney, Catherine Zeta Jones and J.K. Rowling, though a few sportspeople who give interviews in English are sometimes mentioned, such as Martina Hingis (*Changes*, Richards, 1998). Successful L2 users such as Gandhi, Einstein, Picasso, Marie Curie and Samuel Beckett, all taken from François Grosjean's list of bilinguals (1982: 285), are never mentioned. It cannot do the students any harm to show them that the world is full of successful L2 users; indeed, as de Swaan (2001) argues, they are necessary for its functioning. We see later that the goals of language teaching include changing people's attitudes towards other cultures and using second languages effectively. These are hardly advanced by showing students either students like themselves or people who are unable to use more than one language.

8.3 Aptitude: are some people better at learning a second language than others?

Focusing questions

- Why do you think some people are good at learning other languages?
- Do you think the same people learn a language well in the classroom as learn it well in a natural setting, or do these demand different qualities?

Keywords

aptitude: this usually means the ability to learn the second language in an academic classroom

Modern Language Aptitude Test (MLAT): testing phonemic coding, grammatical sensitivity, inductive language learning ability, rote learning

memory-based learners: these rely on their memory rather than grammatical sensitivity

analytic learners: these rely on grammatical sensitivity rather than memory

even learners: these rely on both grammatical sensitivity and memory

Everybody knows people who have a knack for learning second languages and others who are rather poor at it. Some immigrants who have been in a country for twenty years are very fluent. Others from the same background and living in the same circumstances for the same amount of time speak the language rather poorly. Given that their ages, motivations, and so on, are the same, why are there such differences? As always, the popular view has to be qualified to some extent. Descriptions of societies where each individual uses several languages daily, such as central Africa or Pakistan, seldom mention people who cannot cope with the demands of a multilingual existence, other than those with academic study problems. Differences in L2 learning ability are apparently only felt in societies where L2 learning is treated as a problem rather than accepted as an everyday fact of life.

So far, the broad term 'knack' for learning languages has been used. The more usual term, however, is 'aptitude'; some people have more aptitude for learning second languages than others. Aptitude has almost invariably been applied to students in classrooms. It does not refer to the knack that some people have for learning in real-life situations, but to the ability to learn from teaching. In the 1950s and 1960s, considerable effort went into establishing what successful students had in common. The Modern Languages Aptitude Test (MLAT) requires the student to carry out L2 learning on a small scale. It incorporates four main factors that predict a student's success in the classroom (Carroll, 1981). These are:

- *Phonemic coding ability*: how well the student can use phonetic script to distinguish phonemes in the language.

- *Grammatical sensitivity*: whether the student can pick out grammatical functions in the sentence.
- *Inductive language learning ability*: whether the student can generalize patterns from one sentence to another.
- *Rote learning*: whether the student can remember vocabulary lists of foreign words paired with translations.

Such tests are not neutral about what happens in a classroom, nor about the goals of language teaching. They assume that learning words by heart is an important part of L2 learning ability, that the spoken language is crucial, and that grammar consists of structural patterns. In short, MLAT predicts how well a student will do in a course that is predominantly audio-lingual in methodology rather than in a course taught by other methods. Wesche (1981) divided Canadian students according to MLAT and other tests into those who were best suited to an 'analytical' approach and those who were best suited to an 'audio-visual' approach. Half she put in the right type of class, half in the wrong (whether this is acceptable behaviour by a teacher is another question). The students in the right class 'achieved superior scores'. It is not just aptitude in general that counts, but the right kind of aptitude for the particular learning situation. Predictions about success need to take into account the kind of classroom that is involved, rather than being biased towards one kind or assuming there is a single factor of aptitude which applies regardless of situation.

Krashen (1981a) suggests aptitude is important for 'formal' situations such as classrooms, and attitude is important for 'informal' real-world situations. While aptitude tests are indeed more or less purpose-designed for classroom learners, this still leaves open the existence of a general knack for learning languages in street settings. Horwitz (1987) anticipated that a test of cognitive level would go with communicative competence, and a test of aptitude with linguistic competence. She found, however, a strong link between the two tests.

Peter Skehan (1986, 1998) developed a slightly different set of factors out of MLAT, namely:

1 *Phonemic coding ability*. This allows the learner to process input more readily and thus to get to more complex areas of processing more easily – supposing that phonemes are in fact relevant to processing, a possibility that was queried in Chapter 2.
2 *Language analytic ability*. This allows the learner to work out the 'rules' of the language and build up the core processes for handling language.
3 *Memory*. This permits the learner to store and retrieve aspects of language rapidly.

These three factors reflect progressively deeper processing of language and hence may change according to the learner's stage. While true in an overall sense, they relate loosely to the ideas of processing and memory seen in Chapter 7. It is unclear, for example, which model of memory might fit this scheme and how analytic ability relates to parsing.

The lack of this 'knack' is sometimes related to other problems that L2 learners have. Richard Sparks and his colleagues (1989) have observed students whose general problems with language have gone unnoticed until they did badly on a foreign language course. They lacked a linguistic coding ability in their first language as well as their second, particularly phonological, and, like dyslexia, apparently unrelated to their intelligence.

Recent work reviewed by Peter Robinson (2005) has tended to split aptitude into separate components, that is, whether people are better at specific aspects of learning rather than overall learning. A particular sensitivity to language may help with FonF activities, for instance. Second language learning in formal conditions may depend in particular on superior cognitive processing ability. Obviously this sees no relationship between second language acquisition in a classroom and first language acquisition, since none of these attributes matters to the native child.

Aptitude and teaching

The problem for language teachers is what to do once the students have been tested for academic language learning aptitude. There are at least four possibilities:

1 *Select students who are likely to succeed in the classroom* and bar those who are likely to fail. This would, however, be unthinkable in most settings with open access to education.

2 *Stream students into different classes for levels of aptitude,* say high-flyers, average and below-average. The Graded Objectives Movement in England, for instance, set the same overall goals for all students at each stage, but allowed them different periods of time for getting there (Harding *et al.*, 1981).

3 *Provide different teaching for different types of aptitude* with different teaching methods and final examinations. This might lead to varied exercises within the class, say, for those with and without phonemic coding ability, to parallel classes, or to self-directed learning. In most educational establishments this would be a luxury in terms of staffing and accommodation, however desirable.

4 *Excuse students with low aptitude from compulsory foreign language requirements.* In some educational systems the students may be required to pass a foreign language which is unrelated to the rest of their course, as I had to take French and Latin to order to read English at university. An extremely low aptitude for L2 learning may be grounds for exemption from this requirement if their other work passes.

The overall lesson is to see students in particular contexts. The student whose performance is dismal in one class may be gifted in another. Any class teaching is a compromise to suit the greatest number of students. Only in individualized or self-directed learning perhaps can this be overcome.

Box 8.2 Aptitude for L2 learning

- Most aptitude tests predict success in L2 academic classrooms.
- Aptitude breaks down into different factors, such as phonemic coding ability and memory.

8.4 Age: are young L2 learners better than old learners?

Undoubtedly, children are popularly believed to be better at learning second languages than adults. People always know one friend or acquaintance who started learning English as an adult and never managed to learn it properly, and another who learnt it as a child and is indistinguishable from a native. Linguists as well as the general public often share this point of view. Chomsky (1959) has talked of the immigrant child learning a language quickly, while 'the subtleties that become second nature to the child may elude his parents despite high motivation and continued practice'. My new postgraduate overseas students prove this annually. They start the year by worrying whether their children will ever cope with English, and they end it by complaining how much better the children speak than themselves.

This belief in the superiority of young learners was enshrined in the critical period hypothesis: the claim that human beings are only capable of learning their first language between the age of two years and the early teens (Lenneberg, 1967). A variety of explanations have been put forward for the apparent decline in adults: physical factors such as the loss of 'plasticity' in the brain and 'lateralization' of the brain; social factors such as the different situations and relationships that children encounter compared to adults; and cognitive explanations such as the interference with natural language learning by the adult's more abstract mode of thinking (Cook, 1986). It has often been concluded that teachers should take advantage of this ease of learning by teaching a second language as early as possible, hence such attempts to teach a foreign language in the primary school as the brief-lived primary school French programme in England. Indeed, the 1990s saw a growth in the UK in 'bilingual' playgroups, teaching French to English-speaking children under the age of 5.

Evidence for the effects of age on L2 learning

Evidence in favour of the superiority of young children, however, has proved surprisingly hard to find. Much research, on the contrary, shows that age is a positive advantage. English-speaking adults and children who had gone to live in Holland were compared using a variety of tests (Snow and Hoefnagel-Höhle, 1977). At the end of three months, the older learners were better at all aspects of Dutch except pronunciation. After a year this advantage had faded and the older learners were better only at vocabulary. Studies in Scandinavia showed that Swedish children improved at learning English throughout the school years, and that Finnish-speaking children under 11 learning Swedish in Sweden were worse than those over 11 (Eckstrand, 1978). Although the total physical response method of teaching, with its emphasis on physical action, appears more suitable to children, when it was used for teaching Russian to adults and children the older students were consistently better (Asher and Price, 1967).

Even with the immersion techniques used in Canada in which English-speaking children are taught the curriculum substantially through French, late immersion pupils were better than early immersion students at marking number agreement on verbs, and at using 'clitic' pronouns ('le', 'me', etc.) in object verb constructions (Harley, 1986). To sum up, if children and adults are compared who are learning a second language in exactly the same way, whether as immigrants to Holland, or by the same method in the classroom, adults are better. The apparent superiority of adults in such controlled research may mean that the typical situations in which children find themselves are better suited to L2 learning than those adults encounter. Age itself is not so important as the different interactions that learners of different ages have with the situation and with other people.

However, there are many who would disagree and find age a burden for L2 learning. These chiefly base themselves on work by Johnson and Newport (1989), who tested Chinese and Korean learners living in the USA and found that the earlier they had arrived there, the better they were at detecting ungrammatical use of grammatical morphemes such as 'the' and plural '-s', and other properties of English such as wh-questions and word order; indeed, those who arrived under the age of 7 were no different from natives. DeKeyser and Larson-Hall (2005) found a negative correlation with age in ten research studies into age of acquisition and grammaticality judgements, that is, older learners tend to do worse.

Usually children are thought to be better at pronunciation in particular. The claim is that an authentic accent cannot be acquired if the second language is learnt after a particular age, say the early teens. For instance, the best age for Cuban immigrants to come to the USA so far as pronunciation is concerned is under 6, the worst over 13 (Asher and Garcia, 1969). Ramsey and Wright (1974) found younger immigrants to Canada had less foreign accent than older ones. But the evidence mostly is not clear-cut. Indeed, Ramsey and Wright's evidence has been challenged by Cummins (1981). Other research shows that when the teaching situation is the same, older children are better than younger children even at pronunciation. An experiment with the learning of Dutch by English children and adults found imitation was more successful with older learners (Snow and Hoefnagel-Höhle, 1977). Neufeld (1978) trained adults with a pronunciation technique that moved them gradually from listening to speaking. After 18 hours of teaching, 9 out of 20 students convinced listeners they were native speakers of Japanese, 8 out of 20 that they were native Chinese speakers.

It has become common to distinguish short-term benefits of youth from long-term disadvantages of age. David Singleton (1989) sums up his authoritative review of age with the statement:

The one interpretation of the evidence which does not appear to run into contradictory data is that in naturalistic situations those whose exposure to a second language begins in childhood in general eventually surpass those whose exposure begins in adulthood, even though the latter usually show some initial advantage over the former.

Adults start more quickly and then slow down. Though children start more slowly, they finish up at a higher level. My own view is that much of the research is still open to other interpretations (Cook, 1986). The studies that show long-term disadvantages mostly use different methodologies and different types of learners from those conducted into short-term learning. In particular, the long-term research has, by coincidence, mostly used immigrants, particularly to the USA, but the short-term research has used learners in educational systems elsewhere. Hence factors such as immigration cannot at present be disentangled from age. Age in itself is no explanation if we cannot explain which aspect of maturation causes the difference, whether physical, social, cognitive or linguistic.

Age and language teaching

How should a language teacher take the student's age into account? One question is when L2 teaching should start. This also involves how long the learners are going to be studying. If they are intending to spend many years learning the second language, they might as well start as children rather than as adults since they will probably end up better speakers. If they are going to learn the second language for a few years and then drop it, like the majority of learners perhaps, there is an advantage for adults, who would reach a higher standard during the same period. But, as Bernard Spolsky (1989a) points out, 'Educational systems usually arrive first at a decision of optimal learning age on political or economic grounds and then seek justification for their decision.' When to teach children a second language is seldom decided by language teachers or L2 learning experts.

A related question is whether the use of teaching methods should vary according to the age of the students. At particular ages students prefer particular methods. Teenagers may dislike any technique that exposes them in public; role play and simulation are in conflict with their adolescent anxieties. Adults can feel they are not learning properly in play-like situations and prefer a conventional, formal style of teaching. Adults learn better than children from the 'childish' activities of total physical response (Asher and Garcia, 1969) – if you can get them to join in! Age is by no means crucial to L2 learning itself. Spolsky (1989a) describes three conditions for L2 learning related to age:

1 *'Formal' classroom learning requires 'skills of abstraction and analysis'*. That is to say, if the teaching method entails sophisticated understanding and reasoning by the student, as for instance a traditional grammar-translation method, then it is better for the student to be older.

2 *The child is more open to L2 learning in informal situations*. Hence children are easier to teach through an informal approach.

3 *The natural L2 situation may favour children*. The teaching of adults requires the creation of language situations in the classroom that in some ways compensate for this lack. An important characteristic of language spoken to small children is that it is concerned with the 'here and now', rather than with the absent objects or the abstract topics that are talked about in adult conversation – adults do not talk about the weather much to a 2-year-old! That is to say, ordinary speech spoken by adults to adults is too sophisticated for L2 learning. Restricting the language spoken to the

beginning L2 learner to make it reflect the here and now could be of benefit. This is reminiscent of the audio-visual and situational teaching methods, which stress the provision of concrete visual information through physical objects or pictures in the early stages of L2 learning. But it may go against the idea that the content of teaching should be relevant and should not be trivial.

Most adaptation to the age of the learner in textbooks probably concerns the presentation of material and topics. Take *New Headway* (Soars and Soars, 2002): the first lesson starts with photographs of opposite sex pairs of smiling people aged between about 18 and 25, dressed in shirts, and looking lively (riding bicycles, drinking Coke), all in colourfully glossy photographs; the topics in the book include holidays and the Internet – what age would you say this was aimed at? The opening lesson of *Hotline* (Hutchinson, 1992) has a photo-strip story of two young men going along a street, one in a suit, the other with trainers and a purple backpack; topics include soap operas such as *Neighbours* and demos against roadworks – what age is this for? The answers from the blurb are 'adult and young adult' and 'teenagers' respectively. But, as always with published materials, they have to aim at an 'average' student; many teenagers may scorn soap operas, many adults have no interest in discussing holidays.

Box 8.3 Age in L2 learning

- To be older leads to better learning in the short term, other things being equal.
- Some research still favours child superiority at pronunciation, but not reliably.
- Children get to a higher level of proficiency in the long term than those who start L2 learning while older, perhaps because adults slow down.

8.5 Are other personality traits important to L2 learning?

Focusing questions

- Do you tend to straighten pictures if they are crooked?
- What type of personality do you think is the mark of a successful student?

Keywords

cognitive style: a person's typical ways of thinking, seen as a continuum between field-dependent (FD) cognitive style, in which thinking relates to context, and field-independent (FI) style, in which it is independent of context

extrovert and introvert: people's personalities vary between those who relate to objects outside themselves (extroverts) and those who relate to the contents of their own minds (introverts)

Though there has been research into how other variations between L2 learners contribute to their final success, it has produced a mass of conflicting answers. Mostly, isolated areas have been looked at rather than the learner as a whole. Much of the research is based on the non-uniqueness view of language, and so assumes that L2 learning varies in the same way as other types of learning, say learning to drive or to type. One piece of research shows that something is beneficial; a second piece of research following up the same issue shows it is harmful. Presumably this conflict demonstrates the complexity of the learning process and the varieties of situation in which L2 learning occurs. But this is slender consolation to teachers, who want a straight answer.

Cognitive style

The term 'cognitive style' refers to a technical psychological distinction between typical ways of thinking. Imagine standing in a room that is slowly leaning to one side without the people inside it knowing. Some people attempt to stand upright, others lean so that they are parallel to the walls. Those who lean have a field-dependent (FD) cognitive style; that is, their thinking relates to their surroundings. Those who stand upright have a field-independent (FI) style; they think independently of their surroundings. The usual test for cognitive style is less dramatic, relying on distinguishing shapes in pictures and is thus called the embedded figures test. Those who can pick out shapes despite confusing backgrounds are field-independent, those who cannot are field-dependent. My own informal check is whether a person adjusts pictures that are hanging crookedly or does not. These are tendencies rather than absolutes; any individual is somewhere on the continuum between the poles of FI and FD.

A difference in cognitive style might well make a difference to success in L2 learning – another aspect of aptitude. Most researchers have found that a tendency towards FI (field independence) helps the student with conventional classroom learning (Alptekin and Atakan, 1990). This seems obvious in a sense, in that formal education in the West successively pushes students up the rungs of a ladder of abstraction, away from the concrete (Donaldson, 1978). Hansen and Stansfield (1981) used three tests with L2 learners: those that measured the ability to communicate, those that measured linguistic knowledge, and those that measured both together. FI learners had slight advantages for communicative tasks, greater advantages for academic tasks, and the greatest advantages for the combined tasks. However, Bacon (1987) later found no differences between FD and FI students in terms of how much they spoke and how well they spoke. This illustrates again the interaction between student and teaching method; not all methods suit all students.

Cognitive style varies to some extent from one culture to another. There are variations between learners on different islands in the Pacific and between different sexes, though field independence tends to go with good scores on a cloze test (Hansen, 1984). Indeed, there are massive cross-cultural differences in these measures. To take Chinese as an example, first of all there is a general cultural difference between East and West as to the importance of foreground versus background, which affects the issue; second, the embedded figures test does not work, since people who are users of character-based scripts find it much easier to see embedded figures, and other tests have to be used (Nisbett, 2003).

There is no general reason why FI people in general should be better or worse at cognitive functioning than those who are FD. FI and FD are simply two styles of thinking. A challenge has been posed to the use of FI/FD in second language acquisition by Roger Griffiths and Ronald Sheen (1992), who argue that the concept has not been sufficiently well defined in the research and is no longer of much interest within the discipline of psychology, from which it came.

Personality differences

Perhaps an outgoing, sociable person learns a second language better than a reserved, shy person. Again, the connection is not usually so straightforward. Some researchers have investigated the familiar division between extrovert and introvert personalities. In Jungian psychology the distinction applies to two tendencies in the way that people interact with the world. Some people relate to objects outside them, some to the interior world. Rossier (1975) found a link between extroversion and oral fluency. Dewaele and Furnham (1999) found that more complex tasks were easier for extrovert learners. There would seem to be a fairly obvious connection to language teaching methods. The introverts might be expected to prefer academic teaching that emphasises individual learning and language knowledge; the extroverts audio-lingual or communicative teaching that emphasizes group participation and social know-how.

Other individual variation

What else? Many other variations in the individual's mental make-up have been checked against L2 success.

Intelligence

Intelligence has some connection with school performance. There are links between intelligence and aptitude in classrooms, as might be expected (Genesee, 1976).

Sex differences

Sex differences have also been investigated. The UK Assessment of Performance Unit (1986) found English girls were better at French than English boys in all skills except speaking. In my experience of talking with teachers it is true in every country that second languages are more popular school subjects among girls. About 70 per cent of undergraduates studying modern languages in the UK are women (Coleman, 1996). Using SILL, Green and Oxford (1995) found that women overall used more learning strategies than men, particularly social strategies such as 'Ask other person to slow down or repeat', and meaning strategies such as 'Review English lessons often'. Coleman (1996) found that women students were more embarrassed by their mistakes.

Level of first language

Level of first language is also relevant. Some studies support the commonly held teacher's view that children who are more advanced in their first language are better at their second language (Skehan, 1989).

Empathy

Those students who are able to empathize with the feelings of others are better at learning L2 pronunciation, though this depends to some extent on the language the students are acquiring (Guiora et al., 1972).

Of course, all teachers have their own pet beliefs about factors that are crucial to L2 learning. One of my own suspicions is that the time of year when the student was born makes a difference, due in England, not to astrological sign, but to the extra schooling children get if they are born at certain times. But my own checks with the university computer cannot seem to prove a link between choosing a language degree and being born in a particular month.

Many of the factors in this chapter cannot be affected by the teacher. Age cannot be changed, nor can aptitude, intelligence and most areas of personality. As teachers cannot change them, they have to live with them. In other words, teaching has to recognize the differences between students. At a gross level this means catering for the factors that a class has in common, say, age and type of motivation. At a finer level the teacher has to cater for the differences between individuals in the class, by providing opportunities for each of them to benefit in their own way: the same teaching can be taken in different ways by different students. To some teachers this is not sufficient; nothing will do but complete individualization so that each student has his or her own unique course. For class teaching, the aspects in which students are different have to be balanced against those that they share. Much L2 learning is common ground, whatever the individual differences between learners may be.

Box 8.4 Individual differences and language teaching

- The variety and nature of motivations need to be recognized.
- Teachers should work with, not against, student motivation in materials and content.
- Important attitudes in L2 learners include maintaining cultural identity, maintaining relationships with other groups, beliefs about bilingualism, beliefs about monolingualism.
- Students without aptitude can be excluded (if allowable on other grounds).
- Different teaching can be provided for learners with different types of aptitude, even streaming into fast and slow streams.
- Age issues affect when and how to teach the second language.

Discussion topics

1   Suggest three ways in which you would increase (a) positive short-term motivation and (b) integrative motivation in your students.

2   Is it really possible to *change* the students' underlying motivation, as opposed to simply increasing it?

3   What should be done with students who have a low aptitude for L2 learning?

4   What do you think is the best age to learn a foreign language?

5   Name two teaching techniques that would work best with adults, two with children.

6   How can one cater for different personality types in the same classroom?

7   If girls really are better at L2 learning than boys, what could the reason be?

Further reading

Main sources for this chapter are Skehan (1989) *Individual Differences in Second-language Learning;* Gardner (1985) *Social Psychology and Second Language Learning;* and Singleton (1989) *Language Acquisition: The Age Factor.* Coverage from a psychologist's point of view can be found in Dornyei's (2001) *Teaching and Researching Motivation* and (2005) *The Psychology of the Language Learner.*

Classroom interaction and Conversation Analysis 9

9.1 Language and interaction inside the classroom

Focusing questions

- Do people learn a second language best inside or outside a classroom?
- Do you think of the classroom as a real situation of its own or as something artificial?
- How much of the class time does the teacher speak? How much *should* they speak?

Keywords

leader and follower: in some types of conversation one person has the right to lead the conversation while the others follow his or her lead
teacher talk: the speech supplied by the teacher rather than the students
initiation: the opening move by the teacher
response: the student response to the teacher's opening move
feedback: teacher evaluation of the student response
authentic speech: 'an authentic text is a text that was created to fulfil some social purpose in the language community in which it was produced' (Little *et al.*, 1988)

L2 learning inside and outside classrooms

Is L2 learning the same inside the classroom as outside? One extreme point of view sees the L2 classroom as a world of its own. Teachers and books slip into the habit of referring to the world outside the classroom as the 'real world' – *New Cutting Edge* (Cunningham *et al.*, 2005) has a section in each unit called 'Real life' – denying that the classroom is a part of the real world for its participants. What the students are doing in a classroom may be quite different from the 'natural' ways of learning language they would experience in an uncontrolled situation. Thus some teaching exploits deliberately 'unnatural' L2 learning. Focus on form (FonF), for instance, is exploiting the other faculties the mind has available for L2 learning, rather than making use of the 'natural' processes of the language faculty specifically dedicated to language learning. At the opposite extreme is the view that all L2 learning, or indeed all language learning of the first or second language, is the same. The classroom, at best, exploits this natural learning, and at worst puts barriers in its way. What happens in class has to be as 'natural' as possible, dodging the question of the bitter disputes over exactly what natural language learning might be.

What evidence is there one way or the other? Some areas of grammar have been investigated in classrooms as well as in the world outside. Learners appear to go through the same sequence of acquisition in both situations, for example, German children learning English at school compared with those learning outside (Felix, 1981). Three children learning English as a second language in London over a period of time started by producing 'no' by itself as a separate sentence 'Red, no' (Ellis, 1986). They said sentences with external negation, 'No play baseball' before those with internal negation 'I'm no drawing chair.' This happened slowly over the period of a year, only one child producing a single sentence with internal negation 'This man can't read.' The children were passing through the standard stages in the acquisition of negation despite the fact that they were actually being taught negation. So students in classrooms learn some aspects of second languages in much the same way as learners who never go near them.

The language of classrooms in general

Let us start with the language interaction common to all classrooms. In most face-to-face conversation people interact with each other and adapt what they are saying to the listener's reactions. Some situations, however, give one participant a more directive role than the others; one person can be the 'leader' who takes the initiative, the others are 'followers' who respond to it. For example, an interviewer has the right to guide the conversation and to ask questions that would be out of place in other situations. 'How old are you?' addressed to an adult is unthinkable except in an interview. In the classroom this overall 'leader' role falls to the teacher. The exchange of turns between listeners and speakers is under the teacher's overall guidance, overtly or covertly. So, not surprisingly, about 70 per cent of the utterances in most classrooms come from the teacher.

In first language acquisition, adults assume the basic right to direct the conversation when talking to children; 'How old are you?' is a frequent question from adults to children. The same assumption is often true when talking to foreign adults.

The difference between the classroom and other leader-directed conversations lies in the way that the conversation is directed. Let us take a short classroom exchange from Sinclair and Coulthard (1975):

Teacher: Can you tell me why you eat all that food? Yes.
Pupil: To keep you strong.
Teacher: To keep you strong. Yes. To keep you strong. Why do you want to be strong? . . .

This exchange has three main moves:

1 **Initiation**. The teacher takes the initiative by requiring something of the student, say through a question such as, 'Can you tell me why you eat all that food?' The move starts off the exchange; the teacher acts as leader.

2 **Response**. Next the student does whatever is required, here answering the question by saying, 'To keep you strong'. So the move responds to the teacher's initiation; the student acts as follower.

3 **Feedback**. The teacher does not go straight on to the next initiation but announces whether the student is right or wrong, 'To keep you strong. Yes.' The teacher evaluates the student's behaviour and comments on it in a way that would be impossible outside the classroom.

This three-move structure of initiation, response and feedback – or IRF as it is known – is very frequent in teaching; indeed some people see it as an important way in which parents speak to their children. Even in lectures, teachers sometimes attempt feedback moves with comments such as, 'That was a good question.' Some language teaching styles rely heavily on this classroom structure. IRF was, after all, the format of the classic language laboratory drill. Other styles of teaching, such as the communicative, may discourage it because it is restricted to classroom language rather than being generally applicable. Nor is IRF the only characteristic of such exchanges. One common feature, illustrated by the 'Yes' in 'Can you tell me why you eat all that food? Yes', is that the teacher selects and approves who is to speak next, a feature common to all leader/follower situations, ranging from the chairperson at a committee meeting to congressional committees of investigation.

Language in the language teaching classroom

Are language teaching classrooms different from other classrooms? Craig Chaudron (1988) cited figures from various sources which show that teacher talk takes up 77 per cent of the time in bilingual classrooms in Canada, 69 per cent in immersion classes, and 61 per cent in foreign language classrooms. Werner Hullen (1989) found that 75 per cent of the utterances in German classrooms came from the teacher. A massive amount of the language of the classroom is provided by the teacher.

The L2 teaching classroom is unique, however, in that language is involved in two distinct ways. First of all, the organization and control of the classroom take place through language; second, language is the actual subject matter that is being taught; if the teacher asks 'How old are you?' in the second language, the student does not know whether it is a genuine question or a display question practising a question structure. A school subject like physics does not turn the academic subject back on itself. Physics is not taught through physics in the same way that language is taught through language.

This twofold involvement of language creates a particular problem for L2 teaching. The students and teachers are interacting through language in the classroom, using the strategies and moves that form part of their normal classroom behaviour. But at the same time the L2 strategies and moves are the behaviour the learner is aiming at, the objectives of the teaching. The teacher has to be able to manage the class through one type of language, at the same time as getting the student to acquire another type. There is a duality about much language teaching which is absent from other school subjects, because language has to fulfil its normal classroom role as well as making up the content of the class; it functions on two levels. N.S. Prabhu (1987) suggests dealing with this problem by treating the classroom solely as a classroom: 'learners' responses arose from their role as learners, not from assumed roles in simulated situations or from their individual lives outside the classroom': the real language of the classroom is classroom language.

The teacher's language is particularly important to language teaching. Teachers of physics adapt their speech to suit the level of comprehension of their pupils, but this is only indirectly connected to their subject matter. The students are not literally learning the physics teacher's language. Teachers of languages who adapt their speech directly affect the subject matter: language itself. Like most teachers, I have felt while teaching that I was adapting the grammatical structures and the vocabulary I used to the students' level.

But is this subjective feeling right? Do teachers really adapt their speech to the level of the learner or do they simply believe they do so? What is more, do such changes actually benefit the students? Observation of teachers confirms there is indeed adaptation of several kinds. Steven Gaies (1979) recorded student-teachers teaching EFL in the classroom. At each of four levels, from beginners to advanced, their speech increased in syntactic complexity. Even at the advanced level it was still less complicated than their speech to their fellow students. Craig Chaudron (1983) compared a teacher lecturing on the same topic to native and non-native speakers. He found considerable simplification and rephrasing in vocabulary: 'clinging' became 'holding on tightly', and 'ironic' became 'funny'. He felt that the teacher's compulsion to express complex content simply often led to 'ambiguous over-simplification on the one hand and confusingly redundant over-elaboration on the other'. Hullen (1989) found the feedback move was prominent with about 30 per cent of teacher's remarks consisting of 'right', 'ah', 'okay', and so on.

What does this high proportion of teacher talk mean for L2 teaching? Several teaching methods have tried to maximize the amount of speaking by the student. The audio-lingual method fitted in with the language laboratory precisely because it increased each student's share of speaking time. Task-based teaching methods support pair work and group work partly because they give each student the chance to talk as much as possible. Other methods do not share the opinion that teacher talk should be minimized. Conventional academic teaching emphasises factual information coming from the teacher. Listening-based teaching sees most value in the students extracting information from what they hear rather than in speaking themselves. One argument for less speech by the students is that the sentences the students hear will at least be correct examples of the target language, not samples of the interlanguages of their fellow students.

Authentic and non-authentic language

A further distinction is between authentic and non-authentic language. Here is the opening dialogue from *New English File* (Oxenden *et al.*, 2004):

A: Hi. I'm Tom. What's your name?
B: Anna.
A: Sorry?
B: Anna!

This is non-authentic language specially constructed for its teaching potential. People in real-life conversations do not speak in full grammatical sentences and do not keep to a clear sequence of turns. Nor do they tend to go up to complete strangers and introduce themselves, except in certain socially sanctioned situations (speed-dating?).

Instead they speak like these two people, recorded while talking about ghosts for my coursebook *English Topics* (Cook, 1975):

> Mrs Bagg: Oh, how extraordinary.
> Jenny Drew: So...'cos quite a quite a lot of things like that.
> Mrs Bagg: I mean were they frightened? 'Cos I think if I actually...
> Jenny Drew: No.
> Mrs Bagg: ...saw a ghost because I don't believe in them really, I would be frightened, you know to think that I was completely wrong.

This is an example of authentic language, defined by David Little *et al.* (1988) as language 'created to fulfil some social purpose in the language community in which it was produced'. Until recently, teaching provided the students with specially adapted language, not only simplified in terms of syntax and confined in vocabulary, but also tidied up in terms of discourse structure. The belief was that such non-authentic language was vital to L2 learning.

With the advent of methods that looked at the communicative situations the students were going to encounter, it seemed clear that the students were handicapped by never hearing authentic speech in all its richness and diversity. Hence exercises and courses have proliferated that turn away from specially constructed classroom language to pieces of language that have really been used by native speakers, whether tapes of conversations, advertisements from magazines, train timetables, or a thousand and one other sources. In most countries it is possible to use authentic texts based on local circumstances taken from local English-language newspapers, such as the *Jerusalem Post* or the *Buenos Aires Herald*, often available from the Internet these days, for example the *Athens News*, the *Straits Times* (Singapore) or *Granma* (Havana).

 Two justifications for the use of authentic text in communicative teaching are put forward by Little *et al.* (1988):

- **Motivation and interest**. Students will be better motivated by texts that have served a real communicative purpose.

- **Acquisition-promoting content**. Authentic texts provide a rich source of natural language for the learner to acquire language from.

Additional reasons are:

- **Filling in language gaps**. Designers of coursebooks and syllabuses may miss some of the aspects of language used in real-life situations; we often do not know what people actually say in railway stations or offices. This lack can be filled most easily by giving students the appropriate real-life language taken from situations appropriate to their needs.

- **Showing L2 users in action**. While it may be hard for the teacher or coursebook writer to imitate L2 users, authentic L2-use texts can do this readily, for example, the English-speaking newspapers mentioned above.

The fact that the language is authentic does not in itself make it more difficult than specially written language. Difficulty depends partly on the amount of material that is used. A BBC Russian course recorded people on the streets of Moscow saying 'Zdravstvujte' (Hello) to the cameraman – totally authentic, but no problem for the students. The recording or text does not have to consist of many words to be authentic: 'EXIT', 'This door is alarmed', 'Ladies', to take three authentic written signs. Difficulty also depends on the task that is used with the material. You can play a recording of two philosophers discussing the nature of the universe to beginners so long as all you ask them to do is identify which is a man, which a woman, or who is angry, who is calm, or indeed who said 'well' most often.

It is up to the teacher whether authentic language should be used in the classroom or whether non-authentic language reflects a legitimate way into the language. In other words, the choice is between decoding and codebreaking: are the processes of learning similar to those of use, so that authentic language is needed, or are they different, so that appropriate non-authentic language is helpful? Other factors involved in this decision will be the goals of the students and other constraints of the teaching situation. And of course, the classroom is a classroom; authentic language, by definition, is not normal classroom language and is being used for purposes quite other than those of its original speakers, however well intentioned the teacher.

One problem is that many teachers still think of an L2 class as language practice above all else, not related to 'real' communication – mock communication disguising language teaching points or tasks. If the student's answer leads away from the language point that is being pursued, it is ignored, however promising the discussion might seem. Seldom does genuine communication take place in which the students and teacher develop a communicative exchange leading away from the language teaching point. Yet one of the early claims of the direct method pioneers was that genuine interchange of ideas was possible in the classroom. Lambert Sauveur boasted that he could give a beginners' class on any topic; when challenged to give a class on God, he succeeded brilliantly (Howatt, 2004). The IRF exchange, particularly the teacher's evaluation move, is a constant reminder to the students that they are engaged in language practice, not use.

Box 9.1 Language in classroom L2 learning

- Teacher talk makes up around 70 per cent of classroom language.
- Language teaching classrooms are different from other classrooms because language is not just the medium but also the content.
- Authentic speech may motivate and help communicative goals, if decoding equates with codebreaking.
- Non-authentic speech may be specially tailored to students' learning needs if codebreaking is different from decoding.
- Teaching styles of interaction using IRF may interfere with ordinary communicative interaction.

9.2 Language input and language learning

Focusing questions

- How and why should language be simplified for use in the classroom?
- In what ways do you adapt your speech to children? To foreigners?
- When you were at school, did you think of your teachers as wise superior beings or as helpful equals?

Keywords

baby talk, motherese, foreigner talk: forms of language specially designed for listeners without full competence in a language
postfigurative: a culture in which people learn from older, wiser guardians of knowledge
cofigurative: a culture in which people learn from their equals
prefigurative: a culture in which people learn from their juniors

The language of the language teaching classroom is distinctive because its purpose is to enable language learning to take place. All languages have special varieties for talking to speakers who are believed not to speak very well. For example, 'baby talk', or 'motherese', is used when talking to babies. These varieties have similar characteristics in many languages: exaggerated changes of pitch, louder volume, 'simpler' grammar, special words such as those for 'dog': 'bow-wow' (English), 'wan wan' (Japanese) and 'hawhaw' (Moroccan Arabic).

Barbara Freed (1980) found that 'foreigner talk' addressed to non-native speakers also had simple grammar and a high proportion of questions with 'unmoved' question words, for example 'You will return to your country when?' rather than 'When will you return to your country?' But the functions of language in foreigner talk were more directed at the exchange of information than at controlling the person's behaviour, as in baby talk. Most teachers rarely fall totally into this style of speech. Nevertheless, experienced teachers use a distinct type of speech and gesture when speaking to foreigners.

The fact that baby talk exists, however, does not prove that it has any effect on learning. In other words, baby talk and foreigner talk varieties of language reflect what people *believe* less proficient speakers need – but their beliefs may be wrong. Many child language researchers feel that acquiring the first language does not depend on some special aspect of the language that the child hears. The effects of baby talk on children's first language development have so far been impossible to prove. It may well be that its characteristics are beneficial, but this is chiefly a matter of belief, given the many children who acquire the first language despite far from optimal conditions. Some further aspects of input in language learning are discussed in relation to the Universal Grammar (UG) model in Chapter 12.

Teaching and language input

L2 learning differs from L1 learning in that the majority of students fall by the wayside before they get to a high level. An important element in L2 success appears to be how learners are treated: the teaching method they encounter, the language they hear and the environment in which they are learning. The purpose of language teaching in one sense is to provide optimal samples of language for the learner to profit from – the best 'input' to the process of language learning. Everything the teacher does provides the learners with opportunities for encountering the language.

At this point, communicative and task-based methods of teaching mostly part company with the listening-based methods. The communicative methods have emphasized the learners' dual roles as listeners and as speakers. A typical exercise requires students to take both roles in a conversation and not only to understand the information they are listening to, but also to try to express it themselves. They are receiving input both from the teacher and from their peers in the class. The listening-based methods, however, confine the student to the role of listener. In a technique such as total physical response, the students listen and carry out commands, but they do not have to speak. Hence the input they receive is totally controlled by the teacher. An example from Krashen and Terrell's *The Natural Approach* (1983) consists of getting the students to choose between pictures according to the teacher's description: 'There are two men in this picture. They are young. They are boxing.' This approach was encapsulated in Krashen's slogan, 'Maximize comprehensible input' (Krashen, 1981b).

Proponents of communicative teaching methods have often felt that it is beneficial for students to listen to authentic language consisting of judiciously chosen samples of unexpurgated native speech, as we have seen. Authentic speech evidently needs to be made comprehensible in one way or another if it is to be useful. Its lack of any concession to the learner needs to be compensated for in some way, for example, with explanations or visuals.

Implications for teaching

One overall moral is that there is no such thing as *the* classroom, as classrooms vary in so many ways. Some students have been hypnotized, some have studied in their sleep, some have seen Lego blocks built into sentences, some have had the world of meaning reduced to a set of coloured sticks, some have sat in groups and bared their souls, others have sat in language laboratories repeating after the tape. The classroom is a variable, not a constant. Teachers can shape it to suit their students and their aims, within the limits set by their school or educational system. Nor should we forget that instruction does not only take place in classrooms. The self-motivated autonomous student can learn as efficiently as any taught in a class.

What advice can be given about input in the classroom?

- *Be aware of the two levels at which language enters into the classroom.* Overusing the 'leader' pattern of IRF teacher talk undermines a communicative classroom by destroying the usual give-and-take typical outside the classroom.
- *Be aware of the different sources of input.* Language may come first from the teacher, second from the textbook or teaching materials, and third from the

other students, not to mention sources outside the classroom. All these provide different types of language: the teacher the genuine language of the classroom, the textbook purpose-designed non-authentic language or authentic language taken out of its usual context, the other students' interlanguage full of non-native-like forms but at the same time genuine communicative interaction.

- *The input that the students are getting is far more than just the sentences they encounter.* The whole context provides language; this includes the patterns of interaction between teacher and class, and between students in the class, down to the actual gestures used. Many teachers ostensibly encourage spontaneous natural interaction from the students, but they still betray that they are teachers controlling a class with every gesture they make.

- *Students learn what they are taught.* This truism has often been applied to language classrooms: in general, students taught by listening methods turn out to be better at listening; students taught through reading are better at reading. The major source of language available to many learners is what they encounter in the classroom. This biases their knowledge in particular ways. A teacher I observed was insisting that the students used the present continuous; hardly surprisingly his students were later saying things like, 'I'm catching the bus every morning.' The teacher's responsibility is to make certain that the language input which is provided is sufficient for the student to gain the appropriate type of language knowledge and that it does not distort it in crucial ways. While in many respects L2 learners follow their own developmental sequences, and so on, their classroom input affects their language in broad terms.

Much of what we have seen so far implies that language itself is the most important ingredient in the classroom, the core of the syllabus, the basis for the teaching technique, and the underlying skeleton of the class, whether considered as conversational interaction, authentic or non-authentic, simplified grammatical structures, or whatever. This has been challenged by those who see the classroom as a unique situation with its own rationale. Prabhu (1987), for example, talked of how the classroom consisted of particular processes and activities; his celebrated work in Bangalore organized language teaching around the activities that could be done in the classroom: interpreting information in tables, working out distances, and so on. Michael Long and Graham Crookes (1993) describe teaching arranged around pedagogic tasks 'which provide a vehicle for the presentation of appropriate language samples to learners'. A task has an objective and has to be based on tasks that the students need in their lives. Language is far from the crucial factor in the language teaching classroom; the students will suffer if all the teacher's attention goes on organizing language content and interaction. The task-based learning approach is described further in Chapter 13.

Culture and the classroom

Two links with other areas must be made. One concerns the individual in the classroom, the other the classroom as part of the society. The individual's attitudes to the classroom form an important component in L2 learning. The student's attitudes towards the learning situation, as measured by feelings about the classroom teacher and level of anxiety about the classroom, contribute to the student's motivation. This is also discussed in Chapter 8. But there may also be a sharp opposition between different types of teacher. Adrian Holliday (1994) describes the difference between the social context of the expatriate EFL teacher and the non-native teacher who lives in that country. These can have very different interpretations of the same classroom, the one based on the West-dominated 'professionalism' of the EFL tradition, the other on the local educational system. Holliday tells of an encounter in Egypt between Beatrice, an expatriate lecturer, and Dr Anwar, a local member of an EFL project. To the expatriate it was a discussion among equals about their experiences in the language laboratory; to Dr Anwar it was a waste of his expert time. Teachers may then inhabit different cultures of their own, as well as the differences between the cultures of the student and the target language. Differences between native and non-native teachers are discussed in Chapter 10.

So far as the society is concerned, the expectations of the students and teachers about the classroom depend on their culture. Margaret Mead (1970) makes a useful division between **postfigurative** societies in which people learn from wise elders, **cofigurative** societies in which they learn from their equals, and **prefigurative** societies in which they learn from their juniors. Many cultures view education as postfigurative. The classroom to them is a place in which the wise teacher imparts knowledge to the students. Hence they naturally favour teaching methods that transfer knowledge explicitly from the teacher to the student, such as academic teaching methods. Other cultures see education cofiguratively. The teacher designs opportunities for the students to learn from each other. Hence they prefer teaching methods that encourage group work, pair work and task-based learning. Mead feels that modern technological societies are often prefigurative, as witnessed by the ease with which teenagers master computers compared to their parents. There is not, to my knowledge, a language teaching parallel to the prefigurative type, unless in certain 'alternative' methods in which the teacher is subordinated to the students' whims.

So certain teaching methods will be dangerous to handle in particular societies. Whatever the merits of the communicative method, its attempts to promote non-teacher-controlled activities in China were at first perceived as insults to the Confucian ethos of the classroom, which emphasized the benefits of learning texts by heart (Sampson, 1984). In Mead's terms, a cofigurative method was being used in a postfigurative classroom. A teaching method has to suit the beliefs of the society about what activities are proper for classrooms. It is not usually part of the language teacher's brief to decide on the overall concept of the classroom in a society. The different links between L2 learning and societies are followed up in Chapter 10.

Box 9.2 Classroom input and language teaching

- Everything the teacher does provides the learner with opportunities for encountering the language.
- Be aware of the two levels at which language enters into the classroom.
- Be aware of the different sources of input.
- The input that the students are getting is far more than just the sentences they encounter.
- Students learn what they are taught (in some sense).
- What works in the classroom in one cultural milieu may not work in another.

9.3 Describing conversation

Focusing questions

- Think of a way of starting a conversation. When would you use it? How would you teach it?
- What do you do if you realize someone has not understood what you have said?
- How do you respond when someone pays you a compliment?

Keyword

Conversation Analysis: the discipline that studies conversational interaction by close analysis of transcripts (**Note**: this is often abbreviated to CA; in the older SLA literature, however, CA stands for Contrastive Analysis, mentioned in Chapter 1)
adjacency pair: a pair of conversational turns such as question and answer
repair: the way that the speaker or listener gets the interaction back on course when something goes wrong

When people talk to each other, they are constructing a conversation by making particular moves and by responding to the moves of others. For 50 years people have been trying to describe how this works.

The first interest in SLA research came through the work of Evelyn Hatch and her associates, who called her approach 'discourse analysis' (Hatch, 1978). The starting point was how L2 users interact with native speakers. The opening move in a conversation is to get someone's attention:

A: Hi.

Next the participants need to establish what they are talking about – *topic nomination*:

A: Did you see the news in the paper?
At last they can say something about the topic:
A: There's been a bridge disaster.

In a second language we may need to establish the topic more firmly. The listener has to make certain they have grasped what is being talked about – *topic identification*:

B: There's been a what?

To which the other person may respond with *topic clarification*:

A: An accident with a bridge that collapsed.

Often we need *repairs* to keep the conversation going:

B: A fridge that collapsed?
A: No, a bridge.

Conversation is driven by the attempt to get meanings across to someone else; it comes out of the topic we want to talk about.

My beginners' coursebook, *People and Places* (Cook, 1980), was based partly on the ideas of Hatch (1978), using conversational categories such as *initiating topic* ('You know Edna?'), *checking* ('What?'), *repeating* ('Edna?'), *stating facts* ('Edna is an old-age-pensioner') and *confirming* ('Yes, that's right'). These were incorporated into a teaching exercise called a **conversational exchange**. First students get some sample exchanges, with alternative forms for each move:

identifying:	A: My name's Mickey Mouse.
checking:	B: What?
confirming:	A: Mickey Mouse.
acknowledging:	B: Oh I see, Mickey Mouse.

Then they have to invent exchanges with other celebrity names taken from pictures; finally they supply names of their own to put into the exchange. While this teaching exercise reflected conversational interaction, it was highly controlled; the students were not negotiating for meaning so much as learning the patterns and moves for negotiating for meaning. A similar type of exercise is used in *Touchstone* (McCarthy *et al.*, 2005); students match questions and answers in a dialogue, 'Complete the conversations' in fill-in sentences and then practise correct responses to 'Thank you' and 'I'm sorry'.

This view of conversation relates to the speech act theory derived from philosophy or linguistics, which assigns functions to utterances: 'Open the door' is making a command; 'Why is the door open?' is making a question, and so on. This is closer to Lang$_4$, the social side of language. Such functions of speech formed the basis for the communicative teaching approach, seen in the functional/notional syllabus advocated by David Wilkins (1972). Its influence can be seen in almost any coursebook to this day. *Just Right* (Harmer, 2004), for instance, teaches functions such as 'making promises', 'paying compliments' and 'giving opinions'.

The difficulty with teaching functions has often been the disconnection from the structure of conversation involved in teaching one function at a time; how do you practise paying compliments without knowing when to pay a compliment or how to reply to it? Hatch's conversational structure provided one way of connecting functions to conversational moves. Hence *People and Places* taught complimenting as part of a three-move interaction:

stating:	Simon: This is my new jacket.
exclaiming:	Helen: What a smart jacket!
complimenting:	Helen: It suits you.

Students had to continue in this vein by commenting on the other things that Simon and Helen were wearing in their pictures and then describing the clothes of other students.

Paul Seedhouse (2004) points out how this type of approach differs from the discipline of Conversation Analysis (CA) that it superficially resembles. CA does not try to establish categories and units in a fixed structure; instead it looks at a slice of conversational interaction and tries to work out what is going on from the point of view of the participants; 'For those trying to understand a bit of talk, the key question about any of its aspects is – *why that now?*' (Schegloff *et al.*, 2002).

The most obvious feature of interaction is that people take turns to speak. One exchange of turns is the **adjacency pair**:

A: What's the time?
B: Five o'clock.

The move by the first speaker is followed by a related move by the second speaker, chosen out of a limited range of acceptable options. Sometimes, as in question and answer, the second speaker has little choice; after compliments, there may be a less conventional range of responses; after stating opinion:

'I love Picasso's blue period.'

there may be an obvious agreeing/disagreeing move:

'I can't stand it.'

or a more nebulous range of options. While the second speaker may indeed decide to say nothing at all, this is a highly marked option: deliberately failing to respond to 'Good morning' would be the height of rudeness, in CA amounting to a refusal to accept social solidarity.

The two parts of the adjacency pair, however, do not necessarily follow each other:

A: What's the time?
B: Why do you want to know?
A: So I can put this letter in the post.
B: Five o'clock. You're too late.

The speakers keep an ongoing idea of the adjacency pair in their minds even when they are diverting onto side issues. In an early experiment (Cook, 1981), I tried to see the extent to which the concept of the adjacency pair was established in L2 users' minds by getting them to supply first or second moves, finding that the adjacency pair indeed had psychological reality for them.

Central to the idea of interaction is what happens when it goes wrong – the organization of **repair**. According to Emanuel Schegloff *et al.* (2002), this is not the same as the failure to communicate covered by the communication strategies described in Chapter 6, but is an interruption, after which interaction is restored. Usually a distinction is made between *self-initiated* repair by the same person:

A: Where's the saucepan? Sorry, the frying pan.

and *other-initiated* repair by the other speaker:

A: Where's the saucepan?
B: Where's the what?
A: The saucepan.
B: Oh, it's on the bottom shelf.

For the classroom this occurs at two levels; one is the repair of the classroom inter-action itself, where the teacher or students have to make clear what is going on, which may well be in the first language; the other is at the level of the interaction sequence of the language learning activity, which will normally be in the second language. Schegloff *et al.* (2002) point out that repair is the essence of the L2 classroom interaction and that much depends on how people understand and produce self-repair in a second language.

While CA has often been concerned with interaction in constrained institutional settings, this is seen as related to wider settings rather than unique. The language teaching classroom has its own characteristic forms of turn-taking, adjacency pair, repair, and so on. Paul Seedhouse (2004) shows how turn-taking depends on the task involved, particularly crucial in task-based learning. The problem with applying CA to language teaching, however, is that its aim is to describe conversational interaction as it happens, rather like a Lang$_3$ sense of language as a set of external sentences. But it does not say how the participants acquire the ability to interact and so help with how to teach it. It may be possible to deduce how the learner is proceeding and what the teacher should do, but this depends largely on other learning theories and approaches, such as the interaction hypothesis dealt with in Chapter 12, not on Conversation Analysis itself. A CA analysis can tell us whether a repair occurred and whether it was successful, but it cannot in itself say whether anything was learnt.

Box 9.3 Classroom interaction, Conversation Analysis and language teaching

1 In Hatch's discourse analysis the moves of a conversation revolve around a topic, for example:
  - topic nomination;
  - topic identification;
  - topic clarification.
2 Conversation Analysis makes use of concepts such as:
  - the adjacency pair where two conversational moves are linked;
  - repair – how the participants deal with things that go wrong, whether self-initiated repair or other-initiated repair.

Teaching can use these ideas at two levels:

- the pedagogical exchanges of the classroom;
- the target conversational exchanges that the students are aiming at outside the classroom.

Discussion topics

1 To what extent can and should the classroom duplicate the language of the world outside?

2 Should teachers feel guilty if they talk for most of the time in a lesson? Or would students be disappointed if they did not do so?

3 What kinds of authentic speech can you envisage using in a specific classroom? How would you use them?

4 Should you simplify your speech while teaching or not?

5 How would you see your teaching in terms of prefigurative, cofigurative and postfigurative?

6 Do students need to be taught how to make or request repairs?

7 Is the adjacency pair really crucial to language teaching, or is it just saying that people take turns to speak, just as tennis players hit the ball alternately?

Further reading

Two books that give a wealth of information on the language teaching classroom are: Chaudron (1988) *Second Language Classrooms: Research on Teaching and Learning*, and Ellis (1990) *Instructed Second Language Acquisition*. The use of authentic texts in teaching is described in Little *et al.* (1988) *Authentic Texts in Foreign Language Teaching: Theory and Practice*. A useful book on the role of the first language in the classroom is Macaro (1997) *Target Language, Collaborative Learning and Autonomy*; an account of dual language programmes can be found in Montague (1997) 'Critical components for dual language programs' in *Bilingual Research Journal* 21: 4. A clear introduction to Conversation Analysis can be found in Seedhouse (2004) *The Interactional Architecture of the Language Classroom*.

The L2 user and the native speaker

10

This chapter brings together themes about the relationship between people who know more than one language and monolingual native speakers. Are L2 users and monolingual native speakers different types of people? If so, what should be the proper goals of students of second languages and how does this affect how they should be taught? These issues have been debated with great passion. The views here broadly come from within the multi-competence perspective outlined in Chapters 1 and 12. This chapter concentrates on the L2 user as an individual, Chapter 11 on L2 users as part of communities, though there are inevitable overlaps.

Box 10.1 Questions for L2 users

1 Do you use:
   - the two languages in different situations or in the same situation?
   - the two languages to different people or the same people?
   - the L1 at the same time as the L2 (e.g. by translating)?
   - codeswitching during the course of a conversation?
2 Do you feel using two languages has:
   - social advantages or disadvantages?
   - mental advantages or disadvantages?
3 Are you jealous of native speakers?
4 Do you feel you are losing your first language?

10.1 The L2 user versus the native speaker in language teaching

Focusing questions

- Should L2 learners aim to speak like native speakers?
- What kind of role do non-native speakers have in the coursebook you are most familiar with? Powerful successful people? Or ignorant tourists and near-beginner students?

> ### Keywords
>
> **native speaker**: 'a person who has spoken a certain language since early child-
> hood' (McArthur, 1992)
> **L2 user**: a person who uses more than one language, at whatever level

A central issue in SLA research and language teaching is the concept of the native speaker. But what *is* a native speaker? One of the first uses of the term is by Leonard Bloomfield: 'The first language a human being learns to speak is his *native language*; he is a *native speaker* of this language' (Bloomfield, 1933: 43). Being a native speaker in this sense is a straightforward matter of an individual's history; the first language you encounter as a baby is your native language. A typical modern definition is 'a person who has spoken a certain language since early childhood' (McArthur, 1992). You can no more change the historical fact of which language you spoke first than you can change the mother who brought you up. Any later-learnt language cannot be a native language by definition; your second language will never be your native language regardless of how long or how well you speak it.

A second way of defining native speakers is to list the components that make them up. David Stern (1983) lists characteristics such as a subconscious knowledge of rules and creativity of language use: native speakers know the language without being able to verbalize their knowledge; they can produce new sentences they have not heard before. L2 learners may be able to acquire some of these components of the native speaker state. L2 users also know many aspects of the second language subconsciously rather than consciously; L2 users are capable of saying new things in a second language, for example the 'surrealistic aphorisms' of French-speaking Marcel Duchamps such as 'My niece is cold because my knees are cold' (Sanquillet and Peterson, 1978: 111) – not to mention the writings of Nabokov or Conrad. The question is whether it is feasible or desirable for the L2 user to match these components of the native speaker.

A third approach to defining native speaker brings in language identity: your speech shows who you are. In English, a word or two notoriously gives away many aspects of our identity. According to George Bernard Shaw, 'It is impossible for an Englishman to open his mouth without making some other Englishman hate or despise him.' Our speech shows the groups that we belong to, as we see in Chapter 4, whether in terms of age ('wireless' rather than 'radio'), gender (men prefer to pronounce '-ing' endings such as 'running' as /ɪn/, women as /ɪŋ/) (Adamson and Regan, 1991), or religion (the pronunciation of the church service 'mass' as /mɑːs/ or /mæs/ is one giveaway of religious background in England, as is the abbreviation of 'William' to 'Bill' or 'Liam' in Northern Ireland). An English linguist once observed: 'it is part of the meaning of an American to sound like one' (Firth, 1951).

We may be proud or ashamed of belonging to a particular group; politicians in England try to shed signs of their origins by adopting RP as best they can; British pop and folk singers take on American-like vowels. Being a native speaker shows identification with a group of speakers, membership of a language community. In social terms, people have as much right to join the group of native speakers and to adopt a new identity as they have to change identity in any other way. But the native speaker group is only one of the groups that a speaker belongs to, and not of overriding importance; how important is it to be a native speaker of a language compared to being a believer in a religion, a parent, or a supporter of Newcastle United?

The definitions of native speaker then are not helpful for language teachers. In the sense of first language in life, it is impossible for students to become native speakers of a second language. The components definition raises the issue of whether students should be trained to be like native speakers; it therefore limits their components to those that monolingual native speakers possess rather than the additional skills of L2 users, such as translation. In terms of identity, it raises the question of which group we wish the students to belong to – the community of native speakers of which they can never be full members or the communities of L2 users? According to Ben Rampton (1990), language loyalty can be a matter either of *inheritance* (language is something you inherit, you claim and you bequeath) or of *affiliation* (a language is something you belong to), both of them continually negotiated.

Should the native speaker be the target of language teaching?

Most language teachers, and indeed most students, accept that their goal is to become as similar to the native speaker as possible. One problem is the question of *which* native speaker. A language comes in many varieties, according to country, region, class, sex, profession and other factors; this, then, is to do with the Lang$_2$ abstract entity meaning of 'language'. Some varieties are a matter of accent, some of social and regional dialect. The student's target needs to relate to the roles that they will assume when using the second language. Some British students I knew in London were going for job experience in Switzerland; my colleagues accordingly taught them Swiss German. When they used this on the shop floor, their fellow workers found it highly entertaining: foreigners are expected to speak High German, not Swiss German. I was an L2 user of Swiss German as a child and can still comprehend it reasonably, provided the person speaking does not see me as a foreigner and switch to High German.

The problems of which variety to teach is more pressing for a language that is used globally, such as English. England itself contains a variety of class and regional accents, even if vocabulary varies little; the English-speaking countries from Australia to Canada, Scotland to South Africa, each have their own variety, with its own internal range; outside these countries there are well-established varieties of English spoken in countries such as Singapore and India. Which of these native speakers should the students adopt as a role model? The claimed advantages of RP were that, despite its small number of speakers based in a single country, it was comprehensible everywhere and had neutral connotations in terms of class and region. True as this may be, it does sound like the classic last-ditch defence of the powerful status form against the rest. A more realistic native accent nowadays might be Estuary English, encountered in Chapter 4.

Though much of this variation may be a matter of accent, reading an American novel soon shows the different conventions, whether in vocabulary (the piece of furniture called a 'credenza' is known as a 'dresser' in England), spelling (the same hesitation noise in speech is spelled 'uh' in American English and 'er' in British English, because of the 'missing' <r>s in RP) or grammar ('I have got' versus 'I have gotten'). So far as language teaching is concerned, there is no single ideal native speaker for all students to imitate; the choice of model has to take all sorts of variation into account.

However, if L2 users are not the same as monolinguals, as we have been arguing all along, whether in the languages they know or in the rest of their minds, it is inappropriate to base language teaching on the native speaker model, since it may, on the one hand, frustrate the students who soon appreciate that they will never be the same as native speakers, and on the other constrain them to the activities of monolinguals rather than the richness of multilingual use. If we want students to become efficient L2 users, not imitation native speakers, the situations modelled in coursebooks should include examples of successful L2 users on which the students can model themselves. The Japanese syllabus puts forward a goal of 'Japanese with English Abilities', not imitation native speaker (MEXT, 2003). Similarly, the Israeli curriculum 'does not take on the goal of producing near-native speakers of English, but rather speakers of Hebrew, Arabic or other languages, who can function comfortably in English whenever it is appropriate' (*English – Curriculum for all Grades*, 2002).

Successful L2 use is almost totally absent from textbooks. In some courses, students have to compare different cultures. In *Move* (Bowler *et al.*, 2007), students discuss, 'Do men or women usually do these jobs in your country?', linked to cartoons of a chef, a ballet dancer, a soldier, and so on; in *Hotline* (Hutchinson, 1992) students give 'useful expressions' in their own languages. Most coursebooks use England as a backcloth, but they seldom present multilingual English people, even if multiculturalism is sometimes mentioned, as in the discussion of Asian marriages in *The Beginners' Choice* (Mohamed and Acklam, 1992). By the end of a language course, students will never have heard L2 users talking to native speakers, let alone to other L2 users, important as this may be to their goals. When they have finished *Changes* (Richards, 1998), a course with the subtitle 'English International Communication', the only examples of L2 users, except for 'student' figures, the students will have met are brief first-person biographies of people in Taiwan, Madrid and Paris.

Even the celebrities in coursebooks are invariably monolingual rather than bilingual. The characters that are supposedly L2 users fall into two main categories: tourists and visitors, who ignorantly ask the way, desperately buy things or try to fathom strange travel systems, and students who chat to each other about their lives and interests. Both groups use perfectly adequate English for their activities; nothing distinguishes them from the native speakers portrayed in the pages except that their names are Birgit, Klaus or Philippe (*Changes*). Neither group are effective role models of L2 users. *New English File* (Oxenden *et al.*, 2004) features *inter alia* celebrities such as the novelist J.K. Rowling and the model Naomi Campbell, and gives short life histories of people who live in Japan and Rio: it is not thought worth mentioning whether any of them use second languages successfully.

Nor is it only English. Coursebooks for teaching other languages, such as French *Libre Echange* (Courtillon and de Salins, 1995) or Italian *Ci Siamo* (Guarnuccio and Guarnuccio, 1997), present L2 users similarly. L2 users have an unflatteringly powerless status, rather than the extra influence that successful L2 users can wield. The students never see an L2 user in action who knows what they are doing. While the roles of students or of visitors are useful and relevant, they are hardly an adequate reflection of what L2 use can provide. Looking at most EFL and modern language coursebooks, you get the distinct impression that all of them are written by monolinguals who have no idea of the lives lived by L2 users.

Box 10.2 The native speaker

- Many definitions of native speaker exist, based on birth, knowledge and use.
- Since languages have many different types of native speaker, if teaching takes the native speaker as the target it still has to decide which native speaker.
- Under the usual definition of 'a person who has spoken a certain language since early childhood', it is not possible for a second language learner to become a native speaker, and this is not a possible measure of L2 success.

10.2 Codeswitching by second language users

Focusing questions

- When have you heard one person using two languages in the course of the same conversation or the same sentence?
- Is it polite to codeswitch?
- Should students ever switch languages in mid-sentence?

Keywords

codeswitching: going from one language to the other in mid-speech when both speakers know the same two languages
bilingual/monolingual modes: in bilingual mode, the L2 user uses two languages; in monolingual mode, a single language, whether their first or second

The danger of concentrating on the native speaker is that the specific characteristics of L2 users are ignored. L2 users can do things that monolingual native speakers cannot. We are limiting the students' horizons if we only teach them what native speakers can do. An example is a process peculiar to using a second language, namely codeswitching from one language to another. To illustrate codeswitching, here are some sentences recorded by Zubaidah Hakim in a staffroom where Malaysian teachers of English were talking to each other:

- 'Suami saya dulu slim and trim tapi sekarang plump like drum' (Before my husband was slim and trim but now he is plump like a drum).
- 'Jadi I tanya, how can you say that when... geram betul I' (So I asked how can you say that when... I was so mad).
- 'Hero you tak datang hari ni' (Your hero did not come today).

One moment there is a phrase or word in English, the next a phrase or word in Bahasa Malaysia. Sometimes the switch between languages occurs between sentences rather than within them. It is often hard to say which is the main language of such a conversation, or indeed of an individual sentence.

Box 10.3 Examples of codeswitching between languages

- Spanish/English: 'Todos los mexicanos *were riled up.*' (All the Mexicans were riled up.)
- Dutch/English: 'Ik heb een kop *of tea, tea or something.*' (I had a cup of tea or something.)
- Tok Pisin/English: 'Lapun man ia cam na tok, "oh yu poor pussiket".' (The old man came and said, 'you poor pussycat'.)
- Japanese/English: 'She *wa* took her a month to come home *yo.*'
- Greek/English: 'Simera piga sto *shopping centre* gia na psaksw ena *birthday present* gia thn Maria.' (Today I went to the shopping centre because I wanted to buy a birthday present for Maria.)
- English/German/Italian: 'Pinker is of the opinion that the man is singled out as, singled out as, *was?*, as *ein Mann, der reden kann*, singled out as *una specie*, as a species which can. . .'
- English/Italian/French:
  'London Bridge is falling down
  Poi s'ascose nel foco che gli affina
  O swallow swallow
  Le Prince d'Aquitaine á la tour aboli'
  (T.S. Eliot, *The Waste Land*, V)

Codeswitching is found wherever bilingual speakers talk to each other. According to François Grosjean (1989), bilinguals have two modes for using language. In **bilingual mode** they speak either one language or the other; in **monolingual mode** they use two languages simultaneously, by codeswitching from one to the other during the course of speech. Bilingual codeswitching is neither unusual nor abnormal; it is an ordinary fact of life in many multilingual societies. Codeswitching is a unique feat of using two languages at once, which no monolingual can ever achieve, except to the limited extent that people can switch between dialects of their first language. Box 10.3 gives some examples of codeswitching drawn from diverse sources, which also demonstrates its utter respectability by occurring in perhaps the most celebrated twentieth-century poem in English, *The Waste Land*.

The interesting questions about codeswitching are why and when it happens. A common reason for switching is to report what someone has said, as when a girl who is telling a story switches from Tok Pisin (spoken in Papua New Guinea) to English to report what the man said: 'Lapun man ia cam na tok, "oh yu poor pussiket"' (The old man came and said, 'you poor pussycat'). In one sense, whenever a book cites sentences in other languages, or whenever T.S. Eliot uses quotations from other languages, it is codeswitching.

A second reason for switching is to use markers from one language to highlight something in another. The Japanese/English 'She *wa* took her a month to come home *yo*' uses 'wa' to indicate what is being talked about, its function in Japanese.

Another reason is the feeling that some topics are more appropriate to one language than another. Mexican Americans, for example, prefer to talk about money in English rather than in Spanish – 'La consulta era (the visit cost) eight dollars.' One of my Malaysian students told me that she could express romantic feelings in English but not in Bahasa Malaysia, supported by Indians I have met who prefer

---

Box 10.4 Reasons for codeswitching

1 Reporting someone else's speech.
2 Interjecting.
3 Highlighting particular information.
4 Switching to a topic more suitable for one language.
5 Changing the speaker's role.
6 Qualifying the topic.
7 Singling out one person to direct speech at.
8 Ignorance of a form in one language.

English for such emotions – English as the language of romance is a bit surprising to an Englishman!

Sometimes the reason for codeswitching is that the choice of language shows the speaker's social role. A Kenyan man who was serving his own sister in a shop started in their Luiyia dialect and then switched to Swahili for the rest of the conversation, to signal that he was treating her as an ordinary customer. Often bilinguals use fillers and tags from one language in another, as in the Spanish/English exchange, 'Well I'm glad to meet you', 'Andale pues and do come again' (OK swell...).

The common factor underlying these examples is that the speaker assumes that the listener is fluent in the two languages. Otherwise such sentences would not be a bilingual codeswitching mode of language use but would be either interlanguage communication strategies or attempts at one-upmanship, similar to the use by some English speakers of Latin expressions such as '*ab initio* learners of Spanish' (Spanish beginners). Monolinguals think that the reason is primarily ignorance; you switch when you do not know the word, that is, it is a communication strategy of the type mentioned in Chapter 6; yet this motivation seems rare in the descriptions of codeswitching. Box 10.4 lists some reasons people codeswitch, including most of those mentioned here.

When does codeswitching occur in terms of language structure? According to one set of calculations, about 84 per cent of switches within the sentence are isolated words, say the English/Malaysian 'Ana free hari ini' (Ana is free today), where English is switched to only for the item 'free'. About 10 per cent are phrases, as in the Russian/French 'Imela une femme de chambre' (She had a chambermaid). The remaining 6 per cent are switches for whole clauses, as in the German/English 'Papa, wenn du das Licht ausmachst, then I'll be so lonely' (Daddy, if you put out the light, I'll be so lonely). But this still does not show when switches are possible from one language to another; switching is very far from random in linguistic terms.

The theory of codeswitching developed by Shona Poplack (1980) claims that there are two main restrictions on where switching can occur:

- **The 'free morpheme constraint':** the speaker may not switch language between a word and its endings unless the word is pronounced as if it were in the language of the ending. Thus an English/Spanish switch 'runeando' is impossible because 'run' is distinctively English in sound. But 'flipeando' is possible because 'flip' is potentially a word in Spanish.

- **The 'equivalence constraint'**: the switch can come at a point in the sentence where it does not violate the grammar of either language. So there are unlikely to be any French/English switches such as 'a car americaine' or 'une American voiture', as they would be wrong in both languages. It is possible, however, to have the French/English switch 'J'ai acheté an American car' (I bought an American car), because both English and French share the structure in which the object follows the verb.

The approach to codeswitching that has been most influential recently is the matrix language frame (MLF) model developed by Carol Myers-Scotton (2005). She claims that in codeswitching the matrix language provides the frame, and the embedded language provides material to fill out the frame, rather like putting the flesh onto the skeleton. So in 'Simera piga sto *shopping centre* gia na psaksw ena *birthday present* gia thn Maria', the matrix language is Greek, which provides the grammatical structure, and the embedded language is English, which provides two noun phrases. The role for the matrix language is to provide the grammatical structures and the 'system' morphemes, that is, grammatical morphemes that form the basis of the sentence. The role of the embedded language is to provide content morphemes to fit into the framework already supplied. For example, the Russian/English sentence 'On dolgo laia-l na *dog*-ov' (He barked at dogs for a long time) shows matrix Russian grammatical morphemes and structure, but an embedded English content word 'dog' (Schmid *et al.*, 2004).

The later version of this model (Myers-Scotton and Jake, 2000) is known as the 4M model as it divides all morphemes into four types:

- **content morphemes** which have thematic roles, typically nouns such as 'book' and verbs such as 'read';
- **early system morphemes** which have some content meaning, such as articles 'the/a', '(chew) up';
- **late bridge system morphemes** which make necessary connections between grammatical parts but contribute no meaning, say 'the Wife of Bath', or possessive ''s' 'John's friend';
- **late outsider system morphemes** which have connections extending beyond the basic lexical unit, such as agreement 's'; 'Tomorrow never comes'.

(**Note**: 'early' and 'late' apply to the processes of language production, not to the stages of language acquisition.)

According to the 4M model, content and, to a large extent, early system morphemes go with the embedded language in depending on meaning. The late bridge and outsider system morphemes go with the matrix language as they provide the grammatical framework within which the content and early system morphemes can be placed.

Codeswitching and language teaching

What does codeswitching have to do with language teaching? The profile of the proficient L2 user includes the codeswitching mode of language. It is not something that is peculiar or unusual. If the bilingual knows that the listener shares the same two languages, codeswitching is likely to take place for all the reasons given above. For many students, the ability to go from one language to another is highly desirable; there is little advantage in being multi-competent if you are restricted by the demands of a single language in monolingual mode.

A simple point to make to students is that codeswitching between two people who both know the same two languages is normal. There is a half-feeling that people who switch are doing something wrong, either demonstrating their poor knowledge of the L2 or deliberate rudeness to other people present who may not be able to join in, as we see in Figure 10.1. This seems particularly true of children in England. This feeling is not helped by the pressure against codeswitching in many classrooms, as we see in the next section. Occasionally codeswitching may indeed be used for concealment from a third party. However, this may be to preserve the niceties of polite conversation: Philip, a 7-year-old French/English speaker, switches to French to his mother in front of an English guest to request to go to the loo: 'Maman, j'ai envie de faire pipi' (Mummy, I need to have a wee). Too long has codeswitching been seen as something reprehensible (young children who use switching are doing something terrible – they cannot keep their languages separate!), rather than something completely natural and indeed highly skilled, as Fred Genesee (2002) points out. Codeswitching is a normal ability of L2 users in everyday situations and can be utilised even by children as young as 2.

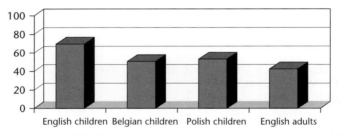

Figure 10.1 Percentage of people who consider codeswitching rude

The Institute of Linguists' examinations in Languages for International Communication (discontinued in 2004) (Institute of Linguists, 2008) assessed whether candidates can mediate between two languages. At beginners' level this may be reading an L2 travel brochure or listening to L2 answerphone messages to get information that can be used in the first language. At advanced stages it might be researching a topic through reading and conducting interviews in order to write a report. To take an Italian example, students are told they are working for an English charity that needs a report on immigration. They are given a dossier in advance of newspaper articles on the topic in Italian. On the day of the test they are given a task-brief, listing points that they should cover; they then have to interview someone in Italian for 15 minutes to establish the information; finally they have two hours to write up a professional report in English based on the dossiers and the interview. In this international use of a second language, the L2 learner is not becoming an imitation native speaker, but is someone who can stand between the two languages, using both when appropriate. While this is not in itself codeswitching, it involves the same element of having two languages readily available rather than functioning exclusively in one or the other.

But codeswitching proper can also be exploited as part of actual teaching methodology. For example, the *New Crown English* course in Japan uses some codeswitching in dialogues (Morizumi, 2002). When the teacher knows the language of the students, whether or not the teacher is a native speaker, the classroom itself often becomes a codeswitching situation. The lesson starts in the first language, or the control of the class takes place through the first language, or it slips in in other ways. In a sense, codeswitching is natural in the classroom if the teacher and students share the same languages: the classroom is an L2 user situation with two or more languages always present, and it is a pretence that it is a monolingual L2 situation; at best, one of the two languages is invisible. Use of the L1 in the classroom is developed in the next section.

Rodolpho Jacobson has developed the *new concurrent approach* (Jacobson and Faltis, 1990), which gets teachers to balance the use of the two languages within a single lesson. The teacher is allowed to switch languages at certain key points. In a class where English is being taught to Spanish-speaking children, the teacher can switch to Spanish when concepts are important, when the students are getting distracted, or when a student should be praised or told off. The teacher may also switch to English when revising a lesson that has already been given in Spanish. The codeswitching is highly controlled in this method.

Box 10.5 Codeswitching exercise

Look at the list of reasons for codeswitching in Box 10.4 (page 176) and then say which applies to each of the following examples of codeswitching, taken from a variety of sources.

1 English-Swedish: *Peak*en var inte bra på *spot*marknaden. (The peak was not good on the spot market.)
2 English-Spanish: But I wanted to fight her *con los puños,* you know. (But I wanted to fight her with my fists, you know.)
3 French-English: *Tu dévisses le bouchon... comme ça... et tu* squirt. (You unscrew the cap... like this... and you squirt.)
4 English-Spanish: No van a *bring it up in the meeting.* (They're not going to bring it up in the meeting.)
5 French/Swedish: Mother: *Tu reprendras un peu de* ca? (Would you like some more?) Emily to her mother in Swedish: 'Jag tror inte att hon tycker om det.' (I don't think she likes it.)
6 Russian-French: Imela *une femme de chambre.* (She had a chambermaid.)
7 Greek/English: ''Ημουν βιβλιοθήκη και ήθελα να πάρω *copycard* και λέω *"five pound phonecard please"*.' (I was at the library and I wanted to buy a copycard and I say 'five pound phonecard please'.)
8 Hindi-English: 'Maine bahut bardas kiya hai *but now it's getting too much.*' (I have withstood a lot but now it's getting too much.)
9 English-Spanish: So you *todavía* haven't decided *lo que vas a hacer* next week. (So you still haven't decided what you're going to do next week.)

Box 10.6 L2 learning and codeswitching

1 Codeswitching is the use of two languages within the same conversation, often when the speaker is:
  - reporting what someone has said;
  - highlighting something;
  - discussing certain topics;
  - emphasizing a particular social role.
2 Codeswitching consists of 84 per cent single word switches, 10 per cent phrases, 6 per cent clauses.

10.3 Using the first language in the classroom

Focusing questions

- When did you last use/encounter the L1 in the L2 classroom?
- Do you think it was a good idea or a bad one?
- When do you think the first language could be used profitably in the classroom? How?

Keywords

compound and **coordinate bilinguals**: compound bilinguals are those who link the two languages in their minds, coordinate bilinguals are those who keep them apart

reciprocal language teaching: a teaching method in which pairs of students alternately teach each other their languages

bilingual method: a teaching method that uses the student's first language to establish the meanings of the second language

Though the teaching methods popular in the twentieth century differed in many ways, they nearly all tried to avoid relying on the students' first language in the classroom. The only exceptions were the grammar-translation academic style of teaching, discussed in Chapter 13, which still survives despite the bad press it has always received, and the short-lived reading method in USA in the 1930s. But everything else, from the direct method to the audio-lingual method, to task-based learning, has insisted that the less the first language is used in the classroom, the better the teaching.

In the early days, the first language was explicitly rejected, a legacy of the language teaching revolutions of the late nineteenth century. Later the first language was seldom mentioned as a tool for the classroom, apart from occasional advice about how to avoid it, for example in task-based learning for beginners: 'Don't ban mother-tongue use but encourage attempts to use the target language' (Willis,

1996: 130). In the 1990s, the UK National Curriculum emphasized this in such dicta as: 'The natural use of the target language for virtually all communication is a sure sign of a good modern language course' (DES, 1990: 58). According to Franklin (1990), 90 per cent of teachers think it is important to teach in the target language.

Arguments for avoiding the first language

While avoidance of the first language is taken for granted by almost all teachers, and is implicit in most books for teachers, the reasons are rarely stated. One is that the teacher's language can be the prime model for true communicative use of the second language. Coming into a classroom of non-English-speaking students and saying 'Good morning' seems like a real use of language for communicative purposes. Explaining grammar in English – 'When you want to talk about something that is still relevant to the present moment use the present perfect' – provides genuine information for the student through the second language. Telling the students, 'Turn your chairs round so that you are in groups of four' gives them real instructions to carry out. Hearing this through the first language would deprive the students of genuine experience of interaction through the second language. The use of the second language for everyday classroom communication sets a tone for the class that influences much that happens.

Yet using the second language throughout the lesson may make the class seem less real. Instead of the actual situation of a group of people trying to get to grips with a second language, there is a pretend monolingual situation. The first language has become an invisible and scorned element in the classroom. The students are acting like imitation native speakers of the second language, rather than true L2 users.

The practical justification for avoiding the first language in many English language teaching situations is that the students speak several first languages and it would be impossible for the teacher to take account of all of them. Hence hardly any British-produced EFL coursebooks use the first language at all. EFL materials produced in particular countries, such as Japan or Greece, where most students speak a common first language, are not restricted in this way. In the EFL context, many expatriate language teachers often do not speak the first language of the students, so the L2 is unavoidable. But this is more an argument about desirable qualities for teachers than about the type of teaching students should receive; an L2 teacher who cannot use a second language may not be the best role model for the students.

The practical reasons for avoiding the first language in a multilingual class do not justify its avoidance in classes with a single first language. It is hard to find explicit reasons being given for avoiding the first language in these circumstances. The implicit reasons seem to be twofold:

- *It does not happen in first language acquisition.* Children acquiring their first language do not have another language to fall back on, by definition, except in the case of early simultaneous bilingualism. So L2 learners would ideally acquire the second language in the same way as children, without reference to another language.

- *The two languages should be kept separate in the mind.* To develop a second language properly means learning to use it independently of the first language and eventually to 'think' in it. Anything which keeps the two languages apart is therefore beneficial to L2 learning.

Neither of these arguments has any particular justification from SLA research. There are indeed many parallels between first and second language acquisition, since both learning processes take place in the same human mind. Yet the many obvious differences in terms of age and situation can affect these processes. The presence of another language in the mind of the L2 learner is an unalterable difference from first language acquisition: there is no way in which the two processes can be equated. If the first language is to be avoided in teaching, this ban must be based on other reasons than the way in which children learn their first language.

The argument assumes that the first and the second languages are in different parts of the mind. An early distinction in SLA research made by Uriel Weinreich (1953) contrasted **compound bilinguals**, who link the two languages in their minds, with **coordinate bilinguals**, who keep them apart. Thus the policy of avoiding the first language assumes that the only valid form of L2 learning is coordinate bilingualism. Even within Weinreich's ideas, this would exclude the compound bilinguals. But mostly the distinction between compound and coordinate bilinguals has been watered down because of evidence that the two languages are very far from separate. However distinct the two languages are in theory, in practice they are interwoven in terms of phonology, vocabulary, syntax and sentence processing, as seen in several chapters of this book.

Ernesto Macaro (1997) observed a number of modern language teachers at work in classrooms in England to see when they used the first language. He found five factors that most commonly led to L1 use:

1 *Using the first language for giving instructions about activities.* As mentioned above, the teacher has to balance the gains and losses of using the first or the second language. Some teachers resort to the first language after they have tried in vain to get the activity going in the second language.

2 *Translating and checking comprehension.* Teachers felt the L1 'speeded things up'.

3 *Individual comments to students*, made while the teacher is going round the class, say, during pair work.

4 *Giving feedback to pupils.* Students are often told whether they are right or wrong in their own language. Presumably the teacher feels that this makes it more 'real'.

5 *Using the first language to maintain discipline.* Saying 'Shut up or you will get a detention' in the first language shows that it is a serious threat, rather than practising imperative and conditional constructions. One class reported that their teacher slipped into the first language 'if it's something really bad!'

In terms of frequency, Carole Franklin (1990) found that over 80 per cent of teachers used the first language for explaining grammar and for discussing objectives; over 50 per cent for tests, correcting written work and teaching background; under 16 per cent for organizing the classroom and activities and for chatting informally.

SLA research provides no reason why any of these activities is not a perfectly rational use of the first language in the classroom. If twenty-first-century teaching is to continue to accept the ban on the first language imposed by the late nineteenth century, it will have to look elsewhere for its rationale. As Swain and Lapkin (2000) put it: 'To insist that no use be made of the L1 in carrying out tasks that are both linguistically and cognitively complex is to deny the use of an important cognitive tool.'

Teaching that uses the first language

A few minority methods during the twentieth century, other than the shunned grammar-translation method, indeed tried to systematise the use of the first language in the classroom. One possibility that has been tried can be called **alternating language methods**. These depend on the presence of native speakers of two languages in the classroom, so that in some way the students learn each other's languages. In **reciprocal language teaching** students switch language at predetermined points (Hawkins, 1987; Cook, 1989). The method pairs students who want to learn each other's languages and makes them alternate between the two languages, thus exchanging the roles of teacher and student. My own experience of this was on a summer course that paired French teachers of English with English teachers of French, and alternated between England and France each year. One day all the activities would take place in French, the next day everything would be in English, and so on throughout the course. In my own case it was so effective that at the end of three weeks I was conversing with a French inspector general – a supreme authority figure for French teachers – without realizing that I was using French. However, while the method worked for me in France, when the course took place in England the following year, it seemed unnatural to use French exclusively.

Other variations on alternating language approaches are the **key school two-way model**, in which classes of mixed English and Spanish speakers learn the curriculum through English in the morning and Spanish in the afternoon (Rhodes *et al.*, 1997), the **alternate days approach**, which teaches the standard curriculum subjects to children with native Pilipino using English and Pilipino on alternate days (Tucker *et al.*, 1971), and **dual language programmes**, in which a balance is struck between two languages in the school curriculum, ranging from say 90 per cent in the minority language versus 10 per cent in the majority languages in the preschool year, to 70 per cent versus 30 per cent in second grade (Montague, 1997). These alternating methods are distinct from the bilingual 'immersion' French teaching programmes developed in English-speaking Canada, which do not have mixed groups of native and non-native students.

Box 10.7 *The Bilingual Method*, C.J. Dodson, 1967

Step 1. Imitation. Pupils learn to speak basic L2 sentences by imitating the teacher; listen to the teacher give L1 meaning

Step 2. Interpretation. The teacher says L1 equivalent of L2 sentence; the pupil replies with L2 sentence, the teacher repeats L1

Step 3. Substitution and extension. Same technique as (1) and (2) but varying the vocabulary within existing patterns

Step 4. Independent speaking of sentences

Step 5. Reverse interpretation (optional)

Step 6. Consolidation of question patterns

More relevant to most language teaching situations are methods that actively create links between the first and the second language; some of these are discussed further in Chapter 13. The **New Concurrent Method**, for example, allows systematic codeswitching under the teacher's control. **Community language learning** (CLL) is an interesting variant which uses translation as a means of allowing genuine L2 use; the second language is learnt in continual conjunction with the first. The most developed is perhaps the **Bilingual Method** used in Wales, outlined in Box 10.7. Here, the teacher reads an L2 sentence and gives its meaning in the first language, called 'interpreting' rather than 'translating', after which the students repeat in chorus and individually (Dodson, 1967). The teacher tests the students' understanding by saying the L1 sentence and pointing to a picture, though the students have to answer in the second language. The two languages are tied together in the students' minds through the meaning.

Some of the ways that teachers have found the first language useful in the classroom (always provided that they know the first language of the students) are:

- *Explaining grammar to the students*. The FonF approach, curiously, has not discussed which language should be used for explaining grammar; Catherine Doughty's influential article on 'the cognitive underpinning of focus on form' (Doughty, 2001) does not once mention that a choice exists. If a French beginners' course such as *Panorama* (Girardet and Cridlig, 1996) includes in Lesson 2 'La conjugaison pronominale', 'Construction avec l'infinitif' and 'Les adjectifs possessifs et demonstratifs', what else are the students supposed to do but use the first language, say via translation? The elementary course *New English File* (Oxenden *et al.*, 2004) includes in its first unit the terms 'pronouns', 'possessive adjectives', 'plurals' and 'prepositions'. Without translation, this is going to make little sense, particularly when the grammar of the student's own culture differs from the English school tradition, as is the case with Japanese students, who do not have a concept of grammatical plural.

- *Explaining tasks and exercises to the students*. If the task is crucial, then whichever language is used, the important thing is to get the students carrying out the task successfully as soon as possible. *Atlas 1* (Nunan, 1995), for example, in Unit 3 has a task chain 'talking about occupations', involving the steps '1 Listen and circle the occupations you hear… 2 Listen again and check [√] the questions you hear…' If the students can understand these instructions in the second language, they probably do not need the exercise. The teacher may find it highly convenient to fall back on the first language for explaining tasks.

- *Students using the first language within classroom activities*. Teachers are often told to discourage students from using their first language in pair and group activities: 'If they are talking in small groups it can be quite difficult to get some classes – particularly the less disciplined or motivated ones – to keep to the target language' (Ur, 1996: 121). Yet codeswitching is a normal part of bilingual life in the world outside the classroom; it is the natural recourse of L2 users when they are with people who share the same languages; stopping codeswitching in the classroom, which is what a ban on the L1 actually amounts to, is denying a central feature of many L2 situations. The students should not be made uncomfortable with a normal part of L2 use. Those working within the sociocultural framework discussed in Chapter 12 have stressed how learning is a collaborative dialogue (Anton and DiCamilla, 1998); the first language can provide part of the scaffolding that goes with this dialogue.

Many other uses of the first language arise naturally in the classroom – keeping discipline, using bilingual dictionaries, administering tests, and many others. If there is no principled reason for avoiding the first language other than allowing the students to hear as much second language as possible, it may be more effective to resort to the first language in the classroom when needed.

Box 10.8 Ways of using the L1 in the classroom

1 Teacher conveying meaning:
   - teacher using L1 for conveying meaning of words or sentences;
   - teacher using L1 for explaining grammar.
2 Teacher organizing the class:
   - teacher using L1 for managing the classroom;
   - teacher using L1 for giving instructions for teaching activities;
   - L1 used for testing.
3 Students using L1 within classroom:
   - students using L1 as part of main learning activity;
   - students using L1 incidentally within classroom activities.

10.4 Are native speakers better language teachers?

Focusing questions

- Would you prefer to be taught by a native speaker teacher or a non-native speaker teacher? Why?
- What are the strengths of native speaker teachers? The weaknesses?
- What are the strengths of non-native speaker teachers? The weaknesses?

A divisive issue in many parts of the world is whether it is better for the teacher to be a native speaker or a non-native speaker. The job ads given in Box 10.9 show the emphasis that EFL recruiters place on native speakers. In many universities

Box 10.9 Online ads for EFL teachers

In London

'Qualified, native speaking English teachers' (a centre in Northfields)
'Please do not apply if you don't have Native English Speaker Competency' (University of East London)
'The candidate should be a native speaker' (the Shakespeare College 'near Liverpool Street')

Outside England

China: 'Are you a native English speaker or "near native". . .?' (University of Southampton ad)
Korea: 'Must be native speaker and UK, Ire, USA, Can, NZ, Aus, SA citizen' (English Teacher Direct)
Ecuador: 'Wall Street Institute Ambato is looking for Native Speakers (no experience needed)'

And it is not just TEFL jobs. An ad on a North London pub wall asks for: 'Assistant Manager. . . English first language'.

around the world, non-native language teachers find it harder to get permanent or full-time positions and are paid less than native speaker teachers. In UK universities it is usual for language teaching to be carried out by native speaker teachers, often on a teaching rather than an academic grade.

Why then are native speakers so desirable? One justification often put forward is that the students themselves demand native speakers. In a survey I conducted in several countries, children in England gave native speaker teachers a 55 per cent preference, in Belgium 33 per cent; 60 per cent of adults in England preferred natives, and in Taiwan 51 per cent. Outside England the preference for native speakers is not overwhelming.

Box 10.10 shows some of the features that Hungarian students valued in native speaker and non-native speaker teachers, researched by Benke and Medgyes (2005). The non-native speaker teacher is seen as an efficient teacher, preparing you for exams, correcting your mistakes and knowing how good you are, but dependent on the coursebook. The native speaker teacher is concerned about spoken language, more friendly and has more flexible and interactive classes.

Box 10.10 Top-rated features of teachers by Hungarian students (Benke and Medgyes, 2005)

The non-native speaker teacher:

- assigns lots of homework;
- prepares conscientiously;
- corrects errors consistently;
- prepares learners well for exam;
- assesses my language knowledge realistically;
- relies heavily on the coursebook.

The native speaker teacher:

- focuses primarily on speaking skills;
- is happy to improvise;
- provides extensive information about the culture;
- is interested in learners' opinions;
- applies group work regularly in class.

The most obvious reason for preferring native speakers is the model of language that the native can present. Here is a person who has reached the apparent target that the students are striving after – what could be better? The native speaker can model the language the students are aiming at and can provide an instant authoritative answer to any language question. Their prime advantage is indeed the obvious one that they speak the language as a first language. Ivor Timmis (2002) found that, given a choice between sounding like a native speaker or having the 'accent of my country', 67 per cent of students preferred to speak like a native speaker.

Do all native speakers present an equally desirable model? A native speaker of British is presumed to speak RP; yet this accent is used by a small minority of people in the UK (as we see in Chapter 4), let alone in the world at large. Is a Welsh accent equally acceptable? A London accent? Both are native accents, but do not have the same status as RP outside their own localities. A Finnish professor I knew reckoned he was the only RP speaker in his university department, despite all his colleagues being native speakers of English. A Middle East university who hired a native speaker teacher were disconcerted when a British speaker of Geordie turned up. And yet he is as much a native speaker of English as I am, or as most of the inhabitants of the UK are.

But as we see throughout this book, gone are the days when the goal of learning a second language was just to sound like a native. Many students need to communicate with other non-native speakers, not with natives, sometimes in different ways from natives. Native speaker speech is only one of the possible models for the L2 student. Students who want to become successful L2 users may want to base themselves on the speech of successful L2 users, not on monolingual native speakers.

Being a native speaker does not automatically make you a good teacher. In many instances the expat native speaker is less trained than the local non-native teacher, or has been trained in an educational system with different values and goals; the local non-native speaker teacher knows the local circumstances and culture. Native speakers are not necessarily aware of the properties of their own language and are highly unlikely to be able to talk about its grammar coherently; one of the 16-year-olds in Benke and Medgyes' study (2005: 207) says: 'They are sometimes not very accurate and they can't spell – especially Americans.' Given equal training and local knowledge, the native speaker's advantage is their proficiency at their native language, no more, no less.

Crucially, the native speaker teacher does not belong to the group that the students are trying to join – L2 users. They have not gone through the same stages as their students and often do not know what it means to learn a second language themselves; their command of the students' own language often betrays their own failings as learners – I was told of a German class in London where much of the time was taken up by the students teaching English to the teacher – perhaps a not uncommon example of reciprocal language teaching. A non-native teacher is necessarily a model of a person who commands two languages and is able to communicate through both; a native speaker teacher is unlikely to know two languages, even if there are exceptions.

Peter Medgyes (1992) highlights the drawbacks of native speakers, who:

- are not models of L2 users;
- cannot talk about L2 learning strategies from their own experience;
- are often not explicitly aware of the features of the language as much as non-native speakers are;
- cannot anticipate learning problems;
- cannot empathize with their students' learning experience;
- are not able to exploit the learners' first language in the classroom.

In addition, students may feel that native speaker teachers have achieved a perfection that is out of their reach; as Claire Kramsch (1998: 9) puts it, 'non-native teachers and students alike are intimidated by the native-speaker norm'. Students may prefer the more achievable model of the fallible non-native speaker teacher.

From my experience, native speakers were overwhelmingly preferred by language schools in London for teaching English, as the job ads imply. It may, however, no longer be legal in England to discriminate against non-native speakers.

In 2000 the Eurotunnel Consortium had to pay compensation to a French national married to an Englishman whose dismissal on grounds of not speaking English was ruled 'an act of unlawful discrimination on the grounds of her race.' The chairman of the employment tribunal said that the job description asking for a native English accent was comparable to having a 'whites-only policy'.

So non-native speaker teachers provide:

- *A model of a proficient L2 user in action.* The students witness someone who is using the second language effectively (one reason for using the L2 in the classroom); they can see that it is possible to operate in a language that is not one's own. The native speaker teacher, on the other hand, is a model of something alien which the students can never be in the second language – a user of a first language.

- *A model of a person who has successfully learnt a second language.* The non-native teacher has acquired another language in the same way as the student, showing that it can be done. They have shared the student's own experience at some time in their lives. The native speaker teacher has followed a completely different route and has not had the students' experiences and problems at first hand.

- *More appropriate training and background.* The native speaker is an outsider and does not necessarily share the culture of the classroom and the values of the educational system in the same way. Many expat EFL teachers are not fully trained, and indeed would not have the qualifications to teach in UK secondary schools.

- *Possible lesser fluency, and so on, in the second language.* Of course, the preceding summary of non-native assets assumes that the non-native speaker teacher can speak fluently and communicate within the classroom, which may be far from true in many classrooms around the world. This is not due to their non-native status, but to inadequate training or ineffective selection for their jobs; they are inefficient L2 users, not poor native speakers.

We can see then that the choice between native and non-native teachers is not a simple matter, but is confounded with language knowledge, teacher training and many other factors. Indeed, if the sole asset of the native speaker is their command of the native language spoken in their home country, this has a short shelf life; after six months or so, English teachers in Spain are starting to use English influenced by the Spanish teaching situation (Porte, 2003).

A compromise is to combine the good points of both native and non-native teachers. Most famously this is through the assistant language teachers on the Japan Exchange and Teaching (JET) programme, in which native speaker teachers with comparatively little experience are teamed with experienced Japanese teachers in the classroom. Typically, the JET assistant is used both as a source of authentic native language and cultural information, and as a foreigner to whom Japanese culture can be explained. The Japanese teacher takes responsibility for the overall direction and control of the class through their experience and local knowledge. More information can be found at the website for MEXT, the Japanese Ministry of Education (www.mext.go.jp/english/).

Alternatively, the presentation of native speaker speech can be through the materials and media. Tapes can use native speaker actors; television programmes, films or tapes can present authentic speech, and so on. The teacher does not have to be the sole source of input in the classroom. Indeed, successful non-native teachers may produce students who speak the language better than they do in native speaker terms, provided that the sole model has not been the teacher's own speech. But of course, the appropriate goal may not be native speaker language in the first place.

Box 10.11 Pros and cons of native and non-native speaker teachers

Expat native speaker teachers	Non-native speaker teachers
provide a model of native speaker use	provide a model of L2 user use
may be fluent in their L1	may not be so fluent in their L2
know the L1 culture from the inside	know the L1 culture from the outside
may become less native over time	may not change or may improve over time
provide a model of someone who has learnt the L2 as an L1	provide a model of someone who has learnt the language as an L2
may not have knowledge of the local educational system	know the local educational system
may or may not have appropriate teacher training and qualifications	have appropriate teacher training and qualifications

---

10.5 International languages: English as lingua franca (ELF)

Focusing questions

- Why do people in your country or another country you know use a second language?
- Is English a peculiar language or is it typical of many other second languages?
- Do you think a language can escape the culture or control of its native speakers?

Keywords

hypercentral language: a language that is used globally for international purposes, as opposed to languages that are used more locally

English as lingua franca (ELF, sometimes LFE): the name for the kind of English that is used globally by non-native speakers for many kinds of international purposes

This section deals with the situation of languages that are used outside the country or area where they originated. Chapter 11 describes the varieties of language in relationship to language teaching. Here we concentrate on English as an international language, rather than say, French or Chinese.

According to Abram de Swaan (2001), languages form a hierarchy (represented in Figure 10.2):

- **Peripheral** languages are used within a given territory by native speakers to each other, such as Welsh spoken in some regions of Wales, or Japanese spoken in the whole of Japan.
- **Central** languages are used within a single territory by people who are both native speakers and non-native speakers, for purposes of education and government, say, English in India used by native speakers of many languages.
- **Supercentral** languages are used across several parts of the world by natives and non-natives, with specialized function, say, Arabic or Latin for religious ceremonies. Often their spread reflects previous colonial empires, French, Spanish, and so on.
- **Hypercentral** languages are used chiefly by non-native speakers across the globe for a variety of purposes. At the moment only one hypercentral language exists, namely English.

To de Swaan (2001), languages exist in 'constellations'. India, for example, has Hindi and English as two supercentral languages, plus 18 central languages, such as Gujarati and Sindhi, nearly all of which have official status within a state; the remaining 780-odd languages are peripheral.

Society as a whole depends on the interlocking of these languages and so is based on multilinguals who can plug the gaps between one level and another, whether within one territory or internationally. According to de Swaan (2001), the learning of second languages usually goes up the hierarchy rather than down: people learn a language that is the next level up. Speakers of a peripheral language

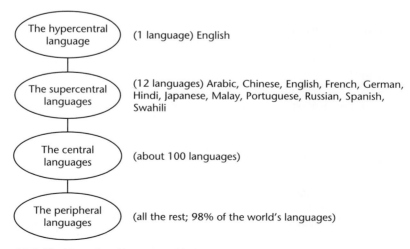

The hypercentral language — (1 language) English

The supercentral languages — (12 languages) Arabic, Chinese, English, French, German, Hindi, Japanese, Malay, Portuguese, Russian, Spanish, Swahili

The central languages — (about 100 languages)

The peripheral languages — (all the rest; 98% of the world's languages)

Figure 10.2 The hierarchy of languages (de Swaan, 2001)

have to learn a central language to function in their own society, such as speakers of Catalan learning Spanish in Spain. Speakers of a central language need to learn a supercentral language to function within their region, say speakers of Persian learning Arabic. Speakers of a supercentral language need the hypercentral language to function globally; anybody but a native speaker of English needs to learn English (and even they may need to learn ELF).

The main reason why people learn a local language (to adopt a slightly more neutral term than de Swaan's 'peripheral') like Finnish as a second language may be to meet Finnish people and take part in life in Finland; the emphasis is on native speakers in their native habitat. The reason for learning a central language is to interact with the rest of the population in multilingual societies: speakers of Ladin need Italian to go to Italian universities outside the South Tyrol. Some of the time users of central languages are dealing with native speakers, some of the time with fellow non-native users with different L1s, within the same country or geographical region. The reasons for acquiring supercentral languages depend on the uses of languages, such as Hebrew for the Jewish faith and Arabic for Islam; the native speaker is of marginal relevance; the location may be anywhere where the language is used in this way, say synagogues or mosques across the globe. The reasons for acquiring the hypercentral language are the global demands of work; international business becomes difficult without English and the native speaker is only one of the types of people that need to be communicated with.

The reasons why languages have got to these particular levels are complex and controversial. Some see the dark side of the dominance of English, regarding it as a way of retaining an empire through deliberate political actions (Phillipson, 1992), and inevitably leading to the death of local languages. Others see the use of English as an assertion of local rights to deal with the rest of the world in their own way rather than as domination (Canagarajah, 2005).

Some of these issues are considered in Chapter 11 in the context of the goals of language teaching. This section concentrates on English, which is unique in that it can be used for any of these levels, from monolingual local to global hypercentral; the closest previous analogues were Latin and Chinese in the empires of Rome and China respectively. Some languages have become global in extremely limited uses, like Japanese for karate. Others have seen their vocabulary adapted to international use – try asking for the Starbucks coffee called 'venti' in a coffee bar in Italy – it actually means 'twenty', rather than 'large'. But English has extended its scope way outside the previous boundaries of the British Empire to a considerable range of functions.

English, then, may be acquired for any or all of the above reasons. Other languages are limited to those appropriate to their position on the hierarchy. The demand for Finnish as an international language is probably small, though it may have some central role for the Finnish-speaking minority in Sweden. Various terms have been proposed for this peculiar status of English, whether 'international English', 'global English' or 'world English'. Recent discussion has preferred the term 'English as lingua franca' (ELF) – English as a means of communication between native speakers of other languages. In this context, 'lingua franca' does not have its historic negative meaning of a mixed language, but means a communication language used by speakers of other languages.

Throughout this chapter, the question that has been posed repeatedly is the status of the native speaker. At one time, native speakers were unquestionably the only true speakers of the language; non-native speakers could only aspire to become like them. The grammars, dictionaries and pronunciation depended on one form or another of native English. Social interaction was assumed to take place between native speakers and non-native speakers.

Nowadays much use of English takes place between fellow non-native speakers; 74 per cent of English in tourism does not involve a native speaker (Graddol, 2006). Many jobs like professional footballers, merchant seamen, call centre workers or airplane pilots require L2 user-to-L2 user interaction. Sometimes indeed the native speaker may find it difficult to join in. L2 users of ELF need primarily to be able to talk to each other rather than to native speakers.

Yet the Chinese person talking to the Brazilian in English, or the German speaker talking to the Arabic speaker in English, do need to share some common form of English or they will not understand each other. While most arguments for the native speaker version of the language are based on ownership and linguistic power, native speaker language at least provides a common standard of reference, so that the Chinese and the Brazilian are sharing the same English. Native speaker English has been extensively studied and described for a hundred years, so a great amount is known about it; we know the sort of grammatical patterns and vocabulary that native speakers use.

But suppose that the English used by non-natives is the target. Compared to the wealth of information on native language, comparatively little is known about non-native English by L2 users; mostly it has been investigated in terms of deviations from native speech rather than in its own right. Chapter 4 discusses Jenny Jenkins' (2002) proposals for an ELF pronunciation syllabus based on students' difficulties with each other's speech, for instance, not bothering with teaching /ð~θ/, but paying particular attention to where the sentence stress occurs. While this severs the link to the native speaker, the phonology is based on students learning language in classrooms rather than on L2 users using language in the world outside education; what students accept or reject may not be the same as what experienced L2 users might feel.

Currently, considerable research is taking place into the characteristics of ELF, for example in the VOICE research at the University of Vienna, based on a variety of L2 users. From this comes the list in Box 10.12, compiled by Barbara Seidlhofer (2004). Characteristics of ELF are different usage of articles from native English,

---

Box 10.12 Features of ELF grammar (based on Seidlhofer, 2004)

- Dropping' the third person '-s'.
- Confusing the relative pronouns 'who' and 'which'.
- Omitting definite 'a/an' and indefinite 'the' articles where they are obligatory in native speech, and inserting them where they do not occur in native speech.
- Failing to use 'correct' forms in tag questions; for example, using 'isn't it?' or 'no?' instead of 'shouldn't they?'
- Inserting redundant prepositions, as in 'We have to study about. . .'
- Overusing certain verbs of high semantic generality, such as 'do', 'have', 'make', 'put', 'take'.
- Replacing infinitive 'to' constructions with that-clauses, as in 'I want that. . .'
- Being over-explicit (e.g. 'black colour' rather than just 'black').

invariable forms of tag questions such as 'isn't it?' and 'are you?', and so on. Many of these have been regarded as persistent mistakes by teachers; how often have I added or deleted 'the' and 'a' from students' work? If, however, this variation simply reflects characteristics of the variety of English that the students are modelling and does not hinder their communication, there is no need to try to change it towards the native form; my urge to correct it is based on my own native speaker usage, not on the ELF variety suitable for the students. If the argument is that these forms are non-native, it is always possible to retort 'Which native?' The invariable tag 'innit?', the omission of third person '-s', and the common spoken overuse of 'do' or 'got' are all found in colloquial British English, only not from the type of native speaker that has been considered appropriate for students.

If L2 users can understand each other despite these differences from native speaker English, there is little point in making them conform to native speech for its own sake. It has often been reported to me that the problem at international meetings where English is used is not so much the L2 users understanding each other as the L2 users understanding the native speakers, who make no concessions to the ELF that is being used. Indeed, it has sometimes been suggested that native speakers themselves should be taught these ELF forms.

Box 10.13 ELF (English as lingua franca)

- The status of English is now peculiar in that it has become a lingua franca hypercentral language largely spoken between non-native speakers.
- A main motive for many learners is to be able to speak with fellow L2 users, not native speakers.
- The target for learners in grammatical and phonological terms will need to be based on successful ELF English, not native speaker English or student English.

Discussion topics

1 Devise a classroom communicative activity depending on use of both languages (other than translation).

2 What do you now believe about the status of the native speaker in language teaching?

3 How would you define a successful L2 learner?

4 When should codeswitching *not* occur in the classroom?

5 How much L1 is the maximum for the L2 classroom? 0 per cent? 10 per cent? 20 per cent? 50 per cent? More?

6 Will the public's demand for native speakers to teach them the second language ever change?

Further reading

The key texts in this area are: Myers-Scotton (2005) in *Handbook of Bilingualism*; Macaro (1997) *Target Language, Collaborative Learning and Autonomy*; de Swaan (2001) *Words of the World: The Global Language System*; and Llurda (2005) *Non-native Teachers*.

The goals of language teaching

This chapter looks at language as the possession of a group and at the L2 user as a member of a specific group. It describes some of the roles that second languages play in people's lives and sees how they can be translated into goals of language teaching. It raises the fundamental questions of why we are teaching a second language and of what students want to be and what groups they want to belong to, things which teachers often neglect to think about in their absorbing teaching lives.

To some people, acquiring a second language is a difficult feat; to others, it is ordinary and unexceptional. Take the real-life history of a boy in Tanzania who spoke Kihaya at home; he needed Kiswahili in elementary school and English in secondary school; he trained to be a priest, for which he needed Latin, but he also learnt French out of curiosity at the same time. Then he went as a priest to Uganda and Kenya, where he needed Rukiga and Kikamba, and he is now in Illinois, where he needs Spanish to communicate with his parishioners. To most monolingual English speakers, this seems a mind-boggling life story. It is extraordinary to us that someone can use more than one language in their everyday life.

Or take a country like Cameroon, which has 2 official languages, 4 lingua francas and 285 native languages (Koenig *et al.*, 1983); most people use four or five languages in the course of a day. Probably more people in the world are like the typical Cameroonian than the typical Englishman. Harding and Riley (1986) point out that 'there are 3000–5000 languages in the world but only about 150 countries to fit them all into'. Even in Europe, 56 per cent of the citizens of the EU know at least one foreign language (EuroBarometer, 2006). Knowing a second language is a normal part of human existence; it may well be unusual to know only one.

A starting point is to look at what a language is. Conventionally, one meaning of 'language' is political in the Lang$_2$ sense of Chapter 1, 'an abstract entity': a language belongs to a nation, whether German, French, English or Chinese. An aphorism attributed to Ulrich Weinreich is that a language is a dialect with an army and a navy. This definition in terms of a nation works when the everyday use of a language effectively stops at the borders of a country, say Japanese in Japan or Korean in Korea. In these cases, the native speakers of the language are born and live within the country. They are local languages spoken within the same area, whether a country or a section of a country. They usually have a single standard form based on a particular region or social class, regardless of dialects: standard Japanese derives from Tokyo, standard Korean from Seoul. The logical target of teaching for those local languages may indeed be the language and culture of the native speaker.

Languages, however, may have native speakers spread across neighbouring countries, not just confined to a single country – supercentral languages in de Swaan's terms, like Swahili, Arabic and Chinese. Some languages do not even have nation homes in that they spread across several countries without being recognized in any of them, say, Romany in many countries of Europe, or Kurdish spread across several frontiers. Other languages spoken within the boundaries of one country may not be the official language of the state, such as Basque and Catalan in Spain or Scottish Gaelic in Scotland. Often this may be a major plank in arguments for political independence, as is the case of Catalonia in Spain. Languages, then, may have very different statuses, as seen in Chapter 10.

11.1 The different roles of second languages in people's lives

Focusing questions

- In the area where you live, how many languages are spoken? Officially or actually?
- How many languages do you know? How many do you use in a day?
- Would you, as a parent, bring up children to speak two languages or not? Why?

Keywords

elite bilingualism: either the decision by parents to bring up children through two languages, or societies in which members of a ruling group speak a second language

official language: language(s) recognized by a country for official purposes

multilingualism: countries or situations where more than one language is used for everyday purposes

linguistic imperialism: the means by which a 'centre' country dominates 'periphery' countries by making them use its language

This section needs to start by defusing the myth that bilingualism in itself has a bad effect on children, typified by Thompson (1952): 'There can be no doubt that the child reared in a bilingual environment is handicapped in his language growth.' This view is still around in some forms; the advice in a pamphlet for parents of children with Down's syndrome, *I Can Talk* (Streets, 1976, reprinted 1991) is: 'Bilingual families: for any child this is confusing – one language should be the main one to avoid confusion.'

However, since the 1960s, research has pointed unequivocally to the advantages of bilingualism: children who know a second language are better at separating semantic from phonetic aspects of words, at classifying objects, and at coming up with creative ideas – far from confused. They also have sharper awareness of language, as we see below; a brief list of bilingual writers, such as Vladimir Nabokov, André Brink and Joseph Conrad, soon confirms this. As for confusion, Einstein used more than one language (and was also a late speaker as a child).

According to Ellen Bialystok and her colleagues (2004), bilinguals are less likely to develop Alzheimer's disease in old age. Diaz (1985) typifies the modern view: 'growing up with two languages is, indeed, an asset to children's intellectual development'. Much of the earlier belief in the deficiencies of the bilingual turned out to be a flaw in the research design of not separating bilingualism out from the poverty and isolation of immigrant groups.

Bilingualism by choice

Some people speak two languages because their parents decided to bring them up bilingually in the home. This so-called 'elite' bilingualism is not forced on the parents by society or by the educational system, but is their free choice. Often one of the languages involved is the central language of the country, the other a local language spoken by one parent as a native. Sometimes both parents speak a minority local language themselves, but feel the majority central language should also be used at home. However, George Saunders (1982) describes how he and his wife decided to bring up their children in German in Australia, though neither of them was a native speaker. Others have three languages in the family; Philip Riley's children spoke English and Swedish at home and French at school (Harding and Riley, 1986).

This parental choice also extends in some countries to educating their children through a second language, for example in International Schools across the world, in the 'European Schools' movement (Baetens Beardsmore, 1993), the French Lycée in London or indeed in the English public schools that now educate large numbers of children from non-English-speaking countries (for the benefit of the non-Brit, a public school in the UK is an expensive private school, not part of the state system). Choosing this type of bilingual education usually depends on having money or on being an expatriate; it is mostly a preserve of the middle classes. While a second language is often considered a 'problem' in the education of lower-status people, it is seen as a mark of distinction in those of higher status. A Chinese child in a state school in England is seen as having a language problem, not helped by being 'mainstreamed' with all the other children; a Chinese child in a public school has been recruited by the school from, say, Hong Kong, and their bilingualism is seen as an asset, to be helped with special English classes.

So bilingualism by choice mostly takes place outside the main educational contexts of L2 teaching, and varies according to the parents' wishes; accounts of these will be found in the self-help manuals written for parents by Arnberg (1987) and by Harding and Riley (1986). A useful source is the Bilingual Families mailing list (www.nethelp.no/cindy/biling-fam.html).

Second languages for religious use

Some people use a second language because of their religion. For centuries after its decline as an international language, Latin functioned as a religious language of the Catholic Church. Muslims read the Koran in Arabic, regardless of whether they live in an Arabic-speaking country like Saudi Arabia or in a multilingual country like Malaysia. Jews outside Israel continue to learn Hebrew so that they can pray in it and study the Bible and other sacred texts. In parts of India, Christianity is identified with English, in Ethiopia with Aramaic. Though the language of religious observances is specialized, it is nonetheless a form of L2 use for supercentral languages. As this type of L2 learning is distinct from most classroom situations, it will not be discussed further here, but it should not be overlooked, since for millions of people it is the most profound use of a second language imaginable.

Official languages and L2 learning

According to Laponce (1987), 32 countries recognize more than one language for official purposes. Switzerland has four languages (German, French, Italian, Romansh) and uses Latin on its stamps ('Helvetia'). The Singapore government uses English, Mandarin, Malay and Tamil.

But the fact that a country has several official languages does not mean that any individual person speaks more than one; the communities may be entirely separate. Mackey (1967) claims that 'there are fewer bilingual people in the bilingual countries than there are in the so-called unilingual countries'. Few Canadians, for instance, use both English and French in daily life. Instead, the French and English speakers live predominantly in different parts of Canada, as do the German, French and Italian speakers in Switzerland, and the French and Flemish speakers in Belgium. It is necessary in many of these countries to teach speakers of one official language to use another official language; Afrikaans-speaking civil servants in South Africa need English; their English-speaking counterparts in Canada need French.

This does not necessarily mean that each official language is equally favoured; few Swiss would bother to learn Romansh as a second language. Nor does it mean that the official language learnt is the version actually used in the country; in Switzerland, French-speaking children learn High German, not the Swiss German mostly spoken in the German-speaking areas, so they can, in a sense, speak with Germans better than they can with their compatriots.

Sometimes a language can become an official language with at first few, if any, native speakers. Hebrew was revived by a popular movement in Israel long before being adopted by the new state. The teaching of Hebrew in Israel did not just educate one group in the language of another, but created a group of people who spoke a second language that would become the first language of their children. In some countries an official language is selected that has, at least to start with, a small proportion of native speakers, for example, Swahili in Tanzania, where only 10 per cent of the population are native speakers. Another pattern is found in the Congo, where French is the official language but there are four 'national languages', Kiswahili, Ciluba, Lingala and Kikongo, which are used as lingua francas among speakers of different mother tongues. To take a final example, in Pakistan four languages are spoken in different provinces: Pashto, Punjabi, Balochi and Sindi. Urdu is used all over the country, as is Arabic for religious purposes. In addition, English is an official language.

Multilingualism and L2 learning

Regardless of whether they have more than one official language, most countries contain large numbers of people who use other languages. According to the Eurydice network (Eurydice, 2005), in Europe, '8 per cent of pupils aged 15 say that at home they speak a language other than the language of instruction.' While England uses one language for official purposes, a survey of London found that 32 per cent of children spoke languages other than English at home and that 300 different languages were spoken (Baker and Eversley, 2000). Some countries nevertheless consist almost entirely of speakers of a single language: 121 million of the 127 million inhabitants of Japan speak Japanese (Gordon, 2005). Others conceal a variety of languages under one official language. Of the 60 million people in France, 1.5 million speak Alemannisch, 1.2 million Arabic, 0.5 million Breton, 0.5 million Kabyle, and so on (Gordon, 2005). In Vancouver, where 46 per cent of the population are immigrants, undoubtedly more bilinguals speak Chinese alongside English than French, and in Toronto 4.9 per cent of the inhabitants speak French at home (Gardner, 2007), despite English and French being the official languages of Canada. In the year 2000, 47 million US residents over the age of 4 spoke a language other than English at home, that is, one in five of the population (US Census Bureau, 2003); this trend has led to a worry about the continuing status and importance of English.

Mobility also plays a part in multilingualism. Some countries, for one reason or other, include static populations of speakers of different languages, sometimes called 'internal colonies'. The UK has had speakers of Welsh, Gaelic and English for many centuries. According to Ethnologue (Gordon, 2005), 24 languages are spoken in South Africa, 415 in India and 102 in Vietnam. In many cases this multiplicity of languages reflects the arbitrary borders imposed on various countries in modern times. Much was the historical result of conquest or movement of people; the empires of Islam and France led to Algeria having speakers of French, Arabic and Berber; the legacy of the British Empire and trade led to Malaysia having speakers of Bahasa Malaysia, Chinese, Indian languages and various indigenous languages, amounting to 140 in total. Recent changes in such groups have sometimes consisted of people going back to their homeland; ethnic Germans returning to Germany, Turkish-speaking Bulgarians returning to Turkey, and so on. A balance between the languages in one country has often been arrived at, though not necessarily with the consent or approval of the speakers of the minority languages: children were at some time forbidden to speak Basque in Spain, Navajo in the USA or Kurdish in Turkey; Koreans in Japanese-occupied territories had to adopt Japanese names; the Turkish minority in Bulgaria had to use Bulgarian names. Indeed, deaf children in England (the use of sign language by the deaf being a form of multilingualism that is often forgotten) have often been made to sit on their hands in class to prevent them using sign language.

The past few decades seem to have accelerated movements of people from one country to another, as refugees, such as the Vietnamese, as immigrants, such as Algerians in France, or as migrants looking for work, such as Moroccans in Germany or Poles in England and Ireland. This has created a vast new multilingualism. New York is said to be the biggest Gujarati-speaking city outside the Indian subcontinent, Melbourne the largest Maltese-speaking city in the world. An Indian student born in Uganda said to me that the first Indian city she had lived in was the London suburb of Southall. A wealth of languages are spoken in every European town today, regardless of the official language of the country; Turkish is spoken in London or in Berlin or in Amsterdam; Arabic can be heard from Paris to Brussels to Berlin; in the west London suburb of Ealing 20 per cent of children speak Punjabi, 10 per cent Hindi/Urdu and 6 per cent Gujarati (Baker and Eversley, 2000). In some cases, these people are temporary birds of passage, intending to return to their country once the political or economic situation changes – Polish taxi drivers in most English cities, for example. In most cases, they are permanent citizens of the country, with the same rights as any other citizen, like Finnish-speaking citizens of Sweden or Bengali-speaking citizens of England.

In many cases, such multilingualism is bound to be short-lived. Paulston (1986) describes how immigrants to the USA from Greece and Italy become native speakers of English over three or four generations. In her view, such a shift from minority to majority language is prevented only when there are strong boundaries around the group, whether social or geographical (Gaelic in the Hebrides), or self-imposed (the Amish in the USA, who speak Pennsylvania Dutch), or when there is a clear separation in social use of the two languages ('diglossia'), as in Standard Arabic versus local versions of Arabic in North Africa. Having one's own ethnic culture as a minority group means speaking the language of that culture, usually different from the majority language, but not necessarily so – as in the use of English by many Scottish nationalists. Language, then, is often part of ethnicity, and hence associated with political movements for the rights of particular groups. Indeed, this extends to the rise of heritage languages in some minority groups, which may not currently be spoken by any of the members; the Confucius Institutes that are springing up around the world for the teaching of Chinese have found that one important group of students consists of Chinese speakers of other dialects wishing to learn Mandarin.

Joshua Fishman (1991) has described this intergenerational shift as a Graded Intergenerational Disruption Scale (GIDS), which has eight stages. At the first stage, a language is used for some 'higher-level' government and mass media, for example, but does not have 'political independence'; an example might be Swiss German. At the second stage, the language is used in the 'lower' levels of government and media, but not 'in the higher spheres of either'. And so on until stage 7, when the users of the language are old and 'beyond child-bearing age', but still talk to each other, such as some speakers of old Italian dialects in Toronto. And it ends with stage 8, when the only language users left are socially isolated and need to transmit their language to people who can teach it to a new generation, like speakers of some Aboriginal languages in Australia or speakers of Cornish in Cornwall.

Internationalism and second languages

For many students, the second language has no real role within their own society; English is not learnt in China because of its usefulness inside China. Instead, the second language is taught in the educational system because of the benefits it brings from outside the home country. Any language may be taught with the aim of promoting relationships with other countries that use it.

So a particular country, or indeed a particular individual, may decide to learn a second language for a purpose outside their own society, whether to do business with other countries, to gain access to a scientific literature or to a cultural heritage, or to be able to work in other countries. In Israel, English is seen as 'the customary language for international communication and for overcoming barriers to the flow of information, goods and people across national boundaries' (*English – Curriculum for all Grades*, 2002). Such use of an international language does not necessarily entail any acceptance of the values of the society from which it originates. Steve Biko justified English as the language of the Black People's Convention in South Africa because it acted as a lingua franca and it was 'analytical' (Biko, 1978). Anti-English graffiti in Belfast were written in English, not Irish. The speaker's attitudes to the target culture are marginal to such uses.

Sometimes, as a legacy of colonialism, the original speakers of an international language feel that they have the right to say what it should be or how it should be taught. We can complement the advertisements for native speaker English teachers in Chapter 10 with the examples of the Alliance Française in London claiming French 'taught by French nationals'; the Eurolingua Institute, 'lessons are given by experienced and fully qualified mother tongue teachers'; and Language Trainers, 'All our German teachers are native speakers (from Germany, Austria or Switzerland)'. While the aims of the UK schools syllabus for French refer to 'French-speaking countries'; this is automatically taken to be France, as a student from the Ivory Coast bitterly pointed out to me.

Setting aside political or commercial motivations, the responsibility for international languages has passed out of the hands of the original owners. Furthermore, the right to say how something should be *taught* is even less a right of the native speaker than the right to say how something should be *said*. An Englishman or an American has no more intrinsic right to tell an Egyptian how to teach English than does a Japanese; the only one who can decide what is right for Egypt is the Egyptian: as a spokesman said in China, 'For China we need a Chinese method.' Whether an idea or an approach to language teaching is useful does not depend on which country it comes from. Its merits have to be accepted or rejected by the experts on the situation – the teachers and students who live and work there.

As we have seen in this section, language is not politically neutral. Deciding which language should be used in a particular country or which other language should be taught affects the economic and cultural life not only of the country itself, but also of the country from which the language comes. Take the example of English. On the one hand, in Singapore the decision to make English its 'first' language must have played a significant part in its economic success. On the other hand, the UK itself can try to keep economic links with many parts of the world by promoting English. This is without taking into account the vast sums of money involved in the language teaching operation itself, whether in the sales of British books or the students coming to UK schools and universities.

Robert Phillipson (1992) calls this 'linguistic imperialism' and sees it as a special case of Galtung's (1980) concept of 'a dominant Centre (the powerful western countries) and a dominated Periphery (the under-developed countries)'. The centre can exert this domination in part by forcing the periphery to use its languages. So English as a centre language is used for business purposes of trading between periphery countries and the centre. However, this use has been so successful that English escaped the hands of its originators and allowed periphery countries to do business with each other rather than with the UK itself.

In addition, educational systems in the periphery emphasize English and indeed have instruction through English, particularly at university; the University of Gaza, for example, uses English as the means of instruction for all subjects, as do universities in Egypt, the Netherlands and Botswana. Above all, English is a requirement for scientific writing and reading: few scientists can make a proper contribution to their field without having access to English, either in person or through translation of one kind or another: 86 per cent of research papers in biology are written in English, and 97 per cent of those on cross-cultural psychology. While the teaching of scientific English may be of vital importance to the individual learners, the pressure to use English for science is a form of linguistic imperialism. Publication in scientific journals depends on getting over an additional obstacle that native speakers do not have to face; journals that come from the centre are not going to value independent views from people outside this area. Even in the SLA research area, this is apparent; it is dominated by literature in English and biased towards accounts of acquisition of English in highly developed countries; an international conference on cross-cultural psychology only used English, despite the fact that many participants did not speak it well. Academics who live in centre countries naturally feel they cannot compromise academic standards – but it is the standards of the centre that are continually perpetuated, not the potentially infinite richness of scientific exploration possible through different cultures and approaches.

Indeed, the influence of the centre is not just on the choice of language that other countries need to learn, but on the very means of teaching them. French audio-visualism was exported to francophone Africa, British communicative teaching to most parts of the globe. Adrian Holliday (1994) points to the permanent guilt feelings of the local teacher who is never able to apply the centre-approved methods to their own satisfaction, basically because they were not designed specifically for the needs of any local situation.

Recently, however, the concept of linguistic imperialism has been criticized on various grounds (Canagarajah, 2005). One is that in many cases English is not so much imposed from outside as requested by the locals themselves, as a way of communicating with the world at large, not just with the centre of an empire – a network with many connections rather than a spider's web leading only to the centre. The other reason is that fears of English replacing other languages seem to have been exaggerated; for instance, in India the shift is not towards English, but towards local regional languages (Bhatt, 2005). Of course, this may be the unique situation of English as the hypercentral language, as seen in Chapter 10, and not necessarily true of supercentral and central languages.

11.2 Language and groups of speakers

Focusing questions

- Do you belong to a community with a single language or a community that uses more than one? Which is preferable?
- Of all the groups to which you belong – family, religion, nation, and so on – how important is the group of L1 speakers? Of L2 users?
- What modern jobs necessarily require the use of a second language?

Let us now turn to the groups of L2 users that people may belong to, that is, membership of a community in the Lang$_4$ sense of language. While language is often seen as a shared core value of the community (Smolicz and Secombe, 2003), it is not always a necessary requirement; Jewish communities, for instance, have historically spoken diverse languages across the world, such as Yiddish (Myhill, 2003). Nor are the members of the community necessarily fluent in its language, as with Scottish Gaelic (Dorian, 1981). People may be part of a community without speaking its language – how many Irish Americans speak Irish?

As well as monolingual communities, there are many communities where it is necessary to use more than one language. India, for example, has a 'three-language formula' 3 ± 1: everyone has to know not only Hindi and English, but also the local language of a particular state. If the local state language is Hindi or English, they only need two languages $(3 - 1)$; if neither Hindi nor English is the state language and they speak another language, they need four languages (3 + 1) (Laitin, 2000). It is taken for granted that the community itself is multilingual, the languages involved varying by individual and by state. The ongoing discussion of ELF recognizes at least one widespread L2 user community, crossing national boundaries and becoming detached from the native speaker, as Latin once separated from Italy.

Groups of language users

Both SLA research and language teaching need to be clear about the differences between language user groups rather than treating all users and learners as the same. Box 11.1 lists some of these groups. Illustrations come primarily from London.

Box 11.1 Language user groups

1 People speaking their native language.
2 People using an L2 within the majority community.
3 People historically from a particular community (re-)acquiring its language as L2.
4 People speaking an L2 as short-term visitors to another country or to short-term visitors to their country.
5 People using an L2 with spouses or friends.
6 People using an L2 internationally for specific functions.
7 Students and teachers acquiring or conveying an education through an L2.
8 Pupils and teachers learning or teaching L2 in school.

People speaking their native language

Some people use their native language exclusively. So monolingual Londoners speak English with each other and potentially with anybody else who speaks English in the world; in London they make up the sea, so to speak. But native speakers may also be an island in a sea; deaf people in London use British Sign Language in the midst of the hearing. And, of course, many native speakers of one language are L2 users of another language rather than monolinguals.

People speaking a second language within a majority community

Some residents use a second language to communicate with the majority language group, say, resident Bengalis in Tower Hamlets using English as a central language for their everyday contacts with other citizens of London. Often this group is permanent and may pre-date the existence of the majority community, such as Aboriginals in Australia. They are using the second language for practical purposes – the classic 'second language' situation – while having a first language for other social and cultural purposes. In addition, many people living in multilingual communities use the second language as a central language with speakers of minority language groups other than their own, essentially as a local lingua franca. The Bengali L1 shop owner in Tower Hamlets uses English for speaking with Arabic L1 customers, both equally English in nationality, true of most of the

L1 speakers of the 300 languages of London (Baker and Eversley, 2000). Sometimes the L2 lingua franca crosses national borders. Swahili has 770,000 native speakers, but 30 million lingua franca speakers spread across several African countries (Gordon, 2005).

People historically from a particular community (re-)acquiring its language as L2

The descendants of a particular cultural or ethnic group may want to learn its language, for instance, to talk to their grandparents who were first-generation incomers. Language maintenance classes take place in London ranging from Polish to Greek. Some people are trying to find their roots through language. Others are returning to their country of historical origin and need to reacquire the language, or sometimes to acquire it for the first time. One example is Puerto Ricans returning from the USA to Puerto Rico (Clachar, 1997), rejoining a community of L1 speakers as L2 users. Another group are the children of expats going back to the country their family originally came from, say, Japanese children returning to Japan (Kanno, 2000); these need to acquire the language of the homeland for practical purposes as well as cultural identity, many finding it an extremely difficult task.

People speaking an L2 either as short-term visitors to another country or to short-term visitors to their country

Some people are short-term visitors to another country, say, tourists. English for tourism is no longer a matter of English-speaking tourists going to non-English-speaking countries, or non-English-speaking tourists going to English-speaking countries, as we have seen. Some tourists may nevertheless try to learn the language of a country before visiting it – English people learning French to go to France, Japanese learning Spanish to visit Spain. English for tourism is a theme in most EFL coursebooks, Spanish for tourism a key attraction for evening classes in England. Other short-term visitors to another country include: athletes going to the Olympic Games, businessmen attending conferences, policemen investigating crimes, pilgrims, retirees visiting their villas in Spain – the list is endless. Again, some may want to use the central language of the country, some a language that will get them by, such as Latin or Klingon at conferences of their devotees. The reverse is people using an L2 with visitors to their country, whether the visitor's L1 as with Japanese people in Tokyo using English with English-speaking L1 visitors, or the visitor's L2 as with Japanese using English with L1 German-speaking visitors.

People using an L2 with spouses, siblings or friends

L2 users may speak their second language within a small social group. People have often joked that the best way of learning a language is to marry someone who speaks it; such married bilingual couples feel they are quite capable of passing for native speakers (Piller, 2002). Parents can choose to use a language with their children that they will not encounter outside the home. Indeed, unrelated pairs of people can decide to use a second language: Henry VIII wrote love letters to Anne Boleyn and Catherine of Aragon in French (Vatican City, n.d.), the language of courtly love.

People using an L2 internationally for specific functions

English as lingua franca (ELF) belongs to a variety of groups of speakers. One is made up of academics, using the language for academic journals and conferences everywhere. Other groups use specially designed varieties of English, like *SeaSpeak* for mariners (Weeks *et al.*, 1988) or *ASD Simplified Technical English*, a carefully restricted English for technical writing (ASD, 2007). And of course, international business uses English regardless of L1, say, Danish businessmen talking to Indians or Syrians on the phone (Firth, 1996). People who speak ELF belong to communities that cross frontiers, united by a common interest. In one view, English no longer counts as learning another language; it is an addition to the three Rs (reading, writing and arithmetic), necessary for primary school children everywhere (Graddol, 2006). But supercentral languages also have specialized transnational uses, for instance, Japanese in martial arts or Arabic for Muslims.

Students and teachers acquiring or conveying an education through an L2

Another group of L2 users are gaining an education through a second language, as we saw earlier. On the one hand, they may be another L2 minority island in an L1 sea; in the Netherlands, universities use English alongside Dutch. In reverse, students go to another country to get their higher education, Zaireans to Paris, Greeks to England. In other words, a second language is the vehicle for education, more or less regardless of its native speakers (except in so far as they can profit by teaching 'their' language). Within this general framework comes the elite bilingualism of children educated in multilingual schools.

Pupils and teachers learning or teaching L2 in school

Finally, children are taught a second language as part of the school curriculum – the classic 'foreign' language situation, whether French in England or Spanish in Japan. The children do not themselves form a community of users – perhaps the only group we can really call 'learners' rather than users. Often the goal is to get through the hurdles set by the examination system – language as a school subject, taught and assessed like other subjects. Members of this group are unique in not having an L2 identity of their own; their use is not an end in itself so much as the route to getting somewhere else.

Doubtless many other groups could be added, for example, interpreters, whether professionals or children helping their parents, a widespread use in minority groups. Some use the second language to native speakers, some to other non-native speakers. The goal of becoming a native speaker or even understanding a native speaker is beside the point; the aim is to become an efficient L2 user. Separating community from the monolingual native speaker leads to new groupings of speakers. Moreover an individual may have multiple memberships in these groups: a professional footballer coming to London needs not just the visitor language to cope with living there, but also the specialized ELF of football for interacting with the rest of the team (Kellerman *et al.*, 2005) – 60 per cent of league footballers in England at the time of writing (2008) are non-native speakers of English.

> **Box 11.2 Language and groups**
>
> - Language users are members of many possible groups, ranging from the family to the nation.
> - Many groups are genuinely multilingual rather than monolingual.
> - It is crucial to see L2 users as belonging to many groups and as being part of a new group of L2 users, rather than as supplicants to join native speaker groups.

11.3 The goals of language teaching

> **Focusing questions**
>
> - Do you think people who go to live in another country should either learn the majority language and forget their own or adopt the majority language for some everyday purposes, or try to keep both the majority language and their L1 going?
> - What goals do you or your students have for their second language outside their own country? Careers? Education? Access to information? Travel?

> **Keywords**
>
> **assimilationist teaching**: teaching that expects people to give up their native languages and to become speakers of the majority central language of the country
> **transitional L2 teaching**: teaching that allows people to function in a central language, without necessarily losing or devaluing the first language
> **language maintenance** and **bilingual language teaching**: teaching to maintain or extend the minority local language within its own group
> **submersion teaching**: extreme sink-or-swim form of assimilationist teaching in which minority language children are put in majority language classes

What does this diversity of functions and group memberships mean for L2 learning and teaching? We can make a broad division between *central goals* which foster the second language within the country, *international goals* which foster it for use outside the country and *individual goals* which aim at developing the potential of the individual learner.

Central goals of teaching

The central goals of language teaching are those that serve the needs of the society within itself, particularly the need for different groups to interact with each other. They can be seen as having three broad divisions, drawing on the distinctions made in *Bilingualism or Not* (Skutnabb-Kangas, 1981): assimilationist, transitional and language maintenance. All these are concerned with the position of minority language children relative to the majority language, that is to say, with speakers of a local language learning the central language for use in the wider community.

Assimilationist language teaching

Assimilationist teaching accepts that society has the right to expect people to give up their native languages and to become speakers of the central language; they are to be assimilated into the rest of the country. One example has been the five-month courses teaching Hebrew to new immigrants to Israel. Here the motivation was to unify people coming from many parts of the world within a single cultural heritage, though this is now changing into vocationally more relevant teaching. UK governments constantly threaten to make residence depend on the ability to speak English. An extreme form of assimilationist teaching is so-called 'submersion' teaching – the 'sink-or-swim' method of 'mainstreaming' minority language children into a central language classroom and forbidding them to use their own language.

Transitional language teaching

The aim of transitional L2 teaching is to allow people to function in the central language of the country, without necessarily losing or devaluing their first language. While resembling assimilationist teaching, the motivation is different. To use Wallace Lambert's terms (Lambert, 1990), assimilationist teaching is 'subtractive' in that the learners feel their first language is being taken away from them; transitional teaching is 'additive' in that it adds the ability to function in the majority language without displacing the first language. With transitional language teaching, the minority language speaker still keeps the right to function in his or her own language, except when communicating with the majority group.

The educational system is one aspect of this. In some countries education takes place almost exclusively through the central official language: English in England, French in France. Hence those who do not speak the language of the school need help in acquiring it. In other countries, special classes enable children to acquire the majority language for the classroom. The Bilingual Education Act in the USA, for example, required the child to have English teaching as an aid in the transition to the ordinary classroom. François Grosjean (1982) says of such classes: 'For a few years at least the children can be in a transitory haven before being "swallowed up" by the regular system.' Ironically, such schemes disappeared in the UK following the Calderdale report finding that separate provision contravenes laws against racial discrimination (Commission for Racial Equality, 1986), thus imposing an assimilationist model on education in England that has lasted ever since. Indeed, this mainstreaming of the immigrant child with some language support is now widespread across Europe, for example, in Denmark, Ireland, Italy, Cyprus, Austria, Portugal and Poland (Eurydice, 2005).

Employment is another aspect. Schemes are set up to help the worker who does not know the language of the workplace; new adult immigrants to Sweden, for example, must be offered the opportunity to study Swedish by their local municipality within three months. Sometimes the needs of the new adult immigrant are taken care of by special initial programmes. The aim of such transitional teaching is not to suppress the first language in the minority language speakers, but to enable them to use the central language sufficiently for their own educational or employment needs. They still keep the values of their first language for all functions except those directly involving speakers of the majority language.

Language maintenance and bilingual language teaching

The aim of language maintenance or 'heritage' teaching is to teach minority languages to speakers of that language. Many ethnic groups want to keep their own language alive in their children. One possibility is the bilingualism by choice of bringing up children with two languages in the home. Many groups also collectively organize language maintenance classes outside the official educational system; in London, classes for children can be found taking place in Chinese, Polish, Greek and other languages, after normal school hours or at weekends. Mandarin Chinese is now being learnt by 30 million adults around the world (Graddol, 2006).

The mainstream educational equivalent is educating minority children through their first language. At one extreme is the notion that children should be taught solely through the minority language – Bantustans in South Africa or Turkish migrants' children in Bavaria – resulting in the minority speakers becoming a segregated enclave. More common, perhaps, is the notion that children have the right to have access to their first language through the educational system. In Sweden, for example, there are playgroups run in minority languages for preschool children and summer camps for older children (Arnberg, 1987). Denmark has 24 German kindergartens and 18 German schools in its German-speaking areas (European Commission, 2006). The position of Maori in New Zealand has been revitalized in part through the provision of 'language nests' – preschool playgroups in which Maori is used (Spolsky, 1989b).

The assumption of maintenance classes is that minority language speakers have the right to continue with their own language and heritage, regardless of the official central language of the country. To quote Tove Skutnabb-Kangas (1981), 'Bilingualism is no longer seen as a passing phase, but rather as something good and permanent, something to be striven for.' Transitional language teaching is neutral about the value of the minority language; bilingual teaching actively encourages a multilingual society. In England, the terms historically evolved from 'English for immigrants' to 'multicultural education' to 'bilingual teaching' to 'English as an additional language'. Changes in slogans, of course, do not necessarily reflect changes in practice.

One form that this emphasis on bilingualism takes is the propagation of other official languages through the school system. In Indonesia, 10 per cent of children speak Bahasa Indonesia as a first language, but 75 per cent learn it at school (Laponce, 1987). Canada has been famous for the experiment of 'immersion' schools, where English-speaking children are educated through the medium of French. Whatever the hotly debated merits or demerits of immersion, it resembles elite bilingualism. Wallace Lambert (1990) opposes its use with minority children, as 'it fuels the subtractive process and places the minority child into another form of psycholinguistic limbo'.

International goals of teaching

Let us now turn to international goals for language teaching which extend beyond the society itself, that is, the territory of supercentral languages such as Chinese and the hypercentral language English, discussed in Chapter 10. The students are assumed to be native speakers of the central language, possibly quite wrongly, say when a person is teaching French in London to the typical multilingual class. There are many types of international goals. Some illustrations will be taken from English syllabuses for Japan (MEXT, 2003) and Malaysia (Pusat Perkembangan Kurikulum, 2003), and the UK National Curriculum for modern languages (DES, 1990).

Careers that require a second language

Without taking into account the situation facing immigrants practising their original profession in another country, such as Hungarian doctors practising in England, there are many careers in which knowledge of another language is important. For certain professions a particular language is necessary – for example, English for air traffic controllers or seamen. The *Angol Nyelv Alapfoken* English textbook in Hungary (Edina and Ivanne, 1987) has a plot-line about travel agents and tourist guides, one kind of career that uses international languages. An important function of language teaching is indeed to train people for the international business world. Degrees in Japanese are popular among London University students because they lead to jobs in the City of London, as it is apparently easier to teach a Japanese graduate finance than a finance graduate Japanese. Nations will always need individuals who are capable of bridging the gap between two countries for economic or political purposes, or indeed for the purposes of war, as in the American crash programme in foreign languages in World War Two which led to the audio-lingual method. This type of goal is not about turning the student into an imitation native speaker, but into an L2 user. It preserves the first language alongside the second so that the student can mediate between them – preparing an L1 report on a meeting held in the second language, for example.

Higher education

Higher education through another language may either be in a country that uses it or sited in particular countries where it is not used, as we saw earlier. Of the 4,249 postgraduates at Newcastle University in 2006–2007, 1,518 were from outside the EU (38 per cent). The importance for the student is not the second language itself, but the knowledge and qualifications that are gained through the second language. Again, the first language is an important part of the situation.

Access to research and information

The Malaysian schools syllabus encourages students to 'Read and understand simple factual texts for main ideas, supporting details'. At a different level is the need for English to support various careers that are not primarily based on language – for scientists, doctors or journalists. To keep up to date or to be well informed, it may be necessary to use English.

Travel

The motivation behind many students' L2 learning is to travel abroad, that is, to belong to the group of visitors. At one level, this is the leisure activity of tourism: two weeks on a beach in Cuba does not require much Spanish. One of the four themes set for the UK GCSE examinations in French is: 'Travelling from the UK to target-language country/community' (AQA, 2007). A goal for my own beginners' course *People and Places* (Cook, 1980) was international travel through English; hence it emphasized talking to strangers about everyday travel functions such as getting money and food or finding the right check-in. The goal of travel is included under international goals here as it involves contact with other countries, though in a sense it is an individual goal belonging in the next section. Sometimes special-ized training has been provided, say, English for tourism workers in Vietnam and Cuba.

Individual goals of language teaching

Some goals are not related to the society itself or its external relations, but to the students' motivations and attitudes examined in Chapter 8. Several individual goals can be recognized.

Understanding foreign cultures

The Japanese syllabus 'aims at instilling a broader perspective and an understand-ing of different cultures, fostering attitudes of respect for such ideas, and the abil-ity to live with people of different cultures'. The UK National Curriculum wants pupils to 'be taught about different countries and cultures by communicating with native speakers', and by 'considering the experiences and perspectives of people in these countries and communities'. Regardless of the actual language that is being learnt, it is often held to be beneficial for the students to understand a foreign culture for its own sake.

Understanding language itself

An educated person should know something of how language itself works as part of the human mind and of society. One of the four main goals of the UK National Curriculum (DES, 1990) is 'Acquiring knowledge and understanding of the target language'. This can be gained through foreign language study or through language awareness training.

Cognitive training

The virtue of learning a classical language such as Latin was held to be that it trained the brain. The logical and reasoning powers of the mind were enhanced through a second language. This is supported by research which shows that children who speak two languages are more flexible at problem solving (Ben Zeev, 1977), and are better able to distinguish form from meaning (Ianco-Worrall, 1972). Ellen Bialystok (1990), for example, asked children to say which was the biggest word in such pairs as 'hippopotamus' and 'skunk'; bilinguals were better able to keep the word size dis-tinct from the object size and to answer the question correctly. After one hour a week of Italian for five months, English-speaking 'bilingual' children were learning to read better than their peers (Yelland *et al.*, 1993). One spin-off from learning any language is indeed the beneficial effects of L2 learning on using the first language. If children are deficient at listening for information, the skills involved can be devel-oped through L2 teaching.

General educational values

Just as sport is held to train children how to work in a team and to promote leadership qualities, so L2 teaching can inculcate moral values. The Malaysian English syllabus (Pusat Perkembangan Kurikulum, 2003) demands that 'Teachers should also use materials that emphasize the principles of good citizenship, moral values, and the Malaysian way of life.'

From another angle, many people support 'autonomous' language learning, where the learners take on the responsibility for themselves because this is in tune with democracy, discussed in Chapter 13. As Leslie Dickinson (1987) puts it: 'A democratic society protects its democratic ideals through an educational process leading to independent individuals able to think for themselves.' A general value that is often cited is the insight that L2 learning provides into the L1 and its culture, or, in the words of the UK National Curriculum, helping the pupils by 'considering their own culture and comparing it with the cultures of the countries and communities where the target language is spoken'.

Learning L2 as an academic subject

Language can also be learnt simply as another subject on the curriculum, another examination to be passed. Japanese teachers are not alone in complaining that they are in thrall to the examination system and cannot teach the English the students really need.

The very learning of a second language can be an important mark of education, another form of elite bilingualism. French had this kind of status in Western Europe, German in Eastern Europe – southern Poland and Hungary are two places where I have occasionally found German more useful than English. Skuttnab-Kangas (1981) paraphrases Fishman's account of bilingualism in the USA as follows:

> If you have learnt French at university, preferably in France and even better at the Sorbonne, then bilingualism is something very positive. But if you have learnt French from your old grandmother in Maine then bilingualism is something rather to be ashamed of.

L2 learning as social change

The goals seen so far in a sense accept the world as it is rather than trying to change it; the student as an individual is expected to conform to their society. But education and L2 teaching can also be seen as a vehicle of social change. According to Paolo Freire (1972), the way out of the perpetual conflict between oppressor and oppressed is through problem-posing dialogues between teachers and students which make both more aware of the important issues in their lives and their solutions. Language teaching on a Freireian model accepts that 'authentic education is not carried out by A for B or by A about B but rather by A with B mediated by the world, giving rise to views or opinions about it'. Language teaching can go beyond accepting the values of the existing world to making it better (Wallerstein, 1983). While the Freireian approach is included here under individual goals because of its liberating effect on the individual, it may well deserve a category all of its own of goals for changing society: language teaching as political action.

Much of what has been said here about the goals of language teaching seems quite obvious. Yet it is surprising how rarely it is mentioned. Most discussions of language teaching take it for granted that everyone knows why they are teaching the second language. 'LP [language pedagogy] is concerned with the ability to use language in communicative situations' (Ellis, 1996: 74). But the reasons for language teaching in a particular situation depend on factors that cannot be summed up adequately just as 'communication', or as 'foreign' versus 'second' language teaching. Even if teachers themselves are powerless to change such reasons, an understanding of the varying roles for language teaching in different societies and for different individuals is an important aid to teaching. A well-balanced set of language teaching goals is seen in the English curriculum for Israel (*English – Curriculum for all Grades*, 2002), summarized in Box 11.3.

Box 11.3 English Curriculum for Israel, 2002 (part of preamble)

The goal of this new curriculum is to set standards for four domains of English language learning: social interaction; access to information; presentation; and appreciation of literature and culture, and language. According to this curriculum by the end of twelfth grade, pupils should be able to:

- interact effectively in a variety of situations;
- obtain and make use of information from a variety of sources and media;
- present information in an organised manner;
- appreciate literature and other cultures and the nature of language.

Teachers should be clear in their minds that they are usually teaching people how to use two languages, *not* how to use one in isolation. The person who can speak two languages has the ability to communicate in two ways. The aim is not to produce L2 speakers who can only use the language when speaking to members of their own group. Myhill (1990), for instance, points out that English materials for Aboriginals in Australia, such as *Tracks* (Northern Territory, 1979), reflect their own lifestyle rather than that of the English-speaking community: what is the point in them speaking to each other in English? Nor should the aim be to produce imitation native speakers, except perhaps for trainee spies. Rather the goal should be people who can stand between two viewpoints and between two cultures, a multi-competent speaker who can do more than any monolingual. Much language teaching has unsuccessfully tried to duplicate the skills of the native speaker in the non-native speaker, as we argue in Chapter 10; the functions of language or the rules of grammar known by the native speaker are taught to the students. The point should be, instead, to equip people to use two languages without losing their own identity. The model for language teaching should be the fluent L2 user – 'Japanese with English Abilities' – not the native speaker. This is called by Michael Byram (1990) 'intercultural communicative competence'. It enables language teaching to have goals that students can see as relevant and achievable, rather than the distant vision of unattainable native speaker competence. One of the significant steps in this direction is the use by the *Common European*

Framework of Reference for Languages (2008) of 'can-do' statements (what I can do), rather than a measure of 'can't-do' based on native speakers.

Box 11.4 The goals of teaching language

1 Central goals foster a second language within a society.
   - *Assimilationist language teaching*: minority speakers learn the majority central language and relinquish their first language.
   - *Transitional language teaching*: minority speakers learn to function in the majority central language for some purposes, without giving up the first language.
   - *Language maintenance and bilingual language teaching*: minority speakers learn to function in both languages.
2 International goals foster a second language for use outside the society.
   - Careers that require a second language.
   - Higher education.
   - Access to research and information.
   - Travel.
3 Individual goals develop qualities in the learner rather than language *per se*.
   - Understanding of foreign cultures.
   - Understanding language itself.
   - Cognitive training.
   - General educational values.
   - Learning the second language as an academic subject.
   - L2 learning as social change.

Discussion topics

1 Why *are* we teaching second languages? Whose decision should it be and which languages should be involved?

2 Are there really bilingual communities, or are there two communities who speak each other's language?

3 Is multilingualism such a new thing, or have a few countries simply been projecting their comparative lack of languages onto the rest of the world?

4 To what extent is second language teaching necessarily political in one way or another?

5 What should be the goals of language teaching in a country where the second language has no obvious use?

6 Does the peculiar position of English as a hypercentral language have anything to say for the teaching of other languages?

7 Have you achieved your goals in second language learning?

Further reading

Apart from specific references in the text, this chapter draws on ideas and examples chiefly from: Grosjean (1982) *Life with Two Languages*; Skutnabb-Kangas (1981) *Bilingualism or Not: The Education of Minorities*; Phillipson (1992) *Linguistic Imperialism*; Canagarajah (2005) *Reclaiming the Local in Language Policy and Practice*; and Brutt-Griffler (2002) *World English: A Study of its Development*.

General models of L2 learning

This chapter applies some general ideas from SLA research to language teaching, complemented by Chapter 13 which goes in the reverse direction. It deals with some of the general models and approaches that researchers have devised to explain how people learn second languages, rather than with individual pieces of research or different areas of language.

12.1 Universal Grammar

Focusing questions

- What kind of language input do you think learners need in order to acquire grammar naturally?
- How much importance do you place on (a) correction by parents in L1 acquisition? (b) correction by teachers in L2 learning?

Keywords

Universal Grammar (UG): 'the system of principles, conditions, and rules that are elements or properties of all human languages … the essence of human language' (Chomsky, 1976: 29)

principles of language: abstract principles that permit or prohibit certain structures from occurring in all human languages

parameters of language: systematic ways in which human languages vary, usually expressed as a choice between two options

pro-drop parameter: a parameter which, set one way, permits a pro-drop language not to have pronoun subjects in the sentence, and set the other, forces a non-pro-drop language to have explicit subjects

Minimalist Program: this is Chomsky's current working model that attempts to simplify the syntax to the minimum necessary for the human computational system to connect sounds and meanings

The Universal Grammar (UG) model, in the version first proposed by Chomsky in the 1980s, bases its general claims about learning on the principles and parameters grammar described in Chapter 2. What we have in our minds is a mental grammar of a language consisting of universal *principles* of language, such as the locality principle which shows why a sentence like 'Is Sam is the cat that black?' is impossible in all languages, and of *parameters* on which languages vary, such as the pro-drop parameter that explains why 'Shuo' (speaks) is a possible sentence in Chinese, but 'Speaks' is not possible in English. Principles account for all the things that languages have in common; parameters account for their differences.

The Universal Grammar model claims that these principles and parameters are built in to the human mind. Children do not need to learn the locality principle because their minds automatically impose it on any language they meet, whether it is English, Chinese or Arabic. However, they *do* need to learn that English sentences have subjects (non-pro-drop), while Chinese and Arabic sentences do not (pro-drop). It is the parameter settings that have to be learnt – to have a subject or not to have a subject. All the learner needs in order to set the values for parameters are a few samples of the language. Hearing 'There are some books on the table', a learner discovers that English has the non-pro-drop setting because 'dummy' subjects such as 'there' and 'it' do not occur in pro-drop languages.

To acquire the first language, the child applies the principles to the input that is encountered and adopts the right value for each parameter according to the input. Learning in the UG model is a matter of getting language input by hook or by crook; the faculty of language needs input to work on; it is the evidence on which the learners base their knowledge of language. This evidence can be either positive or negative. *Positive evidence* consists of actual sentences that learners hear, such as 'The Brighton train leaves London at five'. The grammatical information in the sentence allows them to construct a grammar that fits the word order 'facts' of English that subjects come before verbs (' … train leaves … '), verbs before objects (' … leaves London)', and prepositions before nouns (' … at five'), by setting the parameters in a particular way. The positive evidence in a few sentences is sufficient to show them the rules of English.

Negative evidence has two types. Because children never hear English sentences without subjects, such as 'Leaves', they deduce that English sentences must have subjects – the same evidence of absence as that advanced for curved bananas in the song 'I have never seen a straight banana'. The other type of negative evidence is correction: 'No, you mustn't say, "You was here"; you must say, "You were here".' Someone tells the learners that what they are doing is wrong.

Many linguists are convinced that all a child needs to learn the first language is positive evidence in the shape of actual sentences of the language; negative evidence could only help in marginal instances as it is not uniformly available. Second language learning may be different. The bulk of the evidence indeed comes from sentences the learner hears – positive evidence from linguistic input. But L2 learners also have a first language available to them. Negative evidence can be used to work out what does *not* occur in the second language, but might be expected to if the L2 grammar were like the L1 grammar. Spanish students listening to English will eventually notice that English lacks the subjectless sentences they are used to. The grounds for the expectation is not just guessing, but the knowledge of the first language the learners have in their minds, in other words a form of transfer.

Negative evidence by correction is also different in L2 learning. In the first language, it is not so much that it is ineffective as that it occurs rarely; parents rarely correct their children's speech, and when they do it is usually for meaning rather than for grammar. In the second language classroom, correction of students' grammatical errors can, and often does, occur with high frequency. The L2 learner thus has an additional source of evidence not available to the L1 learner. Furthermore, the L2 learner often has grammatical explanations available as another source of evidence. This reflects a type of evidence that is absent from first language acquisition, at least up to the school years. Finally, the input to the L2 learner could be made more learnable by highlighting various aspects of it – *input enhancement* as Mike Sharwood-Smith (1993) calls it. James Morgan (1986) has talked about 'bracketed input', that is to say, sentences that make clear the phrase structure of the language by pausing or intonation. L2 teaching could try many ways of highlighting input, again an opportunity unique to L2 learning.

The UG model and language teaching

Much UG research has regarded the point of SLA research as being to contribute to linguistic theory rather than the other way round. Hence it is not really concerned with what teachers might make of UG.

Overall, UG theory suggests teachers should concentrate on those aspects of syntax that will not be acquired automatically by the students (Cook, 2001); there is no point teaching things which will be acquired by the students regardless of what the teacher does. As the Universal Grammar in the student's mind is so powerful, there is comparatively little for the teacher to do so far as the aspects of language it covers are concerned. Few mistakes occur with the word order parameters covered by the theory; I have never heard a student making mistakes like 'I live London in' for instance, that is, treating English as a language with postpositions rather than prepositions.

Instead, teaching can concentrate on providing data which the students can use to set the values of the parameters. Thinking of the language of the classroom as a source of input for parameter setting may be a helpful slant for language teachers. So in the case of the pro-drop parameter, UG theory suggests that teachers provide language input which allows the students to find out whether the setting should be pro-drop or non-pro-drop. Quite advanced L2 learners still differ from native speakers when the first and the second language have different settings for the pro-drop parameter. Thus the teacher's awareness of parameter resetting can be helpful. Similarly, syllabuses for language teaching that use grammar need to accommodate such basic syntactic ideas, if only to indicate to teachers which areas they can avoid teaching.

Let us take *Changes* (Richards, 1998) as an example. The input for setting the value for the pro-drop parameter is partly the absence of subjectless sentences, which is shared by all EFL coursebooks as well as *Changes*, and partly the presence of subjects such as 'it' and 'there'. Unit 5 introduces 'it' in time sentences such as 'It's five o'clock in the morning'. Unit 7 has 'There are three bedrooms'. Unit 8 introduces 'weather' 'it', as in 'It rains from January to March' and 'It'll cloud over tomorrow', together with other uses, as in 'It's spring. It's raining'. Everything necessary to set the parameter is introduced within the first weeks of the course. It is hard to imagine language teaching not reflecting these two aspects of the pro-drop parameter, just as it is hard for any small sample of speech not to use all the phonemes of English. Almost any language input should provide the information on which the parameter setting depends in a short space of time.

Many SLA researchers feel that the UG model is the most powerful account of L2 learning. Its attraction is that it links L2 learning to current linguistic ideas about language and language learning. It has brought to light a number of apparently simple phenomena like the pro-drop parameter that are relevant to L2 learning. Yet it would be wrong to draw conclusions from UG theory for anything other than the central area that is its proper domain, the core aspects of syntax. The UG model tackles the most profound areas of L2 acquisition, which are central to language and to the human mind. But there is rather little to say about them for language teaching. The UG principles are not learnt; the parameter settings probably need little attention. Any view of the whole L2 learning system has to take on board more than UG. Classroom L2 teaching too must include many aspects of language that UG does not cover.

Nevertheless, the UG model firmly reminds us that learners have minds and that the form which language knowledge takes in the human mind is crucial. Furthermore, because the type of syntactic description it uses tries to account for the syntax of all languages, it automatically allows for comparison between languages. Pro-drop is easy to explain to students and something like 90 per cent of the languages in the world are pro-drop; telling students of English about the pro-drop parameter can provide a short cut for teachers and students. The useful book *Learner English* (Swan and Smith, 2001) provides examples of mistakes from students with first languages ranging from Italian to Chinese to Thai that linguists would attribute to the pro-drop parameter.

The basis of the UG model is being revised within a theory known as the Minimalist Program (Chomsky, 1995). All language learning is now reduced to the learning of the properties of vocabulary. Take the arguments for verbs described in Chapter 3. Knowing the word 'give' means knowing that it usually has three arguments – an animate subject and two objects: 'Mary [animate subject] gave a book [direct object] to John [indirect object]', that is to say, you cannot say, 'The rock gave him a present' with a non-animate subject 'the rock', or 'The man gave a thousand pounds' without an indirect object saying whom it was given to. The grammar is seen as universal; the differences between languages come down to how words behave in sentences. Even the acquisition of grammatical morphemes such as past tense '-ed' is considered a matter of acquiring the phrases within which these morphemes can function and the parameter settings that go with them. Hence grammatical morphemes are, so to speak, attached to words before they are fitted into the sentence.

A technical account of these developments can be seen in Cook and Newson (2007). The version just presented can be called Minimalism Phase I; the later phases have reduced the apparatus of the grammar to an even barer minimum. Structure is no longer seen as a complex phrase structure, but as built up by an operation called Merge which combines two items into one; all the complexity of the phrase structure tree comes from this simple operation, starting from the properties of the lexical entry such as its arguments, but dispensing with phrases such as noun phrase and verb phrase. Chomsky has also been developing an idea about the perfection of language; the goal is to establish whether language is a perfect instrument for connecting sounds and meanings in the human mind.

The implications for SLA research of the Minimalist Program are as yet little known, except for the anchoring to vocabulary. So the main conclusion of minimalism for language teaching is, oddly enough, not about grammar, but about vocabulary; words should be taught, not as tokens with isolated meanings, but as items that play a part in the sentence by dictating the structures and words they may go with in the sentence.

Box 12.1 The Universal Grammar model of L2 learning

Key themes

- Language is the knowledge in individual minds.
- UG shapes and restricts the languages that are learnt through principles and parameters.
- Language learning is setting values for parameters and acquiring properties of lexical items, but not acquiring principles.

Teaching

- No need to teach 'principles'.
- Design optimum input for triggering parameters.
- Emphasize the teaching of vocabulary items with specifications of how they can occur in grammatical structures.

12.2 Processing models

Focusing questions

- What is the subject of the sentence 'The old man likes bananas'? How do you know?
- How important is it for students to recognize the subject of the sentence?
- Does practice make perfect in second language learning? Is it the same for all aspects of language?

Keywords

Competition Model: this claims that languages have to choose which aspect of language to emphasize in the processing of speech, whether intonation, vocabulary, word order or inflections

declarative/procedural memory: the memory for individual items of information (declarative memory) is different from the memory processes for handling that information (procedural memory)

connectionism: a theory which claims that all mental processing depends on developing and using the connections in the mind

agreement: the grammatical system in which two elements in the sentence show they go together by having appropriate word inflections, and so on, for example singular verb and singular subject in the English present tense

word order: a major element in conveying grammatical meaning in some, but not all languages, is word order; one variation between languages is the order of subject, verb and object: SVO (English), VSO (Arabic), SOV (Japanese), and so on

> **case**: a major grammatical system in many languages in which words show their grammatical function (subject, object, etc.) by different forms; in English, surface case only affects pronouns ('I', 'me', 'my', etc.), but case is still invisibly important
>
> **animacy**: whether a noun is animate or inanimate; not particularly important in English, but vital to Japanese, Italian, and so on

The Competition Model

At the opposite pole from Universal Grammar come models which see language in terms of dynamic processing and communication rather than as static knowledge. These are concerned with how people use language, rather than with sheer knowledge in the mind. One model of this type is the Competition Model developed by Brian MacWhinney and his associates (Bates and MacWhinney, 1981; MacWhinney, 1987, 2005). This derives from psychological theories of language in which L2 learning forms only a minor component.

Whatever the speaker wants to communicate has to be achieved through four aspects of language: word order, vocabulary, word forms (morphology) and intonation. As the speaker can only cope with a limited number of things at the same time, a language has to strike a balance between these four. The more a language uses intonation, the less it can rely on word order; the more emphasis on word forms, the less on word order; and so on. The different aspects of language 'compete' with each other for the same space in the mind. The results of this competition favour one or other of these aspects in different languages. A language such as Chinese, which has complicated intonation, has no grammatical inflections: intonation has won. English, with complicated word order, puts little emphasis on inflections: word order has won. Latin, with a complicated inflection system for nouns, has little use for word order, and so on.

The competition model has mostly been tested by experiments in which people have to find the subject of the sentence. While all languages probably have subjects, they differ in how they signal which part of the sentence the subject is. Take the English sentence 'He likes to drink Laphroaig.' What are the clues that give away which bit is the subject?

Word order

In many languages the subject occurs in a definite position in the sentence: 'he' comes before 'likes' in 'He likes to drink Laphroaig' and is therefore the subject. In English the subject is usually the noun phrase that comes before the verb; hence English is a subject verb object (SVO) language. Arabic and Berber are VSO languages, so the subject usually comes *after* the verb. In languages such as Baure and Tzeltal the subject comes after the object (VOS). Though they differ as to whether the subject comes at the beginning, the middle or the end, in all these languages word order is a good guide as to which noun phrase is the subject. The competition for space is being won by word order.

Agreement

The subject often agrees with the verb in number: both 'he' and 'likes' are singular in 'He likes to drink Laphroaig', as are 'il' and 'aime' in the French 'Il aime Paris'

(He loves Paris). In some languages the agreement of number is the most important clue to the subject; in English it affects only the third person present tense verb forms in '-s' ('He loves' versus 'They love').

Case

English uses the subject case 'he' to show the subject 'He likes Laphroaig', rather than 'Him likes Laphroaig' with the object case 'him'. In some languages the case of the noun is the most important clue to the subject, 'Ich liebe Bier' (I love beer) rather than 'Mich liebe Bier' in German. In English, case is not relevant except for the forms of the personal pronouns, 'he/him', and so on.

Animacy

In languages like Japanese the subject of the sentence is usually animate, that is to say, it refers to someone or something that is alive. The sentence 'The typhoon broke the window' is impossible in Japanese because typhoons are not alive, so 'typhoon' cannot be the subject. In English, whether the subject refers to something alive or not is rarely a clue to the subject. It is possible to say both 'Peter broke the window' and 'The window broke'. The competition is won in some languages by animacy.

So at least four clues potentially signal the subject of the sentence: word order, case, agreement between words, and animacy. The different clues to the subject are not equally important in each language. Rather the competition between them has been resolved in different ways in English, German, Japanese and Spanish.

Children learning their first language are therefore discovering which clues are important for that language and learning to pay less attention to the others. Each of the four competing clues has a 'weighting' that affects how each sentence is processed. Experiments have shown that speakers of English depend chiefly on word order; speakers of Dutch depend on agreement (Kilborn and Cooreman, 1987; McDonald, 1987); Japanese and Italian depend most on animacy (Harrington, 1987; Bates and MacWhinney, 1981). Learning how to process a second language means adjusting the weightings for each of the clues. L2 learners of English transfer the weightings from their first language. Thus Japanese and Italian learners select the subject because it is animate, and Dutch learners because it agrees with the verb. While their processes are not weighted so heavily as in their first languages, even at advanced stages they are still different. On the surface there need not be any sign of this in their normal language use. After all, they will still choose the subject correctly most of the time, whichever aspect they are relying on. Nevertheless, their actual speech processing uses different weightings. Currently, some research is showing how the second language affects the processing of the first language (Cook *et al.*, 2007) with four languages – Korean, Arabic, Japanese and Chinese (two scripts); Japanese people who know English interpret the subject differently in Japanese sentences from those who do not, not only in terms of animacy, but also, oddly enough, in terms of preference for plural subjects rather than singular subjects.

Processing models and cognitivism

The Competition Model deals with some of the performance processes discussed in Chapter 7. The model is related to the behaviourist tradition which claims that language learning comes from outside – from input from others and from interaction and correction – rather than from inside the mind. An early version was Bloomfield's idea that language learning is a matter of associating words with things (Bloomfield, 1933). The child who imitates an adult saying 'doll' is favourably reinforced by adults whenever a doll is seen, and unfavourably reinforced when a doll is absent. The most sophisticated behaviourist account was provided by B.F. Skinner (1957) in the book *Verbal Behavior*, which was savagely reviewed by Chomsky (1959). Language to Skinner was learnt though 'verbal operants' that are controlled by the situation, which includes the social context, the individual's past history and the complex stimuli in the actual situation. One type of operant is the **mand**, which is the equivalent to a command (com+mand) and is reinforced by someone carrying it out; another is the **tact**, which is equivalent to a declarative (con+tact), and which is reinforced by social approval, and so on. The child builds up the complex use of language by interacting with people in a situation for a purpose – rather similar to the rationale of task-based learning.

Other contemporary psychological theories of language learning are also affiliated to behaviourism. John Anderson (1993) has proposed a 'cognitive behaviourist' model called ACTR, which sees learning as building up response strengths through a twofold division into **declarative** memory (individual pieces of information) and **procedural** memory (procedures for doing things). As declarative facts get better known, they are gradually incorporated into procedures, and several procedures are combined into one, thus cutting down on the amount of memory involved. SLA research has often found this distinction convenient; for example, it underlies the work of O'Malley and Chamot (1990) with learning strategies described in Chapter 5. Using a related approach, DeKeyser (1997) demonstrated that the learning of a second language (here an artificial language) conformed to the ideas of improvement with practice in classical psychology in terms of response time and number of errors.

Rumelhart and McClelland (1986) and others have been developing the similar theory of 'connectionism', which sees learning as establishing the strengths between the vast numbers of connections in the mind. It claims that language processing does not take place in a step-by-step fashion, but that many things are being processed simultaneously. The methodology of connectionism research consists of simulated learning by the computer; language data are fed into the computer's network of connections to see whether it will 'learn' the syntactic regularities. The L2 use of connectionism then depends on the computer being able to learn the first language before looking at the second. Blackwell and Broeder (1992) made the computer learn either Arabic or Turkish pronouns based on their frequency in language input to learners; then they added the second of the two languages. They found that the computer indeed duplicated the order of acquisition found in a naturalistic study of four L2 learners. Connectionism may be an important area for future L2 research, but is thinly researched at present.

The main L2 model in this tradition is the information-processing model (McLaughlin *et al.*, 1983). In this, learning starts from controlled processes, which gradually become automatic over time. When you first start to drive a car, you control the process of driving consciously – turning the wheel, using the accelerator, and so on. Soon driving becomes automatic, and for much of the time you have no awareness of the controls you are using. To quote McLaughlin (1987): 'Thus controlled processing can be said to lay down the "stepping stones" for automatic processing as the learner moves to more and more difficult levels.' This is not necessarily the same as being conscious of language rules. A learner who starts by communicating hesitantly, and gradually becomes more fluent, is just as much going from controlled to automatic processes as one who starts from grammatical rules and then tries to use them in ordinary speech.

Clearly, some of the research discussed in other chapters supports this model, for instance the increasing quickness of reaction time as learners make the language more automatic (DeKeyser, 1997). However, the evidence for the information-processing model is mostly based on ideas taken from general psychological theory or on experiments with vocabulary, rather than on L2 learning itself. It requires a continuum from 'higher' to 'lower' skills. Students who do not progress in the second language are not making the lower-level skills sufficiently automatic. Thus children learning to read a second language may be held back by lacking the low-level skill of predicting what words come next. The information-processing model resembles the other processing models in assuming that language learning is the same as the learning of other skills such as car driving. All of them claim language is learnt by the same general principles of learning as everything else – the opposite assumptions to UG.

The main teaching application of these approaches is the emphasis on practice as the key to L2 learning. Practice builds up the weightings, response strengths, and so on, that determine how language is processed and stored. The UG model sets minimal store by practice; in principle, a parameter can be set by a single sentence for ever more. Processing models, however, see language as the gradual development of preferred ways of doing things. Much language teaching has insisted on the value of incremental practice, whether it is the audio-lingual structure drill or the communicative information gap game, described in Chapter 13. The processing models remind us that language is behaviour and skill as well as mental knowledge. Some skills are learnt by doing them over and over again. These ideas are support for the long-held teaching views about the value of practice – and more practice.

Box 12.2 Processing models

Key themes
- Language is processing at different levels.
- Learning involves practising to build up the proper weightings, connections, and so on.

Teaching
- Uses exercises to build up appropriate strengths of response in students.
- The classroom should maximize practice by students.

12.3 The socio-educational model

Focusing questions
- How crucial to success are the attitudes that the students bring to the classroom?
- What stereotype do you think your students have of the target culture?

Many would say that all the models described so far neglect the most important part of language – its social aspect, Lang$_4$. There are two versions of this. One is that L2 learning usually takes place in a social situation where people interact with each other, whether in the classroom or outside. The second version is that L2 learning takes place within a society and has a function within that society. This covers the local and international goals of language teaching discussed in Chapter 11.

A complex view of L2 learning called the socio-educational model has been put forward by Robert Gardner (1985, 2007) to explain how individual factors and general features of society interact in L2 learning. Each of these factors is measured precisely through the research instrument he has developed called the AMTB (Attitudes and Motivation Test Battery), part of which was presented in Chapter 8.

He has always seen the two main ingredients in the learners' success as motivation and ability. Motivation consists of two chief factors: *attitudes to the learning situation*, that is, to the teacher and the course, and *integrativeness*, which is a complex of factors about how the learner regards the culture reflected in the second language. Put together with other factors, these elements yield the model seen in Figure 12.1, which shows the process that leads to a successful or unsuccessful language learning outcome.

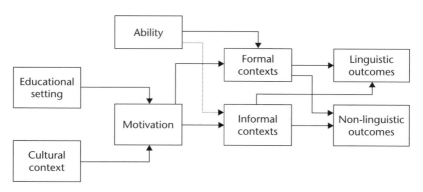

Figure 12.1 Robert Gardner's socio-educational model (Gardner, 2007)

But where do attitudes and integrativeness come from? The answer, according to Gardner, is the educational setting and cultural context within which the students are placed. A society sets a particular store by L2 learning; it has stereotyped views of foreigners and of certain nationalities, and it sees the classroom in a particular way. Hence one way of predicting if students will be successful at L2 learning is to look not at the attitudes of the students themselves, but at those of their parents or indeed of society at large. The crucial factors are how the learner regards the speakers of a second language, as seen in Chapter 8, and how highly he or she values L2 learning in the classroom.

The model also incorporates ability, how good the student is, which primarily affects learning in formal situations rather than in informal situations outside the classroom. These main factors do not lead to L2 success in themselves, except through people's reactions to the actual teaching context, whether formal or informal. The model depicts a process in time, during which the students' background setting affects their motivation, and then their motivation and ability affect their learning situation and so produce a successful or unsuccessful outcome.

The socio-educational model chiefly applies to language teaching for local goals, where the students have definite views on the L2 group whose language they are learning through everyday contact with them within the society, say the position of Chinese learners of English in Vancouver. Students who are learning for international goals may not have such definite opinions. For example, English teaching in Cuba involves little contact with English-speaking groups except tourists.

The implications for teaching mirror the discussion in Chapter 11 of the roles of language teaching in society. The total situation in which the students are located plays a crucial part in their learning. If the goals of teaching are incompatible with their perceptions of the world and the social milieu in which they are placed, teaching has little point. Teachers either have to fit their teaching to the roles of language teaching for that person or that society, or they have to attempt to reform the social preconceptions of their students, difficult as this may be in the teeth of all the pressures that have been exerted on the students by the social milieu for all their lives. If they do not, the students will not succeed. This model also reminds the teacher of the nature of the L2 using situation. The goal of teaching is to enable a non-native speaker to use the language effectively, not to enable him or her to pass as native, as discussed in Chapter 11.

Box 12.3 The socio-educational model

Key themes

Success in classroom second language acquisition depends on the two main factors, integrativeness and attitudes to the learning situation, in a complex interaction with other factors, such as the student's ability and the type of learning context.

Teaching

For some students the emphasis should be on integrativeness; for others, with say ELF goals, it should be on instrumental motivation. Changing long-standing motivations in the students is difficult.

12.4 The interaction approach

Focusing questions

- What do you do when you do not understand what someone else has just said?
- What do you do when you think you have made a mistake in speaking?

Keywords

interaction hypothesis: successful second language acquisition depends crucially on conversational interaction with others
negotiation for meaning: solving mutual difficulties in conversation by means
of various conversational moves
recasts: rephrasing incorrect student utterances

The interaction approach to SLA research has evolved for 30 years, primarily in
the USA; it sees talking to other people as the key to acquiring a language. Three
of its loosely connected tenets are explored below.

Language is acquired through interaction

In the 1960s, considerable research looked at how parents interact with children
in the first language, with largely inconclusive results. Direct correction, in
which the child's sentence is corrected by the parent, occurs very rarely; in one
famous study by Christine Howe (1981), only 1 of 1,711 utterances by mothers
involved correction. Ursula Bellugi and Roger Brown (1964) did find a process of
'imitation with expansion', in which the parent feeds back the child's sentence in
an altered form:

> Child: Baby highchair
> Mother: Baby is in the highchair

Others, however, such as Nelson *et al.* (1973), did not find any beneficial effects
on learning from such exchanges; see Cook and Newson (2007) for a further discussion. Nevertheless some psychologists, like Jerome Bruner (1983), have insisted
that structured interaction is the driving force in first language acquisition.

What is the role of interaction in the learning of second languages? In 1981
Mike Long suggested that it is not what the learner hears but how they are inter-
acted with that matters (Long, 1981). In its full form this became known as the
interaction hypothesis (Long, 1996): essentially, that second language acquisition
depends on profiting from conversation which makes concessions to the learner
through processes of topic clarification and repair.

Learning through interaction involves negotiation of meaning.

The central concept in the interaction approach is 'negotiation of meaning' – 'the
process in which, in an effort to communicate, learners and competent speakers
provide and interpret signals of their own and their interlocutor's perceived comprehension' (Long, 1996: 418). In other words, useful interaction involves keeping
the conversation rolling by continuously resolving any difficulties in comprehension. Some of the different possibilities are: 'repetitions, confirmations, reformula-
tions, comprehension checks, clarification requests etc' (Long, 1996: 418).

Rather like communication strategies, negotiation for meaning is keeping the
channel of communication open – the equivalent of saying, 'Are you still there?'

when the other person on the phone seems to fall silent. Almost invariably, these interactional moves have been discussed in terms of conversation between native and non-native speakers: comprehensibility has been weighted towards the native speaker rather than to successful L2 users. An exception is research by Garcia Mayo (2007), who found that L2 students talking to each other managed to successfully negotiate meaning in a variety of ways, that is, 'scaffolding' each other's use of language.

Teaching involves not only these ordinary conversational moves, but also those specific to the teaching situation in which the aim is learning. One is direct correction. Teachers have perhaps always corrected and always will. In my experience, students usually complain when their teachers do not correct, rather than when they correct them too much.

Box 12.4 Types of feedback by teachers to students (Lyster and Ranta, 1997)

- explicit corrections directly showing correct form
- recasts reformulating the sentence without the error
- clarification requests checking potential misunderstanding
- metalinguistic feedback commenting on wellformedness
- elicitation to get the correct form by pausing, asking questions or making them rephrase
- repetition by repeating the students' sentence, usually with a particular intonation

---

Box 12.4 shows a well-known list of types of correction devised by Roy Lyster and Leila Ranta (1997). In **explicit corrections** the teacher directly provides the correct form:

He goed to the movies.
No, he went to the movies.

In **recasts** the teacher rephrases the student's mistake:

He went to the movies, did he?

In **clarification requests** the teacher tries to clear up possible misunderstandings:

You mean he went to the movies?

Elicitations are when the teacher tries to get the student to make a second attempt:

Eh? What do you mean?

Repetitions involve the teacher repeating but highlighting the mistake:

He *goed* to the cinema?

While all these could occur in non-classroom conversation, they are more focused on the language mistake than the meaning, and doubtless occur with a much higher frequency in teaching than would be acceptable in ordinary conversation.

The idea of recasts has proved popular among researchers. An example from a European Science Foundation (ESF) transcript is:

A: I think one man er very happy only.
B: You think he was a very happy man?

B has recast A's utterance in a way that does not bring the conversation to a halt, as other types of correction would do, but reformulates the L2 user's utterance in a more acceptable way. The full definition by Lyster and Ranta (1997: 46) is: '*Recasts* involve the teacher's reformulation of all or part of a student's utterance minus the error'. One issue is whether the student takes this as a simple aid to the conversation (decoding) or as an aid to learning, singling out something they should be paying attention to (codebreaking). According to Younghee Sheen (2004), 60 per cent of feedback in a variety of language teaching contexts involved recasts. Long (1996) sees this ambiguity as their very usefulness: the student is not sidetracked from the meaning of what is being said, but nevertheless learns about the form of the language. Z.-H. Han (2002) taught tense consistency to students with and without recasts, and suggested that important factors which affected the extent to which students benefited from recasts were intensity of instruction and developmental readiness to acquire the point in question.

The most obvious drawback to the interaction approach is that, while there is considerable research describing how interaction occurs, there is still little proof of its importance to second language learning rather than to second language comprehension, whether correction or recasts. Indeed, Pauline Foster (1998) found that most students in the classroom would avoid making negotiation moves if they possibly could, perhaps because it exposed their ignorance in public. Undoubtedly interaction helps some aspects of second language learning, but it is not clear how crucial this may be compared to all the other factors in the complex second language learning situation. Teachers' interaction patterns are probably based on their experience and training; we do not know if there are better patterns they could adopt than these pre-existing patterns. Moreover, the analysis is usually based on interview-type data or classroom data involving a native speaker and a non-native student; hence it is not representative of normal L2 usage in the world outside the classroom, which often takes place between L2 users. Ernesto Macaro (2005) argues that the 'unswerving faith in the comprehensible input – negotiation – comprehensible output has been entirely due to the fact that the proponents of these theories and hypotheses simply did not speak the first language of their subjects or students'; in a situation where the teacher could speak the same language as the students they would resort to codeswitching. In other words, 'natural' L2 learning would involve an L1 component, and teaching becomes 'unnatural' when its reliance on the L2 forces the learner into these forms of interaction.

The teaching applications are partly to do with communication and task-based learning, discussed in Chapter 13. Mostly the interaction approach to teaching has been seen as encouraging the teacher to interact with students in the classroom and to use activities that require mutual interaction, also discussed in Chapter 13. Lightbown and Spada (2006) recommend recasts rather than corrections with adults, but not with children, as 'learners seem to hear them as confirmation of meaning rather than correction of form'. Since the approach is based on what teachers already do, it seems fairly circular to feed it back to them as advice on what they *should* do; it is only allowable if the expert says so. How many teachers trained in the past 40 years run inflexible classrooms with no interaction with the students or between the students?

Box 12.5 The interaction approach

Key theme

Conversational interaction involving negotiation of meaning is the crucial element in second language learning.

Teaching

- Teaching means setting up tasks that involve negotiation of meaning.
- Teacher or peer feedback is important to interaction, particularly through recasts.

12.5 Sociocultural SLA theory

Focusing questions

- What do you think is the relationship between what you say and what is going on in your mind?
- How much do you think language learning comes from within the child, how much from assistance from other people?

Keywords

internalization: in Vygotsky's theory, the process through which the child turns the external social use of language into internal mental use

zone of proximal development (ZPD): to Vygotsky, the gap between the child's low point of development, as measured individually, and high point, as measured on social tasks; in SLA research often used to refer to the gap between the learner's current stage and the next point on some developmental scale the learner is capable of reaching

scaffolding: the process that assists the learner in getting to the next point in development, in sociocultural theory consisting of social assistance by other people rather than of physical resources such as dictionaries

One of the most influential models since the early 1990s has been sociocultural theory, which emphasises the importance of interaction from a rather different perspective. This theory takes its starting point from the work of Lev Vygotsky, a leading figure in early Soviet psychology who died in 1934, but whose impact in the West came from the translations of his main books into English in 1962 and 1978 (misleadingly, in much of the SLA literature, his works are cited as if they appeared in the 1960s to 1980s, rather than being written in the 1930s). Vygotsky (1934/1962) was chiefly concerned with the child's development in relationship to the first language. His central claim is that, initially, language is a way of acting for the child, an external fact: saying 'milk' is a way of getting milk. Gradually language becomes internalized as part of the child's mental activity: 'milk' becomes a concept in the mind. Hence at early stages children may seem to use words like 'if' and 'because' correctly, but in fact have no idea of their meaning, rather like Eve Clark's features view of vocabulary development seen in Chapter 3. There is a tension between external and internal language, with the child progressively using language for thinking rather than for action. Language is not just social, not just mental, but both – $Lang_4$ as well as $Lang_5$.

Vygotsky also perceived a potential gap between the child's actual developmental stage, as measured by standard tests on individual children, and the stage they are at when measured by tasks involving cooperation with other people. This he called 'the zone of proximal development' (ZPD), defined as 'the distance between the actual developmental level as determined by independent problem solving and the level of potential development as determined through problem solving under adult guidance or in cooperation with more capable peers' (1935/1978: 86). In this zone come things that the child cannot do by himself or herself, but needs the assistance of others; in time these will become part of the child's internal knowledge. This means 'the only good learning is that which is in advance of development'. In one sense the ZPD parallels the well-known idea of 'reading readiness'; in Steiner schools, for example, children are not taught to read until they show certain physical signs of development, such as loss of milk teeth. And it is also a parallel to the teachability concept in processability theory seen in Chapter 3; you cannot teach things that are currently out of the learner's reach. The distinctive aspect of Vygotsky's ZPD is that the gap between the learner's current state and their future knowledge is bridged by assistance from others; learning demands social interaction so that the learner can internalize knowledge out of external action. Any new function 'appears twice: first on the social level, and later on the individual level; first *between* people (interpsychological) and then *inside* the child (intrapsychological)' (Vygotsky, 1935/78: 57).

The ZPD has been developed in SLA sociocultural theory far beyond Vygotsky's original interpretation. In particular, social assistance is interpreted through the concept of scaffolding, taken from one of the major later figures in twentieth-century developmental psychology, Jerome Bruner, who spent much time specifically researching the language of young children. He saw children as developing language in conjunction with their parents through conversational 'formats' that gradually expand over time until they die out; classic examples are nappy-changing routines and peekaboo games, which seem to be universal (Bruner, 1983). The child's language acquisition is scaffolded by the helpful adult who provides a continual supporting aid to the child's internalization of language, what Bruner calls the innate Language Acquisition Support System (LASS), in rivalry with Chomsky's Language Acquisition Device (LAD).

In an SLA context, scaffolding has been used in many diverse senses. For some, anything the learner consults or uses constitutes scaffolding, such as the use of grammar books or dictionaries; virtually anything that happens in the classroom, then, can count as scaffolding, say the traditional teaching style described in Chapter 9 known as IRF (initiation, response and feedback), or any kind of correction by the teacher. Others maintain the original Vygotskyan idea of the ZPD as the teacher helping the student; scaffolding is social mediation involving two people, and is performed by a person who is an expert. Some have extended scaffolding to include help from people at the same level as the student, that is, fellow students. In teaching terms, this includes everything from teacher-directed learning to carrying out tasks in pairs and groups – the liberating effect of the communicative revolution of the 1970s. Swain and Lapkin (2002) combined both approaches by having an expert reformulate students' descriptions and then having the students discuss the reformulation with a fellow student, which turned out to be effective.

For this SLA theory, development seems to mean greater success in doing the task. For example, Amy Ohta (2000) describes the development of a learner of Japanese called Becky in a single classroom session, through detailed grammatical correction and prompting from a fellow student Hal, so that by the end she has reached a new developmental level; she has internalized the social interaction and become more autonomous. In a sense, this is micro-development over minutes rather than the macro-development over years mostly used by developmental psychologists.

Like the interaction hypothesis, sociocultural theory bases itself on the dialogue that learners encounter in the classroom. It is broader in scope in that it emphasises the assistance provided by others, of which the repairs to monolingual L2 conversation form only a small part. It has much higher aims in basing the learning that takes place through social interaction on a whole theory of mental development. Its essence is what Merrill Swain (2000: 102) calls 'collaborative dialogue' – 'dialogue in which speakers are engaged in problem solving and knowledge building'. Hence it is not the dialogue of the interaction hypothesis in which people exchange information, that is, communication, but an educational dialogue in which people create new knowledge, that is, learning. Dialogue provides not so much negotiation for meaning, as assistance in internalization.

The obvious teaching implications are structured situations in the classroom in which the students cooperate with the teacher or with fellow students, as shown in numerous detailed studies of L2 classrooms. In a sense, this is the same message as the other interaction-based teaching applications of SLA research; for instance, it can provide an underpinning in development psychology for the task-based learning movement, discussed in Chapter 13. In another sense it is too vague to give very precise teaching help; it could be used to justify almost anything in the classroom that involved an element of social interaction by the students and teacher. In particular, it is hard to see what the goals of language teaching are for sociocultural theory; it concerns the process of development, not the end point. Apart from the knowledge of language itself as an internalized mental entity, the only other gain from second language learning seems to be the enhanced metalinguistic awareness of the students.

Box 12.6 Sociocultural theory

Key themes

- Language learning is social mediation between the learner and someone else during which socially acquired knowledge becomes internal.
- It takes place through scaffolding by an expert or a fellow learner.

Teaching

- Use collaborative dialogue in the classroom through structured cooperative tasks.

12.6 Multi-competence – the L2 user approach

Focusing questions

- Do you speak your first language any differently because you know a second language?
- Do students want to speak like native speakers? Can they actually achieve it?

Keywords

multi-competence: the knowledge of more than one language in the same mind

L2 user: the person who knows a second language, at whatever level, considered as a user rather than a learner

Most of the models seen so far assume that having a second language is unusual. Whether it is Universal Grammar or the Competition Model, the starting point is knowledge of one language, not knowledge of several languages: a second language is an add-on to a first language model. Only the social-educational model is specifically a model of how L2 learning occurs, rather than an extrapolation from more general models. Thus, mostly they regard L2 learning as inefficient because the learners seldom reach the same level as the L1 child.

But why should they? By definition, L2 learners are not native speakers – at least according to the definition advanced in Chapter 1, 'a monolingual person who still speaks the language they learnt in childhood'. They can never be native speakers of another language, without time travel back to their childhood. There is a need to recognize the distinctive nature of knowing two or more languages without subordinating L2 knowledge to monolingual knowledge. As Sridhar and Sridhar (1986) point out, 'Paradoxical as it may seem, second language acquisition researchers seem to have neglected the fact that the goal of SLA is bilingualism.'

Chapter 1 introduced the term 'multi-competence' to refer to the overall knowledge of both the first language and the L2 interlanguage – two languages in one mind. The multi-competence model develops the implications of this for second language acquisition. The key insight is that the person who speaks more than one language should be considered in their own right, not as a monolingual who has tacked another language on to their repertoire. Since this is the model that I have been concerned with myself, some of the basic ideas are met everywhere in this book, particularly in Chapter 10. First we need to show that L2 users differ from those who use one language.

- *L2 users' knowledge of the second language is not the same as that of native speakers.* Students and teachers are frustrated by their inability to speak like natives. Very few people are ever satisfied by their L2 proficiency. Even bilinguals who can pass for native speakers still differ from native speakers; Coppetiers (1987) found that Americans living in France as bilinguals gave slightly different answers to questions about French from native speakers, even if none of their colleagues had noticed their French was deficient. Only a small proportion of L2 learners can ever pass for natives. SLA research should be concerned with the typical achievement of L2 learners in their own right, rather than with that of the handful of exceptional individuals who can mimic native speakers.

- *L2 users' knowledge of their first language is not the same as that of monolingual native speakers*. While everyday experience clearly shows that the second language has an effect on the first, this is only now starting to be researched; see, for example, *Effects of the Second Language on the First* (Cook, 2003). Yet people's intuitions of their first language, their processing of sentences and even their gestures are affected to some extent by the second language that they know. Chapter 4 reports that French and Spanish learners of English have their voice onset time affected by their knowledge of English, so that to some extent they have a single system they use in both languages. English speakers of Japanese use *aizuchi* (nodding for agreement) when talking English (Locastro, 1987). Experiments with syntax have shown unexpected effects on the first language from knowing a second language. Hartsuiker *et al*. (2004) found, for instance, that hearing passives in one language increased their production in using another.

- *L2 users think in different ways to monolinguals*. Learning another language makes people think more flexibly, increases language awareness and leads to better attitudes towards other cultures. Indeed, these have often been seen as among the educational benefits of acquiring another language. English children who learn Italian for an hour a week learn to read more rapidly in English (Yelland *et al*., 1993).

All in all, learning another language changes people in many ways. The languages exist side by side in the same person, affecting not only the two languages, but also the person as a whole. Acquiring a second language does not mean acquiring the self-contained language system of a monolingual, but a second language system that coexists with the first in the same mind.

The L2 user in language teaching

The multi-competence approach suggests that key factors in language teaching are the L2 user and L2 use of language. Successful L2 users are not just passing for native speakers, but expressing their unique status as people who can function in two cultures. The major consequences for language teaching are set out below.

Teaching goals should be L2 user goals, not approximations to the native speaker

If L2 users differ from monolingual speakers, the benefits of learning a second language are becoming a different kind of person, not just adding another language. This is the basis for the argument presented in Chapter 11 that the proper goal of language teaching should be the proficient L2 user who is capable of using both languages, not the monolingual who functions in only one. The overall goals of language teaching should reflect what L2 users can do; the teaching materials should incorporate situations of L2 use and features of L2 user language, not those belonging to monolinguals. The native speaker teacher is not necessarily a good model for the student, as developed in Chapter 10.

The first language should be recognized in language teaching

If both languages are always linked in the mind, it is impossible for both of them not to be present in the students' minds at all times. It is an illusion that permitting only the second language in the classroom forces the students to avoid their first language; it simply makes it invisible. Hence, as discussed in Chapter 6, teachers should think how teaching can make systematic use of both languages, rather than try to exclude the first language. The insistence of the multi-competence model that the L2 user is at the centre of language teaching frees teaching from some long-standing assumptions. Teachers should be telling students how successful they are as L2 users, rather than implying that they are failures for not speaking like natives.

Box 12.7 Multi-competence and language teaching

Key themes

Multi-competence theory claims that L2 users are not the same as the monolingual native speaker because their knowledge of the second language and their knowledge of their first language is not the same, and they think in different ways.

Teaching uses

Teaching should:

- aim at the goal of creating successful L2 users, not imitation native speakers;
- make systematic use of the first language in the classroom.

12.7 General issues

All these models of L2 learning account persuasively for what it considers the crucial aspects of L2 learning. What is wrong with them is not their claims about their own front yard so much as their tendency to claim that the whole street belongs to them. Each of them is at best a piece of the jigsaw. Do the pieces add up to a single picture? Can a teacher believe (i) that language is mental knowledge (ii) gained by assigning weightings to factors (iii) by those with positive attitudes towards the target culture? This combines three arguably incompatible theories of language acquisition from different disciplines; superficially, it seems a good example of what George Orwell calls doublethink – the belief in two contradictory ideas at the same time. However, the differences between the areas of L2 learning dealt with by each model mean that they are by no means irreconcilable. UG applies only to 'core' grammar; response weightings apply to speech processing; attitudes to behaviour in academic classrooms. Only if the models dealt with the same areas would they come into conflict. There is no overall framework for all the models as yet. When they are fitted together, an overall model of L2 learning will one day emerge. At the moment there are many area-specific models, each of them providing some useful insights into its own province of L2 learning; there is not much point in debating whether a bicycle or an aeroplane is an easier way of getting from place to place; both have their proper uses. Hence there is not much sense in deciding which overall model is best; each has to be developed to its logical limits to see where it might lead.

For the sake of their students, teachers have to deal with L2 learning as a whole, as seen in Chapter 13. It is premature for any one of these models to be adopted as the sole basis for teaching, because, however right or wrong each one may be, none of them covers more than a small fraction of what the students need. As Spolsky (1989a) wisely remarks: 'any theory of second language learning that leads to a single method must be wrong'.

Discussion topics

1   Are there parts of the second language that we do not need to teach, and parts that are based on transfer from our first language?

2   How can vocabulary be taught in relationship to grammatical structure?

3   What parts of the second language can be built up by practice? What parts cannot?

4   How can teachers help students go from the formal language of the classroom to the informal language outside?

5   How much of students' success would you attribute to motivation, and how much to other factors?

6   Is it realistic to claim that the target of L2 teaching should be the L2 user, or do we have to compromise with students' beliefs that they want to be like native speakers?

7   Do you think you have gained more from acquiring a second language than just the language?

Further reading

Teaching applications of the UG model are discussed in Cook (1994) in T. Odlin (ed.), *Perspectives on Pedagogical Grammar*; its link to L2 learning is discussed in Cook and Newson (2007) *Chomsky's Universal Grammar*. Useful overall accounts of some L2 models are in Myles and Mitchell (2004) *Second Language Learning Theories*; and VanPatten and Williams (2006) *Theories in Second Language Acquisition*. A synthesising overview of L2 learning can be found in Spolsky (1989a) *Conditions for Second Language Learning*. The Competition Model is discussed more critically in Cook (1993) *Linguistics and Second Language Acquisition*. The multi-competence model is treated extensively in Cook (2002) *Portraits of the L2 User* and (2003) *Effects of the Second Language on the First*.

Second language learning and language teaching styles

13

This chapter looks at some general questions of teaching methodology in the light of SLA research. It reverses the direction of Chapter 12 by proceeding from teaching to L2 learning. It also provides an overview of the diversity of alternative language teaching methods that teachers should be aware of, if only to remind them that there are many successful ways in which languages can be taught. As Kipling said:

> Here's my wisdom for your use,...
> 'There are nine and sixty ways of constructing tribal lays,
> And-every-single-one-of-them-is-right!'

The term 'teaching method' is used in most of this book as a broad cover term for the different activities that go on in language teaching. Glosses on the main well-known methods are given in Chapter 1 (see page 17). Various suggestions have been put forward over the years for making the term 'method' more precise or for abandoning it. The traditional distinction is between overall *approaches*, such as the oral approach, *methods*, such as the audio-lingual method, and teaching *techniques*, such as drills (Anthony, 1963). Richards and Rodgers (1986) see *approaches* as related through *design* to *procedures*. Marton (1988), on the other hand, talks about four overall teaching 'strategies': the *receptive strategy*, which relies primarily on listening; the *communicative strategy*, in which students learn by attempting to communicate; the *reconstructive strategy*, in which the student participates in reconstructive activities based on a text; and the *eclectic strategy*, which combines two or more of the others. Allen *et al.* (1990) distinguish *experiential activities*, which rely on language use within a situation, from *analytic activities*, which use language study and practice.

To avoid the various associations and prejudices that these terms conjure up, I prefer the more neutral terms 'teaching technique' and 'teaching style', which will be used in this chapter. The actual point of contact with the students is the **teaching technique**. Thus a structure drill in which students intensively practise a structure is one technique; dictation is another; information gap exercises another, and so on. A technique, as Clark (1984) puts it, is a 'label for what we do as teachers'. Teachers combine these techniques in various ways within a particular **teaching style**. Put a structure drill with a repetition dialogue and a role play and you get the audio-lingual style, with its dependence on the spoken language, on practice and on structure. Put a functional drill with an information gap exercise and a role play and you get the communicative style, with its broad assumptions about the importance of communication in the classroom. A teaching style is a loosely connected set of teaching techniques believed to share the same goals of language teaching and the same views of language and of L2 learning. The word 'style' partly reflects the element of fashion and changeability in teaching; it is not intended as an academic term with a precise definition, but as a loose overall label that we can use freely to talk about teaching. A teacher who might feel guilty switching from one 'method' to another or mixing 'methods' within one lesson has less compunction about changing 'styles'; there is no emotional commitment to a 'style'.

This chapter looks at six main teaching styles: the academic teaching style common in academic classrooms; the audio-lingual style that emphasizes structured oral practice; the communicative style that aims at interaction between people both in the classroom and outside; the task-based learning style that gets students doing tasks; the mainstream EFL style which combines aspects of the others; and, finally, other styles that look beyond language itself. These six styles are loose labels for a wide range of teaching rather than clear-cut divisions. The first four are arranged in roughly chronological order, with the oldest style first.

The range of styles highlights the idea that no single form of teaching suits all students and all teachers. Teachers should always remember that, despite the masses of advice they are given, they have a choice. All these methods, techniques and styles are still available for people to use, regardless of whether they are in fashion or not. Indeed, it is doubtless true that never a day goes by when they are not all being used successfully somewhere in the world.

Before looking at these styles in detail, it is useful to assess one's own sympathies for particular styles by filling in the following questionnaire. This is intended as a way in to thinking about teaching styles, not as a scientific psychological test.

Box 13.1 What is your style of language teaching?

Tick the answer that suits your own style of language teaching best (even if it is not the one you are supposed to be using). Try to tick only *one* answer for each question; then fill them in on the grid that follows.

1 *What is the chief goal of language teaching?*
   (a) the students should know the rules of the language ☐
   (b) they should be able to behave in ordinary situations ☐
   (c) they should be able to communicate with other people
      by understanding and transmitting information ☐
   (d) they should be able to carry out a range of tasks in the L2 ☐
   (e) they should both know the rules and be able to behave
      and to communicate ☐
   (f) they should become better people, emotionally and socially ☐
2 *Which of these teaching techniques do you value most highly?*
   (a) explaining grammatical rules ☐
   (b) mechanical drills ☐
   (c) communicative tasks ☐
   (d) meaning-based goal-oriented tasks ☐
   (e) presentation and practice of functions, structures, etc. ☐
   (f) discussion of controversial topics ☐
3 *How would you describe the language you are teaching the students
  in the classroom?*
   (a) rules about the language ☐

(b) grammatical patterns ❏
(c) language functions for communicating and solving tasks ❏
(d) ability to carry out tasks ❏
(e) grammatical structures and functional elements ❏
(f) a way of unveiling the student's own personality ❏
4 *Do you think the students are learning language chiefly by:*
(a) consciously understanding the language rules ❏
(b) forming habits of using the language ❏
(c) communicating in the classroom ❏
(d) achieving tasks in the classroom ❏
(e) understanding rules, forming habits and communicating ❏
(f) engaging in activities that are personally meaningful to them? ❏

Now fill in your answers with ticks in the table below.

Answer	Q1	Q2	Q3	Q4	Teaching style
(a)					academic
(b)					audio-lingual
(c)					communicative
(d)					task-based learning
(e)					mainstream EFL
(f)					others

You should be able to see which of the six teaching styles you are most in tune with by looking for the row with the most ticks. Question 1 tested the overall aims of language teaching you prefer; question 2 the slant on language teaching itself that you like best; question 3 the language content used in the classroom; question 4 the ideas about language learning that you accept. Most people get a line of ticks in the same row. The final column tells you the name of your preferred teaching style, to be expanded below.

13.1 The academic style

Focusing questions

- Do you think grammar explanation should ever be the focus of the lesson?
- Do you think translating texts is a useful classroom activity for the students?
- Do you see any value to using literary texts that have 'deep' meanings?

Keywords

grammar-translation method: the traditional academic style of teaching, which places heavy emphasis on grammar explanation and translation as a teaching technique

---

An advanced language lesson in an academic context often consists of a reading text taken from a newspaper or similar source, for example, the lead story on the front page of today's newspaper under the headline 'PM seeks new curbs on strikes'. The teacher leads the students through the text sentence by sentence. Some of the cultural background is elucidated by the teacher, say the context of legislation about strikes in England. Words that give problems are explained or translated into the students' first language by the teacher or via the students' dictionaries – 'closed shop' or 'stoppage', for example. Grammatical points of interest are discussed with the students, such as the use of the passive voice in 'A similar proposal in the Conservative election manifesto was also shelved'. The students go on to a fill-in grammatical exercise on the passive. Perhaps for homework they translate the passage into their first language.

Consider the situation in a secondary school. In one class the pupils are being tested on their homework. The teacher has written a series of sentences on the board:

The child has (cross /crossed /crossing) the road.
The boy was (help /helped /helping) his father.

… and so on. Then they interact:

Teacher: What's 'child'?
Student: A noun.
Teacher: What's 'cross'?
Student: A verb.
Teacher: What's 'crossed'?
Student: Past participle.
Teacher: So what do we say?
Student: The boy has crossed the road.
Teacher: Good.

In the class next door the pupils have a short text written on the board:

In spring the weather is fine; the flowers come out and everybody feels better that winter is over.

And then they interact:

Teacher: What is 'spring'?
Student: A noun.
Teacher: What's 'spring' in Arabic?
Student: Rabi.
Teacher: So how do we translate 'in spring?

The core aspects of these classrooms are texts, traditional grammar and translation. Conscious understanding of grammar and awareness of the links between the first and the second language are seen as vital to learning. The academic teaching style is sometimes known as the grammar-translation method for this reason. The style is similar in concept to Marton's reconstructive strategy or Allen *et al.*'s analytic activities. It is a time-honoured way of teaching foreign languages in Western culture, popular in secondary schools and widespread in the teaching of advanced students in university systems around the world. James Coleman (1996) said that when he started teaching in an English university, he found the grammar-translation method 'was clearly the most popular approach to language teaching in the universities'. The academic style can involve aspects of language other than grammar. A teacher explains how to apologize in the target language – 'When you bump into someone on the street you say "sorry"'; a teacher describes where to put the tongue to make the sound /θ/ in 'think' – both of these are slipping into an academic style where the pupils have to understand the abstract explanation before applying it to their own speech. The difference from later styles is that, in the academic style, explicit grammar itself is the main point of the lesson.

Translation is the component of the style that has had the least effect on traditional EFL teaching. For historical reasons, EFL has avoided the first language, both in methodology and in the coursebooks produced in England. One reason is the use in many countries of expatriate native speaker teachers who do not know the first language of the students and so cannot translate, one of the handicaps for the native speaker teacher, described in Chapter 11. The other is the prevalence within England of multilingual EFL classes, where the teacher would be quite unable to use the many first languages the students speak. So the translation component of academic teaching tends to be found in countries that use locally produced materials with local teachers – the secondary school lessons mentioned above were actually observed in Gaza, where foreign coursebooks and native speakers of English are in short supply.

The academic style does not directly teach people to use the language for some external purpose outside the classroom; translation, for example, is a means, not an end. To use the division made in Chapter 10 between international, local and national goals, the academic style is ostensibly aimed primarily at the individual goal of L2 learning as an academic subject; in other words, it aims to create Lang$_5$ linguistic competence (sheer language knowledge) in the students' minds, rather than something to be used directly. In addition, it often claims to train the students to think better, to appreciate other cultures and to gain other educational advantages.

But the academic style is nevertheless supposed to prepare the student for the actual use of language. By developing academic knowledge, the student eventually becomes able to use the second language in situations outside the classroom. While the style does not directly practise language use itself, it aims to provide a basis for language use when the student requires it. Hence the undoubted popularity among students of grammar books such as *Basic Grammar in Use* (Murphy, 2002). Despite the lack of explicit grammar in most contemporary teaching methods, students continue to believe that this will help them.

The academic style sees the acquisition of competence as getting hold of traditional rules and lists of vocabulary. Its syllabus largely consists of a list of grammatical points and vocabulary items. One of the first courses I ever taught, *Present-day English for Foreign Students* (Candlin, 1964), is organized around 'sentence patterns' such as 'John has a book', and 'new words' such as 'John Brown'. The style values what people know about the language rather than what they comprehend or produce. Students are seen as acquiring knowledge rather than communicative ability. The learner progresses from controlled conscious understanding of language to automatic processing of speech, as described in Chapter 12. The language teaching classroom is similar to classrooms in other school subjects, with the teacher as a fount of knowledge and advice.

The academic style is appropriate for a society or an individual that treats academic knowledge of the second language as a desirable objective and holds a traditional view of the classroom and of the teacher's role. Its strengths, to my mind, are the intellectual challenge it can present some students, unlike the non-intellectual approach of other styles, and the seriousness with which it views language teaching: the pupils are not just learning how to get a ticket in a railway station, but how to understand important messages communicated in another language, particularly through its literature. The links to literature are then valued. 'Culture' is taught as the 'high culture' of poetry and history rather than the 'low culture' of pop music and football. At the time I was taught Latin I hardly appreciated this; nevertheless, it has remained with me in a way that the functional French I learnt has not. One trivial example is the way that Latin quotations come to mind: Horace's line, 'Caelum non animum mutant qui trans mare currunt' (those who travel across the seas change the weather not their souls), is pithier than any English quotation, as is shown by Christopher Marlowe's use of it in *Dr Faustus*. Likewise, the fact that I had studied Cicero's speeches gave me a good model for appreciating Fidel Castro's devastating defence at the tribunal of those accused in the attack on the Moncado barracks. In other words, I have certainly had my value out of learning Latin in terms of individual goals.

One weakness in the academic style is its description of language. As Michael Halliday *et al.* (1965) pointed out many years ago, you cannot judge the use of grammar in the classroom as wanting if people have not used proper grammars. The linguistic content is usually traditional grammar, rather than more recent or more comprehensive approaches, described in Chapter 2. At advanced levels, it ventures into the descriptive grammar tradition in English, for example *Collins COBUILD Grammar* (Sinclair, 1990). While the treatment of vocabulary in text exercises is far-ranging, it is also unsystematic; the teacher has to cover whatever comes up in the text. Though the academic style laudably strives to build up relationships between vocabulary items encountered in texts, it has no principled way of doing so. Despite being concerned with linguistic forms, it pays little attention to components of language other than grammar and vocabulary, and occasionally pronunciation. The same academic techniques could in fact be applied systematically to other areas, say listening comprehension or communicative function.

The academic teaching style caters for academically gifted students, who will supplement it with their own good language learner strategies, and who will probably not be young children – in other words, they are Skehan's analytic learners from Chapter 8. Those who are learning language as an academic subject – the linguistics students of the future – may be properly served by an academic style. But such academically oriented students form a small fraction of those in most educational settings – the tip of an iceberg. Those who wish to use the second language for real-life purposes may not be academically gifted or may not be prepared for the long journey from academic knowledge to practical use that the style requires.

When should the academic style be used? If the society and the students treat individual goals as primary, language use as secondary, and the students are academically gifted, then the academic style is appropriate. In a country where the learners are never going to meet a French-speaking person, are never going to visit a French-speaking country, and have no career needs for French, an academic style of French teaching may be quite appropriate. But the teacher has to recognize its narrow base. For the academic style to be adequate, it needs to include descriptions of language that are linguistically sound and descriptions that the students can convert into actual use. The academic style would be more viable as a way of L2 teaching within its stated goals if its grammatical and vocabulary core better reflected the ways in which language is described today. Little teaching of English grammar in the academic style, for example, makes use of the basic information from Chapter 2 about grammatical morphemes or principles and parameters. If the intention is that the students are able to use language at the end, the grammar it teaches has to be justified not only by whether it is correct, but also by whether the students can absorb it. Stephen Krashen makes the useful point that we should be teaching 'rules of thumb' that help the student, even if they are not totally true (Krashen, 1985). A quick remark by the teacher that English comparatives are formed with '-er' for monosyllabic words ('big /bigger', 'small /smaller', etc.) and with 'more' for words of more than two syllables ('intelligent /more intelligent', 'beautiful /more beautiful'), leaves the student only to puzzle out words with exactly two syllables, such as 'lovely' or 'obscure'. The rule of thumb will not satisfy the linguists, but it may help the students.

While the individual goals of the academic style are potentially profound, the danger is that teachers can lose sight of them and see grammatical explanations as having no other role than imparting factual knowledge about grammar. The other important goals of language awareness, mental training and the appreciation of other cultures may not be achieved if the teacher does not give them particular attention in planning lessons and in carrying them out.

Box 13.2 The academic style of language teaching

Typical teaching techniques
- grammatical explanation, translation, etc.

Goals
- directly, individual learning of the second language as an academic subject
- indirectly, ability to use language

Type of student
- academically gifted, not young children

Learning assumptions
- acquisition of conscious grammatical knowledge and its conversion to use

Classroom assumptions
- formal, teacher-controlled

Weaknesses from an SLA research perspective
- inadequate use of grammar
- inefficient as a means of teaching language use

Suggestions for teaching
- use it with academic students who have individual goals of self-development rather than international or local goals
- supplement it with other components and processes of language
- remember to develop the powerful individual goals for the students, rather than be carried away by the sheer knowledge of grammar

13.2 The audio-lingual style

Focusing questions

- Do you think language learning is a matter of acquiring 'habits'?
- Do you believe speech necessarily has to be taught before writing?

Keywords

drill: a form of mechanical practice in which words or phrases are substituted within a frame and practised until they become automatic

dialogue: usually a short constructed piece of conversation used as a model of language and to introduce new words or structures

audio-lingual style: the style that stresses language learning as habits and the importance of spoken language

exploitation activity: the formally structured part of the lesson is followed up with freer activities, allowing the students to use what has been learnt in their own speech

four skills: language teaching can be divided into the four skills of listening, speaking, reading and writing; in the audio-lingual style, additionally, listening and reading are considered 'passive' skills, speaking and writing 'active' ones

The name 'audio-lingual' is attached to a teaching style that reached its peak in the 1960s, best conveyed in Robert Lado's thoughtful book *Language Teaching: A Scientific Approach* (Lado, 1964). Its emphasis is on teaching the spoken language through dialogues and drills. A typical lesson in an audio-lingual style starts with a **dialogue**, say about buying food in a shop:

A: Good morning.
B: Good morning.
A: Could I have some milk please?
B: Certainly. How much?

The language in the dialogue is controlled so that it introduces only a few new vocabulary items, 'milk', 'cola', 'mineral water', for instance, and includes several examples of each new structural point: 'Could I have some cola?', 'Could I have some mineral water?' and so on. The students listen to the dialogue as a whole, either played back from a tape or read by the teacher; they repeat it sentence by sentence, and they act it out: 'Now get into pairs of shopkeeper and customer and try to buy the following items …'

Then the students have a **structure drill** in which they practise grammatical points connected with the dialogue, such as the polite questions used in requests: 'Could I …?' This is handled by an adjacency pair of turns, to use terms from Chapter 9. Mostly these are called stimulus and response, taken from behaviourist theory, but I have tended to use the more neutral input and output to fit in with processing theory (Cook, 1968). So the teacher presents a specimen from a tape, or written up on a whiteboard in less strict audio-lingual classes:

Input: Could I have some (milk, water, cola)?
Output: Milk.

The students now answer by constructing appropriate outputs from each input:

Output: Could I have some milk?
Input: Water.
Output: Could I have some water?

… and so on. The drill repeatedly practises the structure with variation of vocabulary; the students hear an input and have to manipulate it in various ways to get an output, here by fitting a vocabulary item into a slot in the structural pattern. Drills developed historically into semi-realistic exchanges, by linking the input and output in conversational adjacency pairs:

Input: What about milk?
Output: Oh yes, could I have some milk?
Input: And cola?
Output: Oh yes, could I have some cola?
Input: And you might need some mineral water.
Output: Oh yes, could I have some mineral water?

Essentially the same technique occurs still in *New Headway* (Soars and Soars, 2002) as a repetition exercise, 'Listen Check and Repeat':

I got up early.
Are you getting up early tomorrow?
I went swimming.
Are you going to swim tomorrow?

Finally, there are **exploitation activities** to make the students incorporate the language in their own use: 'Think what you want to buy today and ask your neighbour if you can have some.' As Wilga Rivers (1964) puts it, 'Some provision will be made for the student to apply what he has learnt in a structured communication situation.' In *Realistic English* (Abbs *et al.*, 1968), we followed up the main audio-lingual dialogue with 'Things to do'. For instance, after practising a dialogue about a traffic accident, the students had to make notes about the witnesses, to imagine what the policeman would say to his wife when he gets home, and to work with a partner to devise advice to give a 5-year-old on how to cross the road. Similarly, a drill about 'infinitive with negative', practising 'And the woman /man/ car not to meet/ see /buy …?' leads into an activity: 'Now offer each other advice about the people you should see and the cars you should buy.'

Chapter 1 mentioned the language teaching assumption that speech should take precedence over writing. The audio-lingual style interprets this in two ways. One is short-term: anything the students learn must be heard before being seen, so the teacher always has to say a new word aloud before writing it on the blackboard. The other is long-term: the students must spend a period using only spoken skills before they are introduced to the written skills; this might last a few weeks or indeed a whole year. This long-term interpretation in my experience led to most problems. Adult students who were used to the written text as a crutch did not know why it was taken from them; I used to present dialogues only from tape until I caught the students writing down the text under their desks; so I decided that, if they were going to have a written text anyway, my correctly spelt version was preferable to their amateur version.

Audio-lingual teaching divided language into the four skills of listening, speaking, reading and writing, and grouped these into active skills which people use to produce language, such as speaking and writing, and passive skills through which they receive it, such as listening and reading. As well as speech coming before writing, passive skills should come before active skills, which leads to the ideal sequence of the four skills given in Figure 13.1: (1) listening, (2) speaking, (3) reading, (4) writing. So students should listen before they speak, speak before they read, read before they write. Needless to say, no one now accepts that listening and reading are exactly 'passive', as Chapter 7 demonstrates.

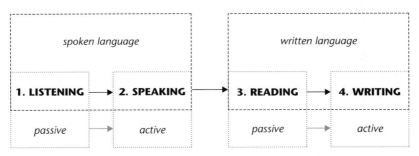

Figure 13.1 The sequence of the four skills in the audio-lingual method

Of all the styles, the audio-lingual most blatantly reflects a particular set of beliefs about L2 learning, which is often referred to as 'habit formation'. Language is a set of habits, just like driving a car. A habit is learnt by doing it again and again. The dialogues concentrate on unconscious 'structures' rather than the conscious 'rules' of the academic style. Instead of trying to understand every word or structure, students learn the text more or less by heart. Learning means learning structures and vocabulary, which together add up to learning the language. Like the academic style, language is seen more as form than meaning, even if its basis is more in structural than traditional grammar. Oddly enough, despite its emphasis on the spoken language, the structures it teaches are predominantly from written language.

The goal of the audio-lingual style is to get the students to 'behave' in common L2 situations, such as the station or the supermarket; it is concerned with the real-life activities the students are going to face. In one sense it is practical and communication-oriented. The audio-lingual style is not about learning language for its own sake, but learning it for actual use, either within the society or without. While the appropriate student type is not defined, the style is not restricted to the academically gifted. Indeed, its stress on practice can disadvantage those with an analytical bias. Nor is the audio-lingual style obviously catering for students of a particular age; adults may do it as happily as children.

Its views of L2 learning are closest to the processing models described in Chapter 12: language is doing things, not knowing things. Partly this comes across in its emphasis on the physical situation: the dialogues illustrate language used in situations such as the travel agent's or the chemist's shop. Most importance is attached to building up the strength of the students' response through practice. Little weight is given to the understanding of linguistic structure or to the creation of knowledge. The ability to use language is built up piece by piece using the same type of learning all the time. Grammar is seen as 'structures' like 'Could I have some X?' or 'This is a Y', within which items of vocabulary are substituted. Courses and syllabuses are graded around structures; drills practise particular structures; dialogues introduce and exemplify structures and vocabulary in context. The style requires a classroom which is teacher-controlled, except for the final exploitation phase when, as Lado (1964) puts it, the student 'has the patterns ready as habits but he must practise using them with full attention on purposeful communication'. Until the exploitation phase of the cycle, students repeat, answer or drill at the teacher's behest. Though they work individually in the language laboratory, all of them still use the same activities and teaching materials. The style demands students who do not expect to take the initiative. All responsibility is in the teacher's hands. The different aspects of the audio-lingual method can be seen in the list made by Wilga Rivers (1964).

Box 13.3 Assumptions of audio-lingual language teaching (Rivers, 1964)

- *Assumption 1*. Foreign Language Learning is basically a mechanical process of habit formation.
- *Assumption 2*. Language skills are learned more effectively if items of the foreign language are presented in spoken form before written form.
- *Assumption 3*. Analogy provides a better foundation for foreign language learning than analysis.
- *Assumption 4*. The meanings which the words of the language have for the native speaker can be learned only in a matrix of allusions to the culture of the people who speak that language.

In Europe, audio-lingualism happened to arrive from the USA at a time when the language laboratory became technically feasible. Many of its techniques indeed worked well with this equipment; repeating sentences and hearing recordings of your repetition, doing drills and hearing the right answer after your attempt, fitted in nicely with the tape recorder and later the language laboratory. Recent styles that emphasise free production of speech and interactive communication have found language laboratories far harder to assimilate, apart from for listening activities. Indeed, any glance at materials for computer-assisted language learning (CALL) on the Web show that they are largely audio-lingual in their emphasis on drill and practice, though they necessarily depend more on the written language because of the computer's limitations in dealing with speech.

One virtue of the academic style is that if it does not achieve its secondary goal of allowing the student to communicate, it might still have educational value via its goals of improving thinking, promoting cross-cultural understanding, and so on. The audio-lingual style has no fallback position. If it does not succeed in getting the student to function in the second language, there is nothing else to be gained from it – no academic knowledge or problem-solving ability. Lado does claim, however, that it teaches a positive attitude of identification with the target culture. Its insistence on L2 learning as the creation of habits is an oversimplification of the behaviourist models of learning that were scorned as explanations for language acquisition for many years. Many would deny that the unique elements of language are in fact learnable by these means; the ability to create or understand 'new' sentences is not acquired by practising 'old' sentences. The principles of Universal Grammar, for example, are impossible to acquire through drills and dialogues.

Syllabuses and textbooks in the audio-lingual style mostly see structures, phonemes and vocabulary items as the sum total of language. Though based on the four skills of listening, speaking, reading and writing, the style pays surprisingly little attention to the distinctive features of each skill. The skill of listening, for example, is not usually broken up into levels or stages that resemble those seen in Chapter 7. Moreover, the communication situation is far more complex than the style implies. If communication is the goal of language teaching, the content of teaching needs to be based on an analysis of communication itself, which is not adequately covered by structures and vocabulary. Even if students totally master the content of an audio-lingual course, they still need much more to function in a real-life situation.

Yet many teachers fall back on the audio-lingual style. One reason may be that it provides a clear framework for teachers to work within. Few other styles could be captured in four assumptions, as Wilga Rivers manages to do. Teachers always know what they are supposed to be doing, unlike more flexible or improvisational styles. Students can relax within a firmly structured environment, always knowing the kinds of activities that will take place and what will be expected of them. After teaching a group of beginners audio-lingually for six weeks, I decided it was time to have a change by introducing some communicative exercises; the students requested to go back to the audio-lingual techniques.

Certain aspects of language may lend themselves best to audio-lingual teaching. Pronunciation teaching has hardly changed its audio-lingual style teaching techniques such as repetition and drill, or its academic style conscious explanation in the past 40 years, unlike the rapid change in other areas of teaching, perhaps because of lack of imagination by teachers, perhaps because the audio-lingual style is indeed the most effective in this area. Lado's (1964) pronunciation techniques of 'demonstration, imitation, props, contrast, and practice' seem as comprehensive as anything presented in Chapter 4. The style reminds us that language is in part physical behaviour, and the total language teaching operation must take this into account.

Though ostensibly out of fashion, the influence of audio-lingualism is still pervasive. Few teachers nowadays employ a 'pure' audio-lingual style; yet many of the ingredients are present in today's classrooms. The use of short dialogues, the emphasis on spoken language, the value attached to practice, the emphasis on the students speaking, the division into four skills, the importance of vocabulary control, the step-by-step progression, all go back to audio-lingualism. Many teachers feel comfortable with the audio-lingual style and use it at one time or another in their teaching.

Box 13.4 The audio-lingual style of language teaching

Typical teaching techniques
- dialogues, structure drills, exploitation activities

Goals
- getting students to 'behave' in appropriate situations

Type of student
- non-analytical, non-academic

Learning assumptions
- 'habit-formation' behaviourist theory

Classroom assumptions
- teacher-controlled classroom

Weaknesses from an SLA research perspective
- inadequate form of grammar
- no position on other aspects of language knowledge or use
- inefficiency of habit formation as a means of teaching use

Suggestions for teaching
- use for teaching certain aspects of language only
- be aware of the underlying audio-lingual basis of many everyday techniques

13.3 The communicative style

Focusing questions

- What do you understand by 'communication'? Do you think this is what students need?
- To what extent do you think the classroom is an educational setting, to what extent a preparation for situations outside?

Keywords

functions and notions: functions are the reasons for which people use language such as persuading and arguing; notions are the general semantic ideas they want to express, such as time and location

information gap: an exercise that gives different students different pieces of information which they have to exchange

communicative style: basing teaching on communication, both as the target that the students need to achieve, and as the means of acquiring it in the classroom

The 1970s saw a worldwide shift towards teaching methods that emphasized communication, seen as the fundamental reason for language teaching. Indeed, communicative teaching has now become the only teaching method that many teachers have experienced; it was the traditional method from the twentieth century as grammar/translation was the traditional method from the nineteenth.

To start with, this style meant redefining what the student had to learn in terms of communicative competence rather than linguistic competence, social Lang$_4$ rather than mental Lang$_5$, to use the terms introduced in Chapter 1. The crucial goal was the ability to use the language appropriately rather than the grammatical knowledge or the 'habits' of the first two styles. The communicative behaviour of native speakers served as the basis for syllabuses that incorporated language functions, such as 'persuading someone to do something', and notions, such as 'expressing point of time', which took precedence over the grammar and vocabulary accepted hitherto as the appropriate specification of the syllabus. Instead of teaching the grammatical structure 'This is an X', as in 'This is a book', students were taught the communicative function of 'identifying', as in 'This is a book'. Though the structure may end up exactly the same, the rationale for teaching it is now very different, not grammatical knowledge but ability to use grammar for a purpose.

The elaboration of communicative competence into functions and notions affected the syllabus but did not at first have direct consequences for teaching methods. The fact that the teaching point of a lesson is the function 'asking directions' rather than the structure 'yes-no questions' does not mean it cannot be taught through any teaching style, just as grammar can be taught in almost any style. The course *Function in English* (Blundell *et al.*, 1982) displayed a list of alternatives for each function categorized as neutral, informal and formal, and linked by codes to a structural index – clearly academic style. The coursebook *Opening Strategies* (Abbs and Freebairn, 1982) made students substitute 'bank', 'post office', 'restaurant', and so on, into the sentence 'Is there a _____ near here?', an audio-lingual drill in all but name.

To many people, however, the end dictates the means: a goal expressed in terms of communication means basing classroom teaching on communication and so leads to techniques that make the students communicate with each other. Consequently, communication came to be seen more as processes rather than static elements like functions and notions. So syllabuses started to be designed around the processes or tasks that students use in the classroom.

Techniques of communicative teaching

The archetypal communicative technique is an **information gap exercise**. *Touchstone* (McCarthy *et al.*, 2005) uses cartoon maps of two imaginary neighbourhoods; students have to find the differences. *Living with People* (Cook, 1983) used pairs of photographs of Oxford street scenes with slight differences – a butcher's shop taken from two different angles, a queue at a bus stop taken a few seconds apart, and so on. Students look at one or other set of photos and have to discover what the differences are, if any, by talking to each other without looking at the other set. This information gap technique originated with language expansion exercises for native English primary school children in the 1970s, in courses such as *Concept 7–9* (Wight *et al.*, 1972), but it soon became a mainstay of EFL teaching. It might use visuals, tapes or models – in fact, anything where the teacher could deliberately engineer two sets of slightly differing information so that the students had an information gap to bridge. The point of the activity is that the students have to improvise the dialogue themselves to solve their communicative task. They have to use their own resources to achieve a communicative goal with other people, thus bringing communication directly into the classroom.

The second standard communicative technique is **guided role play**. The students improvise conversations around an issue without the same contrived information gap. *New Cutting Edge* (Cunningham *et al.*, 2005), for example, suggests: 'Act out a conversation in the tourist information office'. One student role-plays an official, the other their normal character. The aim is practising how to assume particular roles in situations. The situations themselves are virtually the same as those in the audio-lingual method – the doctor's, the station, the restaurant – but instead of starting from the highly controlled, pre-set dialogues of the audio-lingual method, students try to satisfy communicative needs by talking for themselves; it is not the language of the station that is important, it is what you do with it – buying a ticket, asking for the time of a train, and so on.

The third general technique is **tasks**: students carry out tasks in the classroom with a definite outcome. For instance, in Lesson 14 of *Atlas 1* (Nunan, 1995), students go through a linked series of tasks on 'giving reasons', called a 'task chain'. First they listen to a taped conversation and have to tick how many times they hear 'why' and 'because'; then they listen again to find out specific reasons; in pairs, they compare their answers, and after the teacher has given a 'model' conversation, they role-play equivalent conversations about 'asking for things and giving reasons'. Finally, they discuss in groups whether it is appropriate to ask other people to do things like 'buy you a drink' in their own cultures. Students are working together to achieve the task and to share their conclusions with other students: the picture that accompanies this task chain is two smiling students talking to each other, highlighting the classroom-internal nature of the task.

In one sense, these three techniques cover the same ground. The information gap game merges with the role play when the person playing the ticket collector has information the other students do not; the task becomes a role play when they practise fictional requests.

The communicative classroom is a very different place from classrooms using the other two styles encountered so far. The teacher no longer dominates it, controlling and guiding the students every minute. Rather the teacher takes one step back and hands the responsibility for the activities over to the students, forcing them to make up their own conversations in pairs and groups – learning language by doing. A key difference from other styles is that the students are not required to produce speech with the minimum of mistakes in native terms. Instead, they can use whatever forms and strategies they can devise themselves to solve their communication problem, producing sentences that may be entirely appropriate to their task but are often highly deviant from a native perspective. The teacher stands by. While the teacher provides some feedback and correction, this plays a much less central part in his or her classroom duties. The teacher has the role of equal and helper rather than the wise expert of the academic style or the martinet of the audio-lingual.

This jump from the traditional teacher-led class disconcerts or indeed alienates those from cultures who see education differently. The adoption of the communicative style in a particular place always has to recognize this potential cultural obstacle, however ideal communicative language teaching may be on other grounds. Here is a conversation taking place at a parents' evening featuring an Inuk parent and a non-Inuit teacher (Crago, 1992):

Teacher: Your son is talking well in class. He is speaking up a lot.
Inuk parent: I am very sorry.

To the teacher, it is obvious that it is a virtue to speak and contribute in class; to the parent, it is equally obviously that children who show proper respect for the teacher stay silent in class. A communicative style with its emphasis on spontaneous production by the learners is unlikely to go down well in cultures that value silence and respect.

Learning in communicative language teaching

In general, there is surprisingly little connection between the communicative style and SLA research. Its nearest relations are functional theories of how children acquire the first language, like Bruner (1983), rather than models of L2 learning. It assumes little about the learning process, apart from claiming that, if the right circumstances are provided to them, something will happen inside the students' minds.

Historically, the communicative style relates to the idea of interlanguage described in Chapter 1. Teachers should respect the developing language systems of the students rather than see them as defective. Indeed, the major impact of SLA research on language teaching so far may have been the independent language assumption described in Chapter 1, which liberates the teacher from contrived grammatical progressions and allows them to desist from correcting all the student's mistakes: learners need the freedom to construct language for themselves, even if this means making 'mistakes'. So the favoured techniques change the teacher's role to that of organizer and provider, rather than director and controller. The teacher sets up the task or the information gap exercise and then lets the students get on with it, providing help but not control. The students do not have to produce near-native sentences; it no longer matters if something the student says differs from what natives might say.

One strand in this thinking comes from ideas of Universal Grammar, seen in Chapter 12. If the students are using natural processes of learning built into their minds, the teacher can step back and let them get on with it by providing activities and language examples to get these natural processes going. Sometimes this is seen as hypothesis-testing, an early version of the Universal Grammar theory. In this the learner makes a guess at the rules of the language, tries it out by producing sentences, and accepts or revises the rules in the light of the feedback that is provided. However, hypothesis testing in this sense is no longer part of UG theory as it requires more correction than L1 children get from their parents, or indeed most L2 learners from teachers in communicative classrooms.

In a way, this style has a *laissez-faire* attitude: learning takes place in the students' minds in ways that teachers cannot control; the students should be trusted to get on with it without interference. It can lead to the dangerous assumption that any activity is justified which gives students the opportunity to test out 'hypotheses' in the classroom, with no criteria applied other than getting the students talking. However enjoyable the class may be, however much language is provoked from the students, the teacher always has to question whether the time is being well spent: are the students learning as much from the activity as they would from something else?

Language learning in this style is the same as language using. Information gap exercises and role-play techniques imitate what happens in the world outside the classroom in a controlled form, rather than being special activities peculiar to language learning. Later on, students will be asking the way or dealing with officials in a foreign language environment just as they are pretending to do in the classroom. Learning language means practising communication within the four walls of the classroom. You learn to talk to people by actually talking to them: L2 learning arises from meaningful use in the classroom.

The communicative style does not hold a view about L2 learning as such, but maintains that it happens automatically, provided the student interacts with other people in the proper way. Many of its techniques carry on the audio-lingual style's preoccupations with active practice and with spoken language. Communicative tasks belong in the historical tradition of the exploitation phase of the audio-lingual style, in which the students use the language actively for themselves; they have now been developed into a style of their own, task-based learning (TBL), as seen below. This exploitation phase was regarded as essential by all the commentators on audio-lingualism, whether Lado or Rivers. It consisted of 'purposeful communication' (Lado, 1964) such as role playing and games – precisely the core activities of the communicative style. The main difference is that in communicative teaching there is no previous phase in which the students are learning dialogues and drills in a highly controlled fashion.

Like the audio-lingual style, communicative teaching often resembles behaviourist views of learning. I have sometimes introduced the ideas of 'mands' and 'tacts' to teachers without telling them they are verbal operants within Skinner's behaviourist model, as outlined in Chapter 12. Their reaction has been that they sound a useful basis for a communicative syllabus. The main difference between the audio-lingual style and the communicative style is the latter's emphasis on spontaneous production and comprehension.

The style is potentially limited to certain types of student. For instance, it might benefit field-independent students rather than field-dependent students, extroverts rather than introverts, and less academic students. Its cultural implications can also go against students' expectations of the classroom more than other styles; students in some countries have indeed been upset by its apparent rejection of the ways of learning current in their culture, in favour of what they regard as a 'Western' view (though there seems no reason to think of the academic or audio-lingual styles as intrinsically any more or less Western than the communicative – all come from educational traditions in the West). The audio-lingual style, with its authoritarian teacher controlling every move the students makes, fits more with cultures that are 'collectivist', to use Hofstede's term (Hofstede, 1980), say, in Japan; the communicative style, with the teacher setting up and organizing activities, goes more with cultures that are 'individualistic', say, in Australia.

The communicative teaching style covers only some of the relevant aspects of L2 learning, however desirable they may be in themselves. For example, it has no techniques of its own for teaching pronunciation or vocabulary, little connection with speech processing or memory, and little recognition of the possibilities available to the learner through their first language. Pair work and group work among students with the same first language, for example, often lead to frequent codeswitching between the first and the second language, perhaps something to be developed systematically rather than seen as undesirable. In so far as the style uses grammar, it often relies on a structuralist grammar reminiscent of audio-lingualism, for instance in the substitution tables found in many communicative coursebooks, to be discussed below.

In general, communicative language teaching has sophisticated ideas of what students need to learn, which have undoubtedly freed the classroom from the rigours of the academic and audio-lingual styles. It is hard, however, to pin it down in a set of axioms in the way that Wilga Rivers could do for audio-lingual teaching. The best attempt at setting out the basic tenets of communicative language teaching was by Keith Morrow (1981):

1 Know what you are doing.
2 The whole is more than the sum of the parts.
3 The processes are as important as the forms.
4 To learn it do it.
5 Mistakes are not always a mistake.

These clearly do not have the straightforward practicality of the audio-lingual assumptions and would apply to many teaching methods rather than being exclusive to communicative teaching. The basic question of what we do in the classroom next Monday at 11.15 is seldom answered by the generalities of the communicative style. However interesting the techniques we have mentioned may be, there are rather few of them compared to the vast range available in earlier styles. Teachers sometimes feel lost because they have not been told exactly what to do, but essentially have been given some overall guidance and a handful of techniques and told to get on with it. Their preparation time also goes up as they have to devise roles for the students to play, collect pictures for information gap games, or invent ingenious tasks for them to do.

Over time, at least three variants of the communicative style emerged, which we shall call here 'social communicative', 'information communicative' and 'task-based learning'. A conversation requires someone to talk to (social), something to talk about (information), and a reason for talking (task). As the pioneer linguist Ferdinand de Saussure (1916) said: 'Speech has both an individual and a social side and we cannot conceive of one without the other'; $Lang_4$ is bound to $Lang_5$. Social communicative teaching emphasises the joint functioning of two people in a situation, what Halliday (1975) terms the *interpersonal* function of language. Information communicative teaching stresses the exchange of information, of ideas and meanings, rather than the relationships between people – Halliday's *ideational* function of language. These two uses will be dealt with under this style; tasks are expanded as a style of their own below.

Social communicative teaching

Those who put more weight on social communication see language as communication between people, rather than as texts or grammatical rules or patterns: it has a social purpose. Language is for forming relationships with people and for interrelating with them. Using language means meeting people and talking to them. The aim is to give the students the ability to engage in conversations with people. The teaching syllabus is primarily a way of listing the aspects of communication the students will find most useful, whether functions, notions or processes. It is not so much the ideas which people exchange that matter, as the bonds they build up between them.

Social communication mostly aims more at international use of the second language with people in another country than at local goals in multilingual societies. The overall goals of the communicative style have not been specified in great detail in general-purpose language teaching, which usually tries for the generalised situation of visitors to the target country, with the accent on tourism and travel, without specific goals for careers, for education or for access to information. In more specialized circumstances, social communication has been taught for specific careers – doctors, businessmen, oil technicians, or whatever – and for higher education.

In practice, many communicative coursebooks adopt what might be called 'package holiday communication', centred on tourist activities, with the book resembling a glossy holiday brochure and the teacher a jolly package-tour rep organizing fun activities. One entertaining, if light-hearted, method of evaluating courses is to measure the 'smile factor': the average number of smiling faces per page of the textbook, which gives a quick insight into the attitudes being expressed. The higher the smile factor, the closer to 'package holiday communication'. *Headway Elementary* (Soars and Soars, 1993), for example, manages to pack 15 smiling faces onto the first four pages (and seven unsmiling); *Touchstone* (McCarthy *et al.*, 2005) also has 15 smiles on the first four pages; *True to Life* (Collie and Slater, 1995) a mere two. The other genres of printed English where such smiling faces abound are travel brochures and clothes catalogues: the *Landsend Overstocks* catalogue, for example, has 18 on four pages. Whether you consider smiling faces an advantage or not depends on whether you think this makes English a happy, interesting subject or makes the coursebook a trivialization of human existence.

Information communicative teaching

Information communicative teaching departs from the core communicative style in several ways. Overall, it emphasizes the information that is transferred rather than the social interaction between the participants, resembling Marton's receptive strategy and Halliday's ideational function. A typical technique in this style forms the core of Asher's total physical response (TPR) method, that is, acting out commands, as seen in Chapter 7. For example, in *Live Action English* (Romijn and Seely, 2000) an activity called 'sharpening your pencil' gets students to carry out a series of commands: 'Pick up your pencil', 'Look at the point...' There is no real-life social role involved; the point is understanding the information. TPR students are listening in order to discover what actions to carry out; their social interaction with the teacher is unlike that found in any normal language exchange, except for the army drill square. So, unlike social communication, information communicative teaching emphasizes the listening-first approach mentioned in Chapter 7; listening is the crucial key to extracting information from what you hear.

Gary and Gary (1981b) have published a specimen lesson from their listening-based materials ('More English Now!'), which are designed for hotel staff in Egypt. The lesson starts with a 'Preview' section in which the language content of the lesson is explained and in which 'important words' such as 'last week' and 'checked out' are translated into Arabic. In the next section, 'Let's Listen', students hear a tape giving the bookings for a hotel for next week and then carry out a task-listening exercise, first filling in a form with the guests' names and details, and then answering questions such as 'Who was in room 104?' in writing. Finally, a 'Let's Read' section gives them the same tasks with a written text. Such listening-first teaching requires the students to listen actively but not to produce sentences until they are ready. The point here is the information transfer. Students following 'More English Now!' are listening to get specific information to be written down in various forms. While this partly resembles their real-life hotel duties, it deliberately minimizes spoken production and natural social interaction, vital to their actual conversation with guests. The concentration is on the information to be obtained from language, not on the social relationship between listener and speaker. Working out information is the key factor: take care of the message and the learning will take care of itself. Hence the style is compatible with a large range of teaching techniques, united only by their emphasis on information.

The overall goal is to get students to use the language, first by comprehending, then by producing. Comprehension of information, however, is not a goal in its own right, but a way into fuller command of the language in use. Sometimes the overall goal is more specific, as with the Cairo hotel staff. Mostly, however, the goal is non-specific, whether local or international, playing down the individual goals of language teaching and making few claims to general educational values. In terms of classrooms, it is, for good or for ill, much more teacher-dominated than the other communicative variants. The teacher supplies, in person or through materials, the language input and the organization of the students' activities and classroom strategies. The social communicative style is limited by physical factors in the classroom in that it becomes progressively more difficult to organize its activities the larger the group. The listening-based information communicative style lends itself to classes of any size. It is therefore more compatible with the traditional teacher-dominated classroom than is the social communicative style. It also caters for a range of student types, provided they do not mind having to listen rather than speak in the classroom. Again, the students need to be prepared for what the style is trying to do, since it differs from their probable expectations of the classroom.

Finally, information communicative teaching implies that there is information to communicate. An important factor in the style is the choice of information. Many courses rely on 'imaginary' content (Cook, 1983), such as 'For sale' ads for imaginary houses (*Headway*). In a survey I found that this type of content figured on nine pages out of ten in beginners' courses, seven out of ten in intermediate. But it is also possible to have 'real' content based on actual information about the 'real' world: the best-selling mineral waters in different countries (*International Express*), the London Eye (*New English File*), the lives of Calamity Jane (*Just Right*) and Amy Johnson (*Move*), methods for brewing coffee (*Meeting People*). My own feeling is that imaginary content trivializes language learning; the message is conveyed that you do not gain anything significant from your language class apart from the ability to use the language, and this can become just another form of language practice. 'Real' content makes the language lesson have a point; the students have acquired something through the language they would not otherwise have known.

Different types of real information that might be conveyed include:

- *Another academic subject taught through English.* I have recommended to students in England who complained they were stuck at a developmental plateau to go to classes in cookery rather than in English.
- *Student-contributed content.* Getting the students to talk about their own lives and real interests, fascinating in a multilingual class, boring in one where

everybody has known each other since primary school. In the first English class I ever taught, a class discussion brought out how the headman in a student's Vietnamese village had been hanged in front of his very eyes. *People and Places* (Cook, 1980) used a cumulative personal information section at the end of the book, which the student filled in lesson by lesson as they supplied the different aspects of information about themselves.

- *Language*. That is to say, information about the language they are studying. After all, this is the one thing that all the students have in common. *Meeting People* (Cook, 1982), for instance, had a text about the varieties of English spoken in different parts of the world.
- *Literature*. For many years, literature was despised because of its inappropriate language and links to the academic method. It is capable, however, of bringing depth of emotion and art to the classroom that materials written by course-writers can never do. *Living with People* (Cook, 1983) used two short poems by the controversial psychotherapist R.D. Laing to get students discussing their feelings.
- *Culture*. That is to say, discussing the cultural differences between languages – one of the goals of the UK National Curriculum. Are English people aware of showing a polite back (i.e. not obstructing people's view in a stadium) as Japanese are?
- *'Interesting facts'*. These might not be connected to English, but after the lesson the students can say they learnt something: how to treat a nosebleed, how to use chopsticks, how to play cards, how to make coffee, to take examples from *Meeting People* (Cook, 1982).

There is no logical reason why information communicative teaching should rely on listening at the expense of speaking; communication requires a speaker as well as a listener. Reading for gist may be just as much within this style. The use of listening-first techniques, as outlined in Chapter 7, represents the additional assumption that listening is basic to the learning process. There has often been a geographical division in the communicative styles: 'British-influenced' teaching has emphasised that students have to both listen and speak from day one of the course. 'American-influenced', or perhaps more strictly 'Krashen-influenced', teaching has emphasized listening without speaking. As a consequence, 'British' teaching has concentrated more on the interpersonal function; the double role of listener and speaker immediately calls up interactive 'conversation', while the listener-only role resembles people listening to the radio.

In general, the communicative style is appropriate for students and societies that value international goals of a non-specific kind. The teacher using it with a particular class has to remember that it will not appeal to students with other types of goal, say an interest in language structure or a desire for personal liberation. The unexpectedness of the classroom situation it relies on may need selling to the students; they have to realise that the onus is on them to take advantage of the classroom, not on the teacher to spoon-feed them. It needs balancing with other styles to make certain that the coverage of language components is adequate even to achieve its own goal of communicative competence, for example, in the teaching of pronunciation. But at least it sees communication as a dynamic social activity to be acquired by active participation by the students, marking a clear break in this respect from the academic and audio-lingual styles.

One seldom discussed danger has been the academic standing of language teaching as a discipline. The academic style of teaching was to some extent educationally respectable because it stressed intellectual understanding of the language system, studied high art in the form of literature, and used translation as a teaching technique, which was clearly a unique and highly demanding skill. First audio-lingualism, then communicative language teaching, said teaching should be based on everyday use of language. When describing the setting up of the language centre at the University of Essex in the 1960s, David Stern (1964) claimed that it would concentrate on 'learning as a practical skill as distinguished from an academic discipline dependent on the command of the language'. Both at school level and at university level, this view resulted in teachers from other disciplines failing to take language teaching seriously. In schools, some felt that it should no longer be part of the core academic curriculum, but an optional extra, like keyboard skills, because it no longer contributed to the core educational values of the school. At universities in England, if not elsewhere, this has led to a down-valuing in terms of esteem. The consequences of Stern's plan is that an Essex professor said recently that language teaching is only about teaching people to order coffee in a bar in Paris. These dangers are one reason why I have been arguing for the deeper value of language teaching throughout this book. L2 users are different from those who speak one language, not just people who can order a coffee or read a map in another language. L2 teaching is about turning learners into these distinctive types of people.

Box 13.5 The communicative style of language teaching

Typical teaching techniques

- information gap, role plays, tasks

Goals

- getting students to interact with other people in the second language, in the classroom and outside

Type of student

- field-independent students rather than field-dependent students, extroverts rather than introverts, and less academic students

Learning assumptions

- learning by communicating with other students in the classroom: *laissez-faire*
- some use of conscious understanding of grammar

Classroom assumptions

- teacher as organizer, not source of language knowledge

Weaknesses from an SLA research perspective

- lack of views on discourse processes, communication strategies, etc.
- black box model of learning
- lack of role for the first language

Suggestions for teaching

- use with appropriate students in appropriate circumstances
- supplement with other components of language
- avoid trivialization of content and aims

13.4 The task-based learning style

Focusing questions

- What is the ideal way of organizing what students do in the classroom?
- What relationship does what happens in the classroom have to the world outside the classroom?

Keywords

task: 'A task is an activity which requires learners to use language, with emphasis on meaning, to attain a goal' (Bygate *et al.*, 2001)

task-based learning (TBL): the notion that learning and teaching should be organized around a set of classroom tasks

focus on form (FonF): discussion of grammar and vocabulary arising from meaningful language in the classroom

In the past few years the most fashionable style among teaching methodologists has been task-based learning (TBL). In the everyday sense of the word 'task', all language teaching consists of tasks, whether these are translation tasks, structure drill tasks or information gap tasks: a teacher's job is to set up things for the students to do in the classroom, that is, give them tasks to carry out. But TBL uses 'task' in a narrower way, as seen in the definition by Martin Bygate *et al.* (2001): 'A task is an activity which requires learners to use language, with emphasis on meaning, to attain a goal.' This definition illustrates some of the main points of TBL that most of its enthusiasts agreed on. Of course, as with any teaching exercise, the task the teacher plans may be very different from what the students actually do (Hosenfeld, 1976; Seedhouse, 2005b).

According to the definition, a task 'requires learners to use language': students are learning the language by using it, as assumed by the communicative style. This implies that learning is the same as processing, that is, codebreaking is the same as decoding, reminiscent of Krashen's thinking. While the communicative style organizes its tasks and activities around a language point – teaching a function, a communicative strategy, and so on – TBL denies this: the language must come from the learners themselves, not from the teacher. It is solving the requirements of the task itself that counts. So a task is chosen because it is a good task, not because it teaches a particular language point. Suppose we design a class task: 'Make a shopping list for your weekly internet order from a supermarket.' This task requires the students to work together and to report back; but it does not tell them how to interact to achieve this, nor does it supply the vocabulary.

The second part of the definition is that a task has 'an emphasis on meaning'. The teaching focus is not on the structures, language functions, vocabulary items, and so on, of earlier approaches, but on the meaning of what is said. Hence structure drills count as exercises, not as tasks, since they do not involve meaning. Meaning in TBL is one person conveying information appropriate to the particular task to another person, rather like information communicative teaching. There is no requirement for the information to be meaningful in any other way, say by emotionally involving the student, or for it to be useful in the world outside the classroom: meaning relates only to the task at hand. However, it is meaning in a pure information sense, rather like the digits of computer data. As Garcia Mayo (2007: 91) puts it, TBL is 'a computational model of acquisition in which tasks are viewed as devices which can influence learners' information processing'. So the focus in the shopping list task is entirely on the content of the list, the information to be transmitted to the supermarket. It is irrelevant whether the students have ever done or will do online shopping orders.

The last part of the definition requires the student 'to use language … to attain a goal'. The point of the task is not to master a specific language point, but to achieve a particular non-language goal. There has to be an outcome to a task which the students do or do not achieve. Again, this distinguishes tasks from other forms of teaching activities, where a task ends essentially when the teacher says so. The goal of the shopping list task is the shopping list itself; have they succeeded in making a list that will cater for a week's shopping needs?

TBL draws on an eclectic range of sources for its support. It is related to the interaction model in Chapter 12 in that it depends on negotiation of meaning; to the sociocultural model in that it depends on peer-to-peer scaffolding; and to the Conversation Analysis model in that it depends on continuous conversational interaction between the students. It is also related to the various views of processing seen in Chapter 7, in particular to views on the centrality of meaning in processing. Its main support is classroom-based research studies which show in general that TBL does lead to an improvement in fluency and accuracy. However, this is not the same thing as proving that TBL leads to acquisition and to use outside the classroom.

FonF and task-based learning

A central component of TBL for many people is the idea of FonF mentioned in Chapter 2 – discussion of formal aspects of language following non-language-based practice. While the use of tasks in itself is in the direct line of descent from the exploitation phase of audio-lingualism through communicative language teaching, FonF is the distinctive ingredient of the TBL style. In this view, it is beneficial to focus on language form, provided this emerges out of a task rather than being its starting point or sole rationale. To some extent this modifies the basic TBL tenet that language itself is not the focus of the task, by letting language form in through the back door.

Though explanation of forms has been extensively discussed as part of FonF, there are comparatively few examples of what it means in practice. Dave and Jane Willis (2007) give the example of a task based on a text about a suicide attempt. They suggest that the teacher can exploit this to show the various uses of the reflexive pronoun in the text, such as 'Jim Burney himself' and 'kill himself', and to introduce other uses such as 'help yourself'. This is an informal, commonsense view of grammar based on some frequent uses of reflexives. Since the tasks have not been designed with language in mind, such follow-up activities are necessarily ad hoc and unsystematic (unless, of course, the teacher cheats and works a language point into the design of the task).

The FonF idea thus abandons one aspect of audio-lingualism that had still been implicitly accepted by communicative teaching, namely Rivers' assumption

(3): 'Analogy provides a better foundation for foreign language learning than analysis'. The FonF approach harks back to earlier models of language teaching, which also saw explicit grammar as a follow-up activity. FonF is foreshadowed, for example, in Article 4 of the International Phonetics Association manifesto of the 1880s: 'In the early stages grammar should be taught inductively, complementing and generalising language facts observed during reading.' It resembles the traditional teaching exercise known as 'explication de textes', which was an integral part of the grammar-translation methodology for teaching French – and is still apparently encountered by British university students on their year abroad. In this, the teacher goes through a written text to draw out and discuss useful vocabulary and grammar on an ad hoc basis. The difference is that in FonF there is a task to be carried out – and the explication takes place in the second language after the event rather than as it happens. But the underlying question remains, not *whether* grammar should be explained, but *what* grammar should be explained, out of the alternatives presented in Chapter 2, for example.

The nature of tasks

The original impetus for task-based learning came from the celebrated Bangalore Project (Prabhu, 1987), which reacted against both the traditional form of EFL used in India and the type of situational teaching then practised. The main grounds were the refusal to recognize the classroom as a 'real' situation in its own right, rather than as a 'pretend' L2 situation. A real classroom uses activities that are proper for classrooms, that is, educational tasks. If learning is doing tasks, teaching means specifying and helping with the tasks, for example, 'making the plan of a house'. The tasks are not defined linguistically, but in an order based on difficulty.

The whole-class activity consisted of a pedagogic dialogue in which the teacher's questions were, as in other classrooms, invitations to learners to demonstrate their ability, not pretended requests for enlightenment; and learners' responses arose from their role as learners, not from assumed roles in simulated situations or from their individual lives outside the classroom (Prabhu, 1987: 28).

Educational value depends on the validity of the tasks and their usefulness as vehicles for language learning. Hence teaching started to recognize the importance of the classroom itself as a communicative educational setting in its own right and to organize the activities that occurred there in terms of educational tasks rather than tasks that necessarily relate to the world outside the classroom. Prabhu's original list of tasks categorized them as:

- *information gap activities*, such as the picture comparison described above;
- *reasoning gap activities*, deriving new information by inference, such as working out timetables for the class;
- *opinion gap activities*, in which there is no right or wrong answer, only the person's preference, as in 'the discussion of a social issue'.

Jane Willis (1996), on the other hand, lists six main types of task: *listing, ordering and sorting, comparing, problem solving, sharing personal experience* and *creative*. In *Atlas 1* (Nunan, 1995, teacher's book) there are ten types of task, including *predicting* (e.g. 'predicting what is to come on the learning process'), *conversational patterns* ('using expressions to start conversations and keep them going') and *cooperating* ('sharing ideas and learning with other students'). The concept of the task, then, does vary considerably: it seems to be a peg that you can hang many coats on.

Jane Willis (1996) has provided a useful outline of the flow in task-based learning (shown in Box 13.6), which has three main components – pre-task, task-cycle and language focus.

Box 13.6 The flow in task-based learning (Willis, 1996)

The pre-task: the teacher sets up the task.

1 The task cycle
   A. **task**. The students carry out the task in pairs with the teacher monitoring.
   B. **planning**. The students decide how to report back to the whole group.
   C. **report**. The students make their reports.
2 Language focus
   A. **analysis**. Students discuss how others carried out the task on a recording.
   B. **practice**. The teacher practises new language that has cropped up.

This may, however, be a good teaching sequence in any style. In an academic style, for example, the teacher might present an advertisement for translation (pre-task) and set the students the specific task of translating parts of it in pairs (task). They decide how to present it to the group (planning), then compare notes on it with other groups (report), possibly by using networked word-processing. Then the students compare their advertisement with real advertisements (analysis) and they practise new language that has come up (practice). Task-based learning develops communicative language teaching by providing a much greater range of classroom activities and much firmer overall guidance for the teacher.

Issues with TBL

The goals for task-based learning that are usually mentioned are fluency, accuracy and complexity (Skehan, 1998). But people need to be fluent, accurate or complex because they need a second language for buying and selling, for translating poetry, for passing an exam, for listening to operas, for travelling, for praying, for writing a novel, for organising a revolution, or any of the myriad reasons for which people learn second languages. Task-based learning concentrates on what can work in the classroom. Its expressed goal is short-term fluency. It does not appear concerned with overall teaching goals, which are hardly ever mentioned. Presumably there are higher goals to language teaching than fluency, accuracy and complexity, such as the beneficial effects on the students of the second language (personal goals), the usefulness of knowing a second language for the society (local goals), and the benefits for the world in general (international goals), as in Chapter 11. Though classroom tasks may well lead to all these outcomes, this is unlikely to work if they are not explicitly included in the design and implementation.

Nor does TBL require that tasks should mirror what the students have to do in the world outside the classroom. Sometimes it is briefly mentioned that it would be nice if classroom tasks had some relationship to later L2 uses – 'I regard this as desirable but difficult to obtain in practice' (Skehan, 1998: 96). External relevance is an optional extra for task-based learning rather than a vital ingredient, as it would be for most other language teaching. Nor have internal goals been mentioned, for example the beneficial educational effects of learning through tasks on, say, the students' interactional abilities or their cognitive processes.

The information that is conveyed in tasks and the outcomes of the tasks seem essentially trivial; there is no reason why they should matter to anybody. Take the list of specimen tasks given in Ellis (2003):

- completing one another's family tree;
- agreeing on advice to give to the writer of a letter to an agony aunt;
- discovering whether one's paths will cross in the next week;
- solving a riddle;
- leaving a message on someone's answer machine.

These tasks would be fascinating to 10-year-olds, reminding us that information gap activities indeed originated in primary schools. The old-fashioned justification for these topics was the language that they covered, a defence no longer available for TBL since it does not teach specific language points.

The question of the relevance and power of the native speaker model, so eagerly debated by much contemporary SLA research, as seen in Chapter 11, has passed TBL by. It does not seem to care what the long-term purpose may be, provided it gets short-term gains on performance on tasks. It does not see the classroom as an L2 user situation, but follows the traditional line of minimizing the use of the first language. The students are seen as belonging to the learner group described in Chapter 10, rather than as potential or actual members of L2 user groups. For example, Willis and Willis (2007) devote a handful of pages to saying how the teacher can help the students to get over the 'hurdle' of using the language, that is, the first language is seen as a hindrance rather than a help. The reasons for using the second language for any of these classroom-centred tasks seem entirely arbitrary: what is the motive for making a shopping list, discussing suicide or completing your family tree *in a second language*? The students could carry out the tasks far better in the first language: why use the second? In other words, despite its protestations, TBL is essentially language practice, since it provides no motive for the task to be in another language.

The sword that hangs over both the communicative and TBL styles is the question of where the language that the students need for the task comes from in the first place. As exploitation techniques, tasks require the students to draw on their own language resources to carry them out, but they do not provide the resources to do so. The task of completing a family tree requires at least the vocabulary of relatives – 'mother', 'husband', 'aunt', 'cousin', and so on. Many coursebooks use a tree to teach or revise the words for relatives. *Touchstone* (McCarthy *et al.*, 2005: 26) shows an illustrated tree going from grandparents down to children; students practise by stating the various relationships of the people to each other; later they fill out two trees in their 'vocabulary notebook' – all straightforward standard teaching. Indeed, family tree exercises can also be found in *Move*, *New Headway* and *New Cutting Edge* – all, of course, showing a British middle-class view of the nuclear family, rather than the extended family networks of other classes or cultures. But how can the students make a family tree if they have not first had the vocabulary taught to them ('father', 'aunt', 'cousin'...)? In first language acquisition research, this is called 'bootstrapping' – how the child works out the language by pulling itself up with its own boots. TBL must presuppose bootstrapping of the language necessary to the task – the students must have learnt the vocabulary and structures before they can actually perform the task. If this has already been taught, for example in Jane Willis's 'pre-task' stage, this represents the true teaching stage, not the task itself.

So TBL is not concerned with the overall goals or purposes of language teaching, only with short-term fluency gains. Hence it does not have a syllabus for teaching so much as a list of tasks carefully designed and selected to work with the students at a particular stage. It does not cover many areas of language proficiency such as pronunciation. The teacher's role is even more as an organizer and helper than as an expert, since they do not need particular knowledge of anything but task design and the minimal grammar necessary for FonF. The students must be prepared for this type of communal learning through tasks, and be convinced that it is a proper way of acquiring the language and that the teacher knows what they are doing. This approach will not go down well with highly academic students or in certain cultural situations. Students have been concerned when they first encounter this form of teaching where the language content is invisible and not supplied by the teacher, since it is even further from their expectations than the communicative style.

The overall difficulty with the TBL style, then, is its detachment from everything else in language use and language teaching: it is a single-solution approach that tackles the whole of language teaching in the same way. Its tasks are highly useful exploitation activities, and important for teachers to know about and to use with other techniques. But they cannot realistically form the core of any language teaching classroom that sees its students as people engaged with the world.

Box 13.7 The task-based learning style of language teaching

Typical teaching techniques
- meaning-based tasks with definite outcomes

Goals
- fluency, accuracy, complexity

Type of student
- possibly less academic

Learning assumptions
- language acquisition takes place through meaning-based tasks with a specific short-term goal

Classroom assumptions
- teaching depends on organizing tasks based on meaning with specific outcomes

Weaknesses from an SLA research perspective
- lack of wider engagement with goals, learner groups, etc.
- lack of a role for first language
- reliance on a processing model as opposed to a learning model

Suggestions for teaching
- use in conjunction with other styles, not as a style on its own
- useful as a way of planning and preparing lessons

13.5 The mainstream EFL style

Focusing questions

- What does the word 'situation' mean to you in language teaching?
- How much do you think a teacher can mix different teaching styles?

Keywords

situation: some teaching uses 'situation' to mean physical demonstration in the classroom; other teaching uses it to mean situations where the student will use the language in the world outside the classroom

substitution table: a language teaching technique where students create sentences by choosing words from successive columns of a table

The mainstream EFL style has developed in British-influenced EFL from the 1930s up to the present day. Until the early 1970s, it mostly reflected a compromise between the academic and the audio-lingual styles, combining, say, techniques of grammatical explanation with techniques of automatic practice. Harold Palmer in the 1920s saw classroom L2 learning as a balance between the 'studial' capacities by which people learnt a language by studying it like any content subject, that is, what is called here an academic style, and the 'spontaneous' capacities through which people learn language naturally and without thinking, seen by him in similar terms to the audio-lingual style (Palmer, 1926). The name for this style in India was the structural-oral-situational (SOS) method, an acronym that captures several of its main features (Prabhu, 1987) – the reliance on grammatical structures, the primacy of speech, and the use of language in 'situations'. Recently it has taken on aspects of the social communicative style by emphasising person-to-person dialogue techniques.

Until the 1970s, this early mainstream style was characterized by the term 'situation' in two senses. In one sense of 'situation', language was to be taught though demonstration in the real classroom situation; teachers rely on the props, gestures and activities that are possible in a real classroom. I remember seeing a colleague attempting to cope with a roomful of EFL beginners who had unexpectedly arrived a week early by using the only prop he had to hand, a waste-paper basket. In the other sense of 'situation', language teaching was to be organized around the language of the real-life situations the students would encounter: the railway station, the hotel, and so on. A lesson using the mainstream EFL style starts with a presentation phase in which the teacher introduces new structures and vocabulary. In the Australian course *Situational English* (Commonwealth Office, 1967), for example, the teacher demonstrates the use of 'can' 'situationally' to the students by touching the floor and trying unsuccessfully to touch the ceiling to illustrate 'can' versus 'can't'.

The next stage of the lesson usually involves a short dialogue. In this case it might be a job interview which includes several examples of 'can': 'Can you drive a car?' or 'I can speak three languages.' The students listen to the dialogue, they repeat parts of it, they are asked questions about it, and so on.

Then they might see a substitution table such as Table 13.1, a technique suggested by Harold Palmer in 1926 that allows students to create new sentences under tight control. (Historically, the substitution table has been traced back to Erasmus in 1524 (Kelly, 1969).) Chapter 2 discusses the way substitution tables depend on structural grammar analysis. The example comes from a coursebook, *Success with English* (Broughton, 1968), which used lengthy substitution tables as the main teaching technique. Here the students have to make up four true sentences by combining words from different columns – 'I have some grey gloves in my drawer', 'I have some black stockings in my house', and so on. Substitution tables continue to appear in coursebooks. A typical modern substitution table is seen in *Move* (Bowler and Parminter, 2007).

The change is that this has moved to the 'grammar reference' section of the book; the substitution table is now treated as a method of displaying sentence structure, an alternative to a phrase structure tree, to help the students' understanding, not as a way of getting them directly to practise a structure intensively. This depends on the students having some idea of both structural grammar and paradigm displays used in the traditional grammar discussed in Chapter 2.

I have some	new black grey white smart warm	shoes clothes socks stockings gloves hats	in my house. in my cupboard. in my drawer. in my room.

Table 13.1 Substitution table from *Success with English* (Broughton, 1968)

Are	you we they	
Is	he she it	going to set up a new business?

Table 13.2 Substitution table from *Move* (Bowler and Parminter, 2007)

The mainstream style combines Palmer's studial and spontaneous capacities. A coursebook such as *New Headway* (Soars and Soars, 2002), for instance, has elements of the academic style in that it explains structures: 'We use the Present Continuous to talk about actions that last a short time.' It has elements of the audio-lingual style in that it is graded around structures and the 'four skills'. But it has also incorporated elements of social communicative teaching in pair work exercises, such as acting out conversations about solving problems.

The pivot around which the lesson revolves is the grammatical point, couched in terms of structural or traditional grammar. The main difference from the early mainstream style is the use of group work and pair work, and the information orientation to the exercises. A mainstream EFL method is implied every time a teacher goes through the classic progression from presentation to dialogue to controlled practice, whether it is concerned with grammar or communicative function. Many have seen this sequence of presentation, practice, production (PPP) as the chief characteristic of the mainstream style, or indeed of the audio-lingual and communicative styles (Scrivenor, 1994), but not of task-based learning. The mainstream style is the central style described in TEFL manuals such as *The Practice of English Language Teaching* (Harmer, 2007). It represents, perhaps, the bulk of EFL teaching of the past 50 years, if not longer.

The goals are, in a sense, an updated version of audio-lingualism. What counts is how students use language in the eventual real-world situation rather than their academic knowledge or the spin-off in general educational values. The version of learning involved is similarly a compromise, suggesting that students learn by conscious understanding, by sheer practice and by attempting to talk to each other. Some aspects of the knowledge models seen in Chapter 12 are reflected here, as are aspects of the processing models. Mainstream EFL teaching tries to have its cake and eat it, by saying that if the student does not benefit from one part of the lesson, then another part will help. Hence, while I have been using EFL courses here to illustrate particular styles, nearly all of them are actual mainstream mixtures balancing the styles.

In terms of student types as well, this broadens the coverage. One student benefits from grammatical explanation, another from structure practice, another from role play. Perhaps combining these will suit more of the students more of the time than relying on a purer style. Mainstream teaching does not usually encompass the information communicative style, with its emphasis on listening, preferring to see listening and speaking as more or less inseparable. It has the drawbacks common to the other styles – the concentration on certain types of grammar and discourse at the expense of others.

Is such a combination of styles in one mainstream style to be praised or blamed? In terms of teaching methods, the debate has revolved around 'eclecticism'. Some have argued that there is nothing wrong with eclectic mixing of methods provided the mixing is rationally based. Others have claimed that it is impossible for the students to learn in so many different ways simultaneously; the teacher is irresponsible to combine incompatible models of language learning. Marton (1988) argues that only certain sequences are possible. His receptive strategy, for instance, may precede, but not follow, the reconstructive or communicative strategies.

Each of the teaching styles we have seen so far captures some aspects of this complexity and misses out on others. None of the teaching styles is complete, just as none of the models of L2 learning is complete. Eclecticism is only an issue if two styles concern the same area of L2 learning rather than different areas. Hence, at the moment, it is unnecessary to speculate about the good or bad consequences of eclecticism. When there is a choice between competing styles of language teaching, each with a coverage ranging from grammar to classroom language, from memory to pronunciation, from motivation to the roles of the second language in society, then eclecticism becomes an issue. At the moment, all teaching methods are partial in L2 learning terms; some areas of language are only covered by one type of teaching technique; conversely, some methods deal with only a fraction of the totality of L2 learning. The mainstream EFL style cannot be dismissed simply because of its eclecticism, as it is neither more nor less eclectic than any other overall teaching style in terms of L2 learning. My own feeling is that the mainstream style does indeed reflect a style of its own that is more than the sum of its parts.

Box 13.8 The mainstream EFL style of language teaching

Typical teaching techniques
- presentation, substitution, role play

Goals
- getting students to know and use language

Type of student
- any

Learning assumptions
- understanding, practice and use

Classroom assumptions
- both teacher-controlled full classes and internal small groups

Weaknesses from an SLA research perspective
- combination of other styles
- lack of role for the L1
- drawbacks of mixture of styles

Suggestions for teaching
- do not worry about the mixture of different sources
- remember that even this rich mixture still does not cover all aspects relevant to L2 teaching

---

13.6 Other styles

Focusing questions

- To what extent do you think teaching should aim to make students 'better' people?
- How would you strike the balance in language teaching between the students' independence and the teacher's control?

Keywords

community language learning (CLL): a teaching method in which students create conversations in the second language from the outset, using the teacher as a translation resource

suggestopedia: a teaching method aimed at avoiding the students' block about language learning through means such as listening to music

autonomous learning: in this the choice of what and how to learn is essentially handed over to the students, whether immediately or over time

Other teaching styles have been proposed that mark a radical departure from those outlined earlier, either in their goals or in their execution. It is difficult to call these by a single name. Some have been called 'alternative methods', but this suggests there is a common conventional method to which they provide an alternative and that they are themselves united in their approach. Some are referred to as 'humanistic methods' because of their links to 'humanistic psychology', but this label suggests religious or philosophical connections that are mostly inappropriate. Others are called 'self-access' or 'self-directed learning'. In England, the practice of these styles is so rare that they are difficult to observe in a full-blooded form, although every EFL or modern language teaching class probably shows some influence from, say, communicative teaching or TBL. Most of these methods came into being around the 1970s and attracted some enthusiastic supporters who proselytised their message around the world. However, as this generation died out, they do not seem to have been replaced by new adherents or indeed new alternative methods. SEAL (Society for Effective Affective Learning), the association for spreading the ideas of Lozanov, discussed below, once a thriving concern, was actually wound up in 2007.

Let us start with **Community Language Learning** (CLL), derived from the work of Charles Curran (1976). Picture a beginners' class in which the students sit in a circle from which the teacher is excluded. One student starts a conversation by remarking, 'Weren't the buses terrible this morning?' in his first language. The teacher translates this into the language the students are learning and the student repeats it. Another student answers, 'When do the buses ever run on time?' in her first language, which is translated once again by the teacher, and repeated by the student. And the conversation between the students proceeds in this way. The teacher records the translations and later uses them for conventional practice, such as audio-lingual drilling or academic explanation. But the core element of the class is spontaneous conversation following the students' lead, with the teacher offering the support facility of instant translation. As the students progress to later stages, they become increasingly independent of the teacher. CLL is one of the 'humanistic' methods that include **Suggestopedia**, with its aim of relaxing the student through means such as listening to music (Lozanov, 1978), the **Silent Way**, with its concentration on the expression of meaning abstractly through coloured rods (Gattegno, 1972), and **Confluent Language Teaching**, with its emphasis on the classroom experience as a whole affecting the teacher as much as the students (Galyean, 1977).

In general, CLL subordinates language to the self-expression of emotions and ideas. If anything, language gets in the way of the clear expression of the student's feelings. The aim is not, at the end of the day, to be able to do anything with language in the world outside. It is to do something here and now in the classroom, so that the student, in Curran's words, 'arrives at a more positive view of himself, of his situation, of what he wishes to do and to become' (Curran, 1976). A logical extension is the therapeutic use of language teaching for psychotherapy in mental hospitals. Speaking about their problems is easier for some people in a second language than in their first.

The goal of CLL is to develop the students' potential and to enable them to 'come alive' through L2 learning, not to help them directly to communicate with others outside the group. Hence it stresses the general educational value for the individual rather than local or international benefits. The student in some way becomes a better person through language teaching. The concept of 'better' is usually defined as greater insight into one's self, one's feelings and one's relationships with others. Learning a language through a humanistic style has the same virtues and vices as jogging; while it does you good, it is concerned with getting you fit rather than with the care of others, with the individual self, not other-related goals. This type of goal partly accounts for the comparative lack of impact of CLL on the mainstream educational system, where language teaching is often thought of as having more benefit outside the classroom, and where self-fulfilment through the classroom has been seen more as a product of lessons in the mother tongue and its literature. Hence the humanistic styles are often the preserve of part-time education or self-improvement classes. The goals of realizing the individual's potential are perhaps coincidentally attached to L2 teaching; they might be achieved as well through mother-tongue teaching, aerobics, Zen, assertiveness training or motorcycle maintenance. Indeed, Curran says that CLL 'can be readily adapted to the learning of other subjects'; Suggestopedia, similarly, is supposed to apply to *all* education; the Silent Way comes out of an approach to teaching mathematics in primary school.

A strong affinity between them is that they see a 'true' method of L2 learning which can be unveiled by freeing the learner from inhibiting factors. L2 learning takes place if the learner's inner self is set free by providing the right circumstances for learning. If teachers provide stress-free, non-dependent, value-respecting teaching, students will learn. While no one knows what mechanisms exist in the students' minds, we know what conditions will help them work. So the CLL model of learning is not dissimilar to the communicative, laissez-faire, learning-by-doing. If you are expressing yourself, you are learning the language, even if such expression takes place through the teacher's mediating translation.

The other humanistic styles are equally unlinked to mainstream SLA research. Suggestopedia is based on an overall theory of learning and education using ideas of hypnotic suggestion. The conditions of learning are tightly controlled in order to overcome the learner's resistance to the new language. Georgi Lozanov, its inventor, has indeed carried out psychological experiments, mostly unavailable in English, which make particular claims for the effective learning of vocabulary (Lozanov, 1978). Again, where the outlines of an L2 learning model can be discerned, it resembles the processing models seen in Chapter 12.

Oddly enough, while the fringe humanistic styles take pride in their learner-centredness, they take little heed of the variation between learners. CLL would clearly appeal to extrovert students rather than introverts. Their primary motivation would have to be neither instrumental nor integrative, since both of these lead away from the group. Instead, it would have to be self-related or teaching-group related. What happens within the group itself and what the students get out of it are what matters, not what they can do with the language outside. Nor, despite their psychological overtones, do methods such as CLL and Suggestopedia pay much attention to the performance processes of speech production and comprehension.

An opposing trend in teaching styles is the move towards learner autonomy. Let us look at a student called Mr D, described by Henner-Stanchina (1985). Mr D is a brewery engineer who went to CRAPEL (Centre de Recherches et d'Applications Pédagogiques en Langues), in Nancy in France, to develop his reading skills in English. He chose, out of a set of options, to have the services of a 'helper', to have personal teaching materials, and to use the sound library. The first session with the helper revealed that his difficulties were, *inter alia*, with complex noun phrases and with the meanings of verb forms. Later sessions dealt with specific points arising from this, using the helper as a check on the hypotheses he was forming from the texts he read. The helper's role faded out as he was able to progress through technical documents with increasing ease.

The aim, above all, is to hand over responsibility for learning to the student. The teacher is a helper who assists with choice of materials and advises what to do, but does not teach directly. As Henri Holec (1985) from CRAPEL puts it:

> *By becoming autonomous, that is by gradually and individually acquiring the capacity to conduct his own learning program, the learner progressively becomes his own teacher and constructs and evaluates his learning program himself.*

Using autonomous learning depends on devising a system through which students have the choice of learning in their own way. To quote Holec (1987) again:

> *Learners gradually replace the belief that they are 'consumers' of language courses with the belief that they can be 'producers' of their own learning program and that this is their right.*

At North-East London Polytechnic (now University of East London), we had a system in which students could make use of language teaching material of their own choice from the selection provided in a language laboratory at any time. One afternoon per week, helpers were available in all the languages on offer. These could be used by the students in any way they liked, for example, for discussion of which materials to use, for assessment of progress, or for straightforward conversation practice. This system was particularly attractive to people like bus drivers who work varying shifts, as they could fit the timings, and so on, to suit their convenience. Dickinson (1987) describes more sophisticated systems in operation at the Language Laboratory in Cambridge University, at Moray House in Edinburgh, and the one encountered by Mr D at CRAPEL in Nancy. But self-direction can also be offered to children within the secondary school classroom. Leni Dam in Copenhagen uses a system of group-based tasks chosen by the students to suit their own needs and interests, what they want to learn and how they want to learn.

Autonomous learning is not yet widely used, nor is it clear that it would fit in with many mainstream educational systems. One reason is the incompatibility between the individual nature of the instruction and the collective nature of most classrooms and assessment. Autonomous learning takes the learner-centredness of the humanistic styles a stage further in refusing to prescribe a patent method that all learners have to follow. It is up to the student to decide on goals, methods and assessment. That is what freedom is all about. In a sense, autonomous learning is free of many of the criticisms levelled against other styles. No teaching technique, no type of learner, no area of language is excluded in principle. Nevertheless, much depends on the role of the helper and the support system. Without suitable guidance, students may not be aware of the possibilities open to them. The helper has the difficult job of turning the student's initial preconceptions of language and of language learning into those attitudes which are most effective for that student. SLA research can assist autonomous learning by ensuring that the support systems for the learner reflect a genuine range of choices, with an adequate coverage of the diverse nature of L2 learning.

Box 13.9 Other styles of language teaching

Typical teaching techniques
- CLL, Suggestopedia, Confluent Language Teaching, self-directed learning

Goals
- individual, development of potential, self-selected

Type of student
- those with personal motivations

Learning assumptions
- diverse, mostly learning by doing, or a processing model

Classroom assumptions
- learner's freedom of choice

Weaknesses from an SLA research perspective
- either no view of learning or idiosyncratic views
- little attention to learner variation

Classroom assumptions
- usually small groups with cofigurative or prefigurative aims

Suggestions for teachers
- a reminder of the importance of the students' feelings
- open discussions with students over their needs and preferences

---

13.7 Conclusions

The diversity of L2 teaching styles seen in this chapter may seem confusing: how can students really be learning language in so many ways? However, such diversity reflects the complexity of language and the range of student needs. Why should one expect that a system as complex as language could be mastered in a single way? Even adding these teaching styles together gives an inadequate account of the totality of L2 learning. Second language learning means learning in all these ways, and in many more. This chapter has continually been drawing attention to the gaps in the coverage of each teaching style, particularly in terms of breadth of coverage of all the areas necessary to an L2 user – not just grammar or interaction, but also pronunciation, vocabulary and all the rest. As teachers and methodologists become more aware of SLA research, so teaching methods can alter to take them into account and cover a wider range of learning. Much L2 learning is concealed behind such global terms as 'communication', or such two-way oppositions as 'experiential/analytic', or indeed simplistic divisions into six teaching styles. To improve teaching, we need to appreciate language learning in all its complexity.

But teachers live in the present. They have to teach now, rather than wait for a whole new L2 learning framework to emerge. They must get on with meeting the needs of the students, even if they still do not know enough about L2 learning. David Reibel once presented a paper at a conference entitled 'What to do until the linguist gets here'. A psychoanalyst treating an individual patient has to set aside theories in order to respond to the uniqueness of that particular person. Teachers too have the duty to respond to their students. To serve the unique needs of actual students, the teacher needs to do whatever is necessary, not just that which is scientifically proven and based on abstract theory.

And the teacher needs to take into account far more than the area of SLA research; in the present state of knowledge, SLA research has no warrant to suggest that any current teaching is more than partially justified. This book has therefore made suggestions and comments rather than asserted dogmatic axioms. Practising teachers should weigh them against all the other factors in their unique teaching situation before deciding how seriously to take them. Considering teaching from an L2 learning perspective in such a way will, it is hoped, lead in the future to a more comprehensive, scientifically based view of language teaching.

Discussion topics

1 Think of what you did or saw done the last time you visited a class. Would you say the terms to characterize it best were 'techniques', 'approaches', 'styles', or something else?

2 To what extent does the academic style incorporate traditional values of education, say, those held by the man in the street or government ministries, compared to the values of other styles?

3 What aspects of the audio-lingual style are still practised today (whatever they are actually called)?

4 To what extent do students carry over the ability to communicate socially from their first language to their second?

5 If communicative teaching is about transferring 'information', what information do you feel should be conveyed during the language lesson?

6 Should classroom tasks in fact relate to the world outside the classroom?

7 Does task-based learning represent a whole new method of language teaching or is it just a way of organizing some aspects of teaching?

8 In what ways do you think language teaching has changed in the past 70 years, so far as the average classroom is concerned?

9 Does teaching an 'alternative' style mean adopting an 'alternative' set of values?

10 Which aspect of SLA research have you found most useful for language teaching? Which have you found least useful?

Further reading

The models are best approached through the main texts cited in each section, namely Lado, Rivers, Curran, and so on. Any modern teaching methodology book should cover the more recent methods, such as Ur (1996) *A Course in Language Teaching*. For TBL, Willis and Willis (2007) *Doing Task-based Teaching*, is good value. The two articles by Swan (1985, 2005) should remind people to moderate their enthusiasm for new teaching methods, by taking practical issues into consideration.

List of coursebooks mentioned

These are arranged by book title since this is the usual way teachers refer to them. Those which are not for English should be obvious from the title. Older editions of some books that are cited have been listed separately.

Active Intonation (1968) V.J Cook, Harlow: Longman.
Angol Nyelv Alapfoken (1987) B.A. Edina and S. Ivanne, Budapest: Tankonyvkiado.
Atlas 1 (1995) D. Nunan, Boston, MA: Heinle & Heinle.
Basic Grammar in Use (2002) R. Murphy, Cambridge: Cambridge University Press, 2nd edition.
Beginner's Choice, The (1992) S. Mohamed and R. Acklam, Harlow: Longman.
Break into English (1985) M. Carrier, S. Haines and D. Christie, Sevenoaks: Hodder and Stoughton.
Buzz (1993) J. Revell and P. Seligson, London: BBC English.
Cambridge English (1984) M. Swan and C. Walters, Cambridge: Cambridge University Press.
Changes (1998) J.C. Richards, Cambridge: Cambridge University Press.
Ci Siamo (1997) C. Guarnuccio and E. Guarnuccio, Port Melbourne, Australia: CIS Heinemann.
COBUILD English Course 1 (1988) J. Willis and D. Willis, London: Collins.
Concept 7–9 (1972) J. Wight, R.A. Norris and F.J. Worsley, Leeds: E.J. Arnold.
Deux Mondes: A Communicative Approach (1993) T.D. Terrell, M.B. Rogers, B.K. Barnes and M. Wolff-Hessini, New York: McGraw-Hill.
English for the Fifth Class (1988) V. Despotova, T. Shopov and V. Stoyanka, Sofia: Nardodna Prosveta.
English for You (1983) G. Graf, Berlin: Volk und Wissen Volkseigener Verlag.
English Topics (1975) V. Cook, Oxford: Oxford University Press.
Flying Colours 1 (1990) J. Garton-Sprenger and S. Greenall, London: Heinemann.
Function in English (1982) J. Blundell, J. Higgins and N. Middlemiss, Oxford: Oxford University Press.
Handling Spelling (1985) J. Davis, Cheltenham: Stanley Thornes.
Headway (1987) J. Soars and L. Soars, Oxford: Oxford University Press.
Headway Elementary (1993) L. Soars and J. Soars, Oxford: Oxford University Press.
Hotline (1992) T. Hutchinson, Oxford: Oxford University Press.
How to Improve Your Memory (1987) A. Wright, Cambridge: Cambridge University Press.
I Love English (1985) G. Capelle, C. Pavik and M.K. Segal, New York: Regents.
Intercultural Interactions: A Practical Guide (1996) K. Cushner and R.W. Brislin, Thousand Oaks, CA: Sage.
International Express (1996) L. Taylor, Oxford: Oxford University Press.

Just Right (2004) J. Harmer, London: Marshall-Cavendish.
Keep Talking (1984) F. Klippel, Cambridge: Cambridge University Press.
Language Activator (1993) Harlow: Longman.
Learning to Learn English (1989) G. Ellis and B. Sinclair, Cambridge: Cambridge University Press.
Libre Echange (1995) J. Courtillon and G.-D. de Salins, Paris: Hatier/Didier.
Listening File, The (1989) J. Harmer and A. Ellsworth, Harlow: Longman.
Live Action English (2000) E. Romijn and C. Seely, Berkeley, CA: Command Performance Language Institute.
Living with People (1983) V. Cook, Oxford: Pergamon.
Making Sense of Spelling and Pronunciation (1993) C. Digby and J. Myers, Hemel Hempstead: Prentice-Hall.
Meeting People (1982) V. Cook, Oxford: Pergamon.
More English Now! (appendix) (1981) J. Gary and N. Gary, 'Comprehension-based language instruction: practice', in H. Winitz (ed.) *Native Language and Foreign Language Acquisition, Annals of the New York Academy of Sciences*: 379: 332–52. New York: New York Academy of Sciences.
Move (2007) B. Bowler and S. Parminter, Oxford: Macmillan.
New Crown English (2002) E. Morizumi, Tokyo: Sanseido.
New Cutting Edge (2005) S. Cunningham, P. Moor and F. Eales, Harlow: Longman.
New English File (2004) C. Oxenden, C. Latham-Koenig and P. Seligson, Oxford: Oxford University Press.
New Headway Beginners (2002) L. Soars and J. Soars, Oxford: Oxford University Press.
Opening Strategies (1982) B. Abbs and I. Freebairn, Harlow: Longman.
Panorama (1996) J. Girardet and J.-M. Cridlig, Paris: European Schoolbooks.
People and Places (1980) V. Cook, Oxford: Pergamon.
Pre-Intermediate Matters (1995) J. Bell and R. Gower, Harlow: Longman.
Present-day English for Foreign Students (1964) E.F. Candlin, London: University of London Press.
Pronunciation Book, The (1992) T. Bowen and J. Marks, Harlow: Longman.
Pronunciation of English: A Workbook, The (2000) J. Kenworthy, London: Edward Arnold.
Realistic English (1968) B. Abbs, V. Cook and J. Underwood, Oxford: Oxford University Press.
Reward (1994) S. Greenall, Oxford: Heinemann.
Ship or Sheep? (1981) A. Baker, Cambridge: Cambridge University Press.
Situational English (1967) Commonwealth Office of Education, London: Longman.
South Africa – The Privileged and the Dispossessed (1983) G. Davies and M. Senior, Paderborn: Ferdinand Schoningh.
Success with English (1968) G. Broughton, Harmondsworth: Penguin.
Tapestry 1 Listening and Speaking (2000) C. Benz and M. Dworak, Boston, MA: Heinle & Heinle.
Tapestry 1 Writing (2000) M. Pike-Baky, Boston, MA: Heinle & Heinle.
Test Your Spelling (1994) V. Parker, London: Usborne.
Touchstone (2005) M. McCarthy, J. McCarten and H. Sandiford, Cambridge: Cambridge University Press.
Tracks (1979) Northern Territory Department of Education, Northern Territory, Australia.

True to Life (1995) J. Collie and S. Slater, Cambridge: Cambridge University Press.
Use Your Head (1995) T. Buzan, London: BBC.
Using Intonation (1979) V. Cook, Harlow: Longman.
Voix et Images de France (1961) CREDIF [Centre for Information, Documentation, Studies and Research on Women], Paris: Didier.
Words You Need, The (1981) B. Rudzka, J. Channell, Y. Putseys and P. Ostyn, London: Macmillan.

References

Note: coursebooks are listed separately by title (see page 273).
All websites accessed January 2008.

Adams, S.J. (1983) Scripts and second language reading skills. In J.W. Oller, Jr and Richard-Amato, P.A. (eds) *Methods that Work*. Rowley, MA: Newbury House.

Adamson, H. and Regan, V. (1991) The acquisition of community norms by Asian immigrants learning English as a second language: a preliminary study. *Studies in Second Language Acquisition* 13(1): 1–22.

Allen, P., Swain, M., Harley, B. and Cummins, J. (1990) Aspects of classroom treatment: toward a more comprehensive view of second language education. In Harley, B., Allen, P., Cummins, J. and Swain, M. (eds) *The Development of Second Language Proficiency*. Cambridge: Cambridge University Press.

Alptekin, C. and Atakan, S. (1990) Field-dependence–independence and hemisphericity as variables in L2 achievements. *Second Language Research* 6(2): 139–49.

Anderson, J. (1993) *Rules of the Mind*. New Jersey: Lawrence Erlbaum Associates.

Anderson, R.T. (2004) Phonological acquisition in preschoolers learning a second language via immersion: a longitudinal study. *Clinical Linguistics & Phonetics* 18(3): 183–210.

Anthony, E.M. (1963) Approach, method and technique. *English Language Teaching* 17: 63–7.

Anton, M. and DiCamilla, F. (1998) Socio-cognitive functions of L1 collaborative interaction in the L2 classroom. *Canadian Modern Language Review* 54(3): 414–42.

AQA (Assessment and Qualification Alliance) (2007) *GCSE French Specification 2009* (www.aqa.org.uk).

Arnberg, L. (1987) *Raising Children Bilingually: The Pre-school Years*. Clevedon, Avon: Multilingual Matters.

ASD Simplified Technical English Maintenance Group (STEMG) (2007) *Simplified Technical English* (www.simplifiedenglish-aecma.org).

Asher, J.J. (1986) *Learning Another Language Through Actions: The Complete Teacher's Guidebook*. Los Gatos, CA: Sky Oaks Productions.

Asher, J.J. and Garcia, R. (1969) The optimal age to learn a foreign language. *Modern Language Journal* 53(5): 33–41.

Asher, J.J. and Price, B. (1967) The learning strategy of the total physical response: some age differences. *Child Development* 38: 1219–27.

Assessment of Performance Unit (1986) *Foreign Language Performance in Schools: Report on 1984 Survey of French*. London: DES.

Athanasopoulos. P. (2001) L2 acquisition and bilingual conceptual structure. MA thesis, University of Essex.

Athanasopoulos, P., Sasaki, M. and Cook, V.J. (2004) Do bilinguals think differently from monolinguals? Paper presented at EUROSLA, San Sebastian, September.

Atkinson, R.C. (1975) Mnemotechnics in second language learning. *American Psychologist* 30: 821–8.

Bacon, S. (1987) Differentiated cognitive style and oral performance. In VanPatten, B., Dvorak, T.R. and Lee, J.F. (eds) *Foreign Language Learning: A Research Perspective*. Rowley, MA: Newbury House.

Baetens Beardsmore, H. (ed.) (1993) *European Models of Bilingual Education*. Clevedon, Avon: Multilingual Matters.

Bahrick, H.P. (1984) Fifty years of second language attrition: implications for programmatic research. *Modern Language Journal* 68: 105–18.

Baker, P. and Eversley, J. (2000) *Multilingual Capital*. London: Battlebridge.

Bates, E. and MacWhinney, B. (1981) Second language acquisition from a functionalist perspective. In Winitz, H. (ed.) *Native Language and Foreign Language Acquisition. Annals of the New York Academy of Sciences* 379: 190–214. New York: New York Academy of Sciences.

Beauvillian, C. and Grainger, J. (1987) Accessing interlexical homographs: some limitations of a language-selective access. *Journal of Memory & Language* 26: 658–72.

Bellugi, U. and Brown, R. (eds) (1964) *The Acquisition of Language*. Monographs of the Society for Research in Child Development 29: 92.

Benke, E. and Medgyes, P. (2005) Differences in teaching behaviour between native and non-native teachers: as seen by the learners. In Llurda, E. (ed.) *Non-native Teachers*. New York: Springer: 195–216.

Ben Zeev, S. (1977) Mechanisms by which childhood bilingualism affects understanding of language and cognitive structure. In Hornby, P.A. (ed.) *Bilingualism: Psychological, Social, and Educational Implications*. New York: Academic Press: 29–55.

Berlin, B. and Kay, P. (1969) *Basic Color Terms: Their Universality and Evolution*. Berkeley: University of California Press.

Berry, J.W. (1998) Official multiculturalism. In Edwards, J. (ed.) *Language in Canada*. Cambridge: Cambridge University Press: 84–101.

Best, C., McRoberts, G. and Sithole, N. (2001) Discrimination of non-native consonant contrasts varying in perceptual assimilation to the listener's native phonological system. *Journal of the Acoustical Society of America* 109(2): 775–94.

Bhatt, R.M. (2005) Expert discourses, local practices, and hybridity: the case of Indian Englishes. In Canagarajah, A.S. (ed.) *Reclaiming the Local in Language Policy and Practice*. New Jersey: Lawrence Erlbaum Associates: 25–54.

Bialystok, E. (1990) *Communication Strategies: A Psychological Analysis of Second-Language Use*. Oxford: Basil Blackwell.

Bialystok, E., Craik, F.I.M., Klein, R. and Viswanathan, M. (2004) Bilingualism, aging and cognitive control: evidence from the Simon task. *Psychology and Aging* 19(2): 290–303.

Bialystok, E., Majumdar, S. and Martin, M. (2003) Developing phonological awareness: is there a bilingual advantage? *Applied Pyscholinguistics* 24: 27–44.

Biko, S. (1978) *I Write What I Like*. The Bowerdan Press. Reprinted London: Penguin (1998).

Blackwell, A. and Broeder, P. (1992) Interference and Facilitation in SLA: A Connectionist Perspective. Seminar on PDP and NLP, University of California, San Diego, May. Reported in Broeder, P. and Plunkett, P. (1994) Connectionism and second language acquisition. In Ellis, N. (ed.) *Implicit and Explicit Learning of Languages*. London: Academic Press: 421–53.

Bloomfield, L. (1933) *Language*. New York: Holt.

Bonnet, G. (ed.) (2002) *The Assessment of Pupils' Skills in English in Eight European Countries*. The European Network of Policy Makers for the Evaluation of Education Systems.

Bransford, J.D. and Johnson, M.K. (1982) Contextual prerequisites for understanding: some investigations of comprehension and recall. *Journal of Verbal Learning and Verbal Behavior* 11: 717–26.

Breen, M.P. (1984) Process syllabuses for the language classroom. In Brumfit, C.J. (ed.) *General English Syllabus Design*. ELT Documents 118: 47–60.

Broeder, P. and Plunkett, P. (1994) Connectionism and second language acquisition. In Ellis, N. (ed.) *Implicit and Explicit Learning of Languages*. London: Academic Press: 421–53.

Bruner, J. (1983) *Child's Talk*. Oxford: Oxford University Press.

Brutt-Griffler, J. (2002) *World English: A Study of its Development*. Clevedon, Avon: Multilingual Matters.

Buber, M. (1947) *Between Man and Man*. London: Fontana.

Bygate, M., Skehan, P. and Swain, M. (2001) *Researching Pedagogic Tasks, Second Language Learning, Teaching and Testing*. Harlow: Longman.

Byram, M. (1990) Foreign language teaching and young people's perceptions of other cultures. *ELT Documents* 132.

Call, M. (1985) Auditory short-term memory, listening comprehension and the input hypothesis. *TESOL Quarterly* 19(4): 765–81.

Canagarajah, A.S. (2005) Reconstructing local knowledge, reconfiguring language studies. In Canagarajah, A.S. (ed.) *Reclaiming the Local in Language Policy and Practice*. New Jersey: Lawrence Erlbaum Associates: 3–24.

Caramazza, A. and Brones, I. (1980) Semantic classification by bilinguals. *Canadian Journal of Psychology* 34(1): 77–81.

Carney, E. (1994) *A Survey of English Spelling*. London: Routledge.

Carrell, P.L. (1983) Three components of background knowledge in reading comprehension. *Language Learning* 33(2): 183–207.

Carrell, P.L. (1984) Evidence of a formal schema in second language comprehension. *Language Learning* 34: 87–111.

Carroll, J.B. (1981) Twenty-five years of research on foreign language aptitude. In Diller, K.C. (ed.) *Individual Differences and Universals in Language Learning*. Rowley, MA: Newbury House: 83–118.

Carter, R. (1988) Vocabulary, cloze, and discourse. In Carter, R. and McCarthy, M. (eds) *Vocabulary and Language Teaching*. Harlow: Longman.

Chaudron, C. (1983) Foreigner talk in the classroom – an aid to learning? In Seliger, H. and Long, M. (eds) *Classroom-oriented Research in Second Language Acquisition*. Rowley, MA: Newbury House: 127–43.

Chaudron, C. (1988) *Second Language Classrooms: Research on Teaching and Learning*. Cambridge: Cambridge University Press.

Chikamatsu, N. (1996) The effects of L1 orthography on L2 word recognition. *Studies in Second Language Acquisition* 18: 403–32.

Chomsky, N. (1959) Review of B.F. Skinner, *Verbal Behavior*. *Language* 35: 26–58.

Chomsky, N. (1965) *Aspects of the Theory of Syntax*. Cambridge, MA: MIT Press.

Chomsky, N. (1976) *Reflections on Language*. London: Temple Smith.

Chomsky, N. (1980) *Rules and Representations*. Oxford: Blackwell.

Chomsky, N. (1986) *Knowledge of Language: Its Nature, Origin and Use*. New York: Praeger.

Chomsky, N. (1995) *The Minimalist Program*. Cambridge, MA: MIT Press.

Chomsky, N. (2000) *The Architecture of Language*. New Delhi: Oxford University Press.

Clachar, A. (1997) Ethnolinguistic identity and Spanish proficiency in a para-doxical situation: the case of Puerto Rican return migrants. *Journal of Multilingual and Multicultural Development* 18(2): 107–24.

Clark, E. (1971) On the acquisition of 'before' and 'after'. *Journal of Verbal Learning and Verbal Behavior* 10: 266–75.

Clark, M.A. (1984) On the nature of techniques: what do we owe the gurus? *TESOL Quarterly* 18(4): 577–84.

Clement, R., Dornyei, Z. and Noels, K.A. (1994) Motivation, self-confidence, and group cohesion in the foreign language classroom. *Language Learning* 44(3): 417–48.

Cobbett, W. (1819) *A Grammar of the English Language*. Reprinted Oxford: Oxford University Press (1984).

Cohen, A. (1990) *Language Learning: Insights for Learners, Teachers, and Researchers*. New York: Newbury House/Harper Row.

Coleman, J.A. (1996) *Studying Languages: A Survey of British and European Students*. London: CILT (Centre for Information in Language Teaching).

Commission for Racial Equality (1986) *Teaching English as a Second Language: Report of a Formal Investigation in Calderdale Education Authority*. London: CRE.

Commission of the European Communities (1987) *Young Europeans in 1987*. Brussels: EC Commission.

Common European Framework of Reference for Languages (2008) Strasburg: Council of Europe (www.coe.int/t/dg4/linguistic/CADRE_EN.asp).

Cook, V.J. (1968) Some types of oral structure drill. *Language Learning* XVIII: 155–62.

Cook, V.J. (1977) Cognitive processes in second language learning. *International Review of Applied Linguistics* XV(1): 73–90.

Cook, V.J. (1981) Some uses for second language learning research. *Annals of the New York Academy of Sciences* 379: 251–8. New York: New York Academy of Sciences.

Cook, V.J. (1982) Kategorisierung und Fremdsprachenerwerb. *Gegenwärtige Probleme and Aufgaben der Fremdsprachen-psychologie*. Leipzig: Karl Marx University.

Cook, V.J. (1983) What should language teaching be about? *English Language Teaching Journal* 37(3): 229–34.

Cook, V.J. (1986) Experimental approaches applied to two areas of second lan-guage learning research: age and listening-based teaching methods. In Cook, V.J. (ed.) *Experimental Approaches to Second Language Learning*. Oxford: Pergamon: 23–37.

Cook, V.J. (1989) Reciprocal language teaching: another alternative. *Modern English Teacher* 16(3/4): 48–53.

Cook, V.J. (1992) Evidence for multi-competence. *Language Learning* 42(4): 557–91.

Cook, V.J. (1993) *Linguistics and Second Language Acquisition*. Basingstoke: Macmillan.

Cook, V.J. (1994) Universal Grammar and the learning and teaching of second languages. In Odlin, T. (ed.) *Perspectives on Pedagogical Grammar*. Cambridge: Cambridge University Press: 25–48.

Cook, V.J. (1997) *Inside Language*. London: Edward Arnold.

Cook, V.J. (2000) Linguistics and second language acquisition: one person with two languages. In Aronoff, M. and Rees-Miller, J. (eds) *The Blackwell Handbook of Linguistics*. Oxford: Blackwell: 488–511.

Cook, V.J. (2001) Using the first language in the classroom. *Canadian Modern Language Review* 57(3): 402–23.

Cook, V.J. (ed.) (2002) *Portraits of the L2 User*. Clevedon, Avon: Multilingual Matters.

Cook, V.J. (ed.) (2003) *Effects of the Second Language on the First*. Clevedon, Avon: Multilingual Matters.

Cook, V.J. (2004) *The English Writing System*. London: Edward Arnold.

Cook, V.J. (2007) The nature of the L2 user. In Roberts, L. and Gurel, A. (eds) *EUROSLA Yearbook* 7: 205–220.

Cook, V., Al-Ebary, K., Al-Garawi, B., Chang, C.-Y., Huang, K., Lee, S., Li, G., Mitani, H. and Sieh, Y.-C. (2007) Effects of cue processing in the Competition Model on the first language of L2 users. Paper presented at the 17th EUROSLA annual conference, Newcastle upon Tyne.

Cook, V.J. and Bassetti, B. (eds) (2005) *Second Language Writing Systems*. Clevedon, Avon: Multilingual Matters.

Cook, V.J., Bassetti, B., Kasai, C., Sasaki, M. and Takahashi, J.A. (2006) Do bilinguals have different concepts? The case of shape and material in Japanese L2 users of English. *International Journal of Bilingualism* 2: 137–52.

Cook, V.J., Iarossi, E., Stellakis, N. and Tokumaru, Y. (2003) Effects of the second language on the syntactic processing of the first language. In Cook, V.J. (ed.) *Effects of the Second Language on the First*. Clevedon, Avon: Multilingual Matters: 214–33.

Cook, V.J. and Newson, M. (2007) *Chomsky's Universal Grammar. An Introduction*, 3rd edition. Oxford: Blackwell.

Coppetiers, R. (1987) Competence differences between native and near-native speakers. *Language* 63(3): 545–73.

Corder, S.P. (1981) *Error Analysis and Interlanguage*. Oxford: Oxford University Press.

Coulmas, F. (1996) *The Blackwell Encyclopaedia of Writing Systems*. Oxford: Blackwell.

Crago, M. (1992) Communicative interaction and second language acquisition: an Inuit example. *TESOL Quarterly* 26(3): 487–506.

Crookes, G. and Schmidt, R.W. (1991) Motivation: reopening the research agenda. *Language Learning* 41(4): 469–512.

Cruse, D.A. (1986) *Lexical Semantics*. Cambridge: Cambridge University Press.

Cuban Ministry of Education (1999) *Principios que rigen la enseñanza del inglés en la escuela media*. Cuba: Ministry of Education.

Cummins, J. (1981) Age on arrival and immigrant second language learning in Canada: a reassessment. *Applied Linguistics* 2: 132–49.

Curran, C.A. (1976) *Counselling-Learning in Second Languages*. Apple River, IL: Apple River Press.

Cushner, K. and Brislin, R.W. (1996) *Intercultural Interactions: A Practical Guide*. Thousand Oaks, CA: Sage.

de Saussure, F. (1916) *Cours de linguistique générale*. Ed. Bally, C., Sechehaye, A. and Reidlinger, A., Paris: Payot.

de Swaan, A. (2001) *Words of the World: The Global Language System*. Cambridge: Polity.

DeKeyser, R.M. (1997) Beyond explicit rule learning. *Studies in Second Language Acquisition* 19: 195–221.

DeKeyser, R. (2005) What makes learning second-language grammar difficult? A review of issues. *Language Learning* 55: 1–25.

DeKeyser, R. and Larson-Hall, J. (2005) What does the critical period really mean? In Kroll, J. and De Groot, A. (eds) *Handbook of Bilingualism*. Oxford: Oxford University Press: 88–108.

DES (Department of Education and Science) (1990) *Modern Foreign Languages for Ages 11 to 16*. London: DES and the Welsh Office.

Dewaele, J.M. and Furnham, A. (1999) Extraversion: the unloved variable. *Language Learning* 49(3): 509–44.

DfES (Department for Education and Skills) (2001) *The Adult ESOL Core Curriculum*. London: DfES.

Diaz, R.M. (1985) The intellectual power of bilingualism. *Quarterly Newsletter of the Laboratory of Comparative Human Cognition* 7(1): 16–22.

Dickerson, W. (1987) Explicit rules and the developing interlanguage phonology. In James, A. and Leather, J. (eds) *Sound Patterns in Second Language Acquisition*. Dordrecht: Foris.

Dickinson, L. (1987) *Self-instruction in Language Learning*. Cambridge: Cambridge University Press.

Dodson, C.J. (1967) *Language Teaching and the Bilingual Method*. London: Pitman.

Donaldson, M. (1978) *Children's Minds*. London: Fontana.

Dorian, N.C. (1981) *Language Death: The Life Cycle of a Scottish Gaelic Dialect*. Philadelphia: University of Pennsylvania Press.

Dornyei, Z. (1990) Conceptualising motivation in foreign-language learning. *Language Learning* 40(1): 45–78.

Dornyei, Z. (1995) On the teachability of communicative strategies. *TESOL Quarterly* 29(1): 55–83.

Dornyei. Z. (2001) *Teaching and Researching Motivation*. Harlow: Longman.

Dornyei, Z. (2005) *The Psychology of the Language Learner: Individual Differences in Second Language Acquisition*. New Jersey: Lawrence Erlbaum Associates.

Doughty, C. (2001) Cognitive underpinnings of focus on form. In Robinson, P. (ed.) *Cognition and Second Language Instruction*. Cambridge: Cambridge University Press: 206–57.

Doughty, C. and Williams, J. (eds) (1998) *Focus on Form in Classroom Second Language Acquisition*. Cambridge: Cambridge University Press.

Downing, J. (ed.) (1973) *Comparative Reading*. New York: Macmillan.

Dulay, H. and Burt, M. (1973) Should we teach children syntax? *Language Learning* 3: 245–57.

Eckman, F.R., Elreyes, A. and Iverson, G.K. (2003) Some principles of second language phonology. *Second Language Research* 19: 169–208.

Eckstrand, L. (1978) Age and length of residence as variables related to the adjustment of migrant children with special reference to second language learning. In Nickel, G. (ed.) *Proceedings of the Fourth International Congress of Applied Linguistics*. Stuttgart: Hochschulverlag: 3: 179–97.

Ellis, R. (1986) *Classroom Second Language Development*. Oxford: Pergamon.

Ellis, R. (1990) *Instructed Second Language Acquisition*. Oxford: Blackwell.

Ellis, R. (1996) SLA and language pedagogy. *Studies in Second Language Acquisition* 19: 69–92.

Ellis, R. (2003) *Task-based Language Learning and Teaching*. Oxford: Oxford University Press.

English – Curriculum for All Grades (2002) Jerusalem: Ministry of Education (www.education.gov.il/tochniyot_limudim/eng1.htm).

EuroBarometer (2006) *Europeans and their Languages* 243. Brussels: European Commission (http://ec.europa.eu/public_opinion/archives/ebs/ebs_243_sum_en.pdf).

European Commission (2006) *The Euro Mosaic Study* (http://ec.europa.eu/education/policies/lang/languages/langmin/euromosaic/da1_en.html).

Eurydice (2005) *Key Data on Teaching Languages at School in Europe*. Eurydice European Unit (www.eurydice.org).

Faerch, C. and Kasper, G. (1984) Two ways of defining communication strategies. *Language Learning* 34: 45–63.

Favreau, M. and Segalowitz, N.S. (1982) Second language reading in fluent bilinguals. *Applied Psycholinguistics* 3: 329–41.

Felix, S. (1981) The effect of formal instruction on language acquisition. *Language Learning* 31: 87–112.

Firth, A. (1996) The discursive accomplishment of normality: on lingua franca English and conversation analysis. *Journal of Pragmatics* 26: 237–59.

Firth, J.R. (1951) Modes of meaning. In Firth, J.R. *Essays and Studies*. The English Association: 118–49.

Fishman, J.A. (1991) *Reversing Language Shift*. Clevedon, Avon: Multilingual Matters.

Flege, J.E. (1987) The production of 'new' and 'similar' phones in a foreign language: evidence for the effect of equivalence classification. *Journal of Phonetics* 15: 47–65.

Flowerdew, J. and Miller, L. (2005) *Second Language Listening*. Cambridge: Cambridge University Press.

Foster, P. (1998) A classroom perspective on the negotiation of meaning. *Applied Linguistics* 19(1): 1–23.

Franklin, C.E.M. (1990) Teaching in the target language. *Language Learning Journal* September: 20–4.

Freed, B. (1980) Talking to foreigners versus talking to children: similarities and differences. In Krashen, S.D. and Scarcella, R.C. (eds) *Issues in Second Language Research*. Rowley, MA: Newbury House: 19–27.

Freire, P. (1972) *Pedagogy of the Oppressed*. Harmondsworth: Penguin.

Gaies, S.J. (1979) Linguistic input in first and second language learning. In Eckman, F.R. and Hastings, A.J. *Studies in First and Second Language Acquisition*. Rowley, MA: Newbury House.

Gallagher-Brett, A. (n.d.) *Seven Hundred Reasons for Studying Languages*. The Higher Education Academy LLAS Languages, Linguistics, Area Studies, University of Southampton (www.llas.ac.uk/700reasons).

Galtung, J. (1980) *The True Worlds. A Transnational Perspective*. New York: The Free Press.

Galyean, B. (1977) A confluent design for language teaching. *TESOL Quarterly* 11(2): 143–56.

Garcia Mayo, M. del P. (2007) Tasks, negotiation and L2 learning in a foreign language context. In Garcia Mayo, M. (ed.) *Investigating Tasks in Formal Language Learning*. Clevedon, Avon: Multilingual Matters: 44–68.

Gardner, R. (1985) *Social Psychology and Second Language Learning*. London: Edward Arnold.

Gardner, R. (2007) The socio-educational model of second language acquisition. *EUROSLA Yearbook* 6: 237–60.

Gardner, R. and Lambert, W. (1972) *Attitudes and Motivation in Second-language Learning*. Rowley, MA: Newbury House.

Gary, J. and Gary, N. (1981a) Caution: talking may be dangerous to your linguistic health. *International Review of Applied Linguistics* XIX(1): 1–14.

Gary, J. and Gary, N. (1981b) Comprehension-based language instruction: practice. In Winitz, H. (ed.) *Native Language and Foreign Language Acquisition, Annals of the New York Academy of Sciences*: 379: 332–52. New York: New York Academy of Sciences.

Gattegno, C. (1972) *Teaching Foreign Languages in Schools: The Silent Way*. New York: Educational Solutions.

Genesee, F. (1976) The role of intelligence in second language learning. *Language Learning* 26: 267–80.

Genesee, F. (2002) Portrait of the bilingual child. In Cook, V.J. (ed.) *Portraits of the L2 User*. Clevedon, Avon: Multilingual Matters: 161–79.

Goldschneider, J.M. and DeKeyser, R.M. (2001) Explaining the natural order of L2 morpheme acquisition in English: a meta-analysis of multiple determinants. *Language Learning* 51(1): 1–50.

Gordon, R.G., Jr (ed.) (2005) *Ethnologue: Languages of the World*, 15th edition. Dallas, TX: SIL International (www.ethnologue.com).

Grabe, E. and Post, B. (2002) Intonational variation in the British Isles (http://aune.lpl.univ-aix.fr/sp2002/pdf/grabe-post.pdf).

Graddol, D. (2006) *English Next*. London: British Council (www.britishcouncil.org/files/documents/learning-research-english-next.pdf).

Green, J. and Oxford, R. (1995) A closer look at learning strategies, L2 proficiency and gender. *TESOL Quarterly* 29(2): 261–97.

Griffiths, R. and Sheen, R. (1992) Disembedded figures in the landscape: a reappraisal of L2 research on field dependence/independence. *Applied Linguistics* 13(2): 133–47.

Grosjean, F. (1982) *Life with Two Languages. An Introduction to Bilingualism*. Cambridge, MA: Harvard University Press.

Grosjean, F. (1989), Neurolinguists, beware! The bilingual is not two monolinguals in one person. *Brain and Language* 36: 3–15.

Gross, M. (1991) Lexique et syntaxe. *Travaux de Linguistique* 23: 107–32.

Gruneberg, M. (1987) *The Linkword Language System: French*. London: Corgi.

Guiora, A., Beit-Hallahmi, B., Brannon, R., Dull, C. and Scovel, T. (1972) The effects of experimentally induced changes in ego states on pronunciation ability in a second language: an exploratory study. *Comprehensive Psychiatry* 13: 421–8.

Hakuta, K. (1974) A preliminary report on the development of grammatical morphemes in a Japanese girl learning English as a second language. *Working Papers on Bilingualism* 3: 18–38.

Halliday, M.A.K. (1975) *Learning How to Mean*. London: Edward Arnold.

Halliday, M.A.K. (1985) *Spoken and Written Language*. Oxford: Oxford University Press.

Halliday, M.A.K., McIntosh, A. and Strevens, P. (1965) *The Linguistic Sciences and Language Teaching*. Longman: London.

Han, Z.-H. (2002) A study of the impact of recasts on tense consistency in L2 output. *TESOL Quarterly* 36(4): 543–72.

Hannan, M. (2004) A study of the development of the English verbal morphemes in the grammar of 4–9 year old Bengali-speaking children in the London borough of Tower Hamlets. PhD thesis, University of Essex.

Hansen, J. and Stansfield, C. (1981) The relationship of field dependent–independent cognitive styles to foreign language achievement. *Language Learning* 31: 349–67.

Hansen, L. (1984) Field dependence–independence and language testing: evidence from six Pacific island cultures. *TESOL Quarterly* 18(2): 311–24.

Harding, A., Page, B. and Rowell, S. (1981) *Graded Objectives in Modern Languages*. London: CILTR (Centre for Information in Language Teaching and Research).

Harding, E. and Riley, P. (1986) *The Bilingual Family: A Handbook for Parents*. Cambridge: Cambridge University Press.

Harley, B. (1986) *Age in Second Language Acquisition*. Clevedon, Avon: Multilingual Matters.

Harmer, J. (1998) *How to Teach English*. Harlow: Longman.

Harmer, J. (2007) *The Practice of English Language Teaching*, 4th edition. Harlow: Longman.

Harrington, M. (1987) Processing transfer: language-specific processing strategies as a source of interlanguage variation. *Applied Psycholinguistics* 8: 351–77.

Hartsuiker, R.J., Pickering, M.J. and Veltkamp, E. (2004) Is syntax separate or shared between languages? Cross-linguistic syntactic priming in Spanish-English bilinguals. *Psychological Science* 16(6): 409–14.

Hasan, R. (1996) *Ways of Saying: Ways of Meaning*. London: Cassell.

Hatch, E. (ed.) (1978) *Second Language Acquisition: A Book of Readings*. Rowley, MA: Newbury House.

Hawkins, E. (1984) *Awareness of Language*. Cambridge: Cambridge University Press.

Hawkins, E. (1987) *Modern Languages in the Curriculum*, 2nd edition. Cambridge: Cambridge University Press.

Haynes, M. and Carr, T.H. (1990) Writing system background and second language reading: a component skills analysis of English reading by native-speaking readers of Chinese. In Carr, T.H. and Levy, B.A. (eds) *Reading and its Development: Component Skills Approaches*. San Diego, CA: Academic Press: 375–421.

Henner-Stanchina, C. (1985) From reading to writing acts. In Riley, P. (ed.) *Discourse and Learning*. London: Longman: 91–104.

Hofstede, G. (1980) *Culture's Consequences: International Differences in Work-related Values*. London: Sage.

Holec, H. (1985) On autonomy: some elementary concepts. In Riley, P. (ed.) *Discourse and Learning*. London: Longman.

Holec, H. (1987) The learner as manager: managing learning or managing to learn? In Wendon, A. and Rubin, J. (eds) *Learner Strategies in Language Learning*. New Jersey: Prentice-Hall.

Holliday, A. (1994) *Appropriate Methodology and Social Context*. Cambridge: Cambridge University Press.

Horwitz, E. (1987) Surveying student beliefs about language learning. In Wendon, A. and Rubin, J. (eds) *Learner Strategies in Language Learning*. New Jersey: Prentice-Hall.

Hosenfeld, C. (1976) Learning about learning: discovering our students' strategies. *Foreign Language Annals* 9(2): 117–29.

Howatt, A. (2004) *A History of English Language Teaching*, 2nd edition. Oxford: Oxford University Press.

Howe, C. (1981) *Acquiring Language in a Conversational Context*. London: Academic Press.

Hullen, W. (1989) Investigations into classroom discourse. In Dechert, H. (ed.) *Current Trends in European Second Language Acquisition Research*. Clevedon, Avon: Multilingual Matters.

Hyams, N. (1986) *Language Acquisition and the Theory of Parameters*. Dordrecht: Reidel.

Hymes, D. (1972) Competence and performance in linguistic theory. In Huxley, R. and Ingram, E. (eds) *Language Acquisition, Models and Methods*. New York: Academic Press.

Ianco-Worrall, A. (1972) Bilingualism and cognitive development. *Child Development* 43: 1390–400.

Institute of Linguists (2008) *Examinations* (www.iol.org.uk/index.asp).

Ioup, G. and Tansomboon, A. (1987) The acquisition of tone: a maturational perspective. In Ioup, G. and Weinberger, S.H. (eds) *Interlanguage Phonology*. Rowley, MA: Newbury House.

Jacobson, R. and Faltis, C. (eds) (1990) *Language Description Issues in Bilingual Schooling*. Clevedon, Avon: Multilingual Matters: 3–17.

Jenkins, J. (2000) *The Phonology of English as an International Language*. Oxford: Oxford University Press.

Jenkins, J. (2002) A sociolinguistically based, empirically researched pronunciation syllabus for English as an international language. *Applied Linguistics* 23(1): 83–103.

Johnson, J.S. and Newport, E.L. (1989) Critical period effects in second language acquisition: the influence of maturational stage on the acquisition of ESL. *Cognitive Psychology* 21: 60–99.

Kanno, Y. (2000) Kikokushijo as bicultural. *International Journal of Intercultural Relations* 24: 361–82.

Kasper, G. and Kellerman, E. (eds) (1997) *Communication Strategies: Psycholinguistic and Sociolinguistic Perspectives*. London: Longman.

Kellerman, E., Ammerlaan, T., Bongaerts, T. and Poulisse, N. (1990) System and hierarchy in L2 compensatory strategies. In Scarcella, R.C., Andersen, E.S. and Krashen, S.D. (eds) *Developing Communicative Competence in a Second Language*. Rowley, MA: Newbury House: 163–78.

Kellerman, E., Bongaerts, T. and Poulisse, N. (1987) Strategy and system in L2 referential communication. In Ellis, R. (ed.) *Second Language Acquisition in Context*. London: Prentice-Hall.

Kellerman, E., Koonen, H. and van der Haagen, M. (2005) 'Feet speak louder than words': a preliminary analysis of language provisions for professional footballers in the Netherlands. In Long, M.H. (ed.) *Second Language Needs Analysis*. Cambridge: Cambridge University Press: 200–24.

Kelly, L.G. (1969) *25 Centuries of Language Teaching 500 BC–1969*. Rowley, MA: Newbury House.

Kenworthy, J. (1987) *Teaching English Pronunciation*. Harlow: Longman.

Kenworthy, J. (2000) *The Pronunciation of English: A Workbook*. Harlow: Longman.

Kilborn, K. and Cooreman, A. (1987) Sentence interpretation strategies in adult Dutch-English bilinguals. *Applied Psycholinguistics* 8: 415–31.

Kirsner, K., Brown, H.L., Abrol, S., Chadha, N.K. and Sharma, N.K. (1980) Bilingualism and lexical representation. *Quarterly Journal of Experimental Psychology* 32: 585–94.

Koenig, E.L., Chia, E. and Povey, J. (1983) *A Sociolinguistic Profile of Urban Centres in Cameroon*. Kinsey Hall, University of California, Los Angeles: Crossroads Press.

Kramsch, C. (1998) The privilege of the intercultural speaker. In Byram, M. and Fleming, M. (eds) *Language Learning in Intercultural Perspective*. Cambridge: Cambridge University Press: 16–31.

Krashen, S. (1981a) *Second Language Acquisition and Second Language Learning*. Oxford: Pergamon.

Krashen, S. (1981b) The 'fundamental pedagogical principle in second language teaching'. *Studia Linguistica* 35: 5–70.

Krashen, S. (1985) *The Input Hypothesis: Issues and Implications*. Longman: New York.

Krashen, S., Sferlazza, V., Feldman, L. and Fathman, A.K. (1976) Adult performance on the SLOPE test: more evidence for a natural order in adult second language acquisition. *Language Learning* 26(1): 145–51.

Krashen, S. and Terrell, T. (1983) *The Natural Approach*. New York: Pergamon.

Lado, R. (1964) *Language Teaching: A Scientific Approach*. New York: McGraw-Hill.

Laitin, D.D. (2000) What is a language community? *American Journal of Political Science* 44(1): 142–5.

Lambert, W.E. (1981) Bilingualism and language acquisition. In Winitz, H. (ed.) *Native Language and Foreign Language Acquisition, Annals of the New York Academy of Sciences*: 379: 9–22. New York: New York Academy of Sciences.

Lambert, W.E. (1990) Persistent issues in bilingualism. In Harley, B., Allen, P., Cummins, J. and Swain, M. (eds) *The Development of Second Language Proficiency*. Cambridge: Cambridge University Press.

Landry, R.G. (1974) A comparison of second language learners and monolinguals on divergent thinking tasks at the elementary school level. *Modern Language Journal* 58: 10–15.

Laponce, J.A. (1987) *Languages and their Territories*. Toronto: University of Toronto Press.

Larsen-Freeman, D. (1976) An explanation for the morpheme acquisition order of second language learners. *Language Learning* 26: 125–35.

Leather, J. (1987) F0 pattern inferences in the perceptual acquisition of second language tone. In James, A. and Leather, J. (eds) *Sound Patterns in Second Language Acquisition*. Dordrecht: Foris.

Lee, D.J. (1981) Interpretation of morpheme rank ordering in L2 research. In Dale, P. and Ingram, D. (eds) *Child Language: An International Perspective*. Baltimore, MD: University Park Press.

Lenneberg, E. (1967) *Biological Foundations of Language*. New York: Wiley & Sons.

Levenston, E. (1979) Second language lexical acquisition: issues and problems. *Interlanguage Studies Bulletin* 4: 147–60.

Lewis, M. (1993) *The Lexical Approach*. Hove: Language Teaching Publications.

Lewis, M. (1999) *How to Study Foreign Languages*. Basingstoke: Macmillan.

Lightbown, P. and Libben, G. (1984) The recognition and use of cognates by L2 learners. In Alderson, R. (ed.) *A Crosslinguistic Perspective for Second Language Research*. Rowley, MA: Newbury House.

Lightbown, P. and Spada, N. (2006) *How Languages are Learned*. Oxford: Oxford University Press.

Linguistic Minorities Project (1983) *Linguistic Minorities in England*. University of London Institute of Education, distributed by Tinga Tonga.

Little, D., Devitt, S. and Singleton, D. (1988) *Authentic Texts in Foreign Language Teaching: Theory and Practice*. Dublin: Authentik.

Llurda, E. (ed.) (2005) *Non-native Teachers*. New York: Springer.

Locastro, V. (1987) Aizuchi: a Japanese conversational routine. In Smith, L.E. (ed.) *Discourse Across Cultures*. New York: Prentice Hall: 101–13.

Long, J. and Harding-Esch, E. (1977) Summary and recall of text in first and second languages: some factors contributing to performance difficulties. In Sinmaiko, H. and Gerver, D. (eds) *Proceedings of the NATO Symposium on Language Interpretation and Communication*. New York: Plenum Press.

Long, M. (1981) Input. Interaction and second language acquisition. In Winitz, H. (ed.) *Native Language and Foreign Language Acquisition, Annals of the New York Academy of Sciences* 379: 259–78. New York: New York Academy of Sciences.

Long, M. (1991) Focus on form: a design feature in language teaching methodology. In de Bot, K., Ginsberg, R. and Kramsch, C. (eds) *Foreign Language Research in Cross-cultural Perspective*. Amsterdam: John Benjamins: 39–52.

Long, M. (1996) The role of the linguistic environment in second language acquisition. In Ritchie, W.C. and Bhatia, T.K. (eds) *Handbook of Second Language Acquisition*. San Diego, CA: Academic Press: 413–68.

Long, M. and Crookes, G. (1993) Units of analysis in syllabus design: the case for task. In Crookes, G. and Gass, S.M. (eds) *Tasks in a Pedagogical Context*. Clevedon, Avon: Multilingual Matters: 9–54.

Lozanov, G. (1978) *Suggestology and Outlines of Suggestopedia*. New York: Gordon & Breach.

Lyster, R. and Ranta, L. (1997) Corrective feedback and learner uptake: negotiation of form in communicative classrooms. *Studies in Second Language Acquisition* 19(1): 37–66.

Macaro, E. (1997) *Target Language, Collaborative Learning and Autonomy*. Clevedon, Avon: Multilingual Matters.

Macaro, E. (2003) *Teaching and Learning a Second Language: A Guide to Recent Research*. London: Continuum.

Macaro, E. (2005) Codeswitching in the L2 classroom: A communication and learning strategy. In Llurda, E. (ed.) *Non-Native Language Teachers: Perceptions, Challenges and Contributions to the Profession*. Boston, MA: Springer: 63–84.

Macaro, E. (2006) Strategies for language learning and for language use: revising the theoretical framework. *Modern Language Journal* 90: 320–37.

Mackey, W.F. (1967) *Bilingualism as a World Problem*. Montreal: Harvest House.

MacWhinney, B. (1987) Applying the Competition Model to bilingualism. *Applied Psycholinguistics* 8: 315–27.

MacWhinney, B. (2005) Extending the Competition Model. *International Journal of Bilingualism* 9(1): 69–84.

Major, R. (1986) The ontogeny model. Evidence from L2 acquisition of Spanish r. *Language Learning* 36: 453–504.

Major, R.C. (2001) *Foreign Accent: The Ontogeny and Phylogeny of Second Language Phonology*. Mahwah, NJ: Lawrence Erlbaum Associates.

Major, R.C. (2002) The phonology of the L2 user. In Cook, V.J. (ed.) *Portraits of the L2 User*. Clevedon, Avon: Multilingual Matters: 65–92.

Makino, T. (1980) Acquisition order of English morphemes by Japanese secondary school students. *Journal of Hokkaido University of Education* 30: l01–8.

Marton, W. (1988) *Methods in English Language Teaching*. Hemel Hempstead: Prentice Hall.

McArthur, T. (ed.) (1992) *The Oxford Companion to the English Language*. Oxford: Oxford University Press.

McDonald, J. (1987) Sentence interpretation in bilingual speakers of English and Dutch. *Applied Psycholinguistics* 8: 379–413.

McDonough, S. (1995) *Strategy and Skill in Learning a Foreign Language*. London: Edward Arnold.

McLaughlin, B. (1987) *Theories of Second-language Learning*. London: Edward Arnold.

McLaughlin, B., Rossman, T. and McLeod, B. (1983) Second language learning: an information-processing perspective. *Language Learning* 33: 135–58.

Mead, M. (1970) *Culture and Commitment*. London: Bodley Head.

Medgyes, P. (1992) Native or non-native: who's worth more? *English Language Teaching Journal* 46(4): 340–9.

Mennen, I. (2004) Bi-directional interference in the intonation of Dutch speakers of Greek. *Journal of Phonetics* 32: 543–63.

MEXT (Ministry of Education, Culture, Sports, Science and Technology) (2003) *Regarding the Establishment of an Action Plan to Cultivate 'Japanese with English Abilities'*. Tokyo: MEXT.

Montague, N.S. (1997) Critical components for dual language programs. *Bilingual Research Journal* 21: 4.

Morgan, J.L. (1986) *From Simple Input to Complex Grammar*. Cambridge, MA: MIT Press.

Morrow, K. (1981) Principles of communicative teaching. In Johnson, K. and Morrow, K. (eds) *Communication in the Classroom*. Harlow: Longman: 59–66.

Myers-Scotton, C.M. (2005) Supporting a differential access hypothesis: code-switching and other contact data. In Kroll, J. and De Groot, A. (eds) *Handbook of Bilingualism*. Oxford: Oxford University Press: 326–48.

Myers-Scotton, C. and Jake, J. (2000) Four types of morpheme: evidence from aphasia, code-switching and second language acquisition. *Linguistics* 38: 1053–100.

Myhill, J. (2003) The native speaker, identity and the authenticity hierarchy. *Language Sciences* 25(1): 77–97.

Myhill, M. (1990) Socio-cultural content in ESL programmes for newly arrived and NESB and Aboriginal school children in Western Australia. *English Language Teaching Documents* 132: 117–31.

Myles, F. and Mitchell, R. (2004) *Second Language Learning Theories*, 2nd edition. London: Edward Arnold.

Naiman, N., Fröhlich, M., Stern, H. and Todesco, A. (1978) *The Good Language Learner*. Research in Education Series No. 7. The Ontario Institute for Studies in Education, Toronto. Reprinted Clevedon, Avon: Multilingual Matters (1995).

Nation, I.S.P. (2001) *Learning Vocabulary in Another Language*. Cambridge: Cambridge University Press.

Nation, P. (1990) *Teaching and Learning Vocabulary*. New York: Newbury House/Harper Row.

National Curriculum for England: English (2004) London: Qualifications and Curriculum Authority (www.nc.uk.net/nc_resources/html/download.shtml).

Nelson, K.E., Carskaddon, G. and Bonvillain, J.D. (1973) Syntactic acquisition: impact of experimental variation in adult verbal interaction with the child. *Child Development* 44: 497–504.

Neufeld, G. (1978) On the acquisition of prosodic and articulatory features in adult language learning. *Canadian Modern Language Review* 34(2): 163–74.

Nisbett, R.E. (2003) *The Geography of Thought*. London: Nicholas Brealey Publishing.

Odlin, T. (ed.) (1994) *Pedagogical Grammar*. Cambridge: Cambridge University Press.

Ohta, A.S. (2000) Rethinking interaction in SAL: developmentally appropriate assistance in the zone of proximal development and the acquisition of L2 grammar. In Lantolf, J. (ed.) *Sociocultural Theory and Second Language Learning*. Oxford: Oxford University Press: 51–78.

O'Malley, J.M. and Chamot, A.U. (1990) *Learning Strategies in Second Language Acquisition*. Cambridge: Cambridge University Press.

O'Malley, J., Chamot, A.U. and Kupper, L. (1989) Listening comprehension strategies in second language acquisition. *Applied Linguistics* 10(4): 418–37.

O'Malley, J.M., Chamot, A.U., Stewner-Manzanares, G., Kupper, L. and Russo, R.P. (1985) Learning strategies used by beginning and intermediate ESL students. *Language Learning* 35: 21–46.

Oxford, R. (1990) *Language Learning Strategies: What Every Teacher Should Know*. Rowley, MA: Newbury House.

Oxford, R., Crookall, D., Cohen, A.D., Lavine, R., Nyikos, M. and Sutter, W. (1990) Strategy training for language learners: six situational case studies and a training model. *Foreign Language Annals* 22(3): 197–216.

Oxford English Dictionary (1989) 2nd revised edition. Oxford: Oxford University Press (online subscription at www.oed.com).

Palmer, H.E. (1926) *The Principles of Language Study*. London: Harrap.

Paulston, C. (1986) Linguistic consequences of ethnicity and nationalism in multilingual settings. In Spolsky, B. (ed.) *Language and Education in Multilingual Settings*. Clevedon, Avon: Multilingual Matters.

Peters, R.S. (1973) *The Philosophy of Education*. Oxford: Oxford University Press.

Phillipson, R. (1992) *Linguistic Imperialism*. Oxford: Oxford University Press.

Pienemann, M. (1984) Psychological constraints on the teachability of languages. *Studies in Second Language Acquisition* 6(2): 186–214.

Pienemann, M. (1998) *Language Processing and Second-language Development: Processability Theory*. Amsterdam: John Benjamins.

Piller, I. (2002) *Bilingual Couples Talk: The Discursive Construction of Hybridity*. Amsterdam: John Benjamins.

Poplack, S. (1980) Sometimes I'll start a sentence in English y termino en español. *Linguistics* 18: 581–616.

Porte, G. (2003) English from a distance: code-mixing and blending in the L1 output of long-term resident EFL teachers. In Cook, V.J. (ed.) *Effects of the Second Language on the First*. Clevedon, Avon: Multilingual Matters: 103–19.

Postovsky, V. (1974) Effects of delay in oral practice at the beginning of second language learning. *Modern Language Journal* 58: 229–39.

Poulisse, N. (1990) *The Use of Compensatory Strategies by Dutch Learners of English*. Berlin: Mouton de Gruijter.

Prabhu, N.S. (1987) *Second Language Pedagogy*. Oxford: Oxford University Press.

Pusat Perkembangan Kurikulum (2003) *Huraian Sukatan Pelajaran: Kurikulum Bersepadu Sekolah Rendah* [Curriculum specifications for English]. Kementerian Pelajaran Malaysia (http://myschoolnet.ppk.kpm.my).

Quality Control Authority (2004) National Curriculum online (www.nc.uk. net/nc_resources/html/download.shtml).

Queen, R.M. (2001) Bilingual intonation patterns: evidence of language change from Turkish-German bilingual children. *Language in Society* 30: 55–80.

Rampton, M.B.H. (1990) Displacing the 'native speaker': expertise, affiliation and inheritance. *ELT Journal* 44(2): 338–43.

Ramsey, C. and Wright, C. (1974) Age and second language learning. *Journal of Social Psychology* 94: 115–21.

Ranney, S. (1993) Learning a new script: an explanation of sociolinguistics competence. *Applied Linguistics* 13(1): 25–50.

Rhodes, N.C., Christian, D. and Barfield, S. (1997) Innovations in immersion: The Key School two-way model. In Johnson, R.K. and Swain, M. (eds) *Immersion Education: International Perspectives*. Cambridge: Cambridge University Press: 265–83.

Richards, J. and Rodgers, T. (1986) *Approaches and Methods in Language Teaching*. Cambridge: Cambridge University Press.

Riley, P. (ed.) (1985) *Discourse and Learning*. London: Longman.

Ringbom, H. (1982) The influence of other languages on the vocabulary of foreign language learners. In Nickel, G. and Nehls, D. (eds) *Error Analysis, Contrastive Analysis and Second Language Learning*. Heidelberg: IRAL.

Rivers, W.M. (1964) *The Psychologist and the Foreign Language Teacher*. Chicago, IL: Chicago University Press.

Robinson, P. (2005) Aptitude and second language acquisition. *Annual Review of Applied Linguistics* 25: 46–73.

Roller, C.M. and Matombo, A.R. (1992) Bilingual readers' use of background knowledge in learning from text. *TESOL Quarterly* 26(1): 129–40.

Rosch, E. (1977) Human categorisation. In Warren, N. (ed.) *Studies in Cross-Cultural Psychology*. New York: Academic Press.

Rossier, J. (1975) Extroversion-introversion as a significant variable in the learning of English as a second language. PhD thesis, University of Southern California. *Dissertation Abstracts International* 36: 7308A–7309A.

Rubin, J. and Thompson, I. (1982) *How to Be a More Successful Language Learner*. Boston Studies in the Humanities 12. Boston, MA: Heinle & Heinle.

Rumelhart, D.E. and McLelland, J.L. (1986) On learning the past tenses of English verbs. In McLelland, J.L., Rumelhart, D.E. and the PDP Research Group *Parallel Distributed Processing: Volume 2 Psychological and Biological Models*. Cambridge, MA: MIT Press: 216–71.

Sampson, G.P. (1984) Exporting language teaching methods from Canada to China. *TESL Canada Journal* 1(1): 19–31.

Sanquillet, M. and Peterson, E. (eds) (1978) *The Essential Writings of Marcel Duchamps*. London: Thames and Hudson.

Sassoon, R. (1995) *The Acquisition of a Second Writing System*. Oxford: Intellect.

Saunders, G. (1982) *Bilingual Children: Guidance for the Family*. Clevedon, Avon: Multilingual Matters.

Schank, R. and Abelson, R. (1977) *Scripts, Plans, Goals, and Understanding*. New Jersey: Lawrence Erlbaum Associates.

Schegloff, E.A., Koshik, I., Jacoby, S. and Olsher, A. (2002) Conversation Analysis and applied linguistics. *Annual Review of Applied Linguistics* 22: 3–31.

Schmid, M., Kopke, B., Keijzer, M. and Weilemar, L. (eds) (2004) *First Language Attrition*. Amsterdam: John Benjamins.

Schmitt, N. (1997) Vocabulary learning strategies. In Schmitt, N. and McCarthy, M. (eds) *Vocabulary: Description, Acquisition and Pedagogy*. Cambridge: Cambridge University Press: 99–227.

Scrivenor, J. (1994) *Learning Teaching*. Oxford: Heinemann.

Seedhouse, P. (2004) *The Interactional Architecture of the Language Classroom*. Oxford: Blackwell.

Seedhouse, P. (2005a) Conversational analysis and language learning. *Language Teaching* 38(4): 165–87.

Seedhouse, P. (2005b) 'Task' as research construct. *Language Learning* 55(3): 533–70.

Seely, C. and Romijn, E.K. (1995) *TPR is More than Commands*. Berkeley, CA: Command Performance Language Institute.

Seidlhofer, B. (2004) Research perspectives on teaching English as a lingua franca. *Annual Review of Applied Linguistics* 24: 209–39.

Selinker, L. (1972) Interlanguage. *International Review of Applied Linguistics* X(3): 209–31.

Sharwood-Smith, M. (1993) Input enhancement in instructed SLA: theoretical bases. *Studies in Second Language Acquisition* 15(2): 165–79.

Sheen, Y. (2004) Corrective feedback and learner uptake in communicative classrooms across instructional settings. *Language Teaching Research* 8(3): 263–300.

Sinclair, J. (ed.) (1990) *Collins COBUILD Grammar*. London: Collins.

Sinclair, J. and Coulthard, M. (1975) *Towards an Analysis of Discourse*. Oxford: Oxford University Press.

Singleton, D. (1989) *Language Acquisition: The Age Factor*. Clevedon, Avon: Multilingual Matters.

Singleton, D. (1999) *Exploring the Second Language Mental Lexicon*. Cambridge: Cambridge University Press.

Skehan, P. (1986) Cluster Analysis and the identification of learner types. In Cook, V. (ed.) *Experimental Approaches to Second Language Learning*. Oxford: Pergamon: 81–94.

Skehan, P. (1989) *Individual Differences in Second-language Learning*. London: Edward Arnold.

Skehan, P. (1998) *A Cognitive Approach to Language Learning*. Oxford: Oxford University Press.

Skinner, B.F. (1957) *Verbal Behavior*. New York: Appleton-Century-Crofts.

Skutnabb-Kangas, T. (1981) *Bilingualism or Not: The Education of Minorities*. Clevedon, Avon: Multilingual Matters.

Smolicz, J.J. and Secombe, M. (2003) Assimilation or pluralism? Changing policies for minority languages education in Australia. *Language Policy* 2: 3–25.

Snow, C. and Hoefnagel-Höhle, M. (1977) Age differences and the pronunciation of foreign sounds. *Language and Speech* 20: 357–65.

Sparks, R., Ganschow, L. and Pohlman, J. (1989) Linguistic coding deficits in foreign language learners. *Annals of Dyslexia: An Interdisciplinary Journal* 39: 179–95.

Spolsky, B. (1989a) *Conditions for Second Language Learning*. Oxford: Oxford University Press.

Spolsky, B. (1989b) Maori bilingual education and language revitalisation. *Journal of Multilingual and Multicultural Development* 10(2): 89–106.

Sridhar, K.K. and Sridhar, S.N. (1986) Bridging the paradigm gap: second language acquisition theory and indigenised varieties of English. *World Englishes* 5(1): 3–14.

Stern, H.H. (David) (1964) Modern languages in the universities. *Modern Languages* 46(3): 87–97.

Stern, H.H. (David) (1983) *Fundamental Concepts of Language Teaching*. Oxford: Oxford University Press.

Streets, L. (1976, reprinted 1991) *I Can Talk*. London: Down's Syndrome Association.

Swain, M. (2000) The output hypothesis and beyond: mediating acquisition through collaborative dialogue. In Lantolf, J. (ed.) *Sociocultural Theory and Second Language Learning*. Oxford: Oxford University Press: 97–114.

Swain, M. and Lapkin, S. (2000) Task-based second language learning: the uses of the first language. *Language Teaching Research* 4(3): 251–74.

Swain, M. and Lapkin, S. (2002) Talking it through: two French immersion learners' response to reformulation. *International Journal of Educational Research* 37: 285–304.

Swan, M. (1985) A critical look at the communicative approach. *English Language Teaching Journal* 39(2): 6–87.

Swan, M. (2005) Legislation by hypothesis: the case of task-based instruction. *Applied Linguistics* 26(3): 376–401.

Swan, M. and Smith, B. (2001) *Learner English*, 2nd edition. Cambridge: Cambridge University Press.

Takeuchi, O. (2003) What can we learn from good foreign language learners? A qualitative study in the Japanese foreign language context. *System* 31: 385–92.

Tarone, E. (1980) Some influences on the syllable structure of interlanguage phonology. *International Review of Applied Linguistics* 4: 143–63.

Terrell, T.D., Rogers, M.B., Barnes, B.K. and Wolff-Hessini, M. (1993) *Deux Mondes: A Communicative Approach*. New York: McGraw-Hill.

Thompson, G.G. (1952) *Child Psychology*. Boston, MA: Houghton Mifflin.

Timmis, I. (2002) Non-native speaker norms and international English: a classroom view. *English Language Teaching Journal* 56(3): 240–9.

Tomasello, M. (1999) *The Cultural Origins of Human Cognition*. Cambridge, MA: Harvard University Press.

Tomasello, M. (2003) *Constructing a Language*. Cambridge, MA: Harvard University Press.

Tucker, G.R., Otanes, F.E. and Sibayan, B. (1971) An alternating days approach to bilingual education. *21st Annual Round Table Meeting on Linguistics and Language Studies*, Washington, DC: Georgetown University Press.

Underwood, M. (1989) *Teaching Listening*. Harlow: Longman.

Ur, P. (1996) *A Course in Language Teaching*. Cambridge: Cambridge University Press.

US Census Bureau (2003) Nearly 1-in-5 speak a foreign language at home; most also speak English 'very well' (www.census.gov/Press-Release/www/releases/archives/census_2000/001406.html).

VanPatten, W. and Williams, J. (2006) *Theories in Second Language Acquisition*. New Jersey: Lawrence Erlbaum Associates.

Vatican City (n.d.) *Henry VIII Letter to Ann Boleyn* (www.ibiblio.org/expo/vatican.exhibit/exhibit/a-vatican_lib/images/vlib06.jpg).

Venezky, R.L. (1999) *The American Way of Spelling*. New York: Guilford.

Verma, M.K., Firth, S. and Corrigan, K. (1992) The developing phonological skills of Panjabi/Urdu speaking children learning English as a foreign language in Britain. In Leather, J. and James, A. (eds) *New Sounds 92*. Amsterdam: University of Amsterdam.

Vygotsky, L.S. (1934/1962) *Thought and Language*. Cambridge, MA: MIT Press.
Vygotsky, L.S. (1935/1978) *Mind in Society*. Boston, MA: Harvard University Press.
Wallerstein, N. (1983) The teaching approach of Paolo Freire. In Oller, J.W., Jr and Ricard-Amato, P.A. (eds) *Methods that Work*. Rowley, MA: Newbury House.
Watson, I. (1991) Phonological processing in two languages. In Bialystok, E. (ed.) *Language Processes in Bilingual Children*. Cambridge: Cambridge University Press: 25–48.
Weeks, F., Glover, A., Johnson, E. and Strevens, P. (1988) *Seaspeak Training Manual: Essential English for International Maritime Use*. Oxford: Pergamon.
Weinreich, U. (1953) *Languages in Contact*. The Hague: Mouton.
Wesche, M.B. (1981) Language aptitude measures in streaming, matching students with methods, and diagnosis of learning problems. In Diller, K. (ed.) *Individual Differences and Universals in Language Learning*. Rowley, MA: Newbury House, 83–118.
White, J. (1998) Getting the learner's attention: a typographical input enhancement study. In Doughty, C. and Williams, J. (eds) *Focus on Form in Classroom Second Language Acquisition*. Cambridge: Cambridge University Press, 85–113.
White, L. (1986) Implications of parametric variation for adult second language acquisition: an investigation of the pro-drop parameter. In Cook, V.J. (ed.) *Experimental Approaches to Second Language Acquisition*. Oxford: Pergamon: 55–72.
Wieden, W. and Nemser, W. (1991) *The Pronunciation of English in Austria*. Tübingen: Gunter Narr.
Wilkins, D.A. (1972) The linguistic and situational content of the common core in a unit/credit system. Strasburg: Council of Europe. Reprinted in Trim, J., Richterich, R., Van Ek, J. and Wilkins, D.A. (1980) *Systems Development in Adult Language Learning*. Oxford: Pergamon.
Williams, J. and Evans, J. (1998) What kind of focus and on what forms? In Doughty, C. and Williams, J. (eds) *Focus on Form in Classroom Second Language Acquisition*. Cambridge: Cambridge University Press: 139–55.
Williams, L. (1977) The perception of consonant voicing by Spanish-English bilinguals. *Perception and Psychophysics* 21(4): 289–97.
Willis, D. and Willis, J. (2007) *Doing Task-based Teaching*. Oxford: Oxford University Press.
Willis, J. (1996) *A Framework for Task-based Learning*. Harlow: Longman.
Winitz, H. (ed.) (1981) *The Comprehension Approach to Foreign Language Instruction*. Rowley, MA: Newbury House.
Yelland, G.W., Pollard, J. and Mercuri, A. (1993) The metalinguistic benefits of limited contact with a second language. *Applied Psycholinguistics* 14: 423–44.

Index

Page numbers in bold refer to Keywords. Those in italics refer to figures (only indexed separately if there is no other information about the topic on the page). Headings referring to specific groups of language users are constructed in the following way: [L1-L2] language users, e.g. Spanish-English language users.